Boston

written and researched by

David Fagundes and Anthony Grant

this edition researched and updated

Arabella Bowen

ROUGH GUIDES

www.roughguides.com

Introduction to

Boston

Boston is as close to the Old World as the New World gets, an American city that proudly trades on its colonial past, having served a crucial role in the country's development from a few wayward pilgrims right through to the Revolutionary War. It occasionally takes its past a bit too seriously – what might pass for a faded relic anywhere else becomes a plaque-covered tourist sight here – but none of that detracts from the city's overriding historic charm, nor its present-day energy.

Indeed, there are plenty of tall skyscrapers, thriving business concerns and cultural outposts in Boston that are part-and-parcel of modern urban America, not to mention excellent mergers of past and present, such as the bustling Quincy Market, a paradigm for successful urban renewal. And despite the occasional wearisome touch, no other city in America gives a better feel for the events and personas behind the nation's birth, all played out in Boston's wealth of emblematic and evocative colonial-era sights, conveniently linked by the self-guided walking tour (one of a handful in the city) known as the Freedom Trail. As well, the city's cafés and shops, its attractive public spaces and the diversity of its neighborhoods – student hives, ethnic enclaves and stately districts of preserved townhouses – are similarly alluring, going some way to

iii

Fact file

● Boston, founded in 1630, is the capital of the state of Massachusetts, and is named after the town of Boston, England.

● The population of Boston proper is a diminutive 590,000 — up some 16,000 from a decade ago — of whom 57 percent are white, 28 percent black, and 8 percent Asian. The population of the greater Boston area, including Worcester and Lawrence, is over 5.8 million.

● Greater Boston covers about 4466 square miles, much of which is the result of landfill. The original Boston comprised a puny 487 acres.

● Boston is home to America's first public park (Boston Common), university (Harvard), lighthouse (Boston Light), subway (the T), free black church (African Meeting House) and public library (Boston Public Library), as well as the country's oldest pub (the Bell in Hand Tavern), ballpark (Fenway), and restaurant (*Union Oyster House*).

answering the twin accusations of elitism and provincialism to which Boston is perennially subjected.

Boston is also at the center of the American university system — more than sixty colleges call the area home, including illustrious Harvard and MIT, in the neighboring city of Cambridge, just across the Charles River. This academic connection has played a key part in the city's long left-leaning political tradition, which has spawned a line of ethnic mayors, and, most famously, the Kennedy family. Steeped in Puritan roots, local residents often display a slightly anachronistic Yankee pride, but it's one which has served to protect the city's identity. Indeed, the districts around Boston Common exude an almost small-town atmosphere, and, until the past decade or so, were relatively unmarred by chain stores and fast-food joints. Meanwhile, groups of Irish and Italian

descent have carved out authentic and often equally unchanged communities in areas like the North End, Charlestown and South Boston.

Today, Boston's relatively small size – both physically and in terms of population (at under 600,000, it ranks well below most other similarly important US cities) – and its provincial feel actually serve to the city's advantage. Though it has expanded significantly through landfills and annexation since it was first settled in 1630, it has never lost its core, which remains a tangle of streets over old cowpaths clustered around Boston Common (which was itself originally used as cattle pasture). Delightfully, this center can really only be explored properly on foot; for even as Boston has evolved from busy port to blighted city to the rejuvenated and prosperous place it is today, it has remained, fundamentally, a city on a human scale.

> **No other city in America gives a better feel for the events and personas behind the nation's birth**

What to see

The city's epicenter is Boston Common, a large public green that orients **downtown** and holds either on or near its grounds many of Boston's most historic sights, including the Old State House, the Old Granary Burying

Yankee cooking

Despite all sorts of strides made by flash chefs and trendy eateries , traditional cuisine remains strong in Boston, built on the unfussiness of the Puritan ethic and the city's proximity to the Atlantic Ocean. This distinctive brand of Yankee cooking — few other places think baked beans is an appropriate side dish for lobster, for example — can be as comforting as comfort food gets. Fishcakes, seafood chowder, shortcakes and cream pies are the foundations of Boston's cuisine – the best of which can be had at *Durgin-Park* (p.000) and the *Old Union Oyster House* (p.000). Food names can be confusing, however. Scrod, for one, a bastardization of "cod," is a small mystery fish that could be either cod or haddock – it all depends on what costs less at the market that day. Boston clam chowder is more self-explanatory; however, if you're offered a bulkie along with your bowl, know that it's Boston slang for a kaiser-like roll, and that it's the perfect thing to sop up the soup.

Boston nicknames, past and present

Boston has inspired many nicknames over the centuries, from the dignified to the inane. Originally called Tremontaine, after the three hills that punctuated the skyline when the Puritans arrived in the early 1600s (but which have since been razed and used for landfill), the newcomers renamed the spot Boston – itself a shortening of St Botolph – after their hometown, one hundred miles north of London. The name stuck – on maps, anyway – while other, less deferential, monikers took Boston's place in common parlance. These range from the earnest ("Athens of America," after the sixty-plus universities that call the city home), to the hokey ("Beantown," reflecting its inhab-itants' one-time love affair with baked beans), to the overblown ("The Hub," after Oliver Wendell Holmes' infamous 1857 reference to the Massachusetts State House as the "hub of the solar system").

Ground and the Old South Meeting House. Nothing, however, captures the spirit of the city better than nearby **Faneuil Hall**, the so-called "Cradle of Liberty," and the always-animated Quincy Market, adjacent to the hall. Due north, an incomparable sense of Boston's original layout can be found in the cramped **Blackstone Block**. Boston's **waterfront**, on the edge of downtown, offers its fair share of diversions, mostly ideal for traveling families; the action is centered on Long Wharf.

The **North End**, modern Boston's Little Italy, occupies the northeast corner of the peninsula, where, until the Big Dig project is completed, it's cut off from the rest of the city by I-93. The North End is home to a few notable relics, such as **Old North Church** and the **Paul Revere House**, but is equally worth visiting for its animated streetlife, fueled, in large part, by the strong cups of espresso proffered by numerous Italian *caffès*. Just across Boston Inner Harbor from the North End is **Charlestown**, the quiet berth of the world's oldest commissioned warship, the *USS Constitution*, as well as the locus of the **Bunker Hill Monument**, an obelisk commemorating the famous battle that bolstered American morale in the fight for independence.

North of the common are the vintage gaslights and red-brick Federalist townhouses that line the streets of **Beacon Hill**, the city's most exclusive residential neighborhood; it's anchored by the gold-domed **State House**, designed, as were numerous area houses, by Charles Bulfinch. Charles Street runs south from the hill and separates Boston Common from the **Public Garden**, which marks the eastern edge of **Back Bay**, a similarly well-heeled neighborhood which features opulent rowhouses alongside modern landmarks like the **John Hancock Tower**, New England's tallest skyscraper. The neighborhood

Sports fanaticism

You'd be hard-pressed to come up with a city as fanatical about its sports as Boston. Local sports-craziness is something of a paradox, however, given that the Red Sox haven't won the World Series since 1918, the Celtics haven't had a championship since 1986, and the Bruins haven't brought home the Stanley Cup since 1972. At least football's New England Patriots ended the city's title drought in 2002 by winning the Super Bowl. In any case, professional sports are such an integral part of citizens' day-to-day existence that many upscale restaurants have had to incorporate a television or two into their decor just so their patrons can catch the game. For first-hand experience of Boston's notorious hooting and hollering, head to a Red Sox game at Fenway Park (see p.103). The ruckus will be especially vicious if they're playing the New York Yankees – if you're a Yankees fan, be prepared to be taken to task for cheering on the Bronx Bombers; it might be a good idea to just keep it quiet and enjoy the sunshine.

The Big Dig

In a city whose roads follow the logic of colonial cow paths, the added confusion wreaked by Boston's highway reconstruction project – the largest and most expensive in US history – does little to help visitors navigate their way around. The primary purpose of this project, known as the **Big Dig**, is to eliminate the unsightly elevated Central Artery (I-93) – built in the late 1950s without regard for aesthetics, neighborhood dynamics or traffic growth – by replacing it with a wider, underground version. Unfortunately, the undertaking has ignored another crucial factor this time around: cost. In fact, the initial budget of $2.6 billion has now soared to well over $10 billion, and there's doubt over whether the Big Dig will be finished by the slated estimate of 2004.

Still, the project has pumped millions of construction dollars into the city and will eventually free up 150 acres of land for park and recreational use, while supplying dirt to cap landfills where toxins once seeped into Boston Harbor. This comes as little solace to most Bostonians, though, especially those who drive – right now the project is a serious pain to commuters. To get as caught up as the locals, check out ⊛www.bigdig.com, which has all the history, trivia, artwork, plans, politics and gossip connected with the project; it's an interesting site, and has a lot more personality than you might expect.

also hosts some of the city's best shopping along **Newbury Street**. Meanwhile, the stylish enclave of the **South End**, known for its restaurants and streetlife, as well as the ornate ironwork gracing its well-maintained homes, is also worth a visit.

The student domains of **Kenmore Square** and **the Fenway** are found west of Back Bay and the South End: the former is largely overrun with college kids from nearby Boston University; the latter spreads west of Massachusetts Avenue and southwest along Huntington Avenue, home to heavyweight local institutions like the **Museum of Fine Arts**, the **Isabella Stewart Gardner Museum** and **Fenway Park**, home of the Boston Red Sox. Below all these neighborhoods are Boston's vast **southern districts**, which hold little of interest besides the **John F. Kennedy Library and Museum** and the southerly links in Frederick Law Olmsted's series of parks, known as the Emerald Necklace; it includes the **Arnold Arboretum** and **Franklin Park**, setting for the Franklin Zoo. Across the Charles River from Boston is **Cambridge**, synonymous with venerable Harvard University and tech-savvy MIT, but also boasting some of the area's best nightlife and a lively café scene, especially around Harvard Square, which spills over into neighboring **Somerville** to the north.

The waterfront's Long Wharf doubles as a jumping-off point for escaping the city altogether, on cruises to the idyllic Harbor Islands, or to happening **Provincetown**, Cape Cod's foremost destination. Inland, nearby battle sites

in **Lexington** and **Concord** make for easy day-trips, as does a jaunt up the coast to **Salem** and its witch sights, or further on to seafaring towns like **Gloucester** and **Rockport**.

When to go

Boston is at its most enjoyable in the **fall** (September through early November), when the weather is cooler and the long lines have somewhat abated; and in the **spring** (April through mid-May), when the magnolia trees blossom along Commonwealth Avenue and the parks spring back to life. **Summer**, meanwhile, is certainly the most popular time to visit Boston, both for the warmer weather and frequent festivals. However, July and August can be uncomfortably humid, and you'll have to contend with large student-related influxes around graduation (early June) and the

> Nothing captures the spirit of the city better than Faneuil Hall, the so-called "Cradle of Liberty," and the always-animated Quincy Market

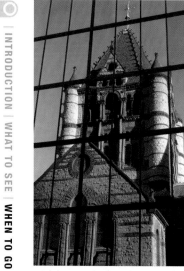

beginning of school (around Labor Day).

At the other end of the spectrum, Boston **winters** can be harsh affairs: they tend to run from late November through March, but, thanks to the moderating influence of the Atlantic, mild spells often break the monotony of long cold stretches, and snowfall is lighter than in the interior regions of New England. No matter when you go, though, be prepared for sudden changes in the weather in the space of a single day: a December morning snow squall could easily be followed by afternoon sunshine and temperatures in the 50s (Fahrenheit).

Average Boston monthly temperature and rainfall

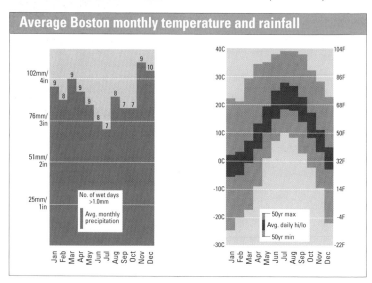

graph taken from the Rough Guide to Weather

things not to miss

It's not possible to see everything that Boston has to offer in one trip – and we don't suggest you try. What follows is a selective and subjective taste of the city's highlights, from impressive museums and bucolic parks to wonderful food and engaging cultural events. They're arranged in five colour-coded categories to help you find the very best things to see, do and experience. All entries have a page reference to take you straight into the Guide, where you can find out more.

02 Ware Collection of Glass Models of Plants
Page **132** • The Harvard Botanical Museum's awesome collection of glass flowers, plants and herbs is truly one-of-a-kind.

01 Charles Bulfinch architecture Page **76**
Among the country's most influential architects, Bulfinch merged Federal and classical styles to create a distinctly Bostonian "look," most notable in the glorious gold-domed Massachusetts State House.

03 Isabella Stewart Gardner Museum Page
111 • Boston's most original museum, with the eccentric Gardner's collection housed round a beautiful courtyard, in her former home.

04 The houses of Beacon Hill Page 74 • Be on the lookout
for purple-tinted windowpanes as you stroll this elegant upper-class neighborhood.

05 A game at Fenway
Park Page 103 • The country's oldest ballpark is home to the Boston Red Sox and the 37-foot-tall "Green Monster."

06 The Omni Parker
House Page 158 • Opulent old-Boston hotel, worth a look regardless of whether you stay there – and also famous as the birthplace of the divine Boston Creme pie.

07 **USS Constitution** Page **69** • The oldest commissioned warship in the world is a must-see for naval buffs and laypersons alike, with tours given by Navy sailors to boot.

08 **Picnicking at the Public Garden** Page **85** • Take the kids down to Back Bay's idyllic Public Garden for a picnic and a ride on the Swan Boats; you might enjoy it as much as they do.

09 **Shopping on Newbury Street** Page 87 • Back Bay's poshest commercial stretch, with everything from colorful boutiques to hip cafés, housed in elegant rowhouses.

10 **Bonsai collection at Arnold Arboretum** Page **121** • The highlight of Jamaica Plain's Arnold Arboretum is the Larz Anderson Bonzai Collection, which features one of the largest assortment of Asian species outside of Asia.

xiii

11 **Head of the Charles Regatta** Page **229** • The annual rowing regatta draws countless spectators to the well-maintained Esplanade on the Charles River.

13 **Blackstone Block** Page **51** • This architecturally untouched bit of old Boston transports you back to an early era of cobblestone streets and low, crooked buildings.

12 **Harvard Square** Page **125** • The epicenter of Cambridge, Harvard Square buzzes with activity day and night.

14 **Walking the Black Heritage Trail** Page **81** • The 1.6-mile Black Heritage Trail, kicked off by the Robert Gould Shaw memorial, is the country's foremost site devoted to pre-Civil War African-American history.

17 A concert at Symphony Hall Page **200**

Home to the Boston Symphony Orchestra, which has been going strong for more than 120 years, this gilded hall is the perfect place in which to hear classical music.

18 Sevens Ale House Page **190** • An authentic Boston neighborhood bar; while the *Bull & Finch* might be more popular, you can be sure that *Sevens* is the real thing.

15 Gibson House Museum Page **86** • This Italian Renaissance townhouse in Back Bay preserves the 1860 home of Catherine Hammond Gibson; it's packed full of curious Victorian-era knick-knacks.

16 Union Oyster House Page **178** • One of the best spots in Boston to get fresh seafood, the *Union Oyster House* also happens to be the oldest continuously operating restaurant in the country.

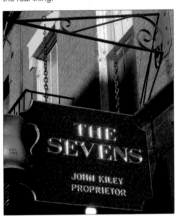

19 Historic burying grounds Pages **41**, **43** & **136**

Holding everyone from revolutionary heroes to literary titans, Boston's colonial burying grounds are idyllic and atmospheric spots to contemplate their contributions.

20 The Christian Science Center Page **92** • These church headquarters are home to several unique and surprising attractions, in particular the Mary Baker Eddy Library and the glass globe Mapparium.

21 Old North Church Page **64** • The oldest church in Boston, this North End landmark was where the lanterns were hung on the night of April 18, 1775 to warn of the advancing British troops.

22 Fanueil Hall Page **50** There's lots of history around Boston, and you get a good sense of it at this vaunted longtime meetingplace, which also abuts the restaurants and shops of Quincy Market.

23 John Singer Sargent Pages **43** & **111** • You'll find paintings and murals by Sargent throughout Boston, to most dazzling effect in the Museum of Fine Arts and the Boston Public Library.

24 A day in Provincetown Page **151** • Though out at the tip of Cape Cod, P-Town (as it's known) is an easy day-trip from the city, its beaches and streetlife popular with families and gay visitors alike.

Contents

Using the Rough Guide

We've tried to make this Rough Guide a good read and easy to use. The book is divided into seven main sections, and you should be able to find whatever you want in one of them.

Front color section

The front **color section** offers a quick tour of Boston. The **introduction** aims to give you a feel for the place and tells you the best times to go. Next, our authors round up their favourite aspects of Boston in the **things not to miss** section – whether it's an important Revolutionary site, a great museum or a fantastic restaurant. Right after this comes the Rough Guide's full **contents** list.

Basics

The Basics section covers all the **pre-departure** nitty-gritty to help you plan your trip and the practicalities you'll want to know once there. This is where to find out about money and costs, city transportation, local media – in fact just about every piece of **general practical information** you might need.

The City

This is the heart of the Rough Guide, divided into user-friendly chapters, each of which covers a different Boston neighborhood or out-of-the-city destination. Every chapter begins with an **introduction** that helps you decide where to go, followed by a chapter map and an extensive tour of the sights.

Listings

Listings contains all the consumer information needed to make the most of your stay in Boston, with chapters on **accommodation**, places to **eat and drink**, **nightlife** and **culture** venues, **shopping**, **sports** and **festivals**. Specialized information for families traveling with children, as well as gay and lesbian visitors, is also provided.

Contexts

Read Contexts to get a deeper understanding of what makes Boston tick, from its colonial past and general **history** to its architectural and urban development. A section on Boston's strong literary history is included, as are reviews of some of the best **books** on the city.

Index + small print

Apart from a **full index**, which includes maps as well as places and people, this section covers publishing information, credits and acknowledgements, and also has our contact details, in case you want to send us updates, corrections or suggestions for improving the guide.

Color maps

The back color section contains seven detailed **maps and plans** to help you explore the city up close, navigate your way on the subway and locate every place recommended in the guide.

Map and chapter list

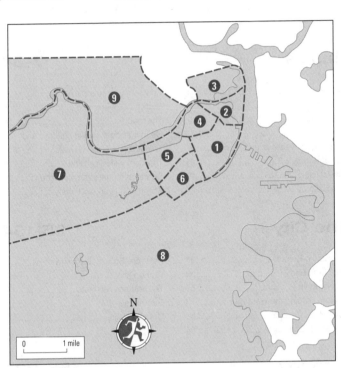

Contents

Contexts

Index + small print

Color maps at back of book

1. Boston and Eastern Massachusetts
2. Boston
3. Downtown and Beacon Hill
4. The North End, Charlestown and the West End

5. Back Bay, the Fenway and the South End
6. Cambridge
7. Boston **T** System

Map symbols

maps are listed in the full index using colored text

— ···	State boundary	⊙	Statue
----	Chapter boundary	⚱	Gardens
▬▬	Expressway	Ⓣ	T system station
══	Main road	◉	Accommodation
══	Minor road	ⓘ	Information office
▬▬	Pedestrianized road	⊞	Hospital
▬▬	Railway	⊠	Post office
– – –	Ferry route	⚲	Church
——	Waterway	■	Building
✈	International airport	⊞	Church (town maps)
◆	Point of interest	▨	Park
🏛	Monument	⸬	Beach
♦	Museum	🪦	Cemetery

Basics

Basics

Getting there

Getting to Boston from most places in North America is fastest and easiest by plane; outside of North America, air travel – at least to somewhere in the States or Canada – is, of course, a near necessity. Flying is also often the least expensive option, especially if you land a last-minute deal, which can save you more than half the regular airfare. Upon arrival, you'll be pleased to find that the Boston airport, Logan International (BOS), is conveniently situated near subways and water taxis that provide fast and efficient city access.

If you're not into flying, or have already arrived from abroad somewhere in the US or Canada, the **railroad** is a decent second option for getting to the city, particularly for visitors traveling along the east coast. **Amtrak** has a reliable high-speed route between Washington DC and Boston; from elsewhere in the country, though, the approaches to Beantown are leisurely at best.

For budget travelers, the **Greyhound** and **Peter Pan bus companies** are good options, and they tend to have more flexible departure times than either train or plane. Keep in mind, though, that long-haul buses can be uncomfortable, and that, unlike on rail or by plane, you're still at the mercy of the traffic.

Lastly, there's **driving**, probably the least palatable option, as car rental in the US is not cheap, and driving in and around Boston a nightmare. If you insist on getting to Boston via car, though, plan on parking your vehicle once you get into the city and leaving it for the duration of your stay; you'll neither want (as Boston is a great walking city) or need the thing again until you leave town.

On a final note, overseas visitors can buy **air**, **train** and **bus passes** for discounted travel throughout the United States; these normally have to be purchased before your trip, and from within your home country. Below, all prices in this section are given in **US dollars**, unless otherwise stated.

Shopping for air tickets and passes

Competition on major routes keeps plane fares at a reasonable level, though prices do vary according to various factors. Within the US, prices for **domestic flights** to Boston are generally determined by the time of departure and seat availability, especially on the busy Northeastern commuter routes between Washington, New York and Boston.

Special seasonal deals or discount fares for students and anyone under 26 can bring the price down, but by far the best deals around are **last-minute fares** for long weekend travel, usually announced mid-week by airlines that haven't filled their full-fare seats. Of course, there's no guarantee that Boston will make the cut on any given week, but if it does, you can count on substantial savings – though ticketing restrictions will affect your departure and return times. You can get first crack at the cheap seats by signing up for email notification at most major airline websites.

If you want a longer stay – or simply the guarantee that you will indeed be going to Boston during your predetermined holidays – you'll get the most savings by booking a mid-week flight two to three weeks in advance, and staying over a Saturday night. Airlines charge $100 to change your departure date once your ticket's been issued, so be sure of your schedule when booking.

From **overseas**, seasonal variations in price are common, with flights at their most expensive from June to August (actually the hottest and most humid time to visit Boston). Spring and autumn are slightly less pricey, while winter (excluding the Christmas and New Year holiday period) is the cheapest time to fly.

Whatever your departure point, if you want to travel during the **major American holiday periods** (around the Fourth of July, Thanksgiving, Christmas, and New Year's Day), you should book well in advance, and

9

expect to pay more. The same is true if you're planning to visit in May or early June, when Boston area universities hold their graduation ceremonies.

Remember also to allow for the extra cost of government **duty fees and airport taxes** whenever, and from wherever, you travel – you'll be quoted an all-inclusive price when you pay for your ticket, but not necessarily when you first make inquiries. On the plus side, Logan doesn't charge a **departure tax** – yet.

Rather than contacting all the separate airlines, you'll save yourself a lot of time, and possibly money, too, by checking out the various **discount travel and flight agents**, which often advertise in the travel sections of the daily and weekend press. Some, such as Council Travel, STA, Travel Cuts and Usit Campus, specialize in **youth/student fares**, but even if you don't fit into that category, they'll do their best to find you the cheapest available flight.

Overseas travelers should also keep in mind that all the main American airlines offer **air passes** for flights within the US. These have to be bought in advance, and are usually sold with the proviso that you reach the US with the same airline. All the deals are broadly similar, involving the purchase of at least three coupons (costing up to $800 for the first three coupons, and $80 for each additional one), each valid for a one-way flight of any duration within the US.

Finally, many airlines and discount travel websites offer you the opportunity to **book your tickets online**, often at a small discount. Keep in mind, though, that you'll need to be flexible about your departure and return dates to get the best prices from these sites. Make sure you read the small print before buying, too, as it can be difficult, if not impossible, to claim refunds or change your ticket, especially on last-minute deals.

Online booking agents and general travel sites

ⓦ**www.cheapflights.com** Bookings from the UK and Ireland only. Flight deals, travel agents, plus links to other travel sites.
ⓦ**www.cheaptickets.com** American discount flight specialists.
ⓦ**www.ebookers.com** and ⓦ**www.ebookers.ie** Low fares on an extensive selection of scheduled flights from the UK and Ireland.
ⓦ**www.etn.nl/discount.htm** A hub of consolidator and discount agent Web links.
ⓦ**www.expedia.com** Discount airfares, all-airline search engine, and daily deals.
ⓦ**www.flyaow.com** UK online air travel info and reservations site.
ⓦ**www.hotwire.com** Bookings from the US only. Last-minute savings of up to forty percent on regular published fares.
ⓦ**www.lastminute.com** Good last-minute holiday package and flight-only deals; UK bookings only.
ⓦ**www.orbitz.com** US bookings only for cut-rate international and domestic flights.
ⓦ**www.priceline.com** and
ⓦ**www.priceline.co.uk** Name-your-own-price website that has deals at around forty percent off standard fares. You cannot specify flight times (although you do specify dates).
ⓦ**www.skyauction.com** Bookings from the US only. Auctions tickets and travel packages using a "second bid" scheme. The best strategy is to bid the maximum you're willing to pay, since if you win you'll pay just enough to beat the runner-up regardless of your maximum bid.
ⓦ**www.smilinjack.com/airlines.htm** Lists an up-to-date compilation of airline website addresses.
ⓦ**www.travel.com.au** and ⓦ**www.travel.co.nz** Discount fares and destination advice for Australian/New Zealand travelers.
ⓦ**www.travelocity.com** and
ⓦ**www.travelocity.co.uk** Destination guides along with deals for car rental, lodging and airfares.
ⓦ**www.travelshop.com.au** Australian website offering discounted flights, packages, insurance, and online bookings.
ⓦ**travel.yahoo.com** Incorporates a lot of Rough Guide material in its coverage of destination countries and cities across the world, with information about places to eat, sleep and so on.
ⓦ**www.unison.otc-ie.com** Irish site with online flight bookings, car rental, insurance and more.

Flights and other approaches from the US and Canada

Unless you're on America's east coast (and perhaps even then, too), you're most likely to **fly** into Boston, which is well-connected to the rest of the country and Canada by air routes. Amtrak trains provide a viable option from places like New York and Washington DC, as do buses from most anywhere, if you're willing to put up with a bit of discomfort (and a significantly longer journey) in exchange for value.

By plane

Boston's only airport, **Logan International**, is New England's busiest. Most service comes from **East Coast shuttles** originating from New York's La Guardia (Delta Airlines; Mon–Fri every 30–60min 6am–9.30pm, Sat–Sun every 2hr 8.30am–8.30pm) and Washington DC's Reagan National Airport (US Airways; Mon–Sat hourly 7.30am–8.30pm, Sun every 2–4hr 8.30am–8.30pm). The following airlines also offer regular, daily service to Boston: Air Canada (from Montréal, Ottawa, Toronto, and Vancouver), American Airlines (from Chicago, Dallas, Miami, Philadelphia, and St Louis), Continental (from Houston, Chicago, Miami, Newark, and Seattle), Delta (from Atlanta, Dallas, and Tampa), United (from Chicago, Los Angeles, and San Francisco), Northwest (from Detroit, Memphis, Minneapolis, San Diego, and Vancouver), and US Airways (from Fort Lauderdale, Orlando, and Philadelphia).

Fares are lowest in the heavily trafficked Northeast corridor; a round-trip fare **from New York** can cost as little as $90–100, although $120–170 is the more usual price fare; **from Washington DC** and **Miami**, the range is usually $200–250; from **Chicago**, $260–300. The price of flights **from the West Coast** is more likely to fluctuate – round-trip fares from LA, San Francisco or Seattle typically cost $450–550, but can go as low as $300. **From Canada**, be prepared to pay around C$400–500 from Toronto and Montréal, and closer to C$700, and as high as C$1200, from Vancouver.

Airlines in the US and Canada

Air Canada ☎1-888/247-2262, @www.aircanada.ca
Air Tran ☎1-800/247-8726, @www.airtran.com
America West ☎1-800/235-9292, @www.americawest.com
American Airlines and **American Eagle** ☎1-800/433-7300, @www.aa.com
American Trans Air ☎1-800/225-2995, @www.ata.com
Cape Air ☎1-800/352-0714, @www.flycapeair.com
Continental ☎1-800/523-3273, @www.continental.com

Delta Air Lines and **Delta Shuttle** ☎1-800/221-1212, @www.delta.com
Delta Express ☎1-866/2-FLYDLX, @www.flydlx.com
Frontier ☎1-800/432-1359, @www.frontierairlines.com
Midwest Express ☎1-800/452-2022, @www.midwestexpress.com
Northwest ☎1-800/225-2525, @www.nwa.com
United ☎1-800/241-6522, @www.ual.com
US Airways, **US Airways Shuttle**, and **US Airways Express** ☎1-800/428-4322, @www.usairways.com

Discount travel and flight agents in the US and Canada

Airtech ☎1-877/247-8324 or 212/219-7000, @www.airtech.com. Standby seat broker.
Council Travel ☎1-800/226-8624, @617/528-2091, @www.counciltravel.com. US organization that mostly, but by no means exclusively, specializes in student/budget travel. Flights from within the US only.
Now Voyager ☎1-800/255-6951, @www.nowvoyager.com. San Francisco-based gay- and lesbian-friendly consolidator with Boston-based tours and packages.
Skylink US ☎1-800/247-6659 or 212/573-8980, Canada ☎1-800/759-5465, @www.skylinkus.com. Consolidator with multiple offices throughout the US and Canada.
STA Travel ☎1-800/777-0112 or 1-800/781-4040, @www.sta-travel.com. Worldwide specialists in independent travel; also student IDs, travel insurance and car rental.
TFI Tours International ☎1-800/745-8000 or 212/736-1140, @www.lowestairprice.com. Consolidator with flights to Boston from Canadian and US cities.
Travelers Advantage ☎1-877/259-2691, @www.travelersadvantage.com. Discount travel club; annual membership fee required (currently $1 for 3 months' trial).
Travel Cuts Canada ☎1-800/667-2887, US ☎1-866/246-9762, @www.travelcuts.com. Canadian student-travel organization.
Worldtek Travel ☎1/800/243-1723, @www.worldtek.com. Discount travel agency.

Package tours

Plenty of travel operators offer **tours** and **camping trips** that typically feature a day or two in Boston as part of a seven-day itinerary that includes several New England desti-

11

nations. Though these are considerably more expensive than a mere weekend in the city (and prices vary wildly according to what's being offered), the Boston element of the trip makes a great backgrounder to a provincial New England vacation.

Tour operators

American Express Vacations ☎1-800/241-1700, ⊛www.americanexpress.com/travel. Flights, hotels, last-minute specials, city-break packages and speciality tours.

Amtrak Vacations ☎1-800/321-8684, ⊛www.amtrak.com/services/amtrak-vacations/html. Train or Amtrak Air-Rail trips through the Northeast, along with hotel reservations, car rental and sightseeing tours.

Collette Vacations ☎1-800/340-5158, ⊛www.collettevacations.com. Boston figures in various escorted or independent tour permutations; from the six-night "Discover Boston" option (from $779) to the "New England Foliage" tour, which also covers provincial NE towns like Lexington, Concord and Killington (from $1369); prices include meals but exclude airfare/travel to Boston.

Contiki Holidays ☎1-888/CONTIKI, ⊛www.contiki.com. Trips for the 18–35-year-old crowd; the 12-day Eastern Canada and the USA tour (from $1159, airfare not included) takes in Boston and Cape Cod.

Globus and Cosmos ⊛www.globusandcosmos.com. Deluxe escorted tours. The "Cape Cod Escape" (eight days, from $1599) and "Great Cities of the East" (ten days, from $2299) tours both include significant time in Boston; the land-only prices include meals. Request brochures online or via a listed travel agent.

Suntrek Tours ☎1-800/SUN-TREK, ⊛www.suntrek.com. Has 7- to 14-day "Eastern Trails" tours that include a couple of days in the Boston region ($439–799), and a three-week "Canadian Pioneer" tour that includes Ontario and Québec in the package, as well ($1252–1322).

Trek America ☎1-800/221-0596 ⊛www.trekamerica.com. Trekking company geared to 18–38 year olds with 7–14-day camping tours through the Eastern US, many with a Canadian leg thrown in (from $469).

By train

For those heading to Boston from within the Washington DC and New York shuttle flight radius, **train** travel is a decent – but likely no less expensive – alternative. On the plus side, the Amtrak trains (☎1-800/USA-RAIL, ⊛www.amtrak.com) that service the Washington to Boston corridor are the fleet's most reliable, and usually stick to their official schedules. Fares from New York to Boston are $128 round-trip, with the trip taking between four and five hours; double the cost gets you a seat on the cushier Acela Express, which, its name notwithstanding, only shaves about thirty minutes off the trip time. From Washington DC, the regular train runs just shy of eight hours ($162 return) while the express gets you there in 6.5 hours ($341 return).

Although it's possible to haul yourself long-distance **from the West Coast**, the Midwest or the South, the trip is anything but fast – count on three days and up from California – nor is it cost-effective, at around $350 for a round-trip ticket. The same applies to visitors trying to approach Boston **from Canada** using Via Rail (☎1-888/842-7245, ⊛www.viarail.ca); you can do so only by connecting in New York City, and on an indirect itinerary at best. The rail journey can take anywhere from twelve to twenty hours from Toronto and Montréal, and over three days from Vancouver. Fares start around C$400 return from the closer points – and at those prices, you might as well fly.

By bus

Given how expensive rail travel is in the US, getting to Boston by **bus** can be an appealing – if less comfortable – option, especially as the buses quite often get there faster than the train does, given the notorious unreliability of rail travel outside of the Northeast corridor. Boston is an especially common stop coming from **New York** or **Washington DC**; barring rush-hour traffic and highway accidents, one-way trips typically take four and a half hours from New York and ten and a half hours from Washington, with round-trip fares costing $80 and $132, respectively. That said, the rates can go down by over half in the summer, when the two main carriers, **Greyhound** (☎1-800/231-2222, ⊛www.greyhound.com) and **Peter Pan**

(☎1-800/237-8747, ⓦwww.peterpanbus
.com) lose their best income source –
Boston university students – and tempt full-
time residents with cut-rate deals. The only
hitch is that these cheap tickets must be
purchased in Boston; even so, you can still
save by buying a one-way ticket to Boston
and getting your return on arrival.

Visitors leaving **from New York** have two
additional choices when it comes to bus
travel. There's **Bonanza** (☎1-888/751-8800,
ⓦwww.bonanzabus.com), which has modestly cheaper tickets year-round (though it
includes a stop in Providence, Rhode Island,
for a total of five hours' road time), and the
Chinatown buses (☎617/338-8222,
ⓦwww.travelpackusa.com), which offer the
cheapest rates, starting as low as $15 one-
way for fully air-conditioned coaches.

Coming from Canada, several daily
buses **from Toronto** reach Boston with at
least one changeover – usually in
Syracuse, New York – contributing to a
minimum twelve-hour ride (C$160 return).
Buses **from Montréal** take around seven
hours and have the added benefit of direct
service (C$116 return). In both cases, con-
tact Greyhound (☎1-800/661-87447,
ⓦwww.greyhound.com).

By car

If you can at all avoid coming into Boston by
car, do. The lane changes and traffic snarls
caused by ongoing work to put the dreaded
I-93 underground, aka the "**Big Dig**" (see
p.viii), can make accessing Boston a sure
recipe for road rage. If you insist on driving,
stay informed of roadwork closures and
reroutings by tuning into 1030 AM (reports
every ten minutes 5am–7pm; every half-hour
7pm–5am) and prepare for interminable
jams and detours.

Aside from frustrating I-93, two other highways lead into town: **I-95**, which circum-
scribes the Boston area (and is also known
as Route-128 between Gloucester and
Boston), and **I-90** (the Massachusetts
Turnpike or "Masspike"), which approaches
Boston from the west and is popular with
those arriving from New York state.

Once you get into Boston, if you're lucky
enough to get rerouted to a street with a 24-

Driving to Boston

From Chicago 16 hours 30 minutes
(982 miles)
From Miami 25 hours (1488 miles)
From New York 4 hours (216 miles)
From San Francisco 52 hours
(3100 miles)
From Montréal 6 hours (310 miles)
From Toronto 9 hours 30 minutes
(552 miles)

hour **parking lot**, use it: you'll probably
never want to drive your car again. For more
on driving in town, see p.24.

Flights from the UK and Ireland

Nine airlines make the seven-hour flight from
Britain to Boston; most leave early to mid-
afternoon and arrive in the late afternoon or
evening, though the odd red-eye flight
leaves the UK at 8pm and arrives later the
same night in Boston. Returning to the UK
and Ireland, you're looking at an early morning or early evening departure; the prevailing
winds tend to make the trip back modestly
shorter than the one over.

British Airways, Virgin Atlantic and
American Airlines have the most daily **non-
stop flights** from London's Heathrow Airport;
travelers from elsewhere in the UK will have
to connect in London. Aer Lingus operates
the only non-stop service **from Ireland**.

As there's not a lot of price differentiation
between the major airlines, you'll have to
shop around to get the best deals. The standard option, the **Apex** ticket, is a non-
refundable return ticket that must be purchased 21 days in advance and requires a
minimum seven-night stay, up to a maximum
of one month; changing departure dates
usually incurs a penalty. With or without an
Apex ticket, fares **from London** hover
around £200 in low season (Oct–Feb), £250
in the spring, and £300 in high season
(May–Sept). All fares are subject to a £63
tax, and weekend flights incur additional sur-
charges. Flights **from Ireland** (Dublin,
Shannon or Cork) on Aer Lingus are somewhat cheaper, and can range from €200 in
low season to €400 in high season.

If you're really penny-pinching, and must go to Boston in high season, you might consider flying as a **courier**. In return for cheaper rates, you'd be responsible for checking a package through with your (carry-on only) luggage. Given heightened security following September 11th, though, the extra hassle over your relation to the package's contents may not be worth the trouble. To offer your services, call Flight Masters (☎020/7462 0022) or Bridges Worldwide (☎01895/465 065). You can also join the International Association of Air Travel Couriers (☎0800/746 481 or 01305/216 920, ⊛www.aircourier .co.uk). Flights leave from either Gatwick or Heathrow, with high-season costs reduced to fares nearing spring rates.

Airlines in the UK and Ireland

Aer Lingus UK ☎0845/973 7747, Republic of Ireland ☎01/705 3333 or 01/844 4777, ⊛www.aerlingus.ie
American Airlines UK ☎0845/778 9789, ⊛www.aa.com
British Airways UK ☎0845/773 3377, Republic of Ireland ☎1800/626 747, ⊛www.british-airways.com
Continental UK ☎0800/776 464, Republic of Ireland ☎1890/925 252, ⊛www.flycontinental.com
Delta UK ☎0800/414 767, Republic of Ireland ☎01/407 3165, ⊛www.delta.com
easyJet UK ☎0870/600 0000, ⊛www.easyjet.com
Go UK ☎0870/607 6543, www.go-fly.com
KLM/Northwest UK ☎08705/074 074, ⊛www.klmuk.com
Ryanair UK ☎0870/156 9569, Republic of Ireland ☎01/609 7800, ⊛www.ryanair.com
United Airlines UK ☎0845/844 4777, Republic of Ireland ☎1800/535 300, ⊛www.ual.com
US Airways UK 0845/600 3300, Republic of Ireland 1890/925 065, ⊛www.usairways.com
Virgin Atlantic UK ☎01293/747 747, Republic of Ireland ☎01/873 3388, ⊛www.virgin -atlantic.com

Discount travel and flight agents in Britain and Ireland

Apex Travel Dublin ☎01/671 5933, ⊛www.apextravel.ie. Specialists in flights to the US.

Bridge the World ☎020/7911 0900, ⊛www.bridgetheworld.com. Specializing in round-the-world tickets, with good deals aimed at the backpacker market.
CIE Tours International Dublin ☎01/703 1888, ⊛www.cietours.ie. General flight and tour agent.
Destination Group ☎020/7400 7000, ⊛www.destination-group.com. Discount airfares, as well as inclusive packages for US travel.
Dial A Flight ☎0870/333 4488, ⊛www.dialaflight.com. Discounts on airfares, as well as car rental, hotels and insurance.
Flightbookers ☎020/7757 2444, ⊛www.ebookers.com. Low fares on an extensive selection of scheduled flights.
Flight Centre ☎08705/666 677, ⊛www.flightcentre.co.uk. Large choice of discounted flights.
Flightfinders Dublin ☎01/676 8326. Discount flight specialists.
Flynow ☎020/7835 2000, ⊛www.flynow.com. Wide range of discounted tickets.
Joe Walsh Tours Dublin ☎01/872 2555 or 676 3053, Cork ☎021/427 7959, ⊛www .joewalshtours.ie. General budget fares agent.
London Flight Centre ☎020/7244 6411, ⊛www.topdecktravel.co.uk. Long-established agent dealing in discount flights.
McCarthy's Travel Cork ☎021/427 0127, ⊛www.mccarthystravel.ie. General flight agent.
North South Travel ☎01245/608 291, ⊛www.northsouthtravel.co.uk. Discounted fares worldwide; profits are used to support projects in the developing world, especially the promotion of sustainable tourism.
Premier Travel Derry ☎028/7126 3333, ⊛www.premiertravel.uk.com. Discount flight specialists.
Quest Worldwide ☎020/8547 3322, ⊛www.questtravel.com. Specialists in round-the-world discount fares.
Rosetta Travel Belfast ☎028/9064 4996, ⊛www.rosettatravel.com. Flight and holiday agent.
STA Travel ☎0870/160 6070, ⊛www.statravel.co.uk. Worldwide specialists in low-cost flights and tours for students and under-26s (other customers welcome); Amtrak passes also available.
Trailfinders ☎020/7628 7628, ⊛www.trailfinders.com. One of the best-informed and most efficient agents for independent travelers; Amtrak passes also available. Dublin ☎01/677 7888, ⊛www.trailfinders.ie. One of the best-informed and most efficient agents for independent travelers; Amtrak passes also available.

Travel Bag ☎0870/900 1350, ⊛www.travelbag.co.uk. Discount flights to the US.
Travel Cuts ☎020/7255 2082, ⊛www.travelcuts.com. Budget, student and youth travel, plus round-the-world tickets; Amtrak passes also available.
Twohigs Travel Dublin ☎01/677 2666. General flight and travel agent.
Usit Now Belfast ☎028/9032 7111, Dublin ☎01/602 1777 or 677 8117, Cork ☎021/4270 900, Derry ☎028/7137 1888, ⊛www.usitnow.ie. Student and youth travel specialists offering flights and Amtrak train passes.
World Travel Centre Dublin ☎01/671 7155, ⊛www.worldtravel.ie. Discount flights and other travel services.

Package tours

There are plenty of companies running package deals **from the UK** to Boston, mostly short city breaks that span three to five days. For a three-day trip, typical rates will run to around £600 per person in summer, though prices drop to around £450 out of high season, and sometimes less than that. It's usually around £100 more for the five-star or superior-grade hotel package. If you plan to see more of the country than just Boston, **fly-drive** deals – which include car rental when buying a transatlantic ticket from an airline or tour operator – are always cheaper than renting a car on the spot. Most of the specialist companies offer fly-drive packages, though watch out for hidden extras, such as local taxes, "drop-off" charges and extra insurance.

Tour operators

American Holidays Belfast ☎028/9023 8762, Dublin ☎01/433 1009, ⊛www.american-holidays.com. Specialists in travel to USA and Canada with independent travel options and escorted tours; a ten-day tour including Boston, Nantucket and Martha's Vineyard costs £1475.
British Airways Holidays UK ☎0870/242 4245, ⊛www.baholidays.co.uk. Using British Airways and other quality international airlines, offers quality package and tailor-made Boston-area holidays by phone; you can book individual amenities like hotel rooms, at a serious discount, online.
Contiki Tours UK ☎0208/290 6777, ⊛www.contiki.com. Trips for the 18–35-year-old crowd; the 12-day Eastern Canada and the USA

tour (from £749, land only) includes Boston and Cape Cod.
Funway USA UK ☎020/8466 0222, ⊛www.funwayholidays.co.uk. Boston city breaks, flight-only deals and car rental .
Kuoni Travel UK ☎01306/742 888, ⊛www.kuoni.co.uk. Flexible package holidays to Boston in a number of price ranges; good family offers.
Media Travel UK ☎01784/434 434, ⊛www.mediatravel.co.uk. Tour operator with various 8-day trips through New England with an option of visiting Canada, too (£799–899).
Thomas Cook UK ☎0870/566 6222, ⊛www.thomascook.co.uk. Long-established one-stop 24-hour travel agency for package holidays, city breaks and scheduled flights, with bureau de change issuing Thomas Cook travelers' checks, travel insurance and car rental.
TrekAmerica UK ☎01295/256 777, ⊛www.trekamerica.com. Youth-oriented (18–38-year-olds) camping tours including Boston as part of larger tours of the region. The one-week "Eastern Highlights" tour, departing from New York, costs from £308 (flights, meals and personal expenses extra).
Unijet UK ☎0870/600 8009, ⊛www.unijet.com. City breaks, hotel reservations and car rental.
United Vacations UK ☎0870/606 2222, ⊛www.unitedvacations.co.uk. One-stop agent for tailor-made holidays, city breaks, fly-drive deals, pre-booked sightseeing tours, and etc. Organized tours include a seven-night "Great American Cities" rail tour with Amtrak, from Boston to DC, from £553 (accommodation, transport and tours included, flights extra).
Virgin Holidays UK ☎0870/220 2788, ⊛www.virginholidays.co.uk. City breaks with hotels in downtown, Back Bay and Cambridge; flights are with Virgin Atlantic.
World Travel Centre Dublin ☎01/671 7155, ⊛www.worldtravel.ie. Specialists in flights and packages to USA and Boston.

Flights from Australia and New Zealand

Flights from **Australia** and **New Zealand** fly into the West Coast before continuing on to Boston, making for a pretty long trip, considering that flying time is about ten hours to the coast and another six to Boston.

Return fares from eastern Australian capitals are usually around $A2000/$NZ2900 in low season (mid-January to February and

Round-the-world tickets

If Boston is only one stop on a longer journey, you might want to consider buying a round-the-world (RTW) ticket. Some travel agents can sell you an "off-the-shelf" RTW ticket that will have you touching down in about half a dozen cities – Boston does figure on some standard itineraries, though New York is a more usual US East Coast stopover. You can also have an agent assemble a tailor-made ticket, though it's apt to be more expensive. Figure on a minimum of A\$2200/\$NZ2800 for a RTW ticket – the most it'll cost you is A\$2800/NZ\$3500. Travelers from the US can expect to pay in the neighborhood of \$1250 for a similar ticket, while Europeans can expect to pay around €1300.

October–November), while tickets from Perth and Darwin can cost up to A\$400 more. You might do better purchasing a direct ticket to either San Francisco or LA and using an air pass to get to Boston. If you choose this route, you must buy a minimum of three flight coupons (at a cost of \$800 total) before leaving your home country. The best connections through the West Coast tend to be with United, Air New Zealand and Qantas.

Airlines in Australia and New Zealand

Air New Zealand Australia ☎13 24 76, New Zealand ☎0800/737 000, ⊛www.airnz.com
American Airlines Australia ☎1300/650 747, New Zealand ☎0800/887 997, ⊛www.aa.com
British Airways Australia ☎02/8904 8800, New Zealand ☎09/356 8690, ⊛www.british-airways.com
Continental Airlines Australia ☎02/9244 2242, New Zealand ☎09/308 3350, ⊛www.flycontinental.com
Delta Air Lines Australia ☎800/500 992, New Zealand ☎0800/440 876, ⊛www.delta-air.com
Japan Airlines (JAL) Australia ☎02/9272 1111, New Zealand ☎09/379 9906, ⊛www.japanair.com
KLM Australia ☎1300/303 747, New Zealand ☎09/309 1782, ⊛www.klm.com
Northwest Airlines Australia ☎1300/303 747, New Zealand ☎09/302 1452, ⊛www.nwa.com
Qantas Australia ☎13 13 13, New Zealand ☎0800/808 767, ⊛www.qantas.com.au
United Airlines Australia ☎13 17 77, New Zealand ☎09/379 3800, ⊛www.ual.com
Virgin Atlantic Australia ☎02/9244 2747, New Zealand ☎09/308 3377, ⊛www.virgin-atlantic.com

Discount travel and flight agents in Australia and New Zealand

Anywhere Travel Australia ☎02/9663 0411 or 018/401 014. General fares agent.
Budget Travel New Zealand ☎09/366 0061 or 0800/808 040, ⊛www.budgettravel.co.nz. Flights, RTW fares and tours.
Destinations Unlimited New Zealand ☎09/373 4033. RTW fares.
Flight Centres Australia ☎02/9235 3522 or for nearest branch 13 16 00, New Zealand ☎09/358 4310, ⊛www.flightcentre.com.au. Specialist agent for budget flights, especially RTW.
STA Travel Australia ☎13 17 76 or 1300/360 960, ⊛www.statravel.com.au; New Zealand ☎09/309 0458 or 366 6673, ⊛www.statravel.co.nz. Discount flights, travel passes and other services for youth/student travelers.
Student Uni Travel Australia ☎02/9232 8444. Good deals for students.
Thomas Cook Australia ☎13 17 71 or ☎1800/801 002, ⊛www.thomascook.com.au; New Zealand ☎09/379 3920, ⊛www.thomascook.co.nz. General flight and holiday agent; Amtrak passes also available.
Trailfinders Australia ☎02/9247 7666, ⊛www.trailfinders.com.au. One of the best-informed and most efficient agents for independent travelers; Amtrak passes also available.
Usit Beyond New Zealand ☎09/379 4224 or 0800/874 823, ⊛www.usitbeyond.co.nz. Youth/student travel specialist; also RTW tickets, train passes and other services.
Walshes World New Zealand ☎09/379 3708. Agent for Amtrak rail passes.

Specialist tour operators

Adventure World Australia ☎02/9956 7766 or 1300/363 055, ⊛www.adventureworld.com.au; New Zealand ☎09/524 5118,

@ www.adventureworld.co.nz. Boston hotel bookings, car rental and organized tours.
American Town and Country Holidays Australia ☎ 03/9877 3322. Tailor-made trips, accommodation, car rental and city breaks.
American Travel Centre/Journeys Worldwide Australia ☎ 07/3221 4788. All aspects of travel to the US.
Australian Pacific Tours Australia ☎ 03/9277 8444 or 1800/675 222, New Zealand ☎ 09/279 6077. Package tours and independent travel to the US.
Canada and America Travel Specialists Australia ☎ 02/9922 4600, @ www.canada -americatravel.com.au. Can arrange flights and accommodation in North America, plus Greyhound

Ameripasses and Amtrak passes.
Contiki Holidays Australia ☎ 02/9511 2200, New Zealand ☎ 09/309 8824, @ www.contiki.com. Frenetic tours for 18- to 35-year-old party animals. Their seven-day "Eastern Explorer" tour includes Boston (from A$1259, NZ$1649).
Creative Holidays Australia ☎ 02/9386 2111, @ www.creativeholidays.com.au. City breaks and other packages.
Sydney International Travel Centre ☎ 02/9299 8000, @ www.sydneytravel.com.au. US flights, accommodation, city stays and car rental.
United Vacations ☎ 02/9324 1000. Tailor-made city stays or wider American holidays, with departures from several Australian airports.

Red tape and visas

Until recently, travelers from Britain, Ireland, Australia and New Zealand needed only a valid passport and proof of departure (in the form of an onward ticket to a country other than a US neighbor) to stay in the US for a period of up to ninety days. Heightened security concerns after September 11th, however, have prompted a review of these entrance formalities, which may result in limiting foreigners' stays to a maximum of thirty days (though as of press time, this hasn't happened yet).

As a result, if you're planning more than a month-long visit, you'd do best to check with your local US embassy to get the latest information on visit terms.

So far, **Canadian citizens** are exempted from the proposed thirty-day limit, and can continue to visit the US for up to six months, as long as they present proof of citizenship (a passport or birth certificate and photo ID). Questions may be put to the US embassy at 100 Wellington St, Ottawa, ON, K1P 5A1 (☎613/238-5335). If you're planning a work- or study-related visit, you may need to get a visa.

US embassies

Foreign consulates in Boston are listed on p.231.
Australia 21 Moonah Place, Yarralumla, Canberra, ACT 2600 ☎02/6214 5600, @usembassy -australia.state.gov/embassy
Britain 24–31 Grosvenor Square, London, W1A 1AE ☎020/7499 9000 or 0891/200 290, 24hr visa hotline ☎09068/200 290, @www.usembassy.org.uk
Canada 490 Sussex Drive, Ottawa, ON K1P 5T1 ☎613/238 5335, @www.usembassycanada.gov
Ireland 42 Elgin Rd, Ballsbridge, Dublin 4 ☎01/688 7122, @www.usembassy.ie
New Zealand 29 Fitzherbert Terrace, Thorndon, Wellington, ☎04/462 6000, @www.usembassy.org.nz

Insurance

Getting travel insurance is definitely recommended, especially if you're coming from abroad and are at all concerned about your health – prices for medical attention in the US can be exorbitant. A secondary benefit is that most policies also cover against theft and loss, which can be useful if you're toting around a laptop or other expensive gear.

Before paying for a new policy, check to see if you're already covered: some all-risks home insurance policies may cover your possessions when overseas, and many private medical schemes include cover when abroad. In Canada, provincial health plans usually provide partial cover for medical mishaps outside of the country, while holders of official student/teacher/youth cards are entitled to meager accident coverage and hospital in-patient benefits. Students will often find that their student health coverage extends during the vacations and for one term beyond the date of last enrollment.

After exhausting the possibilities above, you might want to contact a specialist travel insurance company, or consider the travel insurance deal we offer (see box). A typical travel insurance policy usually provides cover for the loss of baggage, tickets and – up to a certain limit – cash or checks, as well as cancellation or curtailment of your journey. Many policies can be chopped and changed to exclude coverage you don't need – for example, sickness and accident benefits can often be excluded or included at will. If you do take medical coverage, ascertain whether benefits will be paid as treatment proceeds or only after return home, and whether there is a 24-hour medical emergency number. When securing baggage cover, make sure that the per-article limit – typically under $500 – will cover your most valuable possession. If you need to make a claim, you should keep receipts for medicines and medical treatment, and in the event you have anything stolen, you must obtain an official statement from the police.

Rough Guides travel insurance

Rough Guides offers its own travel insurance, customized for our readers by a leading UK broker and backed by a Lloyd's underwriter. It's available for anyone, of any nationality and any age, traveling anywhere in the world.

There are two main Rough Guide insurance plans: **Essential**, for basic, no-frills cover; and **Premier**, with more generous and extensive benefits. Alternatively, you can take out **annual multi-trip insurance**, which covers you for any number of trips throughout the year (with a maximum of 60 days for any one trip). Unlike many policies, the Rough Guides plans are calculated by the day, so if you're traveling for 27 days rather than a month, that's all you pay for. If you intend to be away for the whole year, the Adventurer policy will cover you for 365 days. Each plan can be supplemented with a "Hazardous Activities Premium" if you plan to indulge in sports considered dangerous, such as skiing, scuba diving or hiking.

For a policy quote, call the Rough Guide Insurance Line on US toll-free ☎1-866/220 5588, UK freefone ☎0800/015 0906, or, if you're calling from elsewhere in the world, dial your international access code, followed by ☎44 1243/621 046. Alternatively, get an online quote or buy online at ⊛www.roughguidesinsurance.com.

Health

Visitors from Europe, Australia, New Zealand and Canada don't require any vaccinations to enter the US – what you will require is travel insurance, since medical bills for even the most minor scrape can be outrageously expensive; see p.18 for details. There aren't any out of the ordinary health concerns to consider when coming to the city, other than your own safety; turn to p.33 for a rundown of precautions.

Doctors, pharmacies and hospitals

If you do need to see a **doctor** while in Boston, the Massachusetts General Physician Referral Service (Mon–Fri 8.30am–5pm; ☎726-5800) puts would-be patients together with physicians at Massachusetts General Hospital. For immediate care, Inn-House Doctor (839 Beacon Street, Suite B, ☎267-9407 or 859-1776, ⓦwww.inn-housedoctor.net) makes 24-hour house calls; rates are $150–250 and prescriptions cost more. Gay and lesbian visitors can drop into the Fenway Community Health Center, 7 Haviland St (☎267-0900 or 1-888/242-0900, ⓦwww.fenwayhealth.org), which offers HIV testing during weekdays.

Prescriptions can be filled at the CVS **drugstore** chain: the branches at 155–157 Charles St, in Beacon Hill (☎227-0437, pharmacy ☎523-1028), and 35 White St, in Cambridge's Porter Square (☎876-4037, pharmacy ☎876-5519) are both open 24 hours a day. You can also pick up over-the-counter analgesics here, though bear in mind that if you're partial to a particular brand back home, you should probably bring some with you – you might not find it in the US (this is especially true of codeine-based painkillers, which require a prescription in the US).

Should you be in an accident, an ambulance will take you to a **hospital** and charge you later. For walk-in emergencies, the Massachusetts General Hospital, 55 Fruit St (☎726-2000, ⓦwww.mgh.harvard.edu; Charles/MGH **T**), Beth Israel Deaconess Medical Center, 330 Brookline Ave (☎667-7000, ⓦwww.bidmc.harvard.edu; Longwood **T**), and New England Medical Center, 800 Washington St (☎636-5000, ⓦwww.nemc.org; NE Medical **T**), all have 24-hour emergency rooms. Women travelers with urgent needs can visit the Women's Hospital, 75 Francis St (☎732-5500 or 1-800/BWH-9999, ⓦwww.bwh.partners.org; Longwood or Brigham Circle **T**). Parents can take their children to the Children's Hospital, 300 Longwood Ave (☎355-6000, ⓦwww.tch.harvard.edu; Longwood **T**).

Information, websites and maps

The best place to get Boston information before you go is the Greater Boston Convention and Visitors Bureau's (GBCVB) website, ⓦwww.bostonusa.com, which maintains up-to-date information on events about town, a terrific list of special deals, and an online reservation service; agents can also make recommendations and bookings for you (call ☎1-888/SEE BOSTON).

Tourist information

The **GBCVB** produces the free *Guidebook to Boston*, a 100-page overview of restaurants, hotels and sights, and a slimmer *Travel Planner* booklet; both can be mailed to you by request. For information once there, you can stop by the two GBCVB-run tourism centers: one is in Boston Common, west of the Park **T** stop, facing Tremont Street, while the other is in the Prudential Center, at 800 Boylston St. Both are open daily from 9am to 5pm.

Visitors to **Cambridge** can get all the information they need from the Cambridge Office of Tourism (☎441-2884 or 1-800/862-5678, ⓦwww.cambridge-usa.org), which maintains a well-stocked kiosk in Harvard Square (Mon–Sat 9am–5pm).

The state-wide **Massachusetts Office of Travel and Tourism** (☎727-3201 or 1-800/447-6277, ⓦwww.mass-vacation.usa) produces *Getaway Guide*, a free magazine featuring hotel, restaurant and attraction reviews, and offers a telephone reservation service. Though by no means as comprehensive as the GBCVB, the state tourist office does have a UK phone number (☎020/7978 7429).

Websites

Many **websites** contain travel information about Boston. What follows is a short list of both informative and irreverent sites that'll give you the low-down on what's on around town, local trivia, neighborhood profiles, and other Boston ephemera.

Boston Online ⓦwww.boston-online.com
General info on the city, including a dictionary of Bostonian English and a guide to public bathrooms.
Boston Phoenix ⓦwww.bostonphoenix.com

Easily searched site from the city's alternative weekly, with up-to-date arts, music and nightlife listings, restaurant reviews, and lots of cool links.
The Bostonian Society ⓦwww.bostonhistory.org
The official historical society of the city has info on its museum (see p.47) as well as a complete transcript of the Boston Massacre Trial.
The Greater Boston CVB ⓦwww.bostonusa.com
Everything you'd expect from the city's official site, plus lots of handy links to other sites.
Link Pink ⓦwww.linkpink.com
Comprehensive listings of businesses, hotels, shops, and services catering to New England's gay and lesbian community.
Massachusetts Office of Travel and Tourism ⓦwww.mass-vacation.com
The state-wide tourism bureau is especially useful if you're planning side trips to Cape Cod, Nantucket or Martha's Vineyard.
Urban Photo ⓦwww.urbanphoto.org/boston
Lots of neighborhood photos and profiles, some of which focus on tiny details like wrought-iron railings.

Maps

The **maps** in this book, and those given out at Boston tourism kiosks, should satisfy most of your needs; otherwise, the recently published **Rough Guide Map to Boston** ($8.95), a street atlas with listings of the best restaurants, bars and shopping, should fill in the gaps. Also comprehensive is the small, shiny, fold-out *Streetwise Boston* map ($5.95; ⓦwww.streetwisemaps.com), available from book, travel and map stores in town.

Cyclists might want to pick up the Massachusetts Bicycle Coalition Boston **bike map** ($4.95), available at the Globe Corner Bookstore (28 Church St, ☎497-6277; Harvard **T**) and online at ⓦwww.massbikeboston.org.

Arrival

Those traveling to Boston by airplane will arrive at the city's Logan International Airport, located on Boston's easternmost peninsula, a man-made piece of land sticking far out into Boston Harbor. From there, you can catch the subway or a water shuttle to downtown; taking a taxi is another (but less good) option. For visitors coming into Boston by bus or train, you'll arrive at South Station, near the waterfront at Summer Street and Atlantic Avenue; from there, it's just a short walk or subway ride to downtown.

By air

Busy **Logan International**, servicing both domestic and international flights, has five terminals lettered A through E that are connected by a series of courtesy buses. You'll find currency exchange in terminals C and E (daily 10am–5pm), plus information booths, car rental, and Automatic Teller Machines (ATMs) in all five.

After arriving into Logan, the most convenient way downtown is by **subway**. The Airport stop is a short ride away on courtesy bus #11, which you can catch outside on the arrival level of all five Logan terminals. From there, you can take the Blue Line to State or Government Center stations in the heart of downtown, and transfer to the Red, Orange and Green lines to reach other points; the ride to downtown lasts about fifteen minutes ($1).

Just as quick, but a lot more fun, is the **water shuttle** that whisks you across the harbor to Rowes Wharf near the Blue Line Aquarium stop (Mon–Thurs every 15min 6am–8pm; Fri every 30min 8am–11pm; Sat every 30min 10am–11pm; Sun every 30min 10am–8pm; $10). From the airport, courtesy bus #66 will take you to the pier.

By comparison, taking a **taxi** is expensive – the airport to a downtown destination costs $15–20, plus an extra $4.50 or so in tolls – and time-consuming, given Boston's notorious traffic jams. Save yourself the trouble and avoid them.

By bus or train

The main terminus for both **buses** and **trains** to Boston is Boston's **South Station**, in the southeast corner of downtown at Summer Street and Atlantic Avenue. **Amtrak trains** arrive at one end, in a station with an information booth, newsstands, a food court, and several ATMs (but no currency exchange), while **bus carriers** arrive at the clean and modern terminal next door, from where it's a bit of a trek to reach the subway (the Red Line), which is through the Amtrak station and down a level. Those with sizeable baggage will find the walk particularly awkward, as there are no porters or handcarts. Note that despite its modernity, the bus terminal's departure and arrival screens are anything but up-to-date – confirm your gate with an agent to be sure. Trains also make a second stop at Boston's **Back Bay Station**, 145 Dartmouth St, on the **T**'s Orange Line. If you've taken a **Chinatown bus** from New York (see p.13), you'll arrive at 33 Harrison St, a block from the Chinatown **T** and the Orange Line. Finally, Amtrak's Downeaster train – which connects Portland, Maine with Boston and points in between – arrives at **North Station**, which is located in the West End near the FleetCenter.

By car

Driving into Boston is the absolute worst way to get there, and is sure to put a damper on your trip if you're a first-time visitor. Nevertheless, two highways provide direct access to the city, **I-90** and **I-93** – though the latter, which cuts north–south through the heart of the city, is the focus of the protracted "Big Dig" construction project, designed to put the whole thing underground. The result is notorious traffic jams and indecipherable detours that will invariably stress you out and get you lost. Consequently, if you're coming along the I-90 from **eastern Massachusetts** and **Albany,** you'd do better to get off the highway and head into town before it connects with I-93. Visitors coming from southern points like **New York** or northern states like **New Hampshire** are pretty much stuck, however, as I-93 is the only serviceable road available. A third highway, **I-95**, circumnavigates Boston, and is more useful to drivers trying to avoid the city altogether.

City transit

Much of the pleasure of visiting Boston comes from being in a city built long before cars were invented. Walking around the narrow, winding streets can be a joy; conversely, driving around them is a nightmare. Be particularly cautious in traffic circles known as "rotaries": when entering, always yield the right of way. If you have a car, better park it for the duration of your trip (see p.24) and get around either by foot or public transit – a system of subway lines, buses and ferries run by the Massachusetts Bay Transportation Authority (MBTA, known as the "**T**"; ☎1-800/392-6100, ✆www.mbta.com).

The subway (T)

While not the most modern system, Boston's subway is cheap, efficient, and charmingly antiquated – its Green Line was America's first underground train, built in the late nineteenth century, and riding it today is akin to riding a tram – albeit, underground.

Four **subway** lines transect Boston and continue out into some of its more proximate neighbors. Each line is color coded and passes through downtown before continuing on to other districts. The **Red Line**, which serves Harvard, is the most frequent, intersecting South Boston and Dorchester to the south and Cambridge to the north. The **Green Line** hits Back Bay, Kenmore Square, the Fenway and Brookline. The **Blue Line** heads into East Boston and is most useful for its stop at Logan Airport. The less frequent **Orange Line** traverses the South End and continues down to Roxbury and Jamaica Plain.

All trains travel either **inbound** (towards the quadrant made up of State, Downtown Crossing, Park Street and Government Center stops) or **outbound** (away from the quadrant). If you're confused about whether you're going in or out, the train's terminus is also designated on the train itself; for instance, trains to Harvard from South Station will be on the "Inbound" platform and heading towards "Alewife."

The four lines are supplemented by a bus rapid transit (BRT) route, the Silver Line, which runs above ground along Washington Street from Downtown Crossing **T**. More of a fast bus than a subway, the line cuts through the heart of South End.

The fare to board the **T** is $1, payable by tokens purchased at the station or by exact change; when boarding a subway at a station with no token-seller, you can squeeze your dollar bill into the slot at the bottom left of the **T** conductor's till. If you're planning to use public transit a lot, it's a good idea to buy a **visitor's pass** for one ($6), three ($11), or seven days ($22) of unlimited subway, bus and harbor ferry use.

The biggest drawback to the **T** is the relatively limited hours of operation (Mon–Sat 5.15am–12.30am, Sun 6am–12.30am); the 12.30am closing time means you'll be stuck taking a taxi home after last-call. Free transit maps are available at any station; there's also a subway map at the back of this book.

Color scheming

Each of the **T**'s subway lines is colored after a characteristic of the area it covers. The Red Line evokes Harvard's crimson sports jerseys; the Green Line refers to the Emerald Necklace; the Blue Line reflects its waterfront proximity; and the Orange Line is so named due to the fact that the street under which it runs, Washington Street, used to be called Orange Street, after King William of Orange. The new Silver Line is the only exception to the color scheme: it's colored for speed – like a silver bullet.

Buses

The MBTA manages an impressive 170 **bus** routes both in and around Boston. Though the buses run less frequently than the subway and are harder to navigate, they bear two main advantages: they're cheaper (75¢, exact change only) and they provide service to many more points. It's a service used, however, primarily by natives who've grown familiar with the byzantine system of routes. If you're transferring from the **T**, you'll have to pay the full fare, as the two don't combine fares; transferring between buses is free, however, as long as you have a transfer from your original bus. The **T**'s visitor pass (see opposite), includes unlimited bus access over one, three, or seven days in its package. Be sure to arm yourself with the *Official Public Transport Map*, available at all subway stations, before heading out. Most buses run from 5.30am to 1am, but a few "night owl" buses run until 2.30am, all leaving from the Government Center **T**.

Ferries

Of all the MBTA transportation options, the Inner Harbor **ferry** is by far the most scenic: $1.25 gets you a ten-minute boat ride with excellent views of downtown Boston. The boats, covered 100-seaters with exposed upper decks, navigate several waterfront routes by day, though the one most useful to visitors is that connecting Long Wharf with Charlestown (every 30min Mon–Fri

6.30am–8pm, Sat & Sun 10am–6pm).

Another popular harbor route is the water **shuttle** between Logan Airport and downtown Rowes Wharf, a seven-minute trip that makes for a stunning arrival ($10; ☎951-0255, ⊛www.massport.com); bus #66 (free) from Logan Airport will get you to the quay.

Several larger **passenger boat**s cruise across the harbor and beyond to reach beach destinations such as Provincetown, at the tip of Cape Cod. Two companies make the ninety-minute trip across Massachusetts Bay: Boston Harbor Cruises departs from Long Wharf (daily late May to mid-June departing 9am, returning 4pm; late June to early Oct Mon–Wed departing 9am, returning 4pm; Thurs departing 9am & 6.30pm, returning 4pm & 8.30pm; Fri–Sun departing 9am, 2pm & 6.30pm, returning 11am, 4pm & 8.30pm; $49 return; ☎227-4321, ⊛www.bostonharborcruises.com; Aquarium **T**), while Bay State Cruises leaves, somewhat inconveniently, from the west side of the World Trade Center pier (daily late May to early Oct departing 8am & 5.30pm, returning 2hr later; daily late June to early Oct departing 8am, 1pm & 5.30pm, returning 2hrs later; $49 return; ☎748-1428, ⊛boston-ptown.com). The latter has an excellent **excursion fare** for weekend day-tripping, as well: $15 will get you to P-town and back with a three-hour window to tool around in – keep in mind, though, that the boats take three hours each way (late May to early Sept Fri–Sun departing 9.30am, returning 3.30pm).

Taxis

Given Boston's small scale and the efficiency (at least during the day) of its public transit, **taxis** aren't as necessary or prevalent as in cities like New York or London. If you do find yourself in need, you can generally hail one along the streets of downtown or Back Bay, though competition gets pretty stiff after 12.30am when the subway has stopped running and bars and clubs begin to close. If desperate, go to a hotel where cabs cluster, or where, at the very least, a bellhop can arrange one. In Cambridge, taxis mostly congregate around Harvard Square.

Boston Cab (☎262-2227) and Bay State Taxi Service (☎566-5000) have 24-hour service and accept major credit cards. Other cab companies include Checker Taxi (☎536-7000) and Town Taxi (☎536-5000). In Cambridge, call the dispatcher (☎495-8294) for Yellow Cabs or Ambassador Cabs. As a general rule, the rate starts at $1.50 and goes up by 25¢/mile.

Commuter rail

The only time you're likely to travel by **rail** in Boston is if you're making a day-trip to Revolutionary battlefields in Concord, historical Salem, or South Shore spots like Plymouth. All have stations on the MBTA's **commuter rail** (☎222-3200 or 1-800/392-6100), essentially just a faster, glossier subway than the **T**, with similarly frequent service. Most lines of interest depart from **North Station T**: Rockport, Goucester and Salem lie on the **Rockport Line** (15min–1hr; $3–$5 one way), while Concord is about midway on the **Fitchburg Line** (20min; $4 one way). The exception, Plymouth, is the last stop on the **Plymouth Line** that leaves from **South Station** (55min; $5 one way). Tickets can be bought in advance or aboard the train itself, though doing the latter incurs a service fee of $1.50 to $2, depending on the time of day.

Driving

Don't even try it. The charm of a city that bases its layout on the meandering routes of one-time cowpaths quickly loses its appeal when **driving** enters the picture. Even without the traffic jams caused by the narrow winding streets, the clogs caused by the work on I-93 are enough to drive you batty. Moreover, should you want to pull off the road for a while, the price of parking garages is tantamount to highway robbery ($25–$30 per evening and more overnight). There are metered spots on main streets like Newbury, Boylston and Charles, but the chances of finding an empty one on any given evening are slim at best.

If you must drive, bear these rules in mind: driving is on the right, seatbelt wearing is mandatory, and the ubiquitous "Permit Parking Only" signs along residential streets must be obeyed – without the requisite parking sticker, you will be ticketed $20 or towed (expect to pay well over $50 to get your car

back). Should you get a ticket, you can try sweet-talking the Office of the Parking Clerk (☎635-4410), but it probably won't help.

The cheapest **parking lots** downtown are Center Plaza Garage, at the corner of Cambridge and New Sudbury streets ($9/hr up to $25 max; ☎742-7807) and Garage at Post Office Square ($3.50/30min up to $29 max; ☎423-1430). The parking limit at non-metered spots is two hours, whether posted or not.

As with parking, the cost of **renting a car** in Boston can add up, especially as extra charges, like the $10 Convention Center Finance Fee levied on all rentals, get tacked on to your bill. If you still insist on getting your own wheels, the agencies we list below will happily supply them. A compact car with unlimited mileage will ring in around $42/day ($30 plus $12 in taxes) before insurance ($10).

Car rental agencies

Alamo ☎1-800/522-9696, ⓦwww.alamo.com
Avis ☎1-800/331-1084, ⓦwww.avis.com
Budget ☎1-800/527-0700,
ⓦwww.budgetrentacar.com
Dollar ☎1-800/800-4000, ⓦwww.dollar.com
Enterprise Rent-a-Car ☎1-800/325-8007,
ⓦwww.enterprise.com
Hertz ☎1-800/654-3001, ⓦwww.hertz.com
National ☎1-800/227-7368,
ⓦwww.nationalcar.com
Thrifty ☎1-800/367-2277, ⓦwww.thrifty.com

Cycling

Cycling runs a close second to walking as the preferred mode of city transport. It's especially popular along the riverside promenades in Cambridge, though hustling along downtown streets is quite agreeable by bike as well. The usual precautions – wearing a helmet and carrying a whistle – are advised.

You can rent a bike starting at around $25/day from Community Bicycle Supply, at 496 Tremont St (☎542-8623, ⓦwww.communitybicycle.com; Copley **T**); Back Bay Bicycles, at 333 Newbury St (☎247-2336, ⓦwww.backbaybicycles.com; Hynes **T**); or Wheelworks Bicycle Workshop, at 259 Massachusetts Ave, Cambridge (☎876-6555; Central **T**). Wheelworks also does repairs.

Tours

It's hard to avoid Boston's role in Revolutionary American history – it's proclaimed by landmarks and placards virtually everywhere you go. You could very well spend your entire visit reading every last totem yourself, but a far more enjoyable way to experience the city's lore is by guided tour. Mind you, the walking and bus tours listed below aren't just limited to covering colonial-era Americana; you can also examine the architecture of Charles Bullfinch (Boston by Foot), the city's literary legacy (Literary Trail), and even become an Italian food expert (L'Arte di Cucinare).

Tour companies

L'Arte di Cucinare ☏523-6032, ⓦwww.cucinare.com. Award-winning walking and tasting tours of the North End's Italian salumerias, pasticcerias, and enotecas. Often booked up, so reserve well in advance. Wed & Sat 10am & 2pm, Fri 3pm; $39–42.

Beantown Trolley ☏720-6342 or 236-2148, ⓦwww.brushhilltours.com. One of the oldest and most popular history tours, covering everything from waterfront wharfs to Beacon Hill Brahmins and Fenway museums, with multiple pick-up and drop-off points around town. $18.

Boston by Foot ☏367-2345, ⓦwww.bostonbyfoot.com. Informative ninety-minute walking tours focusing on the architecture and history of Beacon Hill, Copley Square, the South End, North End and the **T**, including disused stations. $8–10.

Boston Duck Tours ☏723-DUCK, ⓦwww.bostonducktours.com. Excellent tours that take to the streets and the Charles River in restored World War II amphibious landing vehicles; kids get to skipper the bus/boat in the water. Tours depart every half-hour from the Prudential Center, at 101 Huntington Ave; reservations advised in summer. $19.

Boston National Historical Park Visitors Center Freedom Trail Tours ☏242-5642, ⓦwww.naps.gov. Educational walking tours of National Landmark sites; the Black Heritage Trail tour is highly recommended. Sept–May call for hours and reservations; June–July 10am, noon & 2pm. Free.

Brush Hill Grayline Tours ☏720-6342 or 236-2148, ⓦwww.brushhilltours.com. Day-long coach tours to surrounding towns such as Lexington, Concord, Plymouth and Salem. Late March to November. $26–45.

Charles River Wheelmen ☏332-8546 or 325-BIKE, ⓦwww.crw.org. Organizes free weekly rides ranging from delightful Wednesday Night Ice Cream rides to hardcore weekend morning fitness rides.

Discover Boston Multilingual Trolley Tours ☏742-1440. Tours in English; audio devices available with French, German, Italian, Japanese and Russian. $24.

Literary Trail ☏350-0358, ⓦwww.lit-trail.org. A three-hour bus tour that takes in all the local hotshots from Henry Wadsworth Longfellow to Henry David Thoreau. $30.

Old Town Trolley Tours ☏269-7010, ⓦwww.trolleytours.com. Another hop-on, hop-off trolley tour of Boston, this one on ubiquitous orange-and-green trolleys with thematic routes like Sons and Daughters of Liberty, and Ghosts and Gravestones. $23.

Costs, money and banks

Boston ranks among the top five most expensive cities in the US to visit. While the high cost of accommodation, food and drink is compensated for, somewhat, by a wealth of inexpensive (and occasionally free) activities, there's no getting around the fact that the former are going to eat up a lot of your budget.

Average costs

Hotels are, by far, the biggest money-grubbers: expect to fork out somewhere in the $200 range just for the privilege of staying in a Boston hotel. This is due somewhat to the limited accommodation the city provides, met by a fairly constant demand. The city's B&Bs do cost less, at around $100, and often have more atmosphere than the chain hotels that make up most of Boston's market; long-term accommodation and hostels can take the price down even further.

Food costs are more reasonable – you could get by on $20 a day, if you stay in a hotel with complimentary breakfast, grab an order of scrod at Faneuil Hall for lunch, and eat only at budget restaurants for dinner. That said, scrimping on food costs when Boston has such terrific restaurants – especially the seafood ones – seems almost a waste of a trip.

The best way to stretch your dollar is to book your hotel through a discount agency like Quickbook (@www.quickbook.com). You should also check the Greater Boston Convention and Visitor Bureau website (@www.bostonusa.com) for deals. You'll also save on admission prices if you have a

student ID card: most attractions in town give discounts when shown an American college ID card or the International Student Identification Card (ISIC; @www.isiccard.com). The ISIC card is available through most student travel agencies for $22 for Americans; C$16 for Canadians; A$16.50 for Australians; NZ$21 for New Zealanders; and £6 in the UK. Otherwise, save money by traveling outside of peak season (Oct–March).

Credit cards and currency

Most of your major purchases, whether hotel or car rental, will require a **credit card** deposit, even if you wind up paying the total in cash. Aside from carrying plastic, you'll also need **US currency**, preferably in denominations of $50 and under, as many places blanch at accepting $100 bills.

Debit cards, ATMs and travelers' checks

Once in Boston, you can withdraw funds from your home account using your **debit card** at any ATM machine equipped with the Cirrus or Plus sign (as most are); conveniently, the machines typically give out $20 bills.

Visa TravelMoney

A compromise between travelers' checks and plastic is **Visa TravelMoney**, a disposable pre-paid debit card with a PIN which works in all ATMs that take Visa cards. You load up your account with funds before leaving home, and when they run out, you simply throw the card away. You can buy up to nine cards to access the same funds – useful for couples or families traveling together – and it's a good idea to buy at least one extra as a back-up in case of loss or theft. There is also a 24-hour toll-free customer assistance number (☎1-800/847-2911). The card is available in most countries from branches of Thomas Cook and Citicorp. For more information, check the Visa TravelMoney website at @usa.visa.com/personal/cards/visa_travel_money.html

Otherwise, you can invest in **travelers' checks**, which have the added security of being replaceable should they be lost or stolen. Checks from Thomas Cooke, American Express and Visa are widely accepted in stores, restaurants and gas stations, though you should always ask before using them, and pay using the low denominations. Make sure to keep the purchase agreement and a record of the check serial numbers safe and separate from the checks themselves. In the event that your checks are lost or stolen, the issuing company will expect you to report the loss forthwith to their office in Boston; most companies claim to replace lost or stolen checks within 24 hours. Foreign travelers should bring checks issued in US dollars.

Wiring money

Having money wired from home should be a last resort, since you (or, at least, the sender of the money) will pay for the privilege. The fee depends on the amount sent, where it's being sent from and to, and the speed of the service. The quickest way is to have someone take cash to the office of a money-wiring service and have it wired to the office nearest you: to the US, this process should take no longer than ten to fifteen minutes. You take along ID and pick up the money in cash. This service is offered by **Travelers' Express Moneygram** (also available at participating **Thomas Cook** branches) and

Western Union. See "Directory" (p.232) for the contact details of local Western Union offices in Boston.

Financial services

American Express UK ☏0870/600 1060, ✆www.americanexpress.co.uk; US and Canada ☏1-888/269-6669, ✆www.americanexpress.com
Thomas Cook Canada ☏1-888/TCDIRECT, ✆www.thomascook.ca; UK ☏01733/294871, ✆www.thomascook.com; US ☏1-800/CURRENCY, ✆www.fx4travel.com
Travelers' Express Moneygram Canada ☏1-800/933-3278, UK ☏0800/6663 9472, US ☏1-800/926-9400; ✆www.moneygram.com
Western Union Australia ☏1800/649 565 or 1800/501 500, New Zealand ☏09/270 0050, Republic of Ireland ☏1800/395 395, UK ☏0800/833 833, US ☏1-800/325-6000; ✆www.westernunion.com

Banks and exchange

Banking hours typically run Monday–Friday 9am–3pm; some banks stay open later on Thursdays and Fridays, and even fewer have Saturday hours. Major banks like Fleet and Bank of Boston will exchange travelers' checks and currencies at the standard exchange rate (one or two percent). Outside of banks, you're limited to exchange bureaus in Cambridge, Boston and the airport (see p.21), which set their own, often higher, commission and rates.

Communications

Staying in touch with friends and family back home won't be a problem in Boston. Every hotel room comes equipped with a phone (though these can be expensive to use), public pay phones are widespread, and many Internet outlets allow you to check your email for free. You can buy stamps at post offices all over town and in Cambridge, and mailboxes are easy to find.

Telephones

Boston's area code is ☏617; you can reach the city from elsewhere in the US or Canada

by dialing 1-617 before the seven-digit number; from abroad, dial your country's international access code, then 1-617 and the seven-digit number.

Local calls cost 35¢ in coin-operated public phones; when making a local call, compose all ten digits, including the area code. Operator assistance (☎0) and directory information (☎411) are toll-free from public telephones (but not from in-room phones).

Calling home from the US

With respect to calling abroad from the US, you've got several options, the most convenient of which is using your **credit card** – most pay phones now accept them. A cheaper option is using a **prepaid phone card**, sold at most convenience stores in denominations of $5 and $10. You'll find a phone number and special PIN number on the back – just dial the number, enter the PIN, and compose the number you're trying to reach (see opposite).

More expensive is using a **telephone charge card** from your phone company back home that will charge the call to your home account. Since most major charge cards are free to obtain, it's certainly worth getting one at least for emergencies, but bear in mind that rates aren't necessarily cheaper than calling from a public phone with a calling card; in fact, they may well be more expensive.

If all else fails, you can call **collect** by dialling ☎0, and then the number you wish to reach; the operator will take it from there. Otherwise, ☎1-800/COLLECT and ☎1-800/CALL-ATT both claim (vehemently) to have the cheapest options.

Mobile phones

If you're from overseas and you want to use your **mobile phone** in Boston, you'll need to check with your phone provider whether it will work abroad, and what the call charges are. Unless you have a tri-band phone, it is unlikely that a mobile bought for use outside the US will work inside the States (and vice versa).

In the UK, for all but the very top-of-the-range packages, you'll have to inform your phone provider before going abroad to get international access switched on. You may get charged extra for this depending on your existing package and where you **are travelling** to. You're also likely to be charged extra

for incoming calls when abroad, as the people calling you will be paying the usual rate. If you want to retrieve messages while you're away, you'll have to ask your provider for a new access code, as your home one is unlikely to work abroad.

For further information about using your phone abroad, check out ❻www.telecoms-advice.org.uk/features/using_your_mobile_abroad.htm

Useful telephone numbers

Area code ☎617
Directory assistance ☎411 or 1-800/555-1212 (for toll-free numbers)
Emergencies ☎911 for fire department, police and ambulance.
Operator ☎0

International calling codes

Calling Boston from abroad international access code + 1 + 617 + seven-digit number.
Calling Canada from Boston 1 + area code + seven-digit number.
Calling Australia from Boston 011 + 61 + city code + number.
Calling New Zealand from Boston 011 + 64 + city code + number.
Calling the Republic of Ireland from Boston 011 + 353 + city code + number.
Calling the UK from Boston 011 + 44 + city code + number.

Email

The best way to check your **email** is to pop into a local university and use one of their free public computers. Harvard's Holyoke Center, at 1350 Massachusetts Ave in Cambridge, has a couple of stations with ten-minute access maximum. The same goes for MIT's Rogers Building, at 77 Massachusetts Ave (also in Cambridge). Boston's main public library, at 700 Boylston St, has free fifteen-minute Internet access on the ground floor of the Johnson building. Cybercafés are limited to Designs For Living, at 52 Queensberry St (Mon–Fri 7am–6.30pm, Sat 8am–6.30pm, Sun 9am–6.30pm; ☎536-6150, ❻www.bosnet.com; $8/hr; Kenmore **T**) and Adrenaline Zone, at 40 Brattle St, lower level (Sun–Thurs 11am–11pm, Fri–Sat 11am–12am; $5/hr; ☎876-1314, ❻www.adrenzone.com; Harvard **T**).

Mail

Boston's postal service is as efficient as most US cities, and has multiple outlets scattered about town. For the best service (as waiting in line for human service can take inordinately long), use the coin-operated machines to buy books of stamps – letters and postcards within the US cost 37¢ and 23¢, respectively.

The biggest post office downtown is J. W. McCormack Station in Post Office Square, at 90 Devonshire St (Mon–Fri 7.30am–5pm; ☎720-4754); Cambridge's central branch is at 770 Massachusetts Ave, in Central Square (Mon–Fri 7.30am–6pm, Sat 7.30am–3pm; ☎876-0620). The General Post Office, 25 Dorchester Ave, behind South Station, is open 24 hours a day (☎654-5326). You can receive mail at the latter by having it addressed to you c/o Poste Restante, GPO, 25 Dorchester Ave, Boston MA, 02205. To collect letters, present some form of photo ID at the window between 10am and 1pm Monday–Saturday. Note that non-acquired letters are thrown out after thirty days.

The media

Despite its legacy as the birthplace of America's first newspaper (*Publick Occurences*, published in 1690), Boston hardly ranks among the country's most media-savvy cities. The better media here is intellectual rather than newsy, and you'll certainly be engaged by *the Atlantic Monthly*, one of the US's most venerable monthly magazines, and a slew of leftist weeklies. For all that, though, Boston's real reporting strength is sports-related: a hurricane may have hit Louisiana, but if the Celtics or the Bruins played the same day, that's what will be on the front page of the city's two daily papers (and the top story on television and radio news). It makes for pretty parochial coverage; you can get your international fix stopping by one the city's excellent newsstands.

Newspapers and magazines

While Boston lacks the media flash of nearby New York City, it's no stranger to intrigue: two *Boston Globe* columnists were busted in 1998 for writing fake stories. Though the news damaged the reputation of the city's oldest **newspaper**, *The Globe* (50¢; ⊛www.boston.com/globe) remains Boston's best general daily; its fat Sunday edition ($2) includes substantial sections on art, culture, and lifestyle. The *Boston Herald* (50¢; ⊛www.bostonherald.com) is the *Globe*'s tabloid competitor and is best for getting your gossip and local sports coverage fix.

The rest of the city's print media consists primarily of listings-oriented and **free weekly papers**. To know what's on, the *Boston*

Phoenix (⊛www.bostonphoenix.com), available at sidewalk newspaper stands around town, is essential, offering extensive entertainment listings as well as good feature articles. Other freebies like *Improper Bostonian* (⊛www.improper.com) and the *Phoenix*'s bi-weekly listings magazine, *Stuff@Night*, both have good listings of new and noteworthy goings-on about town (though the features are primarily ad-driven). *Bay Windows* (⊛www.baywindows.com), a small weekly catering to the gay and lesbian population, is available free at most South End cafés and bars; the cover price is 50¢ otherwise. The *Cambridge TAB* has news articles and listings exclusively about local Cambridge events.

The lone monthly publication, *Boston*

Magazine ($3.95; @www.bostonmagazine.com), is a glossy lifestyle magazine with good restaurant reviews and a yearly "Best of Boston" round-up.

Newspapers from other US cities, as well as **foreign newspapers** and **magazines**, can be bought at Out of Town News, at Harvard Square, and major bookstores like Barnes & Noble and Borders.

TV and radio

You're likely to see more **television** than you might back home just by having a drink or eating out – televisions are as common as pint glasses in Boston bars and restaurants, and they're usually airing home-team games. Most hotels have cable TV, so you'll be able to catch regular **news** on the four major networks: CBS (channel 4), ABC (channel 5), NBC (channel 7), Fox (channel 25), and CNN, as well as keep abreast of your favorite dramas and sitcoms.

The best **radio stations** are on the FM dial, including WGBH (89.7), which carries National Public Radio (NPR) shows, plus jazz, classical, and world music; WBUR (90.9), earnest, leftist talk radio; WJMN (94.5) for good hip-hop beats; WFNX (101.7) for mainstream alternative hits; and WODS (103.3), an oldies station. To get in on Boston's sports fanaticism, tune into WEEI (850AM), for day-long sports talk.

Opening hours, public holidays and festivals

The opening hours of specific visitor attractions, monuments, memorials, stores and offices are given in the relevant accounts throughout the guide. Telephone numbers are provided so that you can check current information with the places themselves.

Opening hours

As a general rule, **museums** are open daily 10am to 5.30pm, though some have extended summer hours; a few art galleries stay open until 9pm or so one night a week. Smaller, private museums close for one day a week, usually Monday or Tuesday. **Federal office buildings** (some of which incorporate museums) are open Monday through Friday 9am to 5.30pm. **Stores** are usually open Monday through Saturday 10am to 7pm and Sunday noon–5pm; some have extended Thursday and Friday night hours. **Malls** tend to be open Monday through Saturday 10am to 7pm (or later) and Sunday noon to 6pm.

In the wake of the terrorist attacks of September 11, 2001 – plus subsequent security scares – some Boston buildings and landmarks have **suspended tours** and **prohibited access** to the general public as they re-evaluate security measures. Throughout the Guide we've noted the places that may be affected by such changes and recommend calling ahead before heading off for a tour at any of these destinations.

Public holidays and festivals

On the **national public holidays** listed below, stores, banks and public and federal offices are liable to be closed all day. The Museum of Fine Arts and Isabella Gardner museums, on the other hand, open on holiday Mondays – but no others – year round. The traditional **summer tourism season**, when many attractions have extended opening hours, runs from **Memorial Day to Labor Day**.

Boston has a huge variety of **annual festivals and events**, many of them historical in scope, like the annual Fourth of July reading of the Declaration of Independence and the mid-June reenactment of the Battle of Bunker

Hill. Such is the range of festivals throughout the rest of the year, it's hard to turn up without your trip coinciding with at least one; Boston's full **festival calendar** is detailed in the "Festivals and events" chapter, p.227.

Do note that during all major festival periods – particularly the Head of the Charles Regatta, Easter, Memorial Day and the Fourth of July – it can be very difficult to find accommodation in the city. Book well in advance if you plan to visit Boston at any of these times.

National holidays

January
1: New Year's Day
3rd Monday: Dr Martin Luther King Jr's Birthday

February
3rd Monday: President's Day
March/April
Easter Monday
May
Last Monday: Memorial Day
July
4: Independence Day
September
1st Monday: Labor Day
October
2nd Monday: Columbus Day
November
11: Veterans' Day
4th Thursday: Thanksgiving Day
December
25: Christmas Day

Travelers with disabilities

People with disabilities will find Boston fairly easy to negotiate – the city is pretty flat, most curbs have dropped lips and many restaurants and attractions are wheelchair-accessible. For all its modernization, however, Boston remains a colonial city with the prerequisite cobblestoned streets and winding roads to match – sections around Faneuil Hall, the Financial District, and Beacon Hill, in particular, may require extra planning.

Planning your trip

It's always a good idea for people with special needs to alert their travel agents when booking: things are far simpler for those with disabilities when the various travel operators or carriers you'll be using are expecting you. A **medical certificate** of your fitness to travel, provided by your doctor, is also useful; some airlines or insurance companies may insist on it. Most **airlines** do whatever they can to ease your journey and will usually let attendants of more seriously disabled people accompany them at no extra charge. Almost every **Amtrak train** includes one or more coaches with accommodation for passengers with disabilities. Guide dogs travel free and may accompany blind, deaf or disabled passengers in the carriage. Be sure to give 24 hours' notice. **Greyhound buses** are not equipped

with lifts for wheelchairs, though staff will assist with boarding, and the "Helping Hand" scheme offers two-for-the-price-of-one tickets to passengers unable to travel alone (make sure to carry a doctor's certificate).

The American Automobile Association produces the *Handicapped Driver's Mobility Guide* for **disabled drivers** (available from Quantum-Precision Inc, 225 Broadway, Suite 3404, New York, NY 10007). The larger car rental companies provide cars with hand controls at no extra charge, though only on their full-size (which is to say, most expensive) models; reserve well in advance.

Disabled access in Boston

For people with mobility impairments, getting around Boston is possible for the simple reason that the city is relatively flat and curb cuts abound. **Public transportation** can also be used: many MBTA buses and **T** stops are wheelchair-accessible; for detailed information, call ☎222-5976/5123 or visit ⊛www.mbta.com. In addition, most major **taxi** companies have some vehicles with wheelchair lifts; Metro Cab (☎242-8000) comes highly recommended.

Very Special Arts (☎350-7713; ⊛www .accessexpressed.net) has superior information on the accessibility of museums, sights, movie theaters, and other cultural venues in the Boston area. For everything else, contact the **Massachusetts Office on Disability**, a one-stop resource for all accessibility issues whether in Boston or further afield; call ☎727-7440 or toll-free on ☎1-800/322-2020.

Useful contacts

US and Canada

Access-Able ⊛www.access-able.com. Online resource for travelers with disabilities.
Directions Unlimited ☎1-800/533-5343 or 914/241-1700. Tour operator specializing in customized tours for people with disabilities.
DisabilityGuide.org A free online source of information for the Washington metropolitan area; lists accessible hotels and shopping venues, rates restaurants in terms of accessibility and provides a referral service. The organization also publishes the *Access Entertainment Guide* ($7; order form available online or write 21618 Slidell Rd, Boyds, MD 20841).
Massachusetts Office on Disability ⊛www.state.ma.us/mod
Mobility International USA ☎541/343-1284, ⊛www.miusa.org. Information and referral services, access guides, tours and exchange

programs. Annual membership ($35) includes quarterly newsletter.
Society for the Advancement of Travelers with Handicaps (SATH) ☎212/447-7284, ⊛www.sath.org. Nonprofit educational organization that has actively represented travelers with disabilities since 1976.
Washington Ear, Inc ☎301/681-6636, ⊛www.washear.org. Supplies large-print ($5) and tactile ($12) atlases of the DC area.
Wheels Up! ☎1-888/389-4335, ⊛www.wheelsup.com. Provides discounted airfares and tour prices for disabled travelers; also publishes a free monthly newsletter.

UK and Ireland

Disability Action Group Northern Ireland ☎028/9049 1011. Provides information about access for disabled travelers abroad.
Holiday Care UK ☎01293/774 535, Minicom ☎01293/776 943, ⊛www.holidaycare.org.uk. Provides free lists of accessible accommodation in the US and other destinations.
Irish Wheelchair Association Republic of Ireland ☎01/833 8241. Useful information provided about traveling abroad with a wheelchair.
RADAR (Royal Association for Disability and Rehabilitation) UK ☎020/7250 3222, Minicom ☎020/7250 4119, ⊛www.radar.org.uk. A good source of general advice on holidays and travel.

Australia and New Zealand

ACROD (Australian Council for Rehabilitation of the Disabled) Australia ☎02/6282 4333. Provides lists of travel agencies and tour operators for people with disabilities.
Disabled Persons Assembly New Zealand ☎04/801 9100. Resource center with lists of travel agencies and tour operators for people with disabilities.

Crime, personal safety and drugs

Boston is one of the safer American cities, making solo travel, even for women, relatively worry-free. There are, as with anywhere, exceptions; at night-time especially, areas like Dorchester, Roxbury, the Fens, Downtown Crossing and parts of the South End can feel deserted and sketchy – but you're unlikely to find yourself in many of these neighborhoods after dark, anyway. The **T** is also safe by day and, for the most part, at night; if you stick to the lines that serve the major nightlife areas (especially the Green and Red lines), you're unlikely to have any trouble.

Pickpocketing is less of a problem in Boston than it is elsewhere in the US, but that doesn't mean it never happens; use common sense and keep an eye on your belongings when at the ATM, on the subway, and paying up at corner stores. If you are robbed, call the police at ☎911. Note that the police may come after you uninvited if they think you're smoking **marijuana** or trading in other narcotics – **drugs** are illegal and you will be fined and possibly sentenced to jail time if caught taking or selling them.

Staying on: work and study

Anyone planning an extended stay in Boston should apply for a special working visa at any American embassy before setting off (see p.17). Different types of visas are issued, depending on your skills and proposed length of stay, but unless you've got parents or children over 21 in the US or a prospective Boston-based employer to sponsor you, your chances of getting a working visa are at best slim.

Illegal work is nowhere near as easy to find as it used to be, and the government has introduced hefty fines for companies caught employing anyone without the legal right to work in the US. Even in the traditionally more casual establishments, like restaurants and bars, things have really tightened up, and if you do find work it's likely to be of the less visible, poorly paid kind – dishwasher instead of waiter.

Another option for work is to acquire a spot as an **intern** – basically an underpaid (and often unpaid) general administrative dogsbody. Various Boston-based biotech firms and media outfits are always on the look-out for interns, especially in the summer, when full-time staff often take their holidays. Applications should be made early in the new year to anyone you can think of who might be interested in your skills and experience.

Large city bookstores carry guides to applying for internships such as the comprehensive annual publication, *Internships USA* (published in the US and UK by Peterson's, Thomson Learning, ⓦwww.petersons.com). *The Atlantic Monthly*'s website (ⓦwww.theatlantic.com) has a good overview of intern-seeking media and publishing companies in the Boston area, as well.

33

Foreign students wishing to **study** at a Boston or Cambridge-area university should apply to that institution directly; if they accept you, you're more or less entitled to unlimited visas so long as you remain enrolled in full-time education.

The City

The City

Downtown Boston

Boston's compact **downtown** encompasses both the colonial heart and the contemporary core of the city. This assemblage of compressed red-brick buildings tucked in the shadow of modern office towers may seem less glamorous than other American big-city centers, but the sheer concentration of historic sights here more than makes up for whatever it lacks in flash. During the day, there's a constant buzz of commuters and tourists, but come nightfall, the streets thin out considerably. A few notable exceptions are the commercialized Quincy Market area, which has a decent, if somewhat downmarket, bar scene; Chinatown, with its popular late-night restaurants; and the Theater District, which is particularly animated on weekends.

As for topography, downtown is flat territory. Hills that once existed here have been smoothed over, though the name of a particularly pronounced peak – Trimountain – lives on in **Tremont Street**, long one of Boston's busiest byways. Today, **King's Chapel**, on Tremont, and the nearby **Old State House** mark the periphery of Boston's earliest town center. The colonies' first church, market, newspaper and prison were all clustered here, though much closer to the shoreline than the plaques that mark their former sites are today. **Spring Lane**, a tiny pedestrian passage off Washington Street, recalls the springs that lured the earliest settlers over to the Shawmut Peninsula from Charlestown. The most evocative streets, however, are those whose essential characters have been less diluted over the years – **School Street**, **State Street** and the eighteenth-century enclave known as **Blackstone Block**, near Faneuil Hall.

The **Freedom Trail**, a self-guided walking tour that connects an assortment of historic sights by a ribbon of red brick embedded in the pavement, begins in **Boston Common**, a king-sized version of the tidy green space at the core of innumerable New England villages. Close by the Common's edge are various churches and old buildings worth a peek on your way toward **Washington Street**, on which the **Old State House** and **Old South Meeting House** provide high-water marks in colonial-era interest. Just east is the **Financial District**, its short streets still following the tangled patterns of colonial village lanes, though now lined with all manner of tall office buildings. Heading up from either Washington Street or the Financial District will take you to the ever-popular meetingplace of **Faneuil Hall**. On the other side of the Financial District, the small but vibrant **Chinatown** and the nearby **Theater District** provide places to head typically after dark; also in the area is the **Leather District**, where empty warehouses and low rents gave rise, in the 1990s, to a series of art galleries. Finally, you can get the flavor of Boston Harbor, once the world's third busiest, along the **waterfront**, where scenic wharfs jut out into Massachusetts Bay; the busiest, **Long Wharf**, is the departure point for **whale-watching** excursions and trips to a handful of offshore **islands** that make relaxing getaways from the center.

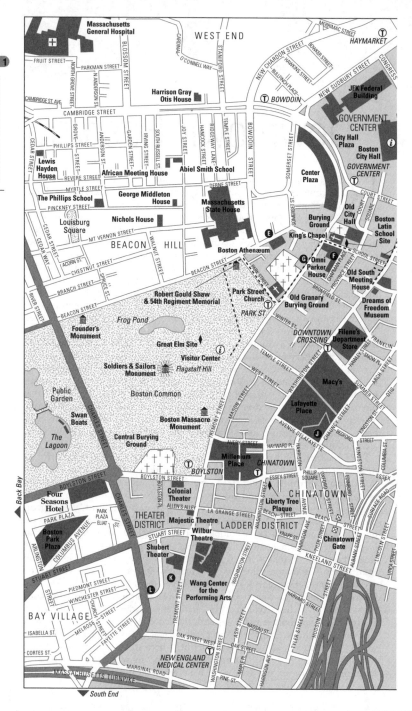

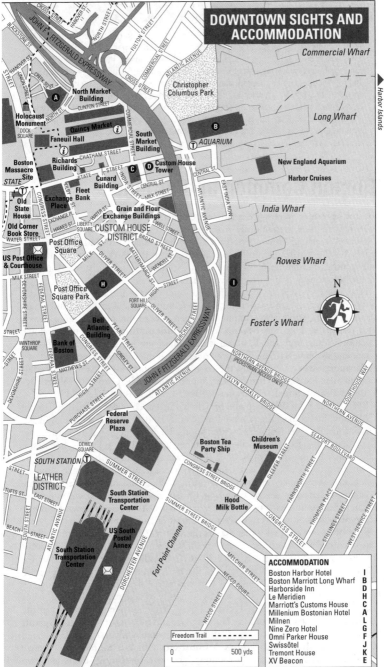

▲ North End   Charlestown ▲

DOWNTOWN SIGHTS AND ACCOMMODATION

Commercial Wharf

Long Wharf

Harbor Islands ▶

Christopher Columbus Park

A North Market Building

Holocaust Monument

Quincy Market (i)

B

Ⓣ AQUARIUM

Faneuil Hall (i)

South Market Building

Richards Building

C

D Custom House Tower

New England Aquarium

Harbor Cruises

Boston Massacre Site

Cunard Building

Fleet Bank

Exchange Place

Grain and Flour Exchange Buildings

Old State House

CUSTOM HOUSE DISTRICT

India Wharf

Old Corner Book Store

Post Office Square

US Post Office & Courthouse

Rowes Wharf

Post Office Square Park

H

I

Bell Atlantic Building

FORT HILL SQUARE

Foster's Wharf

Bank of Boston

N

JOHN F FITZGERALD EXPRESSWAY

NORTHERN AVENUE BRIDGE (PEDESTRIAN ACCESS ONLY)

EVELYN MOAKLEY BRIDGE

COURTHOUSE WAY

Federal Reserve Plaza

NORTHERN AVENUE

Boston Tea Party Ship

Children's Museum

DEWEY SQUARE

SOUTH STATION Ⓣ

SEAPORT BOULEVARD

LEATHER DISTRICT

CONGRESS STREET BRIDGE

South Station Transportation Center

SUMMER STREET BRIDGE

Hood Milk Bottle

CONGRESS STREET

US South Postal Annex

South Station Transportation Center

Fort Point Channel

MELCHER STREET

NECCO COURT

Freedom Trail - - - - - - -

0   500 yds

ACCOMMODATION

Boston Harbor Hotel	I
Boston Marriott Long Wharf	B
Harborside Inn	D
Le Meridien	H
Marriott's Customs House	C
Millenium Bostonian Hotel	A
Milnen	L
Nine Zero Hotel	G
Omni Parker House	J
Swissôtel	K
Tremont House	E
XV Beacon	

Boston Common and around

Boston's premier greenspace is **Boston Common**, a fifty-acre chunk of green, which is neither meticulously manicured nor especially attractive, though it effectively separates downtown from the posher Beacon Hill and Back Bay districts. It's the first thing you'll see emerging from the **Park Street T station**, the central transfer point of America's first subway and a magnet for small demonstrations and, unfortunately, panhandlers.

Established in 1634 as "a trayning field" and "for the feeding of Cattell," as a slate tablet opposite the station recalls, the Common is still primarily utilitarian, used by both pedestrian commuters on their way to downtown's office towers and tourists seeking the **Boston Visitor Information Pavilion**, just down Tremont Street from the **T**, which is the official starting point of the Freedom Trail. The shabbiness of the Tremont Street side of the Common is offset by lovely **Beacon Street**, which runs the length of the northern side, from the gold-domed State House to Charles Street, opposite the Public Garden (for fuller coverage of Beacon Street, see chapter 5, "Beacon Hill and the West End").

Even before John Winthrop and his fellow Puritan colonists earmarked Boston Common for public use, it served as pasture land for the Reverend William Blackstone, Boston's first white settler. Soon after, it disintegrated into little more than a gallows for pirates, alleged witches and various religious heretics; a commoner by the name of Rachell Whall was once hanged here for stealing a bonnet worth 75¢. Newly elected president George Washington made a much-celebrated appearance on the Common in 1789, as did his aide-de-camp, the Marquis de Lafayette, several years later. Ornate eighteenth-century iron fencing encircled the entire park until World War II, when it was taken down for use as scrap metal: it is now said to grace the bottom of Boston Harbor.

One of the few actual sights here is the **Central Burying Ground**, which has occupied the southeast corner of the Common, near the intersection of Boylston and Tremont streets, since 1756. Artist Gilbert Stuart, best known for his portraits of George Washington – the most famous of which is replicated on the dollar bill – died penniless and was interred in Tomb 61. Among the other notables are members of the largest family to take part in the Boston Tea Party, various soldiers of the Revolutionary Army and Redcoats killed in the Battle of Bunker Hill. From the Burying Ground it's a short walk to **Flagstaff Hill**, the highest point on the Common, crowned with the granite, pillared Civil War **Soldiers and Sailors Monument**, which is topped by a bronze statue of Lady Liberty and surrounded by two cap-wearing sailors and two bayonet-toting infantry. A former repository of colonial gunpowder, the hill overlooks the **Frog Pond**, once home to legions of unusually large amphibians and site of the first water pumped into the city. These days, it's nothing more than a kidney-shaped pool, used for wading in summer and ice-skating in winter (see p.221). From here, a path leads to the elegant, two-tiered **Brewer Fountain**, an 1868 bronze replica of one from the Paris Exposition of 1855.

Park Street Church

The **Park Street Church** (July–Aug daily 9am–3pm, rest of year by appointment ☏523-3383; free; Park Street **T**), an oversized version of a typical New England village church, has stood just across from Boston Common since 1809, at the northeast corner of Park and Tremont streets. Though a rather uninteresting mass of bricks and mortar, its ornate 217-foot-tall white telescoping **steeple** is undeniably impressive. To get an idea of the immensity of the building, including the spire, check out the view from tiny Hamilton Place, across Tremont Street. Ultimately, the structure's reputation rests not on its size but on the scope of events that took place inside: the first Sunday School in the country started here in 1818; the next year, the parish sent the first missionaries to Hawaii; a decade later, William Lloyd Garrison delivered his first public address calling for the nationwide abolition of slavery (Massachusetts had already scrapped it back in 1783); and on July 4, 1831, the classic patriotic song *America* ("My country 'tis of thee . . .") was first sung to the church rafters.

Park Street itself slopes upward along the edge of Boston Common toward the State House (see p.46). It was once known as **Bulfinch Row**, for its many brick townhouses designed by the architect Charles Bulfinch (see p.76), but today only one remains, the imposing bay-windowed **Amory-Ticknor House** at no. 9, built in 1804 for George Ticknor, the first publisher of the *Atlantic Monthly*; unfortunately it's not open to the public.

Old Granary Burying Ground

One of the more peaceful stops on the always-busy Freedom Trail is the **Old Granary Burying Ground** (daily 8am–dusk; free; Park Street **T**), the resting place of numerous leaders of the American Revolution. Its odd name comes from a grain warehouse that once stood on the site of the adjacent Park Street Church. The two-acre tract, set a few feet above the busy Tremont Street sidewalk, was originally part of Boston Common; today it's hemmed in by buildings on three sides. The fourth, with its Egyptian Revival arch entrance, fronts Tremont Street.

From any angle, you can spot the stocky **obelisk** at dead center that marks the grave of Benjamin Franklin's parents, but some of the most famous gravesites can only be properly appreciated from the Tremont sidewalk, at the southern rim of the plot. On the side closest to Park Street Church, a boulder with an attached plaque marks the tomb of revolutionary **James Otis**, known for his articulate tirades against British tyranny. A few tombs down rest the bones of **Samuel Adams**, the charismatic patriot whose sideline in beer brewing has kept him a household name. Next to his tomb is the group grave of the five people killed in the **Boston Massacre** of 1770, an event which fueled anti-Tory feeling in Boston (see p.47).

Somewhat more secure burial vaults and table tombs – semi-submerged sarcophagi – were preferred by wealthier families. **Peter Faneuil**, who gave his money and his name to Boston's most famous hall, is interred in one of the latter in the left rear corner of the grounds. Midway along the back path is the grave of famed messenger and silversmith **Paul Revere**, opposite that of Judge **Samuel Sewall**, the only Salem Witch Trial magistrate to later admit that he was wrong. Back across from the judge's grave on the Park Street Church side, a white pillar marks the resting spot of Declaration of Independence signer **John Hancock**. Robert Treat Paine, another signatory, lies along the eastern periphery.

The Freedom Trail

Boston's history is so visible that the city often stands accused of living in its past, and tourist-friendly contrivances like the **Freedom Trail** only serve to perpetuate the notion. It originated when, like many American cities, Boston experienced an economic slump in the postwar years as people migrated to the suburbs; in response, resident William Schofield came up with the idea of a trail highlighting historic Boston sights to lure visitors – and their money – back into town.

Delineated by a 2.5-mile-long red brick stripe in the sidewalk, the trail stretches from Boston Common to Charlestown, linking sixteen points "significant in their contribution to this country's struggle for freedom." It's a somewhat vague qualifier, resulting in the inclusion of several sights that have little to do with Boston's place in the American Revolution. In the relevant column, there's the Revolutionary-era **Old North Church** whose lanterns warned of the British arrival; **Faneuil Hall**, where opposition to the Brits' proposed tea tax was voiced; the **Old South Meeting House** wherein word came that said tax would be imposed; the **Old State House**, which served as the Boston seat of British government; and the site of the **Boston Massacre**. Other stops on the trail, however, have nothing whatsoever to do with the struggle for independence, like the *USS Constitution* built fully two decades after the Declaration of Independence (but which failed, notably, to sink under British cannon fire, earning her the nickname "Old Ironsides"), the **Park Street Church**, built another fifteen years after that, and the **Old Corner Bookstore**, a publishing house for American (and some British) writers. You'll also find two instances of British dominion – the **Bunker Hill Monument**, an obelisk commemorating, ironically, a British victory, albeit in the guise of a moral one for America, and **King's Chapel**, built to serve the King's men stationed in Boston. Finally, you can check out the digs of the gilt-domed **Massachusetts State House** after visiting the gravesites of the Boston luminaries who fought for it – they lie interred in three separate **cemeteries** .

Unfortunately, some of the touches intended to accentuate the attractions' appeal move closer to tarnishing it. The people in period costume stationed outside some of the sights can't help but grate a little, and the artificially enhanced atmosphere is exaggerated by the bright-red brick trail and pseudo-old signage that connects the sights. Still, the Freedom Trail remains the easiest way to orient yourself downtown, and is especially useful if you'll only be in Boston for a short time, as it does take in many "must-see" sights. For more info and an interactive timeline of Boston's history, visit ⓦ www.thefreedomtrail.org. You can also pick up a detailed National Park Service **map** from where the trail begins at the **Visitor Information Pavilion** in Boston Common.

Freedom Trail sights

Boston Athenæum

Around the block from the Old Granary Burying Ground, the venerable **Boston Athenæum**, at 10¹/₂ Beacon St (Mon 8.30am–8pm, Tues–Fri 8.30am–5.30pm, Sat 9am–4pm; free; ☎227-0270, ⊛www.bostonathenaeum.org; Park Street **T**), was established in 1807, and stakes its claim as one of the oldest independent research libraries in the country. In naming their library, the Boston Brahmin founders demonstrated not only their high-minded classicism, but also their marketing sensibility, too, as its growing stature was a potent enough force to endow Boston with a lofty sobriquet – the "Athens of America" – that has stuck.

Recently reopened after extensive renovations to "modernize" the building – a replica of the Palazzo da Porta Festa in Vicenza, Italy – the most significant change (at least, for visitors) is that only the first-floor library is open to non-members. Best known are its special collections, including the original library of King's Chapel – which counted the 1666 edition of Sir Walter Raleigh's *History of the World* among its holdings – as well as books from the private library of George Washington and an impressive array of paintings by the likes of John Singer Sargent and Gilbert Stuart.

King's Chapel Burying Ground and King's Chapel

Boston's oldest cemetery, the atmospheric **King's Chapel Burying Ground**, located at the northeast corner of Beacon and Tremont streets (daily: June–Oct 9.30am–4pm; Nov–May 10am–4pm; free; Park Street **T**), often goes unnoticed by busy passersby. Coupled with its accompanying church, however, it's well worth a tour despite the din of nearby traffic. The graves of several prominent Bostonians are here, and one of the chief pleasures of walking amongst them is to examine the many beautifully etched gravestones, with their winged skulls and contemplative seraphim, such as that of one **Joseph Tapping**, near the Tremont Street side. Others include **John Winthrop**, the first governor of Massachusetts, and **Mary Chilton**, the first Pilgrim to set foot on Plymouth Rock. Near the center of the plot is the tomb of **William Dawes**, the unsung patriot who accompanied Paul Revere on his famous "midnight ride" to Lexington. King's Chapel Burying Ground was one of the favorite Boston haunts of author **Nathaniel Hawthorne**, who drew inspiration from the grave of a certain Elizabeth Pain to create the adulterous character of Hester Prynne for his novel *The Scarlet Letter* (Hawthorne himself is buried in Concord's Sleepy Hollow Cemetery; see p.143).

King's Chapel

The most conspicuous thing about gray, foreboding **King's Chapel**, on the premises of the burying grounds, is its absence of a steeple (there were plans for one, just not enough money). But the belfry does boast the biggest bell ever cast by Paul Revere, which you can't help but notice if you happen to pass by at chime time. A wooden chapel was built on this site first, amid some controversy, when in 1686, King James II revoked the Massachusetts Bay Colony's charter and installed Sir Edmund Andros as governor, giving him orders to found an Anglican parish – a move that for obvious reasons didn't sit too well with Boston's Puritan population. The present chapel, completed in 1754 by Peter Harrison under instructions to create a church "that would be the equal of any in England," is entered through a pillar-fronted portico added in 1789, when it became the country's first Unitarian Church.

The best time to enter the building is during one of the weekly **chamber music concerts** (Tues 12.15–12.45pm; $2 suggested donation). While hardly ostentatious, the elegant Georgian interior, done up with wooden Corinthian columns and lit by chandeliers, provides a marked contrast to the minimalist adornments of Boston's other old churches. It also features America's oldest pulpit, which dates from the late 1600s, and many of its original pews, including a Governor's Pew along the right wall.

Washington Street shopping district

To a Bostonian, downtown proper comes in two packages: the **Washington Street shopping district** (namely the School Street area and Downtown Crossing) and the adjacent Financial District (see p.48). The former, situated east of the King's Chapel Burying Ground, has some of the city's most historic sights – the **Old Corner Bookstore**, **Old South Meeting House** and **Old State House** – but it tends to shut down after business hours, becoming eerily quiet at night. All the stops can be seen in half a day, though you'll obviously need to allow more time if shopping is on your agenda – the stretch around **Downtown Crossing** is decidedly more commercial than historical.

Narrow and heavily trafficked today, in colonial times **Washington Street** connected the Old State House to the city gates at Boston Neck, an isthmus that joined the Shawmut Peninsula to the mainland, thus ensuring its position as the commercial nerve center of Boston. The best way to begin exploring the area is via **School Street**, anchored on its northern edge by the dignified **Omni Parker House**, the city's most venerable hotel. That John F. Kennedy announced his congressional candidacy here in 1946, down the hall from the room in which Charles Dickens first read *A Christmas Carol* are but two of its prestigious accolades; more mystifyingly, Ho Chi Minh and Malcolm X both used to wait tables at the hotel's restaurant. If you'd like, pop in and order a slice of Boston Creme Pie (really a layered cake with custard filling and chocolate frosting all around): it was invented here in 1855, and the hotel reportedly still bakes 25 of them a day.

For the rest of its modest length, School Street offers up some of the best in Old Boston charm, beginning with the antique gaslights that flank the severe west wall of King's Chapel (see p.43). Just beyond is a grand French Second Empire building that served as Boston City Hall from 1865 to 1969; it's near the site of the original location of the **Boston Latin School**, founded in 1635 (a mosaic embedded in the sidewalk just outside the iron gates marks the exact spot). Benjamin Franklin, a statue of whom graces the courtyard, and John Hancock were among the more illustrious graduates of this, America's first public school.

Old Corner Bookstore

A few doors down from the Latin School site, where School Street joins Washington, stands the gambrel-roofed, red-brick **Old Corner Bookstore** (Mon–Fri 9am–6.30pm, Sat 9am–6pm, Sun 11am–6pm; ⊛www.globecorner .com; State Street **T**). In the nineteenth century, Boston's version of London's Fleet Street occupied the stretch of Washington from here to Old South Meeting House, with a convergence of booksellers, newspaper headquarters and publishers; most famous among them was Ticknor & Fields, Boston's hottest-ever literary salon. This highly esteemed publishing house was once

△ Quincy Market and the Custom House District

housed in the bookstore itself and handled the likes of Emerson, Longfellow, Hawthorne and even Dickens and Thackeray. One of America's oldest literary magazines, the staid *Atlantic Monthly*, was published upstairs here for many years, as well; later *The Boston Globe* moved in. It too moved on, but it maintained the site as The Globe Corner Bookstore, an atmospheric travel bookstore until its demise here, in 1997 (a second outlet carries on the trade in Harvard Square; see p.210). Vaingloriously reincarnated as the Boston Globe Store, today the store stocks merchandise stamped with the newspaper's logo and other touristy knick-knacks.

Old South Meeting House

Washington Street's big architectural landmark, the **Old South Meeting House** – a charming brick church building recognizable by its tower, a separate but attached structure that tapers into an octagonal spire – faces the Boston Globe Store one block south, at no. 310 (daily: April–Oct 9.30am–5pm; Nov–March 10am–4pm; $5, Children $1; ☎482-6439, ⓦwww.oldsouthmeetinghouse .org; Downtown Crossing **T**). An earlier cedarwood structure on the spot burned down in 1711, clearing the way for what is now the second oldest church building in Boston, after Old North Church in the North End (see p.64). Its Congregationalist origins prescribed simplicity inside and out, with no artifice to obstruct closeness to God. This also endowed Old South with a spaciousness that made it a leading venue for anti-imperial rhetoric. The day after the Boston Massacre, outraged Bostonians assembled here to demand the removal of the troops that were ostensibly guarding the town. Five years later, patriot and doctor Joseph Warren delivered an oration to commemorate the incident; the biggest building in town was so packed that he had to crawl through the window behind the pulpit just to get inside.

More momentously, on the morning of December 16, 1773, over five thousand locals met here, awaiting word from Governor Thomas Hutchinson on whether the Crown would actually impose duty on sixty tons of tea aboard ships in Boston Harbor. When a message was received that it would, Samuel Adams rose and announced, "This meeting can do nothing more to save the country!" His simple declaration triggered the **Boston Tea Party**, perhaps the seminal event leading to the War for Independence.

The Meeting House served as a stable, a British riding school and even a bar before becoming the **museum** it is today. One of the things lost in the transition was the famous original high pulpit, which the British tore out during the Revolution and used as firewood; the ornate one standing today is a replica from 1808. There's not much to see other than the building itself – take note of the exterior **clock**, the same one installed in 1770, which you can still set your watch by – but if you take the audio tour, included in the admission price, you will hear campy re-enactments of a Puritan church service and the Boston Tea Party debates, among other more prosaic sound effects.

Old State House and around

Skyscrapers dwarf the graceful three-tiered window tower of the red-brick **Old State House** (daily 9am–5pm; $5, children $1; ☎720-1713, ⓦwww.bostonhistory .org; State Street **T**), at the corner of Washington and State streets, amplifying rather than diminishing its colonial-era dignity. This is especially noticeable if you're stuck in traffic on I-93 where the elevated expressway passes by State Street, a view that affords a spectacular juxtaposition of the old and new.

For years, this three-story structure, reminiscent of an old Dutch town hall, was the seat of the Massachusetts Bay Colony and consequently the center of British authority in New England. Later it served as Boston's city hall, and in 1880 it was nearly demolished so that State Street traffic might flow more freely. An attempt was also made to move the site to Chicago for the 1893 World Fair, but the house remains in Boston, its fate spared by the Bostonian Society, the city's official historical society, founded specifically to preserve the building; today the site houses the small but comprehensive **Boston History Museum**.

An impassioned speech in the second-floor Council Chamber by **James Otis**, a Crown appointee who resigned to take up the colonial cause, sparked the quest for independence from Britain fifteen years before it was declared. He argued against the Writs of Assistance, which permitted the British to inspect private property at will. Legend has it that on certain nights you can still hear Otis hurling his anti-British barbs along with the cheers of the crowd he so energized, but museum staff has no comment. The **balcony** overlooking State Street is as famous as Otis' speech, for it was from here on July 18, 1776 that the Declaration of Independence was first read publicly in Boston – a copy having just arrived from Philadelphia. That same night the lion and unicorn figures mounted above the balcony were set ablaze – those currently on display are replicas. Just to show there were no hard feelings, Queen Elizabeth II – the first British monarch to set foot in Boston since the Revolution – read the Declaration of Independence from the balcony as part of the American bicentennial activities in 1976.

As for the **museum**, the permanent ground-level exhibit, "Colony to Commonwealth", chronicles Boston's role in inciting the Revolutionary War. Dozens of images and artifacts track, to varying degrees of interest, the events that led up to the establishment of the Commonwealth of Massachusetts (though not, curiously, to the events leading up to US independence). Displays include a bit of tea from Boston's most infamous party; the plaque of royal arms that once hung over Province House, official residence of the colonial governors; the flag that the Sons of Liberty draped from the Liberty Tree to announce their meetings; and the most galvanizing image of the Revolutionary period, Paul Revere's propagandistic engraving of the Boston Massacre. Upstairs are rotating exhibits on the history of the city and, incongruously, a display on old Boston hotels and restaurants.

Boston Massacre Site

Directly in front of the Old State House, a circle of cobblestones embedded in a small traffic island marks the site of the **Boston Massacre** (State Street **T**), the tragic outcome of escalating tensions between Bostonians and the British Redcoats who occupied the city. Riots were an increasingly common occurrence in Boston by the time this deadly one broke out on March 5, 1770. It began when a young wigmaker's apprentice heckled an army officer over a barber's bill. The officer sought refuge in the Custom House (then opposite the Old State House), but when a throng of people gathered at the scene, the mob grew violent, hurling snowballs and rocks at arriving soldiers. When someone threw a club that knocked a Redcoat onto the ice, he rose and fired. Five Bostonians were killed in the ensuing riot, resulting in Governor Hutchinson's order to relocate occupying troops to Castle Island (see p.117) in Boston Harbor. Two other patriots, John Adams and Josiah Quincy, actually defended the offending eight soldiers in court; six were acquitted, and the two who were found guilty had their thumbs branded.

Downtown views

Whether local or out of town, people can't seem to get enough of Boston's **skyline** – its pastiche of brownstone churches and glass-panelled skyscrapers framing Massachusetts Bay ranks among the country's finest. No wonder then, that so many buildings have public (and often free) viewing floors. You can check out Boston from every angle by ascending the *Marriott's Customs House* (see p.158), One Post Office Square (see p.49), the Prudential Center (see p.91) and the Bunker Hill Monument (see p.71). The best lay of the land, though, is had from the water – board the Charlestown ferry (see p.67) or visit the Harbor Islands (see p.57) and watch the city recede.

Downtown Crossing

Downtown Crossing is a busy pedestrian area centered on the intersection of Washington and Winter streets, whose strip of department stores and smaller shops recalls the time before malls, and it possesses some fine nineteenth-century commercial architecture besides. Brimming with stores that mostly cater to lower-income shoppers and the pushcart vendors and panhandlers that pester them at nearly every street corner, its nucleus is the stalwart **Filene's Basement**, a magnet for bargain hunters of all socioeconomic stripes and the only "attraction" here really worth your time. Otherwise, unless you have the money and inclination to eat at the historic *Locke-Ober* restaurant on Winter Place (see p.178 for review), you may as well move on.

Financial District

Boston's **Financial District**, a small tract of real estate east of Washington Street and bounded by the waterfront, hardly conjures the same interest as those of New York and London, but it continues to wield influence in key fields (like mutual funds, invented here in 1925). The area is not entirely devoid of historic interest, though it's generally more manifest in plaques rather than actual buildings. Like most of America's business districts, it beats to an office hours-only schedule, and many of its little eateries and Irish pubs are closed on weekends (though some brash new restaurants have begun to make inroads).

The mostly immaculate streets follow the same short, winding paths as they did three hundred years ago; only now, thirty- and forty-story skyscrapers have replaced the wooden houses and churches that used to clutter the area. Still, their names are historically evocative: **High Street**, for example, was once known as Cow Lane and led to the summit of the now vanished eighty-foot-tall Fort Hill. **Arch Street** recalls the decorative arch that graced the Tontine Crescent, a block of stately townhouses designed in 1793 by Charles Bulfinch and unfortunately destroyed by the Great Fire of 1872, which began in the heart of the district. Tucked among the relatively generic skyscrapers are several well-preserved nineteenth-century mercantile masterpieces – head down the curve of Franklin Street and you'll see rounded greystone Victorian buildings also designed by Bulfinch.

Milk Street and Post Office Square

The most dramatic approach to the Financial District is east from Washington Street via **Milk Street**. A bust of **Benjamin Franklin** surveys the scene from a recessed Gothic niche above the doorway at no. 1; the site marks Franklin's birthplace, though the building itself only dates from 1874. It now contains the interactive **Dreams of Freedom Museum** (mid-April to Dec daily 10am–6pm; Jan to mid-April Tues–Sat 10am–5pm; $7.50, children $3.50; ☏338-6022, Ⓦwww.dreamsoffreedom.org; State Street **T**), which extols the virtues of immigration via amusing, and often educational, hands-on displays. Though children are obviously the focus here, adults might enjoy testing their knowledge of American history to see if they, too, could pass the citizenship exam.

Further down Milk Street, the somber, 22-story **John W. McCormack Federal Courthouse** building houses one of Boston's larger post offices, with a special section for stamp collectors. An earlier building on this site gave the adjacent **Post Office Square** its name; its triangular layout and cascading fountains are popular with area professionals during the lunch hour. Though it's not officially open to the public, you might try sneaking up to the glass atrium atop the building at **One Post Office Square** for jaw-dropping views of Boston Harbor and downtown. The city's skyline encompasses the architectural excesses of the 1980s and a few Art Deco treats too; the best example of the former is the **Bank of Boston** tower at 100 Federal St with its bulging midsection, nicknamed "Pregnant Alice."

The prime Art Deco specimen, meanwhile, is nearby at 185 Franklin St, the head office of **Bell Atlantic**. The step-top building was a 1947 design; more recently the phone booths outside were given a Deco makeover. If you're here during business hours, check out the fusty nook off the right-hand side of the lobby, home to a replica of the Boston attic room where Alexander Graham Bell first transmitted speech sounds over a wire in 1875; the wooden chamber is a meticulously reassembled version of the original that was installed in 1959 and, with the exception of an evocative diorama of an old Boston cityscape, it looks like nothing's been touched since. Head back to the lobby to see the 360-degree mural that glorifies the exciting world of *Telephone Men and Women at Work*.

Exchange Place, at 53 State St, is a mirrored-glass tower rising from the facade of the old Boston Stock Exchange; the Bunch of Grapes tavern, watering hole of choice for many of Boston's revolutionary rabble-rousers, once stood here. Behind it is tiny **Liberty Square**, once the heart of Tory Boston – the British tax office had its address here, in 1765, and was destroyed by angry colonists – and now mostly of note for its improbable bronze sculpture, called Aspirations for Liberty; it depicts two rebels holding each other up in honor of the Hungarian anti-Communist uprising of 1956.

Government Center

Tremont Street's major tenant, **Government Center**, lies northwest from Exchange Place along Congress Street. Its sea of towering gray buildings on the former site of Scollay Square – once Boston's most notorious den of porn halls and tattoo parlors – is by far the least interesting section of downtown

Boston. As part of a citywide face-lift, Scollay was razed in the early 1960s, eliminating all traces of its salacious past and, along with it, most of its lively character. Indeed, the only thing that remains from the square's steamier days is the Oriental Tea Company's 227-gallon **Steaming Kettle** advertisement, which has been clouding up the sky across from the Government Center **T** stop since 1873. The area is now overlaid with concrete, thanks to an ambitious plan developed by I.M. Pei, and towered over by two monolithic edifices: **Boston City Hall**, at the east side of the plaza, and the **John F. Kennedy Federal Building**, on the north. Unless the workings of bureaucracy get you going, the only conceivable reason to stop here is to go to the **visitor's center** on the fourth floor of City Hall, which has the usual array of travel information, and some aberrantly clean public restrooms.

Faneuil Hall Marketplace and around

Popular with locals and tourists alike, the **Faneuil Hall Marketplace** (rhymes with "Daniel"), set on a pedestrian zone east of Government Center, is the kind of active, bustling public gathering place that's none too common in Boston nowadays. Built as a market during colonial times to house the city's growing mercantile industry, it declined during the nineteenth century and, like the area around it, was pretty much defunct until the 1960s, when it was quite successfully redeveloped as a restaurant and shopping mall.

Faneuil Hall

Much-hyped **Faneuil Hall** (Mon–Sat 10am–9pm, Sun noon–6pm; ☏523-1300, ⓦwww.faneuilhallmarketplace.com; State Street **T**) itself doesn't appear particularly majestic from the outside; it's simply a small, four-story brick building topped with a Georgian spire – hardly the grandiose auditorium one might imagine would have housed the Revolutionary War meetings that earned its "Cradle of Liberty" sobriquet.

The structure once housed an open-air market on its first floor and a space for political meetings on its second, a juxtaposition that inspired local poet Francis Hatch to pen the lines, "Here orators in ages past / Have mounted their attacks, / Undaunted by the proximity / Of sausage on the racks." Faneuil Hall was where revolutionary firebrands such as Samuel Adams and James Otis whipped up popular support for independence by protesting British tax legislation. The first floor now houses a panoply of tourist **shops** that make for a less-than-dignified memorial; you'll also find an information desk, a post office and a BOSTIX kiosk. The auditorium on the second floor has been preserved to reflect modifications made by Charles Bulfinch in 1805, the focal point being a massive – and rather preposterous – canvas depicting an imagined scene of Daniel Webster speaking in Faneuil Hall as a range of luminaries from Washington to de Tocqueville look on. More down-to-earth, perhaps, is the story of how Beantown residents suspected of being spies during the War of 1812 were asked what flew atop Faneuil Hall as a weathervane. Those who knew it was a grasshopper were trusted as true Bostonians; those who didn't were regarded with suspicion, and sometimes – in extreme cases – even decapitated.

Dock Square, Blackstone Street and the Holocaust Memorial

Immediately in front of Faneuil Hall is **Dock Square**, so named for its original location directly on Boston's waterfront; carvings in the pavement indicate the shoreline in 1630. The square's center is dominated by a statue of **Samuel Adams**, interesting mostly for its somewhat over-the-top caption: "A Statesman, fearless and incorruptible." A dim, narrow corridor known as Scott's Alley heads north of the market to reach Creek Square, where you enter **Blackstone Street**, the eastern edge of a tiny warren of streets bounded to the west by Union Street. The area has, so far, been bypassed by urban renewal and maintains a reasonably authentic representation of central Boston's original architectural character. Its uneven cobblestoned streets and low brick buildings have remained largely untouched since the 1650s; many of them, especially those along Union Street, now house restaurants and pubs. The one touch of modernity here is nearby on Union Street, where you'll see six tall, hollow, glass pillars erected as a **memorial** to victims of the Holocaust. Built to resemble smokestacks, the columns are etched with quotes and facts about the human tragedy – with an unusual degree of attention to its non-Jewish victims. Steam rises from grates beneath each of the pillars to accentuate their symbolism, an effect that's particularly striking at night.

Quincy Market

The markets just behind Faneuil Hall – three parallel oblong structures that house restaurants, shops and office buildings – were built in the early eighteenth century to contain the trade that had quickly outgrown its space in the hall. The center building, known as **Quincy Market** (Mon–Sat 10am–9pm, Sun noon–6pm; ☎523-1300, ⓦwww.faneuilhallmarketplace.com; 5 State Street **T**), holds a super-extended corridor lined with stands vending a variety of decent if pricey take-out treats – the mother of the city's modern food courts, it was built in 1822 under the direction of Boston's mayor at the time, Josiah Quincy. To either side of the market are the **North** and **South Markets**, which hold restaurants and popular chain clothing stores. The cobblestone corridors between them host a number of vendor carts selling curios and narrow specializations (one sells only plaid clothing, another nothing but puppets). You'll also find the usual complement of street musicians, fire-jugglers and mimes, weather permitting. There's not much to distinguish it from any other shopping complex, although there are several good restaurants and a nice concentration of bars (see p.174 & 188 for reviews), which are scarce elsewhere in the downtown area. All in all, though, sitting on a bench in the carnivalesque heart of it all on a summer day, eating scrod while the mobs of townies and tourists mill about, is a quintessential, if slightly contrived, Boston experience.

The Custom House District

The not-quite-triangular wedge of downtown between State and Broad streets and the Fitzgerald Expressway is the unfairly overlooked (and rather loosely named) **Custom House District**, dotted with some excellent architectural draws, chief among them is the **Custom House Tower**. Surrounded by 32 huge Doric columns, it was built in 1847, though the thirty-story Greek

Revival tower was only added in 1915. Not surprisingly, it is no longer the tallest skyscraper in New England – a status it held for thirty years – and it's dwarfed by the John Hancock Tower (see p.91); that said, it still has plenty of character and terrific views nonetheless – you can check them out from the 360-degree observation deck free of charge (daily 10am & 4pm).

Another landmark is the **Grain and Flour Exchange Building**, a block away at 177 Milk St, a fortress-like construction that recalls the Romanesque Revival style of prominent local architect H.H. Richardson. Its turreted, conical roof, encircled by a series of pointed dormers, is a bold reminder of the financial stature this district once held. **Broad Street**, built on filled-in land in 1807, is still home to several Federal-style mercantile buildings designed by Bulfinch, notably those at numbers 68–70, 72 and 102.

On **State Street**, long a focal point of Boston's maritime prosperity, get a look at the elaborate cast-iron facade of the **Richards Building** at no. 114 – a clipper ship company's office in the 1850s – and the **Cunard Building** at no. 126, its ornamental anchors recalling Boston's status as the North American terminus of the first transatlantic steamship mail service. Trading activity in the nearby harbor brought a thriving banking and insurance industry to the street in the 1850s, along with a collection of rather staid office buildings. A modern exception is the opulent **Fleet Bank** headquarters at no. 75, a medium-sized skyscraper crowned with 3600 square feet of gold leaf and containing a six-story lobby decked out in marble, mahogany and bronze.

Theater District

Just south of Boston Common is the slightly seedy **Theater District**, the chief attractions of which are the flamboyant buildings that lend the area its title, such as the Wilbur, Colonial and Majestic theaters. Not surprisingly, you'll have to purchase tickets in order to inspect their grand old interiors (see p.201), but it's well worth a quick walk along Tremont Street to admire the facades. The **Colonial** – still the *grande dame* of Boston theater – is just off **Piano Row** – a section of Boylston Street between Charles and Tremont that was the center of American piano manufacturing and music publishing in the nineteenth and early twentieth centuries. There are still a few piano shops around, but the hip restaurants and clubs in the immediate vicinity are of greater interest; many, like *Finale* and *Mistral* (see review p.172 and p.184), are tucked between Charles and Stuart streets around the mammoth **Massachusetts Transportation Building** and cater to the theater-going crowd.

South along Tremont from the Colonial, the **Majestic Theatre** is, as of press time, closed for restoration; it should be open for its centennial season in 2003. Just down the street you'll also find the porticoed **Wilbur Theatre**, the place to go for Broadway shows (see p.202); when it opened in 1914, it was the first Boston theater to have its own guest lounge, which today is used by the nightclub *Aria*. Adjacent to the Wilbur is the old **Metropolitan Theater**, a movie house of palatial proportions, which survives as the glittering **Wang Center for the Performing Arts**, home of the Boston Ballet (see p.202). Across the street is the darling **Shubert Theater**, the so-called Little Princess of the Theater District; its plush, 1600-seat auditorium is home to the Boston Lyric Opera, as well as some Broadway productions.

Banned in Boston

Boston's Puritan founders would be horrified to find that an area called the **Theater District** exists. Their ingrained allergy to fun resulted in theatrical performances actually being outlawed in Boston until 1792, and in 1878, the Watch & Ward Society was formed to organize boycotts against indecent books and plays. Still, the shows went on, and in 1894 vaudeville was born at the lavish (now extinct) B.F. Keith Theater. Burlesque soon followed, prompting the city licensing division in 1905 to deny performances that didn't meet their neo-Puritan codes – thus the phrase "Banned in Boston." In fact, as recently as 1970, a production of *Hair* was banned for a month due to its desecration of the American flag.

Despite this censorship, Boston still managed to become the premier theater try-out town that it is today – high production costs on Broadway have dictated that hits be sifted from misses early on, and Boston was a cost-efficient testing ground. During the 1920s – the heyday of theater in the city – there were as many as forty playhouses in the Theater District alone. However, the rise of film meant the fall of theater, and after brief stints as movie halls, many of the grand buildings – most notably, the Art Deco **Paramount**, the crumbling **Opera House** (formerly the Savoy) and the **Modern Theater**, all on lower Washington Street – slid into disrepair and eventual abandonment.

The Ladder District

The tenor around Washington Street between Essex and Kneeland was, until quite recently, relatively dodgy. Designated as an "adult entertainment zone" in the 1960s (when it replaced Scollay Square as the city's "Red Light" district; see p.49) and known, enigmatically, as the Combat Zone, the latter-day **Ladder District** was home to a few X-rated theaters and bookshops until trendy restaurants and nightclubs designated it the new "It" spot and pushed the less reputable businesses out. PR hacks successfully renamed the area after its ladder-like layout (Tremont and Washington form the rails; Winter and Avery streets, the top and bottom rungs), but failed to alter its daylight character, which, despite the recent addition of a *Ritz-Carlton* at the corner of Tremont and Avery streets, remains rather desolate. At night, the place has slightly more energy as theater-goers come to dine before or after shows. Other than this, the only real sight of note is the plaque at the corner of Essex and Washington streets that marks the site where the so-called **Liberty Tree** stood. This oak, planted in 1646, was a favored meeting point of the Sons of Liberty; as such, the British chopped it down in 1775.

Chinatown

Boston's colorful and authentic **Chinatown** lies wedged into just a few square blocks between the Financial and Theater districts, but it makes up in activity what it lacks in size. Just lean against a pagoda-topped payphone on the corner of **Beach** and **Tyler streets** – the neighborhood's two liveliest thoroughfares – and watch the way life here revolves around the food trade at all hours. By day, merchants barter in Mandarin and Cantonese over the going price of produce; by night, Bostonians arrive in droves to eat in Chinatown's restaurants. Walk down either street, and you'll pass most of the restaurants, bakeries and markets in whose windows you'll see the usual complement of roast ducks hanging from hooks and aquariums filled with future seafood dinners. The area's at its most vibrant during various **festivals**, none more so than **Chinese New Year** (late Jan, early Feb), when frequent parades of papier-mâché dragons fill the streets and the acrid smell of firecrackers permeates the air. During the **Festival of the August Moon**, held, as you may have guessed, in August, there's a bustling street fair. Call the Chinese Merchants' Association for more information (☎482-3972).

The prosperity of Boston's Chinatown has increased dramatically in recent years, so much so that the district is expanding to the north, taking up some of the land that lies between it and Downtown Crossing. Despite this growth, the heart of Chinatown contains little in the way of sights, and the atmosphere is best enjoyed by wandering around with no particular destination in mind. Still, there are a few important landmarks, such as the impressive **Chinatown Gate**, a three-story red-and-gilt monolith guarded by four Fu dogs, located at the intersection of Hudson and Beach streets, a gift from Taiwan in honor of Chinatown's centennial. Adjacent **Tian An Men Park** provides a place to rest, but it's poorly kept, generally littered with trash and inhabited by fearsomely aggressive pigeons.

Leather District

Just east of Chinatown, the six square blocks bounded by Kneeland, Atlantic, Essex and Lincoln streets form the **Leather District**, which takes its name from the time when the material was shipped through warehouses here to keep the shoe industry – a mainstay of the New England economy – alive. Since then, the Financial District – with which it is frequently lumped – has taken over as economic hub, and the leather industry has pretty much dried up. The distinction between the Financial and Leather districts is actually quite sharp, and most evident where High Street transitions into **South Street**, the Leather District's main drag. Stout brick warehouses replace gleaming modern skyscrapers, and a melange of merchants and gallery owners take over from the suited bankers. Some of the edifices still have their leather warehouse **signs** on them. Check out the Boston Hide & Leather Co at 15 East St, and the Fur and Leather Services Outlet at 717 Atlantic – but don't expect to see too much going on behind the facades. The nearby **South Street Station**, Boston's main train and bus terminus, has little to recommend it architecturally.

Otherwise, the Leather District doesn't have much of historical interest to offer, but its abundance of cheap warehouse space in the 1990s attracted a number of **art galleries** and trendies, making it the capital of Boston's modest contemporary arts scene (though the South End is trying to take over that title). For a list of galleries, see p.213.

The waterfront

Stretching from the North End to South Street **T** station, Boston's **waterfront** is still a fairly active area, though no longer the city's focal point, as it was up until the mid-1800s. The city's decline as a port left the series of wharves stretching along the harborside below Christopher Columbus Park with no real function, and the construction of the elevated central artery in the 1950s physically separated the area from the rest of the city. Today, the waterfront thrives instead on tourism, with stands selling tacky T-shirts, furry lobsters and the like, concentrated around **Long Wharf**. Nevertheless, strolling the atmospheric **Harborwalk** that edges the water affords unbeatable views of Boston, and is a pleasant respite from the masses that can clog Faneuil Hall and the Common. You'll also find plenty of diversion if you've got little ones in tow, as the **Children's Museum** and **Aquarium** are both found here. Otherwise, you can do some watery exploring on a number of **boat tours**, or escape the city altogether by heading out to the **Harbor Islands**.

Long Wharf

Long Wharf has been the waterfront's main drag since its construction in 1710. Summer is, not surprisingly, its busiest season, when the wharf is dotted with stands vending kitschy souvenirs and surprisingly good ice cream. This is also the main point of departure for Boston Harbor Cruises (☎227-4321; ⓦwww.bostonharborcruises.com), which runs **whale-watching** excursions (summer; 3hr; call for times; $29, children $23) as well as ferries to the Harbor Islands (see p.58).

Walk out to the end of Long Wharf for an excellent vantage point on **Boston Harbor**. Since the city is surrounded by other land masses, you'll only see a series of peninsulas and islands, which are generally smoky and grinding with industry. It's perhaps most enjoyable – and still relatively safe – at night, when even the freighters appear graceful against the moonlit water.

New England Aquarium

Next door to Long Wharf is the waterfront's major draw, the **New England Aquarium** (July–Aug Mon, Tues & Fri 9am–6pm, Wed & Thurs 9am–8pm, Sat, Sun & holidays 9am–7pm; Sept–Jun Mon–Fri 9am–5pm, Sat & Sun 9am–6pm; weekdays $12, kids $6; weekends $13.50, children $7; City Pass accepted; ☎973-5200, ⓦwww.neaq.org; Aquarium **T**). Like many of the Boston

The Harborwalk

Like the Freedom Trail, the **Harborwalk** was designed to lure tourist dollars with the promise of an historic theme. On this particular trip back in time, blue plaques illustrate the relevance of various points in Boston's role as a major commercial port – a face of the city that seems ever more a thing of the past, especially with the Harbor's recent notoriety for pollution. While the walk's sights don't have the all-star quality of the historic points on the Freedom Trail (some would need spicing up to pass for mundane), the red-brick waterside promenade does provide a decent excuse to take a picturesque stroll along the water, with any enhanced historical context serving as a bonus. Visitor center maps can help steer you on the self-guided stroll that starts at the corner of State Street and Merchant's Row, proceeds along the wharves, passing by scads of swanky condominiums, upscale hotels like the *Boston Harbor Hotel* (see p.158), and countless moored sailboats, before ending up on the Congress Street bridge at the Boston Tea Party Ship. The views of the harbor are pretty spectacular, what with modern glass buildings reflecting towering boat masts in their facades.

waterfront attractions, this one is most fun for kids, though engaging enough for anyone whose sights aren't set too high. Currently in the midst of an ambitious, multimillion-dollar expansion, which has already seen the addition of an **IMAX theater** with an emphasis on marine-based films (daily 9.30am–9.30pm; $8, children $6; ☎973-5200, ⓦwww.neaq.org).

The indoor aquarium has plenty of good exhibits, too, such as the penguins on the bottom floor. Be sure to play with the special laser device that maneuvers a red point of light around the bottom of their pool; the guileless waterfowl mistake the light for a fish and follow it around obediently. In the center of the aquarium's spiral walkway is an impressive collection of marine life: a three-story, 200,000-gallon cylindrical tank packed with moray eels, sharks, stingrays and a range of other sea exotica that swim by in unsettling proximity. The aquarium also runs excellent **whale-watching** trips into the harbor (early April through late Oct; 3.5–5hr, call for times and specific dates; $27, children $17; ☎973-5281).

Children's Museum and the Seaport District

It's hard to miss the larger-than-life 1930s-era **Hood Milk Bottle** across the Congress Street bridge from downtown, though the only dairy product the 40-foot structure serves is ice cream – most of its trade is in hot dogs and hamburgers. Behind it, the engaging **Children's Museum**, 300 Congress St (daily 10am–5pm, Fri till 9pm; $7, children $6, Fri 5–9pm $1; ☎426-8855, ⓦwww.bostonkids.org; South Station **T**) comprises five floors of deceptively educational exhibits designed to trick kids into learning about a huge array of topics, from kinematics to the history of popular culture. The key here is interactivity: displays are meant to be touched rather than observed, like the climbing maze in the central shaft that no one over 14 could possibly get into. Other exhibits are amusing even for adults, particularly those on Japanese youth culture and the replica of "Grandma's House," replete with authentic 1950s furniture, vintage commercials on the television, and a meatloaf in the oven.

The Children's Museum sits in the **Seaport District**, which loosely refers to the harborside area across the Northern Avenue bridge from Boston, accessible by a free shuttle from the South Station **T**, where businesses have recently banded together in an attempt to forge a collective identity. The only real draw here, however, is the excellent range of restaurants near Boston's **Fish Pier** (see p.174 for reviews). There is also a number of odoriferous **lobster wholesalers** on the pier and along Northern Avenue. If you happen to be in the area and love crustaceans, you'll avoid paying standard market price by braving the harrowing sights and smells of these seafood warehouses.

Boston Tea Party Ship

Moored in the Fort Point Channel alongside the Congress Street bridge is a replica of the notorious **ship** that launched the Boston Tea Party. There's not much to see nowadays, as the vessel, along with its neighboring museum (☎338-1773, ⓦwww.bostonteapartyship.com), were hit by lightning in August 2001, and have been closed ever since – you're not missing out on much, since the exhibits were pretty hokey anyway. Spirited re-creations of the Tea Party itself are still held on occasion here, but don't be taken in: this is not the site of the actual event. The Tea Party took place on what is today dry

The Boston Tea Party

The first major act of rebellion preceding the Revolutionary War, the **Boston Tea Party** was far greater in significance – especially as a popular symbol – than it was in duration. On December 20, 1773, a longstanding dispute between the British government and its colonial subjects, involving a tea tax, came to a dramatic head. At nightfall, an angry mob of about a thousand, which had been whipped into an anti-British frenzy by Samuel Adams at Old South Meeting House, converged on Griffin's Wharf. Around a hundred of them, some dressed in Indian garb, boarded three brigs and threw the cargo of tea overboard. The protestors disposed of 342 chests of tea each weighing 360 pounds – enough to make 24 million cups, and worth more than one million dollars by today's standards. While it had the semblance of spontaneity, the event was in fact planned beforehand, and the mob was careful not to damage anything but the offending cargo. In any case, the "party" transformed protest into revolution; even Governor Hutchinson agreed that afterwards, war was the only recourse. The ensuing British sanctions, colloquially referred to as the "Intolerable Acts," along with the colonists' continued resistance, further inflamed the tension between the Crown and its colonies, which eventually exploded at Lexington and Concord several months later.

land, near the intersection of Atlantic and Congress streets. Indeed, at the **Harbor Plaza**, 470 Atlantic St, there's a commemorative plaque engraved with a lively – but silly – patriotic poem expressing outrage at "King George's trivial but tyrannical tax of 3p. per pound."

Harbor Islands

Extending across Massachusetts Bay from Salem south to Portsmouth, the thirty islands that comprise the bucolic **Harbor Islands** originally served as strategic defense points during the American Revolution and Civil War. It took congressional assent to turn them into a national park, in 1996, with the result that six are now easily accessible by ferry from Long Wharf. Even so, they're still lightly trafficked in comparison to most Boston sights, which makes them ideal getaways from the city center, especially on a hot summer day, when their **beaches** and **hiking** trails will easily help you forget urban life altogether. Their wartime legacy has left many of their winding pathways and coastal shores dotted with intriguing fortress **ruins** and **lighthouses**, which makes for some pretty attractive scenery; the views of Boston from this distance are simply sublime, as well.

The most popular and best serviced of the lot, the skipping-stone-shaped **George's Island** was a heavily used defensive outpost during the Civil War era, as attested by the remains of **Fort Warren** (April to mid-Oct daily dawn–dusk; free), a mid-nineteenth-century battle station covering most of the island. Constructed from hand-hewn granite, and mostly used as a prison for captured Confederate soldiers, its musty barracks and extensive fortress walls are on the eerie side, while the parapets offer some stunning downtown views. You'll get more out of a visit by taking a Park Ranger tour (free), where you'll learn the legend of the Lady in Black – a prisoner's wife who was hanged while attempting to break her husband out of jail.

The remaining Harbor Islands needn't rank high on your must-see list unless you can spare a day island-hopping – getting to them by shuttle from George's

Island requires some flexibility. The densely wooded and sand-duned **Lovell** is probably your best bet after George's, as it hosts the islands' only life-guarded sand beach near the remains of Fort Standish, an early-twentieth-century military base. The largest of all, the 134-acre **Peddock**, is laced with hiking trails connecting the remains of Fort Andrews, a harbor defense used from 1904 to 1945, with a freshwater pond and wildlife sanctuary. Romantic **Bumpkin** was once the site of a children's hospital whose ruins, along with the casements of an old stone farmhouse, lie along raspberry bush-fringed pathways. More berries grow on **Grape**, making it ideal bird-watching territory. Furthest at sea, **Little Brewster Island** hosts the 1716 Boston Light, the country's last man-powered beacon (call ☎223-8666 to arrange a visit).

Island-bound

A 45-minute ride connects Long Wharf with central **George's Island** (July–Aug daily on the hour 10am–5pm; May & Sept to mid-Oct daily 10am, noon & 2pm; June daily 10am, noon, 2pm & 4pm; $10, children $7; ☎227-4321, ⊛www.bostonharborcruises .com; Aquarium Ⓣ), the hub from which water taxis (free) shuttle visitors to the remaining five. The islands lack a freshwater source, so be sure to bring **bottled water** with you. You should also consider packing a picnic lunch (best arranged through nearby *Sel de la Terre*, see review p.178), though if you've come without, you can make do on beachfare from George's **snackbar** or – for a small snack – go **berry-picking** on **Grape** and **Bumpkin** islands. In the interest of preserving island ecology, no bicycles or in-line skates are allowed. You can **camp**, for a nominal fee, on four of the islands (May to mid-Oct; Lovell & Peddock ☎727-7676; Bumpkin & Grape 1-877/422-6762); you'll need to bring your own supplies. In all cases, good walking shoes are required as most of the pathways consist of dirt roads. The Harbor Islands **information** kiosk, at the foot of Long Wharf, keeps a detailed shuttle **schedule** and stocks excellent **maps**.

The North End

he **North End**, a small yet densely populated neighborhood whose narrow streets are chock-a-block with Italian bakeries, restaurants, and some of Boston's most storied sights, is bordered by Boston Harbor and separated from downtown by the noisy, elevated John F. Fitzgerald Expressway (aka I-93 or the Central Artery). Its detached quality goes all the way back to colonial times, when the neighborhood was actually an island, later to be joined by short bridges to the main part of town, known then as the South End (and not to be confused with today's South End, which is covered in chapter 6). This physical separation bred antagonism culminating every November 5th in Pope's Day, when North and South Enders paraded effigies of the Pope through their neighborhoods to a standoff on Boston Common where the rival groups attempted to capture each other's pontiff. If the North Enders won, they would burn the South Ender's effigy atop Copp's Hill. Though landfill temporarily ended the district's physical isolation, it remained very much a place apart, and when the Central Artery tore through the city in 1954, the North End became permanently insulated.

As such, the North End may seem an inaccessible district at first, and indeed the protracted "Big Dig" construction project will make getting there a challenge for years to come (see p.viii), but you can avoid the hassle – and get a much better sense of the area's attractiveness – by entering from the waterfront Christopher Columbus Park, then taking Richmond Street past quiet North Square to Hanover Street, the North End's main drag. Alternatively, get off the subway at the Haymarket **T** stations and negotiate the poorly indicated pedestrian detours to bypass the construction. Once there, you can cover the must-sees fairly quickly – the **Paul Revere House**, **Old North Church**, and **Copp's Hill Burying Ground**. Also take time to explore the area's vibrant cafés and food shops (see reviews pp.167–212) in this, Boston's most authentically **Italian** neighborhood. This Italian flavor is most pronounced during the eight annual summer *festas*, during which members of private charity clubs parade figurines of their patron saints (usually the same as those of their home towns in Italy) through the narrow streets. The processions, complete with marching bands, stop every few feet to let people pin dollar bills to streamers attached to the statues.

Some history

In its early days, North End was the residence of choice for the wealthy merchant class: Massachusetts Bay Colony governors Hutchinson and Phips owned spacious homes here, as did the notoriously Puritanical Mather family. But most of the British Loyalists who called the North End home fled to Nova Scotia after the Revolution, hastening de-gentrification. In 1840, Irish immigrants – just the first of several immigrant groups to put down roots in the

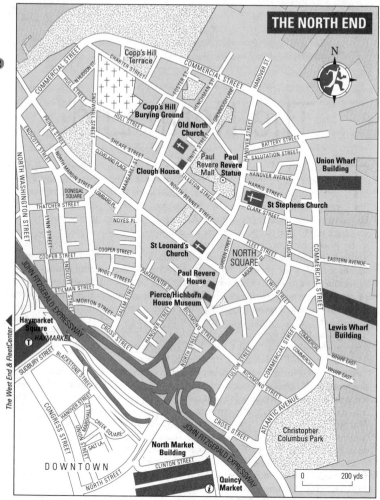

Downtown & The Waterfront ▼

North End – poured in after the potato famine of 1840; John F. Fitzgerald, JFK's grandfather, was born on Ferry Street, and the late president's mother, Rose, on nearby Garden Street. In the 1850s, the Irish were displaced by Eastern European Jews, who were in turn edged out by Southern Italians in the early twentieth century, who have, for the most part, stayed put.

Over the years, local Mafia types ensured that crime (of the unorganized kind) was virtually nonexistent here, and helped make the neighborhood one of the safest in the city. This, combined with comparatively low rents, made the area attractive to yuppies, who gentrified the waterfront and rehabilitated tenements in the heart of the district. However, despite this more recent influx of outsiders, life in North End continues much as it has for decades – complete with laundry dangling from upper-story windows, grandmothers gossiping in Italian in front of their apartment buildings, and folks whiling away the hours in local cafés and bars.

Hanover Street

Hanover Street has long been the main connection between the North End and the rest of Boston. Along its length – especially where it meets Parmenter and Richmond – are many of the area's trattorias, cafés and bakeries, giving the street a distinctly European flavor (albeit now somewhat diluted by chain stores, the first of which was a CVS drugstore). However, classic Italian spots remain, including *Mike's Pastry*, at no. 300, and the quieter side of the North End reasserts itself on the short blocks north of the Paul Revere Mall (not a "mall" in the modern sense; rather a cobblestoned park). But even this area is home to an increasing number of restaurants, geared as much to locals as tourists. Though there's little in the way of proper sights, it's easy to spend half a day just lingering at cafés and browsing in shops here.

North Square and the Paul Revere House

The triangular wedge of cobblestones and gaslights known as **North Square**, found one block east of Hanover between Prince and Richmond streets, is one of the most historic and appealing pockets of Boston. Here the eateries recede in deference to the **Paul Revere House**, the oldest residential address in the city, at 19 North Square (mid-April to Oct daily 9.30am–5.15pm; Nov to mid-April Tues–Sun 9.30am–4.15pm; $2.50; ☏523-2338, ⓦwww.paulreverehouse .org). A North Ender for most of his life, Revere lived here from 1770 to

Paul Revere

It wasn't until decades after his death that **Paul Revere** achieved fame for his nighttime journey to Lexington to warn John Hancock and Sam Adams of the impending British march inland to seize colonial munitions. When he did, it was thanks to a fanciful poem by Henry Wadsworth Longfellow, which failed to note that another patriot, **William Dawes**, made the trip as well. Its opening line, "Listen, my children, and you shall hear / Of the midnight ride of Paul Revere," is as familiar to American schoolchildren as the Pledge of Allegiance. But during his lifetime, this jack-of-all-trades was principally known for his abilities as a silversmith (with a side business in false teeth) and a propagandist for the patriot's cause – not so much as a legendary messenger.

As a propagandist, Revere's engraving of the Boston Massacre did much to turn public opinion against the Tories, and he even went so far as to stage an exhibition of more patriotic engravings at his North End home on the first anniversary of the incident. He also rode on horseback to carry news of the Boston Tea Party to New York and Philadelphia – only hours after participating in the event. Furthermore, in December 1774, four months before the legendary ride to Lexington, Revere rode to Portsmouth, New Hampshire, to notify locals of the British intent to shore up fortifications there, precipitating the first organized American assault on a royal fortress flying the king's flag. After the Revolution, he engraved the first American currency – though a more profitable venture was his bell and cannon foundry in the present-day town that bears his name, located just north of Boston. He died in 1818 at the age of 83, and rests among his Revolutionary peers in the Old Granary Burying Ground (see p.41).

1800 (except for much of 1775, when he hid out from the British in Watertown), and during these thirty years he sired a sixteen-member brood. Prior to being restored to its seventeenth-century appearance in 1908, the small Tudor-style, post-and-beam structure, which dates from about 1680, had served in turn as a grocery store, tenement and cigar factory. It stands on what once was the site of the considerably grander home of Puritan heavyweight Increase Mather (father of Cotton), which burned down in the Great Fire of 1676.

Though the building is more impressive for its longevity than its appearance, the second-story overhang and leaded windows provide quite a contrast to the red-brick buildings around it. The inside is a letdown, however, as none of the artifacts are original to the house. The first-floor "hall," or living room, is curious, though: it resembles a hunting lodge, complete with low ceiling and enormous fireplace. In addition, recent examples of Revere's self-made silverwares are found upstairs, as is a small but evocative exhibit about the mythologizing of Revere's horseback ride to warn patriots that the British were coming.

The Pierce/Hichborn House and North Street

Back out on the street, a small courtyard, the focus of which is a glass-encased 900-pound bell that Revere cast, separates the Paul Revere House from the **Pierce/Hichborn House** (tours by appointment only; $2.50; ☎523-2338). A simple Georgian-style residence – and the oldest brick house in Boston – it was built in 1710 by glazier Moses Pierce, and later owned by Paul Revere's cousin, Nathaniel Hichborn, who was considerably wealthier than his more famous relative. As such, the sparsely furnished interior of the prosperous shipbuilder's modest home, with its unremarkable period tables and chairs, along with a few decorative lamps and pieces of cabinetry, speaks volumes about Yankee thrift.

South from North Square, Garden Court Street (on which the Revere House and the Pierce/Hichborn House are located) runs into **North Street**, which was somewhat of a red-light district in the early nineteenth century, but today is only an average residential side street. Its one distinguishing feature, the **oldest sign** in Boston, is affixed to the third floor of a building at the corner of Richmond Street – the initials "W, T, S" refer to the owners of an inn that stood here in 1694.

St Stephen's Church and Paul Revere Mall

Further north, at Hanover's intersection with Clark Street, you'll find the striking three-story recessed brick arch entrance to **St Stephen's Church**, the only church built by Charles Bulfinch in Boston that's still standing. Originally called New North Church, it received its present-day name in 1862, in order to keep up with the increasingly Catholic population of the North End. Though it seems firmly planted today, the whole building was actually moved back sixteen feet when Hanover Street was widened in 1870. A more recent

△ Paul Revere Statue

claim to fame is that Rose Kennedy's funeral ceremony was held in the under-stated, whitewashed apse, in 1995.

Just across Hanover, the famous bronze **statue** of Paul Revere astride his bor-rowed horse marks the edge of the **Paul Revere Mall**, a cobblestoned park known as the Prado. This much-needed open space was carved out of a chunk of apartment blocks in 1933 and runs back to tiny **Unity Street** – home of the small 1712 red-brick **Clough House**, at no. 21, a private residence built by the mason who helped lay the brick of the nearby Old North Church.

Old North Church

Rising unobstructed above the surrounding homogeneous blocks of red-brick apartments, few places in Boston have as emblematic a quality as the simple yet noble **Old North Church** at 93 Salem St (daily: June–Oct 9am–6pm; Nov–May 9am–5pm; free; ⓦwww.oldnorth.com). Built in 1723, and inspired by St Andrew's-by-the-Wardrobe in Blackfriars, London, it's the oldest church in Boston, easily recognized by its gleaming 191-foot **steeple**. The weathervane perched on top is the colonial original, though the steeple itself is actually a replica – hurricanes toppled both its first, in 1804, and its replacement, in 1954.

It was a pair of lanterns that secured the structure's place in history, though. The church sexton, Robert Newman, is said to have hung both of them inside ("One if by land, two if by sea") on the night of April 18, 1775, to signal the movement of British forces from Boston Common, which then bordered the Charles River. However, some historians speculate that the lanterns were actu-ally hung from another church, also called Old North, which occupied the North Square spot where the Sacred Heart Italian Church now stands, at no. 12; that irate Tories burned it for firewood in 1776 adds fuel to the theory. What is certain is that Paul Revere had already learned of the impending British advance and was riding to Lexington by the time the lanterns were in place – he simply needed Newman's help to alert Charlestown in case his mis-sion was thwarted. As it turned out, both he and fellow patriot William Dawes were detained by British patrols, but each managed to continue his ride.

The interior of the churc – spotlessly white and well lit thanks to the Palladian windows behind the pulpit – holds many interesting historical footnotes. The first, just inside the entrance, is a sign affixed to a collection box that suggests that were it not for the Old North Church, "You Might be Making Donations in Pound Notes." Other details include twelve bricks from a prison cell in Boston, England, where an early group of Pilgrims were incarcerated, that are set into the vestibule wall, and the four eighteenth-century cherubim near the organ that were looted from a French vessel. You can also check your watch by the clock at the rear – made in 1726, it's the oldest one still ticking in an American public building. Have a wander, too, among the high box pews: no. 62 belonged to General Thomas Gage, commander-in-chief of the British army in North America, while descen-dants of Paul Revere still lay claim to no. 54. Beneath your feet, the timber on which the pews rest is supported by 37 basement level brick crypts; one of the 1100 bodies encased therein is that of John Pitcairn, the British major killed in the Battle of Bunker Hill. His remains were tagged for Westminster Abbey, but they never quite made it home to England. Finally, the eight bells inside the belfry – which is unfortunately not open to the public – were the first cast for the British Empire in North America and have since tolled the death of every US President.

On your way out, the church's quirky **souvenir shop** is worth a stop if only for a look at some of its not-for-sale items, such as a vial of Boston Tea Party tea and the bellringers' contract that Paul Revere signed as a mere lad in 1750. Some of Old North's greatest charms are actually outside the church itself, notably the diminutive **Washington Memorial Garden**, the brick walls of which are bedecked with commemorative plaques honoring past church members, and the inviting **eighteenth-century garden**, its terraces packed with lilies and roses, as well as some curious umbrella-shaped flowers known, ironically, as archangels.

Salem Street

While the Old North Church is certainly its star attraction, **Salem Street** – especially the lower blocks between Prince and Cross – is arguably the North End's most colorful artery. The actual street – whose name is a latter day bastardization of "Shalom Street," as it was known to the earlier European Jewish settlers – is so narrow that the red-brick buildings seem to lean into one another, and light traffic makes it a common practice to walk right down the middle of the road. Traveling south, an agreeable onslaught of Italian grocers, aromatic pasticcerias and cafés begins rather abruptly at Salem's intersection with Prince, starting with *Bova's Bakery* at no. 134 (see review p.212); above this point the street is primarily residential. At the southern end, as soon as you traverse Cross Street (which snakes alongside the construction on I-93), the Naplesesque bustle ends; continuing on under what's left of the expressway will lead you to the commercialized Quincy Market and bland Government Center in downtown.

Prince Street

Parallel to Salem Street is appealing **Prince Street**, a narrow road cutting through the heart of the North End on an east–west axis. Like most streets in the neighborhood, it's also lined with salumerias and restaurants, but tends to be more social – locals typically while away the day along the pavement here on folding chairs brought from home.

At the corner of Hanover Street, **St Leonard's Church**, 14 N Bennet St (☎523-2110), was supposedly the first Italian Catholic church in New England. The ornate interior is a marked contrast to Boston's stark Protestant churches, while the so-called "Peace Garden" in front, with its prosaic plantings and tacky statuary, is – in a sense – vintage North End.

Copp's Hill Burying Ground

Up Hull Street from Old North Church, **Copp's Hill Burying Ground** (daily dawn–dusk), with its eerily tilting slate tombstones and stunning harbor views, makes up in atmosphere what it lacks in the way of illustrious deceased. The first burial here, on the highest ground in the North End, took place in

1659. Among the ten thousand interred are nearly a thousand men who had lived in the "New Guinea Community," a long-vanished colonial enclave of free blacks at the foot of the hill. The most famous gravesite here is that of the Mather family, just inside the wrought-iron gates on the northern Charter Street side. Increase Mather and his son Cotton – the latter a Salem Witch Trial judge – were big players in Boston's early days of Puritan theocracy, a fact not at all reflected in the rather diminutive, if appropriately plain, brick vault tomb. As for other noteworthy graves, Robert Newman, who hung Paul Revere's lanterns in the Old North Church, is buried near the western rim of the plot, as is Edmund Hartt, the builder of the famous ship Old Ironsides (see p.69).

You'll notice, too, that many gravestones have significant chunks missing – a consequence of British soldiers using them for target practice during the 1775 Siege of Boston. The grave of one Captain Daniel Malcolm, toward the left end of the third row of gravestones as you enter the grounds, bears particularly strong evidence of the English maneuvers: three musketball marks scar his epitaph, which hails him as a "true son of liberty" and an "enemy of oppression."

Copp's Hill Terrace

The granite **Copp's Hill Terrace**, a plateau separated from the burial ground on the northern side by Charter Street, was the place from which British cannon bombarded Charlestown during the Battle of Bunker Hill. Here, too, on a particularly hot day in 1919, a 2.3-million-gallon steel storage tank of molasses – used in the production of alcoholic beverages – exploded nearby, creating a syrupy tidal wave fifteen feet high that engulfed entire buildings and drowned 21 people along with a score of horses. Old North Enders – the kind you'll see playing bocci in the little park at the bottom of the terrace – claim you can still catch a whiff of the stuff on an exceptionally hot day.

3

Charlestown

harlestown, across Boston Harbor via Charlestown Bridge from the North End, is a largely Irish working-class neighborhood that stands quite isolated from the city, despite its annexation more than a century ago. Separated from Boston not only by the water, its historic core of quiet streets and elegant rowhouses is now all but surrounded by elevated highways and construction projects. Changes resulting from the "Big Dig" should reshape the landscape dramatically for the better when concluded, however; the most obvious alteration is the brand new, ten-lane **Leonard P. Zakim Bridge** that will funnel traffic underground when the burying of I-93 is complete. Even so, the best way to reach Charlestown remains the short $1.25 ferry trip from the waterfront's Long Wharf, which bypasses the most unsightly areas of the district and deposits you on the eastern outskirts of the Charlestown Navy Yard, where the area's big draw, the **USS Constitution**, is berthed.

Just a few minutes' walk northwest from the Navy Yard is Charlestown's center and **City Square**, the point from which most notable streets in the area radiate out. Directly north is the neighborhood's only other major sight (as well as the last stop on the Freedom Trail, which runs across the Charlestown Bridge from the North End), the **Bunker Hill Monument**. Aside from this, the rest of the district is fairly nondescript and even somewhat dodgy in parts – though this shouldn't cause much worry: if you stick to the *USS Constitution* and the monument, you needn't spend more than a morning in Charlestown. A relative lack of appealing restaurants or bars, save the renowned *Olives* (and its offshoot, *Figs*), makes it unlikely you'll be coming back in the evening.

Some history

The earliest **Puritan settlers** had high hopes for developing Charlestown when they arrived in 1629, but an unsuitable water supply pushed them over to the Shawmut Peninsula, which they promptly renamed Boston (see Contexts, p.235). Charlestown grew slowly after that, and had to be completely rebuilt after the British burned it down in 1775; almost as many houses were lost in that blaze as had been burnt in the entire Revolution.

The mid-1800s witnessed the arrival of the so-called "lace-curtain Irish" – who were somewhat better off than their North End compatriots – and the district remains an Irish one at heart. The neighborhood was long a haven for criminals, too – if a bank was robbed in Boston, the story goes, police would simply wait out on the Charlestown Bridge for their quarry to come home. Today, though, the criminal element has all but disappeared from the area since urban professionals took over many of the Federal and Colonial-style townhomes south of the Bunker Hill Monument. The resulting mood in Charlestown now is one of amiable neighborliness imbued with an air of quiet affluence, especially along the southern blocks of Main Street, where the better restaurants are found.

CHARLESTOWN

Freedom Trail

0   500 yards

Pier 9
Pier 8
Pier 7
Pier 6
Pier 5
Pier 4
Pier 3
Pier 2
Pier 1

Foundary

Charlestown Navy Yard

Shipyard Park

Ropewalk Building

MBTA ferry to Long Wharf, Downtown

USS Cassin Young

USS Constitution Museum

Boston National Historical Park

USS Constitution (Old Ironsides)

Constitution Inn YMCA

Bunker Hill Pavilion

Bed & Breakfast Afloat

Breed's Hill

Bunker Hill Monument

33 Cordis Street

Larkin House

Warren Tavern

Charlestown Public Library

Charlestown Five Cents Savings Bank Building

John Harvard Mall

City Square

Phipps Street Burying Ground

Bunker Hill Community College

TOBIN BRIDGE

CHELSEA STREET

RUTHERFORD AVENUE

NEW RUTHERFORD AVENUE

JOHN F FITZGERALD EXPY

CONSTITUTION ROAD

MAIN STREET

North End

West End & Downtown

Community College

Charlestown Navy Yard and the USS Constitution Museum

The sprawling **Charlestown Navy Yard** was one of the first and busiest US naval shipyards – riveting together an astounding 46 destroyer escorts in 1943 alone – though it owes most of its present-day liveliness to its grandest tenant, the frigate *USS Constitution* at Constitution Wharf. Today, under the aegis of the Boston National Historical Park, an umbrella association preserving Boston sights deemed nationally significant, the yard has largely been repurposed as marinas, upscale condos and offices. None of these will really attract your attention, save the **USS Constitution Museum** (daily: May–Nov 9am–6pm; Nov–Apr 10am–5pm; free; Ⓦwww.ussconstitutionmuseum.org), housed in a substantial granite structure a short walk from the *Constitution* and across from Pier 1. The museum is worth visiting before you board the ship itself, as its excellent exhibits help contextualize the vessel and her unparalleled role in American maritime history. One especially evocative display consists of curios which sailors acquired during a two-year, round-the-world diplomatic mission begun in 1844, creatively arranged under a forest of faux palm fronds. Also among the souvenirs are wooden carved toys from Zanzibar, a chameleon from Madagascar preserved in a glass jar, and a Malaysian model ship made of cloves. Upstairs you'll find temporary exhibits, as well as replicas of the sailors' hammock-style bunks.

The USS Constitution ("Old Ironsides")

As tall as a twenty-story building and three hundred feet long from bowsprit to back end, the **USS Constitution** is an impressive sight from any angle (daily 10am–4pm; free; Ⓦwww.ussconstitution.navy.mil). Launched two centuries ago to safeguard American merchant vessels from Barbary pirates and, later on, from the French and British navies, the ship earned her nickname during the War of 1812, when cannonballs fired from the British *HMS Guerrière* bounced off the hull (the "iron" sides were actually hewn from live oak, a particularly sturdy wood from the southeastern US), leading to the first and most dramatic American naval conquest of that war. The ship went on to clinch victory in more than forty battles before she was retired from active service in the 1830s. Since then, her fate flipped back and forth during various congressional and presidential administrations, until the ship had her full naval commission returned in 1940, making her the oldest commissioned warship afloat in the world; as a result of this active commission, the guides onboard are real US Navy sailors. When in 1997 she went on her first unassisted sail in 116 years, news coverage was international in scale, a measure of the worldwide respect for the symbolic flagship of the US Navy.

Authentic enough in appearance, the *Constitution* has certainly taken its hits – roughly ninety percent of the ship has been reconstructed. Even after extensive renovations, though, Old Ironsides is still too frail to support sails for extended periods of time, and the only regular voyages she makes are annual Fourth of July turnarounds in Boston Harbor. There's often a line to visit the ship – especially in the summer – and access has been further slowed by increased security checks, but it's nonetheless worth the wait to get a close-up view of the elaborate rigging that can support some three dozen sails totaling almost an acre in area. After ambling about the main deck, you can scuttle down nearly vertical stairways to the lower deck, where you'll find an impressive array of cannons, many of them christened with fighting names like Raging Eagle and Jumping Billy, arranged in two long rows. Most of the ship's 54 cannon are actually replicas – when Old Ironsides ceased to be a fighting vessel her ammunitions were removed for use in battle-worthy ships – but two functional models face downtown from the bow of the main deck. They still get a daily workout, too, shooting off explosive powder to mark mast raising and lowering (dawn and dusk respectively); were they to fire the 24-pound balls for which they were originally outfitted, they'd topple the Customs House tower across the bay in downtown Boston.

The rest of the Navy Yard

Berthed in between Old Ironsides and the museum is the hulking gray mass of the World War II destroyer **USS Cassin Young** (daily: June–Oct 10am–5pm; Nov–May 10am–4pm; free). While several similar destroyers were made in Charlestown, the *Cassin Young* was actually built in San Pedro, California, and served primarily in the Atlantic and Mediterranean before eventually being transferred to the National Park Service for use as a museum ship in 1978. There's not much of interest to see here, though, aside from the expansive main deck's depth chargers and tiny infirmary. The cramped chambers below, the Captain's rooms and "head," or restroom, among them, are mostly of interest to World War II buffs, who can inspect them by taking a 45-minute guided tour (June–Oct hourly 10am–5pm; Nov–May 11am, 2pm & 3pm; free).

At the northern perimeter of the Navy Yard, there's not much to recommend a visit to quarter-mile-long, two-story, granite **Ropewalk Building**, where most of the cordage used by the US Navy was made after 1837. Though closed to the public, Navy aficionados may be interested to know that the narrow building is the last remaining complete structure devoted to rope-making in the country. At the opposite end of the Yard, near the point where the Freedom Trail dips under an overpass to continue toward the Bunker Hill Monument, the **Bunker Hill Pavilion** screens a rather dated, twenty-minute program entitled *The Whites of Their Eyes* (daily 9.30am–4.30pm; $3; ☎241-7575), which attempts to recreate the infamous battle that took place here with blinking lights and voiceovers passing for multimedia.

City Square and around

Charlestown's center is a few minutes' walk northwest of Navy Yard, at the end of a scenic, if barren, harborfront walk that wends under I-93 to reach **City Square**, a park space that doubles as a traffic circle. The square is anchored at its northern tip by *Olives*, one of Boston's most popular restaurants (see p.179 for review).

Adjacent **Harvard Street** – named for John Harvard, the young Charlestown-based minister whose library and funds launched the Cambridge-based university after his death – curves through the small **Town Hill** district, site of Charlestown's first settled community. Here you'll also find John Harvard Mall and Harvard Square (not to be confused with the one in Cambridge), both lined with well-preserved homes.

Main Street

Main Street extends north from the square; at no.55 you'll find the wooden 1795 house of **Deacon John Larkin**, who lent Paul Revere his horse for the ride to Lexington and never got it back. You can't go inside, so press on to the atmospheric **Warren Tavern**, at no. 105, a small three-story wooden structure built soon after the British burned Charlestown in the Battle of Bunker Hill. It's named for doctor Joseph Warren, personal physician to the Adams (as in President John Adams) family before he was killed in the Battle of Bunker Hill, and still functions as a popular tavern today (see p.189 for review).

West of the tavern, the monumental 1876 **Charlestown Five Cents Savings Bank Building**, at 1 Thompson Square, boasts a steep mansard roof and Victorian Gothic ornamentation, even though it now houses street-level convenience stores; the modest external vault belonging to its original tenants still protrudes from the eastern wall. A good ten minutes' walk further west takes you to the **Phipps Street Burying Ground**, which dates from 1630. Its unusual layout allegedly corresponds to that of Charlestown itself, and finds quirky gravestones, like that of Prince Bradstreet, memorialized as "an honest man of color." While many Revolutionary soldiers are buried here, it lacks the historical resonance of some other burying grounds in the city, and you need not go out of your way to visit.

Devens and Cordis streets

From Warren Tavern, crooked **Devens Street** to the south (called Crooked Lane in 1640) and **Cordis Street** to the north are packed with historic, private houses, many of which are lovely to look at if you've got the time to dawdle, though they don't offer anything in the way of tours. Of these, the worn Revival mansion at 33 Cordis St is the most striking, with its white Ionic columns standing tall amidst its quaint New England neighbors.

Monument Avenue and Winthrop Square

North from Main Street toward the Bunker Hill Monument, the red-brick townhouses along **Monument Avenue** – long the dividing line between the moneyed and blue-collar classes in Charlestown – are some of the most exclusive residences in Boston. Though no house really stands out, strolling past the medley of Federal and Revival structures en route to the Bunker Hill monument holds low-key appeal. Nearby along Winthrop Street is **Winthrop Square**, Charlestown's unofficial common; the prim rowhouses overlooking it form another upscale enclave. Appropriately enough, considering its proximity to Bunker Hill, the common started out as a military training field – a series of bronze tablets at its northeastern edge list the men killed just up the slope in the Battle of Bunker Hill.

Bunker Hill Monument

Commemorating the Battle of Bunker Hill is the **Bunker Hill Monument** (daily 9am–4.30pm; free), a gray, dagger-like obelisk that's visible from just about anywhere in Charlestown thanks to its position atop a butte confusingly known as Breed's Hill (see box below). It was here that revolutionary troops positioned themselves on the night of June 16, 1775, to wage what was ultimately a losing battle – despite its recasting by US historians as a great moral victory in the fight for independence. The latter, rather than the former, is commemorated by the obelisk, which is notable for being both the country's first monument funded entirely by public donations and the first to popularize the obelisk style epitomized by the Washington Monument in DC. Centrally positioned in Monument Square and fronted by a strident, sword-bearing statue of Colonel William Prescott, a lodge at its base houses dioramas of the battle, while inside, 294 steps ascend to the top of the 221-foot granite shaft. Hardy climbers will be rewarded with sweeping views of Boston, the Harbor, surrounding towns and, to the northwest, the stone spire of the **St Francis de Sales Church**, which stands atop the real Bunker Hill, but which is too out-of-the-way to warrant a visit.

The Battle of Bunker Hill

The Revolutionary War was at its bloodiest on the hot June day in 1775 when British and colonial forces clashed in Charlestown. In the wake of the battles at Lexington and Concord two months before, the British had assumed full control of Boston, while the patriots had the upper hand in the surrounding counties. The British, under the command of generals Thomas Gage and "Gentleman Johnny" Burgoyne, intended to sweep the countryside clean of "rebellious rascals." Americans intercepted the plans and moved to fortify **Bunker Hill**, the dominant hill in Charlestown. However, when Colonel William Prescott arrived on the scene, he chose to occupy **Breed's Hill** instead, either due to confusion – the two hills were often confused on colonial-era maps – or tactical foresight, based on the proximity of Breed's Hill to the harbor. Whatever the motivation, more than a thousand citizen-soldiers arrived during the night of June 16, 1775, and fortified the hill with a 160-foot-long earthen redoubt by morning.

The next day, spotting a Yankee fort on what they took to be Bunker Hill, the Redcoats, each carrying 125 pounds of food and supplies in preparation for a three-day military foray in the country, rowed across the harbor to take the rebel-held town. On the patriots' side, Colonel William Prescott issued an order to his troops not to fire "'til you see the whites of their eyes," such was their limited store of gunpowder. Though vastly outnumbered, the Americans successfully repelled two full-fledged assaults, the even rows of underprepared and overburdened Redcoats making easy targets. Some British units lost more than ninety percent of their men, and what few officers survived had to push their troops forward with their swords to make them fight on. However, the tide began to turn by the third British assault, as the Redcoats shed their gear and reinforcements arrived. The Americans' supply of gunpowder was dwindling, too, though they continued to fight with stones and musket butts; meanwhile, British cannon fire from Copp's Hill in the North End had turned Charlestown into an inferno. Despite the eventual American loss, the battle did much to persuade the patriots – and the British, who lost nearly half their men who fought in this battle – that continued armed resistance made independence inevitable.

Beacon Hill and the West End

Beacon Hill, a dignified stack of red brick rising over the north side of Boston Common, is Boston at its most provincial. Once home to numerous historical and literary figures – including John Hancock, John Quincy Adams, Louisa May Alcott, Oliver Wendell Holmes, and Nathaniel Hawthorne – the area has remained the address of choice for the city's elite, and looking around, it's not hard to fathom why. The narrow, hilly byways are lit with gaslamps and lined with quaint, nineteenth-century townhouses, all part of an enforced preservation that prohibits modern buildings, architectural innovations, or anything else from disturbing the carefully cultivated atmosphere of urban gentility.

In colonial times, Beacon Hill was the most prominent of three peaks, known as the Trimountain, which formed Boston's geological backbone. The sunny south slope was developed into prime real estate and quickly settled by the city's political and economic powers, but the north slope was traditionally closer in spirit to the **West End**, a tumbledown port district populated by free blacks and immigrants. The north slope was home to so much salacious activity, in fact, that outraged Brahmins – Beacon Hill's moneyed elite – termed it "Mount Whoredom."

During the twentieth century, this social divide was largely eradicated, though it can still be seen in the somewhat shabbier homes north of **Pinckney Street** and in the tendency of members of polite society to refer to the south slope as "the good side." Still, both sides have much to offer, if of very different character. On the south slope, there's the grandiose **Massachusetts State House**, residences of past and present luminaries, and attractive boulevards like **Charles Street** and **Beacon Street**, the former full of quaint antique shops and cafés, the latter snugly crowded with prim townhouses; this is the Boston of popular image, and an integral part of most any visit. More down-to-earth, the north slope has its share of atmospheric blocks as well, plus some signature sights of the **Black Heritage Trail**, including the **African Meeting House**, the warren of alleyways used by fleeing slaves to escape arrest, and the superb **Robert Gould Shaw/54th Regiment Memorial**.

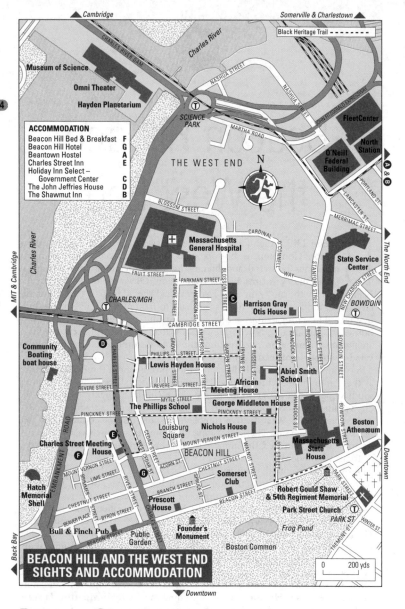

ACCOMMODATION

Beacon Hill Bed & Breakfast	F
Beacon Hill Hotel	G
Beantown Hostel	A
Charles Street Inn	E
Holiday Inn Select – Government Center	C
The John Jeffries House	D
The Shawmut Inn	B

THE WEST END

N

BEACON HILL AND THE WEST END
SIGHTS AND ACCOMMODATION

0   200 yds

Beacon Street

Running along the south slope of Beacon Hill above the Common, **Beacon Street** was described by Oliver Wendell Holmes in the late nineteenth century as Boston's "sunny street for the sifted few." Its lofty character remains today: a row of stately brick townhouses, fronted by ornate iron grillwork, presides regally over the area. The ground level of one of these homes holds what might be the most famous address on the block, that of the *Bull & Finch Pub*, better known as the inspiration for the TV show *Cheers*, and one that unabashedly trades on the association.

Continuing along, look out for **purple panes** in some of the townhouses' windows, especially at nos. 63 and 64; the story behind this odd coloring evinces the street's long association with Boston wealth and privilege. When panes were installed in some of the first Beacon Street mansions, they turned purple upon exposure to the sun, due to an excess of manganese in the glass. At first an irritating accident, they were eventually regarded as the definitive Beacon Hill status symbol due to their prevalence in the windows of Boston's most prestigious homes; some residents have gone so far as to shade their windows purple in imitation.

Prescott House, Founder's Monument and Somerset Club

It may lack purple-tinted panes, but the elegant bowfronted 1808 **Prescott House**, at no. 55 (May–Oct Wed, Thurs & Sat noon–4pm, tours every 30min; $4; ☏742-3190, ⊛www.nscda.org/ma; Park St **T**), is the only house on Beacon Street with public access to its inner chambers. Designed by Asher Benjamin, one of Charles Bulfinch's most prolific understudies, for Boston merchant James Colburn, its most distinguished inhabitant was renowned Spanish historian and Harvard professor William Hickling Prescott, whose family occupied its five floors from 1845 to 1859. Hung above the pastiche of Federalist and Victorian furniture inside are two crossed swords belonging to Colonel William Prescott and British Captain John Linzee – the professor and his wife's respective grandfathers. The men fought against each other at Bunker Hill, and the sight of their munitions here inspired William Thackeray, a frequent house visitor, to write his novel, *The Virginians*.

Across the street, the **Founder's Monument** commemorates Boston's first European settler, William Blackstone, a Cambridge-educated loner who moved from England with his entire library to a piece of wilderness he acquired for next to nothing from the Shawmut Indians – the site of present-day Boston. A stone bas-relief depicts the apocryphal moment in 1630 when Blackstone sold most of his acreage to a group of Puritans from Charlestown.

Back on the north side of Beacon Street, and a few steps past Spruce Court, is the last of a trio of **Charles Bulfinch** houses (see box p.76) commissioned by lawyer and future Boston mayor Harrison Gray Otis over a ten-year period; the four-story Classical house has been home to the American Meteorological Society since 1958. Just east of here, it's hard to miss the twin-swelled granite building at nos. 42–43, built for Colonel David Sears' family by Alexander Parris of Quincy Market fame (see p.51). Its stern Greek Revival facade has welcomed members of the exclusive **Somerset Club** since 1872, a club so elitist that when a fire broke out in the kitchen, the firemen who arrived were ordered to come in via the cumbersome servants' entrance, a heavy iron-studded portal.

Robert Gould Shaw/54th Regiment Memorial

Further up Beacon Street, a majestic monument honors **Robert Gould Shaw** and the **54th Massachusetts Regiment**, America's first all-black company (except for its commander) to fight in the Civil War. Led by Shaw, scion of a moneyed Boston Brahmin clan, the regiment performed its service bravely, though it was isolated from the rest of the Union army, given the worst of the military's resources, and saddled alternately with menial and dangerous assignments. Most of its members, including Shaw, were killed in a failed attempt to take Fort Wagner from the Confederates in 1863. Augustus Saint-Gaudens' outstanding 1897 high-relief bronze sculpture depicts the 54th's Boston down Beacon Street, with the Angel of Death flying above them. The names of the soldiers who died in action were belatedly added in 1982 in a list on its reverse side. Robert Lowell won a Pulitzer Prize in 1964 for his poem about the monument, "For the Union Dead," and the regiment's story was depicted in the 1989 film *Glory*. The monument is also the starting point of the excellent National Park Ranger-led walking tour of the **Black Heritage Trail** (see box p.81).

Massachusetts State House

Across from the memorial, at the confluence of Park and Beacon streets, rises the large gilt dome of the **Massachusetts State House** (Mon–Fri 10am–4pm, last tour at 3.15pm; free; Park Street **T**), the scale and grandeur of which recalls the heady spirit of the newly independent America in which Charles Bulfinch designed it. The original 1795 design actually makes up only a small portion of the existing structure – the huge wings jutting out on either side, as well as the extension in the rear, were added much later. An all-star team of Revolution-era luminaries contributed to the original construction. Built on land donated by John Hancock, its cornerstone was laid by Samuel Adams, and the copper for its dome was rolled in Paul Revere's foundry in 1802 (though it was covered over with 23-karat gold leaf in the 1870s). Its front lawn is dotted with statuary honoring favorite sons such as Henry Cabot Lodge and JFK. More interesting is the statue of Mary Dyer, which overlooks the spot on Boston Common where she was hanged for adhering to her Quaker faith.

The architecture of Charles Bulfinch

America's foremost architect of the late eighteenth and early nineteenth centuries, **Charles Bulfinch** developed a distinctive style somewhere between Federal and Classical that remains Boston's most recognizable architectural motif. Mixing Neoclassical training with New England practicality, Bulfinch built residences characterized by their rectilinear brick structure and pillared porticoes – examples remain throughout Beacon Hill, most notably at **87 Mount Vernon St** and **45 Beacon St**. While most of his work was residential, Bulfinch, in fact, made his name with the design of various government buildings, such as the 1805 renovation of **Faneuil Hall** and, more significantly, the **Massachusetts State House**, whose dome influenced the design of state capitols nationwide.

Bulfinch's talents extended to urban planning, as well. He designed the layout of Boston's **South End**, as well as an area known as **Tontine Crescent**, a half-ellipse crescent planned around a small park that won Bulfinch praise but ruined him financially; what vestiges that remain are found around the Financial District's **Franklin** and **Arch streets**. Bulfinch was also adept at designing massive greystone mercantile warehouses in both Victorian and Federal styles, examples of which can be seen at **68–70 Broad St**, and churches – the North End owes **St Stephen's** to Bulfinch. Furthermore, his wide-ranging skill caught the attention of President Adams, who in 1818 commissioned Bulfinch to serve as the architect of Washington DC's **US Capitol**; it only cost the country a paltry $2500 – plus, of course, expenses.

Once inside the labyrinthine interior, make your way up a flight to the second floor, where tours start from **Doric Hall** – though you'd do as well to grab a free map and show yourself around. Littered with statues and murals celebrating even the most obscure Massachusetts historical events and the statesmen who shaped them, the floor's central hallway leads to the impressively sober **Hall of Flags**, a circular room surrounded by tall columns of Siena marble, lit by a vaulted stained-glass window bearing the state seal and hung with the original flags carried by Massachusetts soldiers into battle. On the third floor, a carved wooden fish known as the **Sacred Cod** hangs above the Senate chambers. The state senators take this symbol of maritime prosperity so seriously that when Harvard pranksters stole it in the 1930s, they shut down the government until it was recovered.

Behind the State House, on Bowdoin Street, lies pleasant, grassy **Ashburton Park**, centered on a pillar – a replica of a 1789 Bulfinch work – indicating the hill's original summit, which was sixty feet higher. Beacon Hill got its name from the makeshift warning light to ships in the night that once stood in the pillar's place; an iron skillet filled with combustibles and dangled from a 65-foot iron post.

Nichols House

Not far from the State House, at 55 Mount Vernon St, is the only Beacon Hill residence open year round to the public, the **Nichols House** (May–Oct Tues–Sat 12.15–4.15pm; Nov–Dec & Feb–April Mon & Thurs–Sat noon–4.15pm, tours start fifteen minutes past the hour; $5; ☎227-2993; Park Street **T**). Yet another Bulfinch design, the building was most recently the home of eccentric spinster and accomplished landscape gardener Rose Standish Nichols, who counted among her allegiances Fabian Socialism and the International Society of Pen Pals. Miss Rose, as she is known to posterity, lived in the house until her death in the early 1960s – though the faint odor of roses permeating the air here today is supposed to imply that she may still be haunting the hallways. While the detailed tour given by the curator may be gripping only for those with an abiding interest in antique furnishings and decorations – though there are some striking Asian tapestries, Federal-period furniture, and an original self-portrait by John Singleton Copley – it does give a brief glimpse of the overstuffed life of leisure led by Beacon Hill's moneyed elite.

Louisburg Square and around

Farther down the street, between Mount Vernon and Pinckney streets, **Louisburg Square** – the "s" is not silent, as any Hill resident will tell you should you ask about "Louie-burg Square" – forms the gilded geographic heart of Beacon Hill. An oblong green space flanked on either side by rows of stately brick townhouses, it's the city's only private park, owned by the surrounding residents. Encompassed by wrought-iron fencing to keep out non-resident plebeians, and featuring statues of Columbus and Aristides the Just, the square owes its distinction less to its architectural character than to a history of illustrious residents, among them novelist Louisa May Alcott and members of the Vanderbilt family. Today, a sense of elite civic parochialism makes this Boston's most coveted address for a select few: Senator John Kerry and his wife, ketchup heiress Teresa Heinz, are among those who call the square home.

Acorn and Chestnut streets

Just below Louisburg Square, narrow **Acorn Street** still has its original early-nineteenth-century cobblestones. Barely wide enough for a car to pass through, it was originally built as a minor byway to be lined with servants' residences. Locals have always clung to it as the epitome of Beacon Hill quaint; in the 1960s, residents permitted the city to tear up the street to install sewer pipes only after exacting the promise that every cobblestone would be replaced in its original location. One block down, **Chestnut Street** features some of the most intricate facades in Boston, particularly Bulfinch's **Swan Houses**, at nos. 13, 15 and 17, with their recessed arches and marble columns, and delicate touches like scrolled door knockers and wrought-iron lace balconies.

Pinckney Street

North of Louisburg Square runs **Pinckney Street**, once the sharp division between the opulent south and ramshackle north sections of Beacon Hill – which is how the original developers planned it, arranging their stables and estates so that only the back entrances fringed the street. As recently as the 1920s, resident Robert Lowell expressed shock at the proximity of his home at 91 Revere St to these shadier environs, claiming that while he lived only fifty yards from Louisburg Square, he was nevertheless "perched on the outer rim of the hub of decency." The distinction is no longer so sharp, and now Pinckney is yet another picturesque Beacon Hill street, all the more worth a stroll thanks to its location at the crest of the hill; on a clear day, from its intersection with Anderson Street, you can see all over the West End and clear across the Charles River to Cambridge – not the prettiest view, but good for getting the lay of the land.

Charles and Mount Vernon streets

Just west of the square is **Charles Street**, the commercial center of Beacon Hill, lined with scores of restaurants, antique shops and pricey specialty boutiques (see p.181 and p.208 for reviews). A walk on Mount Vernon Street along the flat of the hill brings you past some of Beacon Hill's most beautiful buildings. The Federal-style **Charles Street Meeting House**, with its setback, cupolaed roof, is at the corner of the two roads; a hotbed of political activity in the nineteenth century, it has been repurposed as an office building with a basement café. At Mount Vernon's intersection with Brimmer Street, you'll find the vine-covered **Church of the Advent** (Ⓦwww.theadvent.org); with its pointed arches and starkly contrasting building materials – stone and polychrome red bricks – it's a striking example of High Victorian Gothic. If you poke your head in during one of their frequent weekly masses, you can check out the decadent gold altar and detailed grillwork along the apse.

△ Beacon Hill townhouse and gaslamp

The Esplanade

To the west of Beacon Hill, spanning nine miles along the Charles River, the **Esplanade** is yet another of Boston's well-manicured public spaces, complete with requisite playgrounds, landscaped hills, lakes and bridges. The nicest stretch runs alongside Beacon Hill – and continues into Back Bay – providing a unique, scenic way to appreciate the Hill from a distance, as well as being a leading hotspot for the city's young and attractive. On summer days the Esplanade is swarming with well-toned joggers and rollerbladers, many of them seemingly on the prowl for a partner. Just below the Longfellow Bridge (which connects to Cambridge, across the river; see chapter 9) is the Community Boating boathouse, the point of departure for sailing, kayaking and windsurfing outings on the Charles (April–Oct daily 9am-5pm; two-day visitor's pass $50; ☎523-1038). The two-day pass gets you unlimited use of their equipment.

The white half-dome rising from the riverbank along the Esplanade is the **Hatch Shell**, a public performance space (call ☎727-9547 or check ⓦwww.state.ma.us/mdc for schedules and upcoming events; Charles **T**) best known for its Fourth of July celebration, which features a free concert by the Boston Pops, a pared-down version of the Boston Symphony Orchestra. The popularity of this event has caused it to become terribly overcrowded, but the other summer happenings at the Shell, such as free movies and jazz concerts, occur almost nightly and can be far more accessible.

Smith Court and the African Meeting House

Back along Pinckney Street from the Esplanade, **Smith Court** was the center of Boston's substantial pre-Civil War black community, back when the north slope was still a low-rent district; now it's home to a few crucial stops on Boston's **Black Heritage Trail** (see box opposite).

Free blacks who were denied participation in Boston's civic and religious life until well into the nineteenth century worshiped and held political meetings in what became known as the **African Meeting House**, at 8 Smith Court (July–Aug daily 10am–4pm; Sept–June Mon–Sat 10am–4pm; donation requested; ⓦwww.afroammuseum.org; Park Street **T**). Informally called the Black Faneuil Hall, it was a hotbed for abolitionist activity in the mid-1800s; in fact, William Lloyd Garrison founded the New England Anti-Slavery Society in the building's simple, second-floor auditorium, in 1832.

Today, the sober former church is home to the **Museum of Afro-American History** which, considering the importance of the site it occupies, is rather a disappointment. You won't find much in the way of displays, only a rotating exhibit on the first floor – usually contemporary African-American art – and the meeting house on the second, which has been restored to look like the most basic of churches it once was. Well-informed rangers lead **free tours** and can add much to contextualize what little you actually see.

At the end of Smith Court, you can walk along part of the old Underground Railroad used to protect escaped slaves, who once ducked into the doors along narrow **Holmes Alley** that were left open by sympathizers to the abolitionist

The Black Heritage Trail

In 1783, Massachusetts became the first state to declare slavery illegal, partly as a result of black participation in the Revolutionary War. Subsequently, large communities of free blacks and escaped slaves swiftly sprang up in the North End and Beacon Hill. The neighborhoods' proximity to the shipyards was convenient for the men, while the nearby upper-class houses meant household work for the women. Very few blacks live in either place nowadays, but the **Black Heritage Trail** traces Beacon Hill's key role in local and national black history – and is the most important historical site in America devoted to pre-Civil War African-American history and culture.

The 1.6-mile loop takes in fourteen historical sights which are detailed in a useful **guide** available at the African Meeting House (see opposite) and the information center in Boston Common (see p.40). Much of what there is to see, however, is quite ho-hum on its own; the best way to experience the trail is by taking a National Park Service **walking tour** (late May to early Sept Mon–Sat 10am, noon & 2pm, Sept–June call to reserve; free; ☏742-5415, ⓦwww.nps.gov/boaf; Park St Ⓣ), which superbly contextualizes the community. Starting from the **Robert Gould Shaw Memorial** (see p.75) the two-hour tour passes the modest 1797 clapboard **George Middleton House**, Beacon Hill's first African American-built private dwelling; the red-brick **Phillips School**, the first integrated school in Boston; and the cupola-topped **Charles Street Meeting House**, the last black institution to leave Beacon Hill in 1939. Near the end of the walk, you'll find the superficially unremarkable, but historically significant, **Lewis and Harriet Hayden House** at 66 Phillips St, whose owner, a former escaped slave himself, regularly opened his door to fugitive abolitionists and slaves alike as part of the Underground Railroad, and **Smith Court**, home to the **African Meeting House** and **Abiel Smith School** (see below) at the end of **Holmes Alley**, a common escape route used by runaway slaves.

cause. The **Abiel Smith School**, at 46 Joy St, built in 1834, was the first public educational institution established for black schoolchildren in Boston. It now showcases exhibits for the Museum of Afro-American History; check out "Separate Schools, Unequal Education," which traces, as the name indicates, the history of racial inequality in the American school system. There's also a **gift shop** with a wide range of literature related to the African-American experience.

The West End

North of Cambridge Street, the tidy rows of townhouses transition into a more urban spread of office buildings and old brick structures, signaling the start of the **West End**. Once Boston's main port of entry for immigrants, this area was populated by a broad mix of ethnic groups as well as transient sailors who brought a rough-and-tumble sex and tattoo industry with them. However, the eventual drift of Boston's ethnic populations to the southern districts, along with 1960s urban renewal, has effaced the district's once-lively character with sterile, modern facades.

That said, a vestige of the old West End remains in the small tangle of byways – namely Friend, Portland and Canal streets – behind the high-rise buildings of Massachusetts General Hospital, where you'll see urban warehouses interspersed with numerous Irish bars. *The Irish Embassy* and *McGann's* both have particularly authentic atmosphere (see "Drinking," p.190), but every bar swells to a fever pitch after Celtics basketball and Bruin hockey games at the nearby **FleetCenter**, the slick, corporate-named arena on top of North Station at 150 Causeway St (tours daily at 11am, 1pm & 3pm; $5).

➍ Harrison Gray Otis House

Back along Cambridge Street at no. 141, the brick **Harrison Gray Otis House** (Wed–Sun 11am–5pm, tours hourly; $5; ☎227-3956, ⊛www.spnea .org; Charles **T**), originally built for the wealthy Otis family in 1796 by Bulfinch, sits incongruously among minimalls and office buildings (another of the family's houses can be seen on Beacon Street; see p.75). In the 1830s, this building served as a Turkish bath before its transformation into a medicine shop and later a boarding house. In the 1920s, the structure was literally rolled back from the present-day median strip to make way for the highway. Its unadorned exterior gives no hint of the painstaking 1970s restoration that returned the house's interior to its original, eye-numbing Federal-style colors.

Museum of Science

Situated on the Charles River Bridge, at the northernmost part of the Esplanade, Boston's **Museum of Science** (July to early Sept daily 9am–7pm, Fri till 9pm, Sept–June daily 9am–5pm, Fri till 9pm; $12, children $9; CityPass accepted; ☎723-2500, ⊛www.mos.org; Science Park **T**) consists of several floors of inter-active – if patchy and often well-worn – exhibits illustrating basic principles of natural and physical science. There's enough here to entertain kids for most of a day, though that doesn't make it off-limits to fun-loving adults, either.

The best exhibit is the Theater of Electricity in the Blue Wing, a darkened room full of optical illusions and glowing displays on the presence of electricity in everyday life; the world's largest Van de Graaf generator gives daily electricity shows in which simulated lightning bolts flash and crackle. You can also play virtual volleyball here: the outline of your body appears on a wall-sized screen as you attempt to hit a virtual ball with your virtual shadow. More cerebral is Mathematica, in which randomly dropped balls fall neatly into a bell curve to demonstrate the notion of probability, and Virtual FishTank, a trippy underwater exhibit that encourages visitors to create and care for their own virtual sealife. Check out the Big Dig exhibit on the lower level, as well, where videos and interactive displays provide an engaging chronicle of Boston's Sisyphean attempt to put the unsightly elevated I-93 underground (see box, p.viii).

The museum also holds the **Charles Hayden Planetarium** and the **Mugar Omni Theater** ($8, children $6, $1.50 discount Thurs–Sun after 6pm; call ☎723-2500 or check ⊛www.mos.org for showtimes), though neither has too much to recommend it. The planetarium hosts talks and presentations through-out the day – free with museum admission – but it's better known for its laser shows, usually set to a soundtrack of classic rock and shown before an audience of precocious children and teenagers. In a similarly showy vein, the Omni Theater's enormous domed IMAX screen and state-of-the-art sound system provide plenty of stunning sensory input (though not the most hard-and-fast actual information).

Back Bay

The meticulously planned neighborhood of **Back Bay** – where elegant tree-lined streets form a pedestrian-friendly area that looks much as it did in the nineteenth century, right down to the original gaslights and brick sidewalks – manages a far more cosmopolitan air than similarly affluent Beacon Hill, with which it inevitably draws comparisons. A youthful population helps offset stodginess and keeps the district, which begins at the **Public Garden**, buzzing with chic eateries, trendy shops and the aura of entitlement that goes with both. Aside from the trust-fund vibe, the other main draw here is a trove of exquisite Gilded Age rowhouses; walking around, it seems as if there's no end to the fanciful bay windows and ornamental turrets. With a few exceptions, the brownstones get fancier the farther from the garden you go (the order in which they were built), a result of one-upmanship on the part of architects and those who employed them.

Running parallel to the Charles River in neat rows, Back Bay's east–west thoroughfares – **Beacon**, **Marlborough**, **Newbury** and **Boylston streets**, with **Commonwealth Avenue** in between – are transsected by eight shorter streets. These latter roads have been so fastidiously laid out that not only are their names in alphabetical order, but trisyllables are deliberately intercut by disyllables: Arlington, Berkeley, Clarendon, Dartmouth, Exeter, Fairfield, Gloucester and Hereford (though Gloucester, purists protest, only looks trisyllabic) – until Massachusetts Avenue breaks the pattern at the western border of the neighborhood. The grandest rowhouses are to be found on Beacon Street and Commonwealth Avenue, while Marlborough, with its tree-lined blocks, is more atmospheric, and Boylston and Newbury are the main commercial drags. In the midst of it all is a small green space, **Copley Square**, surrounded by the area's main sights: **Trinity Church**, the imposing **Boston Public Library** and the city's skyline-defining **John Hancock Tower**.

Some history

Back Bay was fashioned (as was its neighbor, the South End; see chapter 6) in response to a shortage of living space in Boston, a problem still somewhat unresolved. An increasingly cramped Beacon Hill prompted developers to revisit a failed dam project on the Charles River which had made a swamp of much of this area. With visionary architect and urban planner Arthur Gilman at the helm of a huge landfill project, the sludge began to be reclaimed in 1857. Taking his cue from Paris – Haussmann had just designed wide new boulevards for the French capital under Napoléon III – Gilman decided on an orderly street pattern extending east to west from the Public Garden, which itself had been sculpted from swampland only two decades before. By 1890, the cramped

BACK BAY SIGHTS AND ACCOMMODATION

▲ *Downtown*

◀ *Beacon Hill*

◀ *Cambridge*

▼ *Kenmore Square*

The South End ▶

Ducklings Statue

Public Garden

Swan Boats

Ether Memorial

George Washington Statue

Gibson House Museum

First Lutheran Church

Baylies Mansion

Emmanuel Church of Boston

Arlington St. Church

C

ARLINGTON

CHARLES STREET

RIVER STREET

BYRON STREET

BRIMMER STREET

BEAVER PLACE

CHESTNUT STREET

CHARLES ST

BRANCH ST

BEACON STREET

ARLINGTON STREET

BERKELEY STREET

BOYLSTON STREET

PARK PLAZA

F

H

PROVIDENCE STREET

Church of the Covenant

Ames-Webster Mansion

MARLBOROUGH STREET

COMMONWEALTH AVENUE

First Baptist Church

NEWBURY STREET

Trinity Church

John Hancock Tower

ST JAMES AVENUE

STUART STREET

COLUMBUS AVENUE

CLARENDON STREET

CLARENDON STREET

STANHOPE ST

DARTMOUTH STREET

COPLEY

Copley Square

BOYLSTON STREET

J

Newbury Street Mural

New Old South Church

E

Boston Public Library

L

K

DARTMOUTH STREET

BACK BAY

Copley Place

Tent City

YARMOUTH STREET

WEST CANTON ST.

CHANDLER STREET

LAWRENCE STREET

EXETER STREET

EXETER STREET

G

HUNTINGTON AVENUE

N

HOLYOKE ST.

WEST NEWTON STREET

FAIRFIELD STREET

FAIRFIELD STREET

GARRISON ST.

O

P

Q

ST BOTOLPH STREET

FOLLEN ST.

Burrage Mansion

D

GLOUCESTER STREET

Prudential Center

RING ROAD

CUMBERLAND ST.

PRUDENTIAL

T

Reflecting Pool

Institute of Contemporary Art

HEREFORD STREET

BOYLSTON STREET

Hynes Convention Center

Christian Science Center

M

DALTON STREET

Christian Science Mother Church

Oliver Ames Mansion

MARLBOROUGH STREET

COMMONWEALTH AVENUE

COMMONWEALTH AVENUE

Stable Shops

NEWBURY STREET

HYNES/ICA

T

SCOTIA ST.

BELVIDERE STREET

ST CECILIA ST.

ST GERMAIN STREET

CLEARWAY STREET

I

Mapparium

Berklee College of Music

HAVILAND ST.

MASSACHUSETTS AVENUE

MASSACHUSETTS AVENUE

WESTLAND AVENUE

NORWAY ST.

EDGERLY ROAD

HUNTINGTON AVENUE

B

Storrow Lagoon

JAMES STORROW MEMORIAL DRIVE

N

ACCOMMODATION

463 Beacon Street Guest House	**A**
Back Bay Hilton	**H**
Boston Park Plaza Hotel & Towers	**E**
Charlesmark Hotel	**O**
The Colonnade	**D**
Copley House	**Q**
Copley Inn	**P**
Copley Square Hotel	**K**

Eliot	**B**
Fairmont Copley Plaza	**J**
Four Seasons	**F**
The Lenox	**G**
Marriott at Copley Place	**N**
Newbury Guest House	**D**
Ritz-Carlton	**C**
Sheraton Boston Hotel	**M**
Westin	**L**

0 — 200 yds

peninsula of old Boston could claim 450 new acres, on which stood a range of churches, townhouses and schools.

It should come as no surprise, either, that Back Bay quickly became one of Boston's most sought-after addresses – although its popularity subsided somewhat during the Great Depression, when single families were unable to afford such opulence. During this period, developers converted many of the spaces into apartments, often gutting the interiors in the process; other properties were purchased by colleges and universities. The 1990s saw the arrival of gentrification, and the demand for whole houses led to developers actually knocking out many of the apartment walls their predecessors erected.

No matter what may have happened on the inside, the exteriors of most buildings remain unaltered, due largely to landmark preservation laws, and many retain their old wood ornamentation and Victorian embellishments. All this authentic charm contributes to high rents which feed, in turn, the consumer-driven culture on Newbury Street – a far cry from the traditional image of Boston – with its hundreds of upscale shops, designer hair salons and tiny gourmet eateries. The district has its share of urban problems, too, from a shortage of parking space and bad traffic jams to homeless people trawling for designer garbage. But the pervasive grace of the bowfronts and wrought-iron terraces masks these issues and proffers an air of well-heeled serenity.

The Public Garden

The value of property in Boston goes up the closer its proximity to Back Bay's lovingly maintained **Public Garden**, a 24-acre park first earmarked for public use in 1859. Of the garden's 125 types of trees – many identified by little brass placards – most impressive are the weeping willows that ring the picturesque man-made **lagoon**. Here you can take a fifteen-minute ride in one of six **Swan Boats** (April to late June daily 10am–4pm; late-June to early Sept daily 10am–5pm; early to mid-Sept Mon–Fri 12pm–4pm, Sat–Sun 10am–4pm; $2; ⓦ www.swanboats.com), which trace gracious figure-eights in the oversized puddle. The campy, pedal-powered conveyances, inspired by a scene in Wagner's opera *Lohengrin*, have been around since 1877 – long enough to become a Boston institution. The boats carry up to twenty passengers at a time, and in the height of summer there is often a line to hop on board – instead of waiting, you can get just as good a view of the park from the tiny **suspension bridge** that spans the lagoon.

The park's other big family draw also happens to be fowl-related: a cluster of popular bronze birds collectively called **Mrs Mallard and Her Eight Ducklings**. The sculptures were installed in 1987 to commemorate Robert McClosky's 1941 *Make Way for Ducklings*, a children's tale set in the Public Garden. Of the many other statues and monuments throughout the park, the oldest and oddest is the thirty-foot-tall **Good Samaritan** monument along the Arlington Street side of the garden; the granite and red-marble column is a tribute to, of all things, the anesthetic qualities of ether. Controversy as to which of two Boston men invented the wonder drug led Oliver Wendell Holmes to dub it the "Either Monument." Finally, a dignified equestrian statue of **George Washington**, installed in 1869 and the first of him astride a horse, watches over the garden's Commonwealth Avenue entrance.

Beacon Street

As a continuation of Beacon Hill's stately main thoroughfare, **Beacon Street** was long the province of blueblood Bostonians. Despite being so close to the Charles River, however, its buildings turn their back to it, principally because in the nineteenth century the river was a stinking mess. One such building, the Italian Renaissance townhouse at no. 137, holds the remarkable **Gibson House Museum** (Wed–Sun 1–3pm, tours hourly; $5; ☎267-6338, ⊛www.thegibsonhouse.org), which preserves the home built for Catherine Hammond Gibson in 1860, twenty years after the death of her well-to-do husband. In the somber interior, there's a curious host of Victoriana, including a still-functioning dumbwaiter, antique globes and writing paraphernalia (one of the Gibsons was a noted travel writer), and gilt-framed photos of Catherine's relatives. Notable among the various chinoiserie is the stunning gold-embossed "Japanese Leather" wallpaper that covers a good portion of the abode, and a sequined pink velvet cat house or, if you prefer the Gibsons' term, "pet pagoda."

Things get less interesting at the far end of Beacon Street (furthest from the Public Garden); the one structure of note is the turreted **Charlesgate Building** at no. 535, a former hotel that's been nicknamed "The Witch's Castle" – for obvious reasons – by the Emerson College students who now call it home.

Marlborough Street

Sandwiched between Beacon Street and Commonwealth Avenue is quiet **Marlborough Street**, which with its brick sidewalks and vintage gaslights is one of the most prized residential locales in Boston – asking prices here can top $2.5 million – after Beacon Hill's Louisburg Square and the first few blocks of Commonwealth Avenue. Even though the townhouses here tend to be smaller than elsewhere in Back Bay, they display a surprising range of stylistic variation when it comes to ornamentation, especially along the blocks between Clarendon and Fairfield streets; check out **no. 362**, for starters, outfitted as it is with elegant windows topped by trompe l'oeil arches.

Commonwealth Avenue

Commonwealth Avenue, the 220-foot-wide showcase street of Back Bay, was modeled after the grand boulevards of Paris, and its tree-lined, 100-foot-wide median forms the first link in Frederick Law Olmsted's so-called **Emerald Necklace** (see box on p.105), which begins at Boston Common and extends all the way to the Arnold Arboretum in Jamaica Plain (see p.120). The flagship *Ritz-Carlton* hotel on Arlington Street forms a fittingly upscale backdrop to the promenade, itself peppered with several elegantly placed **statues**, though with the exception of a particularly dashing likeness of Revolutionary War soldier John Glover – who helped Washington cross the Delaware in 1776 – between Berkeley and Clarendon streets, few of these hold any interest. "Comm Ave," as locals ignobly call it, is at its prettiest in early May, when the magnolia and dogwood trees are in full bloom, showering the brownstone steps with their fragrant pink buds.

Baylies, Ames-Webster and Burrage mansions

One set of these steps – the first as you walk along Commonwealth Avenue – belongs to the **Baylies Mansion**, at no. 5, which now houses the Boston Center for Adult Education. Feel free to slip inside for a look at the opulent Louis XV ballroom built expressly for Baylies' daughter's coming-out party (in the old-fashioned sense). You'll have to be content to see the Queen Anne-style **Ames-Webster Mansion**, a few blocks down at the corner of Dartmouth St, from the outside. Built in 1872 for railroad tycoon, Massachusetts governor, and US congressman Frederick Ames, it features a two-story conservatory, central tower and imposing chimney. Down the street is the **Burrage Mansion**, at no. 314, a fanciful synthesis of Vanderbilt-style mansion and the French château of Chenonceaux. The exterior of this 1899 urban palace is a riot of gargoyles and sundry carved cherubim; inside, it's less boisterous, currently serving as a retirement home. Further on, the Beaux Arts chateau at no. 355 is the **Oliver Ames Mansion** (no relation to the railroad tycoon), topped by multiple chimneys and dormer windows; its interior is now comprised of offices, and as such, is not open to the public.

First Baptist Church of Boston

Rising above the south side of the avenue at no. 110 is the landmark belfry of the **First Baptist Church of Boston** (Mon–Fri 10am–4pm), designed by architect H.H. Richardson in 1872 for a Unitarian congregation – though at bill-paying time only a Baptist group was able to pony up the necessary funds, hence the name. The puddingstone exterior is topped off by a 176-foot **bell tower**, which is covered by four gorgeous friezes by Frédéric-Auguste Bartholdi, of Statue of Liberty fame – he and Richardson became friends when the two studied together at the École des Beaux Arts in Paris. More interesting than what the tableaux depict (baptism, communion, marriage and death) are some of the illustrious stone-etched visages, particularly those of Emerson, Longfellow, Hawthorne, and Lincoln. Trumpeting angels protrude from each corner, inspiring its inglorious nickname, "Church of the Holy Bean Blowers."

The interior is exceedingly plain in comparison to the detailed facade, but its high ceiling, exposed timbers and Norman-style rose windows are still worth a peek if you happen by when someone's in the church office. If you've a mind to visit, ring the bell on the Commonwealth Avenue side and hope for the best.

Newbury and Boylston streets

Newbury Street, just south of Comm Ave, takes in eight blocks of alternately traditional and eclectic boutiques, art galleries and restaurants, all tucked into Victorian-era brownstones. It's an atmospheric place to browse, though the encroachment of big chain stores like the Gap and NikeTown has eroded some of its charm. Wealthy foreign students have colonized cafés like *29 Newbury* and

Café Armani, but despite the occasional nod to pretentiousness, the strip's overall mood is surprisingly inviting. And not all is shopping or dining: Newbury and neighboring **Boylston Street** – a less commercially oriented boulevard – are home to most of the old schools and churches built in the Back Bay area.

Emmanuel Church of Boston and Church of the Covenant

On the first block of Newbury Street, sandwiched between hair salons and upscale retail stores, is the **Emmanuel Church of Boston**, an unassuming rural Gothic Revival building. Of greater interest is the full-blown Gothic Revival **Church of the Covenant**, further down the street on the same side. Most passersby are too intent on window shopping to notice the soaring steeple, so look up before checking out the interior, famous – like its neighbor, the Arlington Street Church (see below) – for its Tiffany stained-glass windows, some of which are thirty feet high. The NAGA (Newbury Associated Guild of Artists) gallery, in the chapel (Tues–Sat 10am–5.30pm; ☎267-9060, Ⓦwww.gallerynaga.com) is one of Boston's biggest contemporary art spaces, and stages new exhibits of works by artists from Boston and New England; it's also a nice setting for chamber music performances – the Boston Pro Arte Chamber Orchestra was founded here.

The rest of Newbury Street

Designed as an architect's house, the medieval flight-of-fancy at **109 Newbury St** is arguably more arresting for its two fortress-like brownstone turrets than the Cole Haan footwear inside. A block down and across the street, at **no. 144**, is the Rodier Paris boutique, but again the burnt sienna-colored building with mock battlements hunkered over it steals the show. Originally the Hotel Victoria in 1886, it looks like a combination Venetian-Moorish castle, not a bad place to have a condo (which is how it serves the neighborhood today). A block further along, on the exposed side of no. 159, is the **Newbury Street Mural**, a fanciful tribute to a hodgepodge of Boston notables from Sam Adams to Sammy Davis Jr; a key to who's who is affixed to the parking attendant's booth in the lot next to it.

Newbury gets progressively funkier west of Exeter Street; the shoppers are more often students and locals than wealthy ladies venturing in from the suburbs. This is where you'll find Boston's most original fashion boutiques and alternative record stores (see p.215), in addition to several decent restaurants with popular summer sidewalk terraces (for reviews, see pp.181–184). On the final block, between Hereford Street and Massachusetts Avenue, a span of nineteenth-century **stables** has been converted to commercial space; check out the cavernous Patagonia clothing shop at no. 346 for the best example.

Arlington Street Church and the New England Mutual Life Building

Right on the corner of Boylston and Arlington streets is Back Bay's first building, the **Arlington Street Church** (Mon–Fri 10am–5pm), a minor Italianesque masterpiece whose construction in 1861 started a trend that resulted in many downtown congregations relocating to posher quarters in Back Bay. Arthur Gilman, chief planner of Back Bay, designed the clay-colored, squat structure, marked by a host of Tiffany stained-glass windows, added from 1895 to 1930. A history of progressive rhetoric has also earned it some note: abolitionist minister William Ellery Channing intoned against slavery here just a year before the Civil War erupted, and the church was a favored venue of peace activists during the Vietnam War; nowadays there's an active gay congregation. A block down is the prison-like **New England Mutual Life Building**, with some national chain stores on the first floor that do little for its character. It's worth nipping inside, though, for a look at the **murals**, which depict such historic regional events as John Winthrop sailing from Old to New England aboard the *Arbella*, Paul Revere sounding his famous alarm ("The British are coming! The British are coming!"), and the Declaration of Independence being read in Boston for the first time, from the balcony of the Old State House (see p.46).

Institute of Contemporary Art

Well down Boylston Street nearer Massachusetts Avenue, the **Institute of Contemporary Art**, at no. 955 (Wed & Fri–Sun noon–5pm, Thurs till 9pm; $7, free Thurs 5–9pm; ☎266-5152, ⓦ www.icaboston.org), is Boston's main modern art venue, though it has no permanent collection to speak of. Housed in half of an odd Romanesque-style police and fire station built in 1886 – the other half of which is still home base for Back Bay's firefighters – the ICA hosts about four exhibits and installations a year, many of them meeting with mixed success. Its small size – two floors plus a basement theater (see p.202) – is ideal for showcasing solo artists, but their thematic exhibits are vastly more accessible.

Copley Square and around

Bounded by Boylston, Clarendon, Dartmouth and St James streets, **Copley Square** is the busy commercial center of Back Bay. Various design schemes have come and gone since the square was first filled in the 1870s; the present one is a remnant from 1984, a nondescript, central grassy expanse and a heavy, slab-like fountain anchored by two stone obelisks on the Boylston Street side. A farmers' market materializes opposite the *Fairmont Copley Plaza Hotel* on Fridays in the spring and summer. Fortunately, the square's periphery holds more interest than the space it surrounds.

Trinity Church

In his meticulous attention to detail – from the polychromatic masonry on the outside to the rather generic stained-glass windows within – Boston architect H.H. Richardson seemed to overlook the big picture of his 1877 **Trinity Church** at 206 Clarendon St (daily 8am–6pm; $3; ⓦ www.trinityboston.org), which, as one 1923 guidebook averred, "is not beautiful." Critics in Richardson's time disagreed, dubbing it a masterpiece of the Romanesque Revival style, which Richardson initially attempted with his First Baptist Church (see p.87). The hulking exterior is a bit easier on the eye when approached from Clarendon instead of Dartmouth, where you'll get the classic, dead-on view; gazing up at the chunky centered tower from behind affords an unusual, even dizzying, perspective. From here, you'll also have an easier time of finding the church's cloister and hidden garden, one of Back Bay's more enchanting quiet spots. Skip the rather spartan interior, which feels more empty than awe-inspiring – unless, of course, you happen to be there on Friday at 12.15pm, in which case there are often **free organ recitals**. Indeed, the most interesting aspect of Trinity Church is probably its juxtaposition to the John Hancock Tower, in whose mirrored panes it's reflected; a shot of them together is a classic Boston image. Interesting, too, is the fact that the church rests rather precariously on 4500 submerged wood pilings – before the advent of modern construction techniques this was the only way for buildings to stay put in the very moist depths of Back Bay.

Boston Public Library

A decidedly secular building anchoring the end of Copley Square opposite Trinity Church, the **Boston Public Library** (Mon–Thurs 9am–9pm, Fri–Sat 9am–5pm; ☎536-5400, ⓦwww.bpl.org) is the largest public research library in New England and the first one in America to permit the borrowing of books. McKim, Mead & White, the leading architectural firm of its day, built the Italian Renaissance Revival structure in 1852; the visibility of its Dartmouth Street entrance is heightened by the presence of the spiky yet sinuous lanterns over-hanging it. The massive inner bronze doors were designed by Daniel Chester French (sculptor of the Lincoln Memorial in Washington DC); beyond them, a musketeer-like statue of Sir Henry Vane stands guard. This early governor of the Massachusetts Bay Colony believed, or so the inscription relates, that "God, law and parliament" were superior to the king, which apparently didn't do much for his case in 1662, when his freethinking head got the chop.

Beyond the marble grand staircase and beneath the extensively coffered ceilings are a series of **murals**, most impressive of which is a diaphanous depiction of the nine Muses. To its right stands a statue of a smiling, naked woman holding a baby in one hand and a bunch of grapes in the other, a replica of an original bacchante which, due to neo-Puritan prudishness, never graced the library's inner courtyard as intended. Just right of that is the gloomy **Abbey Room**, named for Edwin Abbey's murals depicting the Holy Grail legend, and where Bostonians once took delivery of their books. Most of these were kept in the imposing **Bates Reading Room**, which with its 218-foot-long sweep, 50-foot-high barrel-vaulted ceiling, dark oak paneling and incomparable calm, hasn't changed much since its debut more than a century ago. The library's most remarkable aspect is tucked away on the top floor, however, where the darkly lit **Sargent Hall** is covered with more than fifteen astonishing murals painted by John Singer Sargent between 1890 and 1916. Entitled the *Triumph of Religion*, the works are a mastery of detail incorporating appliquéd metal, paper and jewels – most striking in the north end's stunning twin *Pagan Gods* ceiling vaults – and plaster relief, evident in Moses's twin tablets which project from the east wall. First-time visitors should pick up a floor plan and explanatory pamphlet at the top of the stairs to guide you through the works – they're quite overwhelming without. Afterwards, you can take a breather in the library's open-air central **courtyard**, modeled after that of the Palazzo della Chancelleria in Rome.

New Old South Church

Just opposite the library, on the corner of Boylston and Dartmouth streets, is one of Boston's most attractive buildings, the **New Old South Church** (Mon–Fri 9am–5pm). There's actually some logic to the name: the congregation in residence at downtown's Old South Meeting House outgrew it and decamped here in 1875. You need not be a student of architecture to be won over by the Italian Gothic design, most pronounced in the ornate, 220-foot bell tower – rebuilt in 1940 after the original started leaning – and copper-roof lantern, replete with metallic gargoyles in the shape of dragons. The dramatic zebra-striped archways on the Dartmouth Street side are unfortunately partially obscured by the entrance to the Copley **T** station. It's not just to be admired from the outside, either: its interior is an alluring assemblage of dark woods set against a forest green backdrop, coupled with fifteenth-century, English-style stained-glass windows.

John Hancock Tower

At 62 stories, the **John Hancock Tower**, at 200 Clarendon St, is the tallest building in America north of New York City and, in a way, Boston's signature skyscraper – first loathed, now loved, and taking on startlingly different appearances depending on your vantage point. In Back Bay, the characteristically angular edifice is often barely noticeable, due to deft understatement and wafer-thin design in deference to adjacent Trinity Church and the old brownstones nearby. This modern subtlety in the face of historic landmarks is a signature quality of architect I.M. Pei (of the Louvre Pyramid and Bank of China, Hong Kong fame). From Beacon Hill, the tower appears broad-shouldered and stocky; from the South End, taller than it actually is; from across the Charles River, like a crisp metallic wafer. One of the best views is from the **Harvard Bridge**, which connects the western edge of Back Bay and Massachusetts Avenue with MIT in Cambridge; from there, you'll be able to see clouds reflected in the tower's lofty, fully mirrored coat. With such a seamless facade, you'd never guess that soon after its 1976 construction, dozens of windowpanes popped out, showering Copley Square with glass, due to a design flaw that prompted the replacement of over 10,000 panes.

There's no real reason to enter anymore; most of the building is given over to offices, and its main attraction, the sixtieth-floor **observatory**, which afforded some of the most stunning views around, is now closed due to security concerns. You'll have to head instead to the Prudential Skywalk (see below) for deluxe Boston vistas. Next door to the tower is the old Hancock Tower, which cuts a distinguished profile in the skyline with its truncated step-top pyramid roof. It's locally famous for the neon weather beacon on top which can be decoded with the help of the jingle, "Solid blue, clear view; flashing blue, clouds are due; solid red, rain ahead; flashing red, snow instead" (except in summer when red signifies the cancellation of a Red Sox game).

Prudential Tower

Not even the darkest winter night can cloak the ugliness of the **Prudential Tower** ("The Pru") at 800 Boylston St, just west of Copley Square. The 52-story gray intruder to the Back Bay skyline is one of the more unfortunate by-products of the urban renewal craze that gripped Boston and most other American cities in the 1960s – though it did succeed in replacing the Boston & Albany rail yards, a blighted border between Back Bay and the South End.

Today, apart from being the starting point for Duck Tours (see p.25), its chief selling point is its fiftieth-floor **Skywalk** (daily 10am–10pm; $7; ☏859-0648,

ⓦwww.prudentialcenter.com), which, at 700 feet, is not quite as high as the nearby John Hancock Observatory, but it does offer the only 360-degree aerial view of Boston. On a clear day you can make out Cape Cod across the waters of Massachusetts Bay and New Hampshire to the north. If you're hungry (or just thirsty) you can avoid the admission charge by ascending two more floors to the *Top of the Hub* restaurant; your bill may well equal the money you just saved, but during most daytime hours it's fairly relaxed, and you can linger over coffee or a drink. Well below, the crowded first-floor **Shops at Prudential Center** is about as generic as malls come, adjoining the hulking mass of the equally bland **Hynes Convention Center**.

Christian Science buildings

People gazing down at Boston from the top of the Prudential Tower are often surprised to see a 224-foot-tall Renaissance Revival basilica vying for attention amidst the urban outcroppings lapping at its base. This rather artificial-looking structure is the central feature of the world headquarters of the sprawling **First Church of Christ, Scientist**, at 175 Huntington Ave (Mon–Sat 10am–4pm; free; ⓦwww.tfccs.com; Symphony **T**). With seating for 3000 (and an enormous pipe organ), it dwarfs the earlier, prettier Romanesque **Christian Science Mother Church** just behind it, built in 1894 and decked out with spectacular opalescent stained-glass windows. The nice thing about wandering round the central plaza, a huge concrete block hammered out around the two churches by I.M. Pei in the early 1970s, is that no one tries to convert you. In fact there may be no better place in Boston to contemplate the excesses of religion than around the center's 670-foot-long, red-granite-trimmed **reflecting pool** (which, through some high-tech miracle, manages to cool water for the complex's air-conditioning system).

The highlights of a visit here, though, are on the ground floor of the **Mary Baker Eddy Library**, at 200 Massachusetts Ave (Tues–Fri 10am–9pm, Sat–Sun 10am–5pm, closed Mon; $5; ☎1-888/222-3711, ⓦwww.marybakereddylibrary .org; Symphony **T**). The entrance foyer alone is worth a peek, as the grand Art Deco lobby recently added a trippy glass and bronze fountain that appears to cascade with words rather than water; the sayings – mostly to do with peace and humanity – are projected from the ceiling for an effect that verges on holographic. Another unique marvel is the **Mapparium** tucked behind the lobby; you can walk across the thirty-foot diameter of this curious stained-glass globe on a glass bridge. The technicolor hues of the six hundred-plus glass panels, illuminated from behind, reveal the geopolitical reality of the world in 1935, when the globe was constructed, as evidenced by country names such as Siam, Baluchistan and Transjordan. Intended to symbolize the worldwide reach of the Christian Science movement, the Mapparium has perhaps a more immediate payoff: thanks to the spherical glass surface, which absorbs no sound, you can whisper, say, "What's Tanganyika called today?" at one end of the bridge and someone on the opposite end will hear it clear as a bell – and perhaps proffer the answer.

The upstairs **library**, on the other hand, is less interesting, primarily concerned as it is with amassing every piece of writing, videotape and audio ever produced by or involving Mary Baker Eddy; unless you're a devotee, you can easily give it a miss.

Bay Village

Back near the Public Garden, one of the oldest sections of Boston, **Bay Village**, bounded by Arlington, Church, Fayette and Stuart streets, functions now as a small atmospheric satellite of Back Bay. This warren of gaslights and tiny brick houses has managed to escape the trolley tours that can make other parts of the city feel like a theme park; of course, that's in part because there's not all that much to see. The area is, however, popular with Boston's gay population, who colonized it over a decade ago, before the current vogue for nearby South End.

The neighborhood's overall resemblance to a miniature Beacon Hill is no accident, as many of the artisans who pieced that district together built their own, smaller houses here throughout the 1820s and 1830s. A few decades later, water displaced from the filling in of Back Bay threatened to turn the district back into a swamp, but Yankee practicality resulted in the lifting of hundreds of houses and shops onto wooden pilings fully eighteen feet above the water level. Backyards were raised only twelve feet, and when the water receded many building owners designed **sunken gardens**. One of the most unusual remnants from the nineteenth century is the **fortress** at the intersection of Arlington and Stuart streets at Columbus Avenue. Complete with drawbridge and fake moat, it was built as an armory for the First Corps of Cadets, a private military organization, and has since been relegated to use as an exhibition hall and convention facility for the *Park Plaza Hotel* (see review p.159).

The obvious streets to explore are **Piedmont**, **Winchester** and **Church**, which spread out from the *Park Plaza* anchoring the neighborhood. Lightly trafficked **Melrose** and **Fayette streets**, footsteps beyond them, are also worth inspection: it's here you'll find the last remaining sunken gardens – tiny, and often gated, private lawns lying just below street level. There's little else to see here by day. Bay Village really wakes up after the sun sets, when men of all ages zero in on places like the *Luxor*, one of the more popular gay clubs in Boston; for reviews of the hotspots, see chapter 14, Nightlife, and chapter 16, Gay and lesbian Boston.

The South End

The **South End**, a predominantly residential neighborhood extending below Back Bay from Huntington Avenue to I-93, is one of those neighborhoods somewhere between quaint and trendy; both tags pretty much fit. At its heart is an area lovingly nicknamed the "Golden Triangle" by South End realtors; bounded by Tremont Street, Dartmouth Street and Columbus Avenue, this posh enclave boasts a spectacular concentration of Victorian architecture, unmatched anywhere in the US. In fact, the sheer number of such houses here earned the South End a National Landmark District designation in 1983, making the 500-acre area the largest historical neighborhood of its kind in the country. In addition to its architecture, the area is also known for its well-preserved ironwork; a French botanical motif known as Rinceau adorns many of the houses' stairways and windows (see box p.98). Unsurprisingly, details like these made the area quite popular with upwardly mobile Bostonians in the mid-1990s, who moved in and gentrified the neighborhood. Among them was a strong gay and lesbian population, ensuring at least some diversity remained when long-term Puerto Rican and Dominican residents were forced out. The upshot has been some of the most upbeat and happening streetlife in town, not least of which exists in the proliferation of art galleries and hip **restaurants**; indeed, this has become the breeding ground for chefs looking to push the boundaries of haute cuisine. The activity is most visible on **Tremont Street** and on pockets of **Washington Street**, a few blocks below the Back Bay **T**, the neighborhood's only **T** stop.

A couple of notable exceptions to the gentrification rule still exist in a small quadrant below Tremont Street, still home to a long-standing Puerto Rican community, and a patch along Dartmouth Street near Copley Place, where the low-income housing co-op of Tent City presides. As well, the surrounding areas such as Roxbury are some of the poorest in the city, and have not benefited from the economic comforts of gentrification. Along the outer reaches of the neighborhood, the tension can be palpable, and appropriate caution should be taken especially at night. Stick to the Golden Triangle area, though, and you'll have nothing to worry about.

Some history

Like Back Bay, the South End was originally a marshland that now sits on landfill. Though the mud-to-mansion process kicked off in 1834 – predating Back Bay by more than twenty years – the neighborhood really took shape between 1850 and 1875, when it was laid out according to 1801 plans designed by Charles Bulfinch. The neighborhood's similarity to Beacon Hill, completed just two years prior to development here, is striking, though the South End "look" is more homogeneous and streamlined, dominated by red-brick bowfront

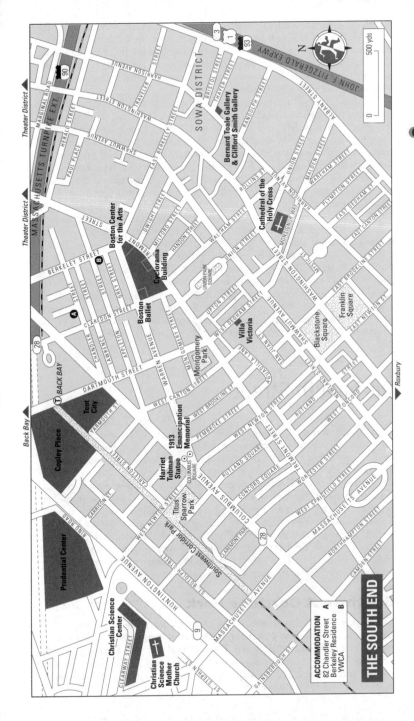

THE SOUTH END

ACCOMMODATION
A 82 Chandler Street
B Berkeley Residence YWCA

Prudential Center

Christian Science Center

Christian Science Mother Church

Copley Place

Tent City

Boston Center for the Arts

Cyclorama Building

Boston Ballet

Harriet Tubman Statue

Titus Sparrow Park

1913 Emancipation Memorial

Montgomery Park

Villa Victoria

Cathedral of the Holy Cross

Bernard Toale Gallery & Clifford Smith Gallery

SOWA DISTRICT

Union Park Square

Blackstone Square

Franklin Square

Theater District

Back Bay

Roxbury

0   500 yds

townhouses that are modestly taller than their Beacon Hill predecessors. As for green space, quaint slivers like Union Park Square were created to attract wealthy buyers who had progressively been moving to the Boston countryside; the marketing campaign to draw them southward included, among other schemes, naming neighborhood arteries like Appleton and Chandler streets after well-to-do merchant families.

This initial success began to flag, however, when many of these families experienced financial decline after the Panic of 1873. Following the Panic, what nouveau riche were left headed for the newly created Back Bay, while waves of immigrants moved in to take their place, turning numerous South End townhouses into boarding houses, or razing them altogether to make room for low-income living space. The lure of affordable housing attracted large numbers of the city's African-American population, too, at the turn of the twentieth century, who left expensive Beacon Hill digs to install themselves here. Their presence would produce Sammy Davis Jr and Louis Mayer (of MGM fame), who both grew up here, and lead Dr Martin Luther King Jr and his wife, Coretta Scott King, to rent an apartment in the neighborhood while the future civil rights leader attended Boston University.

In the 1970s, the African-American population was in turn pushed out to Roxbury, being replaced by Puerto Ricans and Dominicans, who instigated the creation of local community housing projects like Villa Victoria. Two decades later, the aforementioned gentrification commenced in earnest, leading to, among other things, the opening of several art galleries in the streets south of Washington Street, a geographical concentration latterly going by the name of SoWa (South of Washington), recalling New York's über-trendy SoHo.

Dartmouth Street

The South End's main access point, the Back Bay **T**, opens up onto **Dartmouth Street** – anchored by Copley Place on the far side – which gets more upscale the closer it comes to Tremont Street, a few blocks southeast. Immediately below Copley Place, at no. 130, is the street's most important tenant, **Tent City**, a mixed-income housing co-op that owes its name to the 1968 sit-in protest – tents included – staged on the formerly vacant lot by residents concerned about the neighborhood's dwindling low-income housing. Their activism thwarted plans for a parking garage to be built here, and the result is a terrific example of environmental architecture planning. Built in 1988, the section of the co-op closest to Copley Place blends seamlessly with the mall's modern facade, while that closer to Columbus Avenue incorporates a series of Victorian houses for which the neighborhood is known; the proposed parking lot, incidentally, lies underground.

Southwest Corridor Park

The pocket of land separating Tent City from Copley Place marks the start of the five-mile **Southwest Corridor Park**, a grassy promenade (whence "corridor") that connects the Back Bay **T** with the Forest Hill **T** station near the beautiful Arnold Arboretum in Jamaica Plain (see p.121). The park is another creative urban project, as the strip expertly covers the tracks of a long-gone nineteenth-century railroad corridor.

Columbus Avenue

Defining the northern edge of the Golden Triangle, **Columbus Avenue** is lined with handsome Victorian houses; the main interest, however, is a tiny wedge of parkland known, obviously enough, as **Columbus Square**. The square, more or less the outer boundary of the triangle, contains two out-standing bronze relief sculptures, commemorating Boston's role as part of the Underground Railroad. The nine-foot-tall **Harriet Tubman "Step on Board" Memorial** depicts the strident abolitionist leading several weary slaves to safety, while the nearby 1913 **Emancipation Memorial** is a more harrowing portrait of the slaves' plight: the foursome here are achingly thin and barely clothed. More African-American history is found behind the park, along Warren Avenue; the Gothic red-brick **Concord Baptist Church**, at no. 190, welcomed Martin Luther King Jr as a guest minister during his Boston University days.

Appleton and Chandler streets

Cobblestoned **Appleton Street** and quiet **Chandler Street**, which jut off to the northeast from Dartmouth, are the most sought-after South End address-es. The appeal is obvious: the tree-lined streets are graced with refurbished flat- and bowfronted rowhouses that would easily be at home in London's Mayfair. In addition, unlike many of their neighbors, the houses here have an extra, fourth story, and are capped off by mansard roofs. Keep an eye out for the Frisbee-sized bronze discs embedded in the sidewalk in front of the houses, too – they're remnants of coal-heating days, when the stuff was delivered through the portals and straight into the basement.

The best way to see the houses in this area is as part of the South End Historical Society's annual October **house tour** (check Ⓦ www.southend historicalsociety.org or call ☎ 536-4445 for the exact date and price), in which residents open their doors to the public. The rest of the year, you can still enjoy the ambiance by grabbing a pastry from the *Appleton Bakery*, at 123 Appleton St, and watching the streetlife from its sidewalk benches.

Clarendon and Tremont streets

South End's architecture is more working-class along **Clarendon Street**, one block northeast of Dartmouth Street. There's little to see here until you reach Warren Street, anchored by a 1991 arch-windowed red-brick building used as a practice space by the world-renowned **Boston Ballet** (call ☎ 695-6950 to sched-ule a studio tour). The building gets some of its architectural inspiration from the substantial red-brick **Second Baptist Church** across the way, with its late-1860 Gothic facade. It no longer serves as a church, however, since the interior was razed by fire and its surviving walls incorporated into a condominium in 1991.

The heart of the South End, and the linchpin of the Golden Triangle, is at the intersection of Clarendon and **Tremont** streets, where an upmarket pseudo-square is flanked by some of the trendiest restaurants in Boston; the acclaimed *Hamersley's Bistro*, at 553 Tremont St, holds fort at the square's southern corner. The area's only real sight, per se, is smack in the middle, the domed **Cyclorama Building**, built in 1884 to house an enormous, 360-degree painting of the Battle of Gettysburg (since moved to Gettysburg itself). Later used as a carousel space, a boxing ring, and even the site of the Boston Floral Exchange in 1923, repurposing here continued until 1972, when its current tenants, the **Boston Center for the Arts** (☎426-7700, Ⓦ www.bcaonline.com), moved in and created three basement theaters devoted to modern performances; the old "Gettysburg" space now showcases temporary art exhibits. And finally, if the ornate kiosk in front of the building looks somewhat oversized, that's because it originally served as the cupola of an 1850s Roxbury orphanage; it was moved here in 1975, when the orphanage was demolished.

The rest of Tremont Street, foremost among South End's major arteries, carries on the high-end restaurant theme set by *Hamersley's*, especially at luxurious eateries like *Aquitaine* and *Truc* (see p.184 for South End restaurant listings). Worth a quick peek en route to gastronomic heaven is the old **St Cloud Hotel**, at 567 Tremont St, a French Second Empire building dating from 1872 that still boasts a facade of white marble and green bay windows; most of its former flats now house real-estate offices.

Union Park Square

Charming **Union Park Square**, east of Tremont along Union Park Street, is a tiny decorative park which, in typical English fashion, you can walk around but not through – an elegant wrought-iron fence encircles it to make sure you keep off the grass. The ovalesque park is framed by about twenty refined brownstone rowhouses, representing a pastiche of styles from Italianate to Greek Revival, all of them with bigger windows and more elaborate cornice-work than houses on surrounding streets. Of these, the residence at **14 Union Park St**, with its overhanging portico and rounded bay windows, is worth a nod – it's among the few single-family homes to escape condo-conversion in this deluxe area.

Know your irons

As you walk around the South End, you'll notice a slew of brownstones adorned with curlicued cast iron on everything from stairway railings and flower boxes to windowsills and balconies. A distinctive South End feature, the fancy ironwork was, like the area's street-naming convention, intended as a perk to attract upwardly mobile residents back from the suburbs. The arboreal-themed lacing is known as the Rinceau style (from the French, and meaning "small branch"), and the neighborhood boasts around seven variations on the serpentine scroll, ranging from a simple run of acanthus leaves to elaborate arabesques sprouting off from a central rosette. Some of the best can be seen on West Canton Street (a few blocks southwest along Tremont St), where a series of sandstone stairways are trimmed with a wavy version inset with garden roses that create quite an eye-catching ensemble. Don't let their intricacy fool you, though – by the mid-1850s, technological innovations meant that scrolls such as these were about as easy to stamp out as notebook paper.

Just past the square along Union Park Street is the whitewashed **St John the Baptist Church** (open for Sunday mass only); a pretty blue-hued Nativity mosaic on its facade adds the only splash of color. Edward Everett Hale, author of *Man without a Country*, a short story about a self-exiled man sentenced to a lifetime alone at sea (made into a film in 1973), was minister here from 1856 to 1909; a statue of him can be seen in the Public Garden (see p.85).

Washington Street and around

The South End's other major artery, **Washington Street**, intersects with Union Park Street and extends southwest to Roxbury. Though intended to resemble a French grand boulevard, the only real similarity is its width; the street itself is worn and devoid of the bustle of Tremont Street. What activity exists tends to focus on its major tenant, the 1875 **Cathedral of the Holy Cross**, at no. 1400, which in 2002 unfortunately found itself at the center of the Catholic priest sex abuse scandal. Distinguished by uneven and truncated twin towers – intended as steeples until the parish ran out of money – the vast neo-Gothic interior seats two thousand, and boasts some fine stained-glass work, including a multicolored rose window depicting the Bible's King David.

The only other sight nearby is a few blocks southwest of the church, at the corner of West Brookline Street, where the charmless **Blackstone Square**, named for Boston's original settler William Blackstone (see p.235), occupies a city block. Like much in the neighborhood, it, too, is laid out in English fashion, with diagonal spokes leading to a central fountain. This public space, with equally ramshackle **Franklin Square** across the street, was once the official entry-point to Boston, but nowadays is rather seedy, and really not worth your time.

Villa Victoria and around

North from Blackstone and Franklin squares, a decidedly lackluster bronze **plaque** at the corner of Washington and West Dedham streets commemorates the 56th infantry of World War II, a largely Puerto Rican regiment, and serves as an unofficial marker of the community's southern frontier.

The real heart of the enclave, though, is two blocks up West Dedham at **Villa Victoria**, a housing project serving 3000 members of the community. This place, like Tent City, was also the result of late-1960s public activism. And, though the buildings suffer from 1970s architectural aesthetics, their coral hues and setting around a central square, **Plaza Betances**, demonstrate a Hispanic sensitivity that sets them apart from the rest of the South End's Victoriana. The main draw here is in the square itself, where the **Ramón Betances Mural** occupies a whopping 45 feet long by 14 feet high of wall space. Created in 1977 by 300 local children, the brightly colored mosaic has less to do with its namesake (a leader in Puerto Rico's fight for independence from Spain) than simple childlike hope and optimism, as demonstrated by myriad cartoonish faces and flowers that surround a massive sun; it may be Boston's best piece of public art.

Harrison and Thayer streets

Around the intersection of **Harrison** and **Thayer** streets, near the eastern edge of the South End, a handful of **art galleries** have showrooms in cavernous loft spaces. Wandering around the self-styled **SoWa** district could easily distract you for an hour or so. Certainly, the **Bernard Toale Gallery** at 450 Harrison St (Tues–Sat 10.30am–5.30pm) is worth a peek; when its namesake, one of Boston's foremost art connoisseurs, moved here from his tony Newbury Street digs in 1998, he effectively sanctified the area as the new arts hotspot. Another happening art space, **Clifford-Smith Gallery**, is upstairs; it showcases tech-savvy installations along with more traditional media like painting and photography. For a more complete list of galleries, see p.213.

Kenmore Square, the Fenway and west

At the western edge of Back Bay, the decorous brownstones and smart shops fade into the more casual **Kenmore Square** and **Fenway** districts. While both areas are somewhat removed from the historical-sights-of-Boston circuit, they're good fun nonetheless, with a youthful vibe and, a bit surprisingly, some of the city's more notable cultural landmarks. The Fenway spreads out beneath Kenmore Square like an elongated kite, taking in a disparate array of sights ranging from **Fenway Park**, where baseball's star-crossed Red Sox play, to some of Boston's finest high-culture institutions: **Symphony Hall**, the **Museum of Fine Arts** and the **Isabella Stewart Gardner Museum**. Further west and more residential are the communities of **Allston–Brighton** and **Brookline**; the former is home to a young, hip crowd, and the latter features the birthplace of JFK, though in truth there's not all that much to do in either.

Kenmore Square and around

Kenmore Square, at the junction of Commonwealth Avenue and Beacon Street, is the unofficial playground for the students of Boston University, as most of its buildings can be found here. Back Bay's Commonwealth Avenue Mall leads right into this lively stretch of youth-oriented bars, record stores and casual restaurants that cater to the late-night cravings of local students; as such, the square is considerably more alive when school's in session. Many of the buildings on its north side have been snapped up by BU, such as the bustling six-story Barnes & Noble bookstore at 660 Beacon St, on top of which is perched the monumental **Citgo Sign**, Kenmore's most noticeable landmark. This sixty-square-foot neon advertisement, a pulsing red triangle that is the oil company's logo, has been a popular symbol of Boston since it was placed here in 1965.

Southwest along Brookline Avenue from the square, you can cross over the Massachusetts Turnpike (via bridge) to the block-long Lansdowne Street, on the

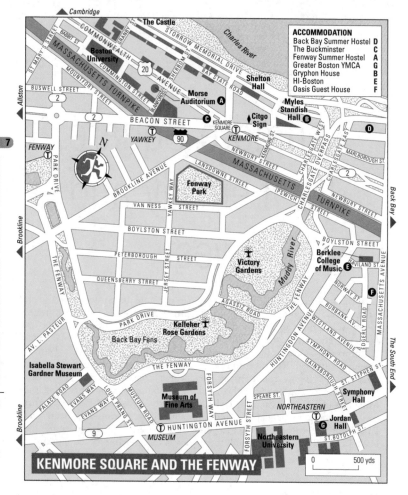

KENMORE SQUARE AND THE FENWAY

ACCOMMODATION
Back Bay Summer Hostel   D
The Buckminster   C
Fenway Summer Hostel   A
Greater Boston YMCA   G
Gryphon House   B
HI-Boston   E
Oasis Guest House   F

0   500 yds

northeast side of Fenway Park, a grungy but perennially popular stretch of show-your-ID bars and nightclubs (see reviews pp.197–198). There's little point in coming here during daylight hours, though, as the place really only wakes up at midnight.

Boston University

Boston University, one of the country's biggest private schools, has its main campus alongside the Charles River on the narrow stretch of land between Commonwealth Avenue and Storrow Drive. Though it boasts a few Nobel-prize winners among its faculty, such as Derek Walcott and Elie Wiesel, the school is more interesting for its inventive reuse of old buildings, such as the dormitory **Myles Standish Hall**, at 610 Beacon St, a scaled-down version of New York's Flatiron Building that once was a hotel where notables like Babe Ruth camped out. One of its rooms also served as the fictional trysting place of

Willy Loman in Arthur Miller's *Death of a Salesman*. Behind the building on **Bay State Road**, many of the turn-of-the-century brownstones serve as BU graduate institutes and smaller residence buildings, such as **Shelton Hall**, also a former hotel with an illustrious past: playwright Eugene O'Neill spent his last days, in 1953, in one of the rooms here. The ornate High Georgian Revival mansion at no. 149, meanwhile, holds the office of the current university president. Bay State Road ends at **The Castle**, an ivy-covered Tudor mansion now used for university functions. Just beyond is one of BU's few green spaces, the **Warren Alpert Mall** and its so-called "BU Beach," a sliver of lawn that's been purposefully upswept at the edge to shield busy Storrow Drive from view.

Back on Commonwealth, the domed Morse Auditorium, formerly a synagogue, continues the repurposing theme, nowadays hosting student graduations, lectures, and occasional performances. One long block down is the closest thing the BU campus has to a center, Marsh Plaza, with its Gothic Revival chapel and memorial to Martin Luther King Jr, one of the university's more noted alumni.

Fenway Park

Baseball is treated with reverence in Boston, so it's appropriate that it is played here in what may be the country's most storied stadium, Fenway Park, at 24 Yawkey Way, whose giant 37-foot-tall left-field wall, aka the "Green Monster," is an enduring symbol of the quirks of early ballparks. Constructed in 1912 in a tiny, asymmetrical wedge just off Brookline Avenue, the park's resulting famously awkward dimensions include an abnormally short right-field line (302 feet) and a fence that doesn't at all approximate the smooth arc of most outfields. That the left-field wall was built so high makes up for some of the short distances in the park and also gives Red Sox left-fielders somewhat of an advantage over their counterparts – it takes time to get accustomed to the crazy caroms a ball hit off the wall might take.

Fenway's fate is somewhat up in the air these days as developers and conservationists quarrel over the cost-effectiveness and feasibility of renovating the existing park versus building a new one; it's one of the few from its era that has not been replaced by a more spacious, and commercially conscious modern park. Meanwhile, you can still take tours of the stadium (April–Oct Mon–Fri 10am, 11am, 1pm & 2pm, no 2pm tour on game days; $8, children $6; T236-6666; www.redsox.com; Kenmore or Fenway T), the highlight of which is getting up close with the famed Green Monster, and visiting the locker room once occupied by one-time Red Sox greats like Ted Williams, Carl Yazstremski and Babe Ruth, before he became a Yankee. That said, your best bet is to come see a game – a must for any baseball fan and still a reasonable draw for anyone remotely curious. The season runs from April to October, and tickets are quite affordable, especially if you sit in the bleachers; check out chapter 19, Sports and outdoor activities, for more details on tickets and the team.

The Back Bay Fens

The Fenway's defining element, the snakelike Back Bay Fens (daily 7.30am–dusk; www.emeraldnecklace.org/fenway.htm), occupies land due

The Curse of the Bambino

In 1903, Boston's baseball team (then called the Pilgrims) became the first to represent the American League in the World Series; their continued financial success allowed them to build a new stadium, **Fenway Park**, in 1912. During their first year there, Boston won the Series again and repeated the feat in 1915, 1916 and 1918, led in the latter years by the young pitcher **George Herman "Babe" Ruth**, who also demonstrated an eye-opening penchant for hitting home runs.

The team seemed poised to become a dynasty, until its owner, Harry Frazee, turned his finances towards a Broadway play starring his ingenue girlfriend and sold off most of the players at bargain prices, including Ruth, who went to the New York Yankees, which went on to become the most successful franchise in professional sports history. On the other hand, Frazee's play, *No, No, Nanette*, flopped. So did his Red Sox team.

Since then, fans have suffered one letdown after another, so much so that they affectionately – and only half-jokingly – refer to the Sox fate as "The Curse of the Bambino," in honor of the Babe. One of the more notable instances of the curse rearing its ugly head occurred in 1978, as a late-season collapse was capped off when the Yankees' light-hitting shortstop Bucky Dent slugged a three-run homer to beat the Sox in a one-game playoff; another in 1986, when, just one strike away from clinching the World Series in Game Six against the New York Mets, the Sox began a series of infamous miscues that brought about another crushing loss. As recently as 1999, the team made it to the American League Championship Series, only to be dashed by – who else – the Yankees. Current star pitcher Pedro Martinez, when asked about the Curse in June of 2001, replied that the Babe could "kiss his butt." Shoulder problems then shut him down for two months.

To read about the Curse of the Bambino being put to the test, pick up local sportswriter Dan Shaughnessy's book of the same name (see "Books," p.247).

east of the stadium, starting where the prim Commonwealth Avenue Mall leaves off. This segment of Frederick Law Olmsted's Emerald Necklace was fashioned from marsh and mud in 1879, a fact reflected by frequent vistas of swaying reeds and the name of the waterway that still runs through the park space today – the Muddy River – a narrow channel crossed in its northernmost part by an H.H. Richardson-designed medievalesque puddingstone bridge. In the northern portion of the park, local residents maintain small garden plots in the wonderfully unmanicured Victory Garden, the oldest community garden in the US. Nearby, below Agassiz Road, the more formally laid out Kelleher Rose Garden boasts colorful hybrid species bearing exotic names like Voodoo, Midas Touch and Sweet Surrender. The area also makes an agreeable backdrop for some of Boston's smaller colleges, such as Simmons and Emmanuel, as well as the Harvard Medical School.

Berklee College of Music and Symphony Hall

The renowned Berklee College of Music makes its home east of the Fens near Back Bay, its campus buildings concentrated mostly on the busy stretch of Massachusetts Avenue south of Boylston Street, an area with several appropriately budget-friendly eateries. Looming a few short blocks south, Symphony Hall, where the Boston Symphony Orchestra plays, anchors the corner of Massachusetts and Huntington avenues. The inside of the 1900 McKim, Mead & White design, modeled after the no longer extant Gewandhaus in Leipzig, Germany, resembles an oversized cube, apparently just the right shape to lend it its perfect acoustics. The big English Baroque-style building across the street is Horticultural Hall (℡933-4900, ⍾www.masshort.org) headquarters of the Massachusetts Horticultural Society, which occasionally stages herbaceous events on site, but is better known for hosting the annual New England Spring Flower Show (see p.227). Jordan Hall, venue of the New England Conservatory of Music's chamber music concerts, is a few blocks down on Huntington, at nos. 290–294. The modern campus of Northeastern University spreads out on both sides of the avenue about a half-mile further south. There's not much to see here, though; it's largely a commuter campus, and as such lacks the collegiate atmosphere of Boston's more happening universities.

Museum of Fine Arts

Rather inconveniently located in south Fenway – but well worth the trip – the Museum of Fine Arts, at 465 Huntington Ave (Mon–Tues & Sat–Sun 10am–4.45pm, Wed–Fri 10am–9.45pm, Thurs–Fri West Wing only after 5pm; $15, $13 Thurs–Fri after 5pm, by contribution Wed after 4pm; CityPass accepted; ℡267-9300, ⍾www.mfa.org; Museum **T**), is New England's premier art space. Founded in the 1850s as an adjunct of the Boston Athenæum when that organization decided to focus more exclusively on local history rather than art, the collection was given public imprimatur and funding by the Massachusetts Legislature in 1870. After moving around at the end of the nineteenth century, it found its permanent home here in 1906.

The Emerald Necklace

The string of vegetation that stretches through Boston's southern districts, known as the **Emerald Necklace**, grew out of a project conceived in the 1870s, when landscape architect **Frederick Law Olmsted** was commissioned to create for Boston a series of urban parks, as he had done in New York and Chicago. A Romantic naturalist in the tradition of Rousseau and Wordsworth, Olmsted conceived of nature as a way to escape the ills wrought by society, and considered his parks a means for city-dwellers to escape the clamor of their everyday life. He converted much of Boston's remaining open space, which was often disease-ridden marshland, into a sequence of meticulously manicured outdoor spaces beginning with the **Back Bay Fens**, including the **Riverway** along the Boston–Brookline border, and proceeding through **Jamaica Pond** and the **Arnold Arboretum** to Roxbury's **Franklin Park**. While Olmsted's original skein of parks was limited to these, further development linked the Fens, via the Commonwealth Avenue Mall, to the Public Garden and Boston Common, all of which now function as part of the Necklace, and which make it all the more impressive in scale. However, the Necklace's sense of pristine natural wonder has slipped in the century since their creation – the more southerly links in the chain, starting with the Fens, have grown shaggy and are unsafe at night.

The **Boston Park Rangers** (daily 9am–5pm; ℡635-7383) organize free walking tours covering each of the Necklace's segments, and hardcore Olmsted fans won't want to miss the **Frederick Law Olmsted National Historic Site** at 99 Warren St (see p.114).

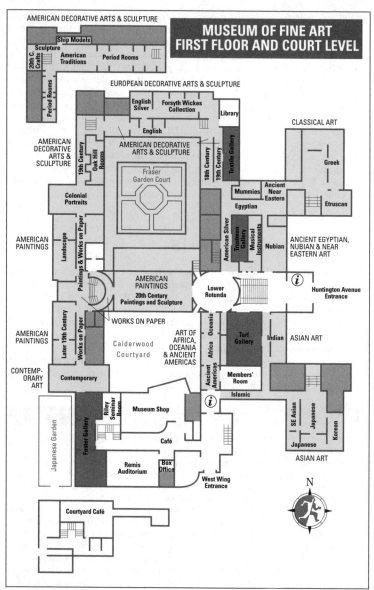

MUSEUM OF FINE ART
FIRST FLOOR AND COURT LEVEL

Most recently, the sprawling three-floor granite complex has proven too small for its extensive collections, despite measuring near 550,000 square feet, and is in the throes of a remedial five-year expansion period – the ninth such enlargement since the museum's 1909 opening. While one projected goal is the improvement of museum "wayfinding" – navigating the labyrinthine corridors and galleries as they are now is utterly bewildering, even with the museum map in hand – the better layout promises more inconvenience in the interim,

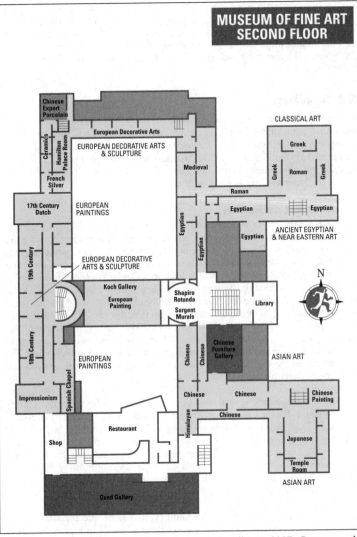

**MUSEUM OF FINE ART
SECOND FLOOR**

Chinese Export Porcelain

European Decorative Arts

EUROPEAN DECORATIVE ARTS & SCULPTURE

Ceramics

Hamilton Palace Room

French Silver

Medieval

CLASSICAL ART

Greek

Greek

Roman

Greek

17th Century Dutch

EUROPEAN PAINTINGS

Roman

Egyptian

Egyptian

Egyptian

ANCIENT EGYPTIAN & NEAR EASTERN ART

19th Century

EUROPEAN DECORATIVE ARTS & SCULPTURE

Egyptian

Egyptian

Koch Gallery

European Painting

Shapiro Rotunda

Sargent Murals

Library

N

18th Century

EUROPEAN PAINTINGS

Chinese

Chinese

Chinese Furniture Gallery

ASIAN ART

Impressionism

Spanish Chapel

Chinese

Chinese

Himalayan

Chinese

Chinese Painting

Restaurant

Shop

Japanese

Temple Room

ASIAN ART

Gund Gallery

with gallery closures and relocations scheduled well into 2007. Consequently, if you're looking for a particular piece, be sure to ask where it is; well-informed staffers maintain ground-floor booths near the Huntington Avenue and West Wing entrances and float around the galleries as well.

The collection is massive – and trying to see it all in one day is a daunting prospect at best; conveniently, though, the entrance fee entitles you to visit the museum twice in a thirty-day period on presentation of your original ticket. Perhaps the easiest way to stay focused is by concentrating on one particular main building: the West Wing holds the marvelously dense American painting collection, substantial Impressionist art, and blockbuster special exhibits; the adjoining Huntington Building contains one of the world's best collections of arts of the ancient world and Asia. The two buildings are joined by interconnecting galleries which culminate in the Huntington Avenue-side rotunda, the second floor of which is a must-see for the outstanding John Singer Sargent murals decorating its walls and ceilings. Completing the current layout are several smaller wings with an emphasis on decorative arts.

West Wing

Yet another I.M. Pei design, the modern, greystone West Wing lacks a bit of personality, but it draws the bigger crowds of the two MFA buildings thanks to its important collection of American paintings, Impressionist works, and stellar temporary exhibits. The former takes up most of the first floor starting chronologically, but annoyingly, layout-wise, near the rear, in the Colonial Portraits gallery; the latter two are housed on the second floor.

American art collections

The **American** gallery features important paintings from the two major figures of the **Colonial** period: Copley, whose portraits of Revolutionary figures – among them Paul Revere, John Hancock, and Sam Adams – while instructive, are less engrossing than his gruesome narrative *Watson and the Shark*; and Gilbert Stuart, whose nationalistic *Washington at Dorchester Heights* is on display along with his portrait of the first US president which graces the one-dollar bill. The works lining the long hallway that heads back to the front entrance are of lesser interest than the adjoining rooms, which find Romantic naturalist **landscapes** from the first half of the nineteenth century, of which Albert Bierstadt's quietly majestic *Lake Tahoe, California* is a fine example, mixed in with Neoclassical representations of sea battles like Thomas Birch's jubilant *The Constitution and the Guerrière*, which depicts the engagement from whence the USS *Constitution*'s nickname, "Old Ironsides," originates.

From the latter half of the century are Whistler's ephemeral *Nocturne in Blue and Silver: the Lagoon* and several works from the Boston School, notably Childe Hassan's gauzy *Boston Common at Twilight* and John Singer Sargent's provocatively spare *The Daughters of Edward Darley Boit*. The era's highlights, a trio of haunting seascapes painted by Winslow Homer shortly before his death, hang midway along the corridor, by the stairway to the upper galleries. **Early twentieth-century** American work is displayed in the last room on the left, where Edward Hopper's dour *Drugstore* hangs beside his uncharacteristically upbeat *Room in Brooklyn*; check out as well Maurice Prendergast's sentimental renderings of genteel life, *Sunset* and *Eight Bathers*.

Rounding out the wing, the **Lane Gallery**, tucked behind the stairs to the second floor and extending to the ground floor of the Huntington Building, is particularly strong on early to mid-twentieth century American works. The standout, Jackson Pollock's tense, semi-abstracted *Troubled Queen*, pre-dates his famous splatter-painting style and overlooks Alexander Calder's wire *Cow* stabile. The gallery's far walls count Georgia O'Keefe's majestically antlered *Deer's Skull with Pedernal* hanging kitty corner to Charles Sheeler's ironically titled *View of New York* – which you'll have to see for yourself to appreciate the joke. The exit between these last two works puts you in the Lower Rotunda of the Huntington Avenue Building (see p.110), face-to-face with underwhelming Boston School works; the most intriguing, William McGregor Paxton's oriental-themed *The New Necklace*, depicts a well-to-do young woman disinterestedly receiving the gift of a necklace.

European art collections

The stairs leading from within the American galleries to the second-floor **European** galleries put you smack in the middle of the collection. Like the first floor, it actually begins chronologically to the far right, in a room show-casing Dutch paintings from the **Northern Renaissance**, including two out-standing Rembrandt works, which emphasize his mastery of light and shadow, *Artist in his Studio* and *Old Man in Prayer*. A gruesome work by David Teniers the Younger, *Butcher's Shop*, hangs nearby. Several rooms of grandiose **Rococo** and **Romantic** work from the eighteenth and early nineteenth centuries lead off to the right of the central hallway; most interesting are Pannini's self-refer-ential *Picture Gallery with Views of Modern Rome*, Jean-Baptiste Greuze's erotic *Young Woman in White Hat*, Tiepolo's complex allegory, *Time Unveiling Truth*, and Turner's fire and brimstone *Slave Ship*. The rooms across the hall contain a good survey of **European modern art**, among them Henri Matisse's resplen-dent *Vase of Flowers*, Max Beckman's morbid *Still-Life with Three Skulls* – declared degenerate by the Nazis – and Braque's autumnal *Still Life with Peaches, Pears and Grapes*.

The culmination of the wing is the late-nineteenth-century collection, which begins with works by **early Impressionists**: Manet's *Execution of Emperor Maximilian* and Degas' *Edmond and Thérèse Morbilli* exhibit the stark use of color and interest in common subjects that characterized later French artists. The subsequent **Impressionist** room also contains Monet's heavily abstracted *Grainstack (Snow Effect)* and *Rouen Cathedral (Morning Effect)*, though his tongue-in-cheek *La Japonaise*, a riff on Parisian fashion trends, steals the show. Degas figures prominently here again with his agitated *Pagans and Degas' Father* and a bronze cast of the famous *14-Year Old Dancer*, as does Renoir, whose renowned *Dance at Bougival* looks onto *Psyche*, a delicate Rodin marble. The room's highlight, however, is its selection of **Post-Impressionist** art, best of which is Picasso's coldly cubist *Portrait of a Woman*, Van Gogh's richly hued *Enclosed Field with Ploughman* and *Houses at Auvers*, and Gauguin's bizarre relief wood sculpture, *Be in Love and you will be Happy*, in which the artist casts him-self seizing a woman's outstretched hand and ordering her to do as the title instructs.

The Koch Gallery

Halfway back along the main corridor, the **Koch Gallery**, which connects the West Wing with the second floor of the Huntington Building's rotunda, ranks among the museum's more spectacular showings. Designed to resemble a European palace hallway, its wood-inlaid ceilings cap walls hung two-high with dozens of portraits and landscapes of varying sizes. The southern wall finds largely **religious** pieces, three of which belong to El Greco, whose sparse *Fray Hortensio Felix Paravicino* contrasts sharply with Francesco del Cairo's *Herodias with the Head of St John the Baptist*, a macabre depiction that'll have you think-ing twice about tongue-piercing.

The opposite wall showcases predominantly **portraits** and **landscapes**, most emblematic of which is Velazquez's austere *Philip IV King of Spain*, dating from the artist's time as court painter. Another standout is Poussin's harmonious *Mars and Venus*, which provides an uplifting counterpoint to nearby Ruben's *Head of Cyrus Brought to Queen Tomyris*, an epic story of retribution in which his sons served as models for the Queen's pages. The doors at the far end put you in the upper Rotunda, under John Singer Sargent's superb murals (see overleaf).

Huntington Avenue Building

Connected to the West Wing by both the Lane and Koch galleries, the 500-foot granite-faced **Huntington Avenue Building** was the first building to open on this site in 1909. It's significantly gloomier than the West Wing addition, due to a lack of natural light that's been used to advantage to preserve the museum's impressive – and often overwhelming – collection of **ancient world** and **Asian** arts.

Ancient world galleries

A series of MFA-sponsored digs at Giza have made its **Egyptian collection** the standout of the museum's **ancient world** holdings, with eight galleries over two floors devoted to sculpture, pottery and sarcophagi ranging from prehistoric times to the Roman period. Best among the first-floor findings is the small gallery on **Egyptian Funerary Arts**, with gorgeous blue canopic jars, pristine shrouds and mummies – including one for a baby crocodile that likely served as a well-to-do family's pet.

While rather modest by comparison, the **Nubian collection** preceding the Funerary Arts gallery is nevertheless the largest of its kind outside Africa. Most of the pieces, such as the *Granite Stela of King Tanyidamani*, are funerary and actually quite similar to their Egyptian contemporaries. Upstairs are several imposing statues of King Mercerinus and Queen Kha-Merer-Nebty – notable for their strongly defined features – a colossal head of Ramses II, a strident King Anlamani from the Great Temple of Amen, and two fully reconstructed burial chambers of Old Kingdom royalty.

Not nearly as well represented, the **Classical** section is worth a glance mostly for its numerous Grecian urns, a fine Cycladic *Female Figure*, and several Etruscan sarcophagi with elaborately wrought narrative bas-reliefs.

Shapiro Rotunda

Between the second-floor Egyptian and Asian galleries is the outstanding **Shapiro Rotunda**, its dome and en-suite colonnade inset with multiple **murals** and **bas reliefs** by John Singer Sargent, who undertook the commission following his Boston Public Library work. Operating under the belief that mural painting – not portraiture – was the key to "artistic immortality," this installation certainly guaranteed the artist a lasting place in the MFA and some attending controversy to boot: when the ten-year project was completed shortly before Sargent's death in 1925, his Classical theme was falling out of vogue and his efforts were considered the "frivolous works of a failing master." Today, after a 1999 refurbishment that revitalized the works, his twenty murals and fourteen bas-reliefs – many of which depict debates between Classical and Roman Art using figures from Greek mythology – mask an often obtuse subject matter with a visual feast of fluid lines and color schemes.

Asian galleries

South of the rotunda, the **Asian galleries** – though they're among the best of their kind in the world – don't get near the attention they deserve, in all likelihood due to their awkward layout and hard-to-find galleries. Two in particular are worth ferreting out and none more so than the magnificent recreation of Japan's oldest surviving Buddhist temple, complete with gray stone floors, tapered wooden columns and coffered ceiling. Seven Buddhas dating to the ninth century recline inside the darkened temple; two of them represent the Buddha of Infinite Illumination. The antechambers contain a marvelous array of Japanese scrolls and

△ Seats at Fenway Park

screens, including ornamental munitions that date back to the thirteenth century. The woodblock print cityscapes of Ando Hiroshige, with their sharply delineated chromatic schemes, influenced Van Gogh, Gauguin and Whistler.

The **Chinese** section is equally superb, with scrolls decorated with spare naturalist abstractions as well as finely detailed graphic narratives, and several life-size statues; that of *Guanyin, Bodhisattva of Compassion* is one of the best-preserved pieces from the twelfth-century Jin dynasty. Also, don't leave before checking out the remarkable Chinese Furniture Gallery, a dull name for what is in fact a life-size staging of an upper-class Chinese house. Arranged beneath its pagoda-style roof are ornate examples of sixteenth- and seventeenth-century Chinese furniture, such as handsomely carved teak day beds, lacquered tables inlaid with birds and flowers, and household items like the strategy game Wiegi, in which the goal is to surround other players' pieces.

Isabella Stewart Gardner Museum

Less broad in its collection, but more distinctive and idiosyncratic than the MFA, is its neighbor, the **Isabella Stewart Gardner Museum**, at 280 The Fenway (Tues–Sun 11am–5pm; $10, $11 on weekends; Citypass accepted; ☎566-1401,

Eccentric Boston socialite Gardner collected and arranged more than 2500 objects in the four-story Fenway Court building she designed herself – right down to the marbleized paint technique she demonstrated to her workers atop a ladder – making this the country's only major museum that is entirely the creation of a single individual. It's a hodge-podge of works from around the globe, presented without much attention to period or style; Gardner's goal was to foster the love of art rather than its study, and she wanted the setting of her pieces to "fire the imagination."Your imagination does get quite a workout: there's art everywhere you look, with many of the objects unlabeled, placed in corners or above doorways, for an effect that is occasionally chaotic, but always striking and at times quite effective.

To get the most out of a visit, aim to join the hour-long Friday **tours** (free; 2.30pm), but get there early as only twenty people are allowed on a first-come-first-served basis. Alternatively, the **gift shop** sells a worthwhile **guide** ($5) detailing the location and ownership history of every piece on display.

The first floor

The Gardner is best known for its spectacular central courtyard styled after a fifteenth-century Venetian palace; the second-century Roman mosaic of Medusa at its center is fittingly surrounded by stone-faced statuary and fountains, and brightened up, year round, by flowering plants and trees. However, the museum's greatest success is the Spanish Cloister flanking the courtyard, a long, narrow corridor just through the main entrance which perfectly frames John Singer Sargent's ecstatic representation of Spanish dance, *El Jaleo*, and also contains fine seventeenth-century Mexican tiles, as well as Roman statuary and sarcophagi. A discreet door nearby leads to the **Monks Garden**, a Mediterranean outdoor garden bursting with palms and bougainvillaea.

The first floor's remaining side-rooms hold Gardner's small collection of **European modern art**: Degas' tiny *Madame Gaujelin* and Matisse's sun-streaked *The Terrace, St Tropez*, are in the **Yellow Room**, while Manet's stern portrait of his mother, *Madame Auguste Manet*, is in the appropriately dim **Blue Room**. The floor's final room, the **Macknight**, was Gardner's writing room when she was in residence and frequently doubled as John Singer Sargent's guestroom; atop one of the bookshelves is a poignant late-life portrait of his hostess, *Mrs Gardner in White*, that reveals the closeness of their friendship.

The second floor

Up a floor, what was once a first-rate array of **seventeenth-century Northern European** works was debilitated by a 1990 **art heist** in which two Rembrandts and a Vermeer were among ten canvases stolen.You can spot the missing artworks by their empty frames, an ingenious way of circumventing Gardner's will, which stipulated that every piece in the collection stay put, or else the entire kit and kaboodle was to be shipped to Paris for auction and the proceeds given to Harvard. Even with these glaring absences – the works have yet to be found – the second-floor **Dutch Room** retains Rembrandt's early *Self-Portrait* across from Rubens' heavily ornamented *Thomas Howard, Earl of Arundel*.

The magnificent **Tapestry Room** next door is hung with rich mid-six-teenth-century Brussels tapestries, including the *Abraham Series*, illustrating the life of the prominent Bible figure; it's a sumptuous backdrop for the weekend chamber orchestra concerts held here from September to May (call ☎566-1401 for details). The **Short Gallery** extending north from the Tapestry

Room is devoted primarily to **etchings**, many of which hang on hinged wooden panels; one bears a sign noting the theft of four Degas from its spot – his chalk *Racehorse* remains behind it, at the bottom of the rear panel. Rounding out the floor, the colorful **Raphael Room** finds its namesake's officious *Portrait of Tommaso Inghirami*, the Vatican's rotund chief librarian, above his early *Lamentation over the Death of Christ*, which sits, unassumingly, on the desk below. The nearby walls find a couple of Botticellis as well, most notably his highly stylized *Tragedy of Lucretia*.

The third floor

Gardner had an affinity for **altars**, and her collection contains several, cobbled together from various religious artifacts. A dramatic concentration of these surrounds the third-floor stairwell and includes a medieval stone carving of the beheading of John the Baptist, a particularly agonized twelfth-century wood carving of *Christ from a Deposition Group* from Spain, and Giovanni Minelli's maudlin altar painting, *Entombment of Christ*. Perhaps the most notable sacred art on display, however, is in the **chapel**, also on the third floor, which incorporates sixteenth-century Italian choirstalls and stained glass from Milan and Soissons cathedrals, as well as assorted religious figurines, candlesticks and crucifixes, all surrounding Paul-César Helleu's moody representation of the *Interior of the Abbey Church of Saint-Denis*.

Between the stairwell and the chapel is the **Gothic Room**, a somberly decorated chamber whose chief attraction is John Singer Sargent's controversial life-size *Portrait of Isabella Gardner* that prompted the public to rename her "Saint Isabella" – and the sobriquet wasn't intended as a compliment. Completing the third floor, the **Titian** and **Veronese rooms** comprise a strong showing of **Italian Renaissance** and **Baroque** work, including Titian's famous *Europa*, and Crivelli's Mannerist *St George and the Dragon*. Also in the Veronese room are four minute Whistlers, including *Little Note in Yellow and Gold*, yet another portrait of the museum's doyenne, albeit a softer and more feminine version.

Allston-Brighton and Brookline

There's little doing west of the Fenway, just a few largely residential areas which seem more or less extensions of Boston and Cambridge. In fact, **ALLSTON-BRIGHTON**, a triangular community that spreads south from the Charles River down to Beacon Street, was originally conceived as a Cambridge adjunct. Nowadays, it's a funkier community than its neighbor across the river, with laid-back restaurants, a plethora of Jewish delis and bakeries – hit up *Kupel's*, at 421 Harvard St, for exceptional bagels – and innovative shops crammed into a couple of blocks along Harvard Street. It hardly ranks as a destination in its own right, however.

Marginally more interesting is the affluent town of **BROOKLINE**, where much the focus of activity is around bustling **Coolidge Corner**, at Beacon and Harvard streets. Of note in these parts is the **Coolidge Corner Theater**, at 290 Harvard St, a refurbished art-house cinema sustained by the many students living in the area. The main draw, though, is the nearby **John F. Kennedy National Historic Site**, at 83 Beals St (Wed–Sun 10am–4.30pm; $2), which preserves the unremarkable home where JFK happened to be born on May 29, 1917. Inside, a narrated voiceover by the late president's mother, Rose, adds some spice to the plain, roped-off rooms. To get to the heart of Brookline take the Green Line's C branch to Coolidge Corner or D branch to Brookline Village.

It's a bit of hike to the last of Brookline's attractions; along the suburb's southern fringe is the **Frederick Law Olmsted National Historic Site**, at 99 Warren St (Fri–Sun 10am–4.30pm; free; ⓦwww.nps.gov/frla). Known as Fairsted, this expansive house doubled as Olmsted's family home and office. Though almost one million landscape schemes are archived here, ranging from his work on Yosemite Valley to New York's Central Park, it's a dry retrospective that will appeal mostly to Olmsted buffs. That said, the surrounding grounds are (unsurprisingly) quite idyllic; you could hardly ask for better strolling territory.

8

The southern districts

The parts of Boston that most visitors see – downtown, Beacon Hill, Back Bay and the North End – actually only cover a small portion of the city's geography. To the south of the city center lies a vast spread of residential neighborhoods known collectively as the **southern districts**, including **South Boston**, **Dorchester**, **Roxbury** and **Jamaica Plain**, whose oft-downtrodden character can come as quite a shock after Boston's polished colonial center. Though they do offer a more complete picture of urban life in Boston, they're unlikely to divert your interest for long (or at all), especially if you're short on time. Nevertheless, JFK-junkies will be rewarded by Dorchester's worthwhile **John Fitzgerald Kennedy Library and Museum**, and almost anyone should be able to take delight in Jamaica Plain's superb **Arnold Arboretum**, with its world-renowned array of bonsai trees; the two combine to make a terrific half-day outing, and are easily accessible by the **T**.

Once rural areas dotted with the swank summer resort homes of Boston's privileged, in the late nineteenth century the southern districts became populated by middle- and working-class families pushed from the increasingly crowded downtown area. Three-story rowhouses soon replaced mansions, and the moniker "streetcar suburbs" – after the trolley that debuted in 1899 and connected these once remote areas with downtown – was coined as a catch-all for the newly redefined neighborhoods. In the years immediately following World War II, each was hit to varying degrees by economic decline, and the middle class moved farther afield, leaving the districts to the mostly immigrant and blue-collar communities that remain today. Personal safety has always been an issue here, and the streets can feel desolate by day and dodgier still by night. The exception, Jamaica Plain, has become more gentrified in recent years, and its main drag, Centre Street, has a pleasant, laid-back vibe and some good lunch options.

South Boston

Across Fort Point Channel from downtown and east into Boston Harbor lies **South Boston**, affectionately referred to as "Southie" by its large Irish-

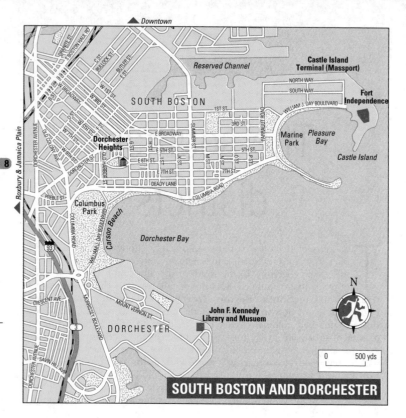

SOUTH BOSTON AND DORCHESTER

American population. Originally a peninsula separated from Boston proper by waterways, it was connected to the city by bridge in 1805, and throughout the nineteenth century expanded geographically, via landfill, and in population, thanks to a steady influx of Irish immigrants. South Boston remained solidly blue-collar and Irish until just after World War II, when it was particularly hard hit by recession, and its makeup began to change. Despite some subsequent economic revival – especially in the shipbuilding industry – it is better known today for tensions between its old-timers and the newer communities of African-Americans, Hispanics, and gays that have moved into the area. Indeed, the radical AIDS Coalition to Unleash Power met with staunch resistance when the group petitioned in 1994 to march in Southie's annual St Patrick's Day parade; the battle went to the Supreme Court, which upheld the exclusion. To be fair, though, South Bostonians showed a different side in a less publicized incident shortly afterward, when the Ku Klux Klan marched in the area and were met with jeers and protests from local residents.

The area's Celtic heritage is quite evident on the main commercial boulevard, **Broadway**, where seemingly every laundry, convenience store, and even Chinese restaurant has a sign plastered with shamrocks. You'll also find an unsurprising profusion of Irish bars and pubs along West Broadway that make up in enthusiasm for the mother country what they lack in authenticity. The *Blackthorn*, at no. 471, comes closest to the real feel of an Irish pub.

Castle Island

South Boston narrows to an end in Boston Harbor on a 22-acre strip of land called **Castle Island** (even though it's actually a peninsula), off the terminus of William J. Day Boulevard, a favorite leisure spot for Southie residents and, in fact, for many Bostonians. Park and beaches cover the spit, though you wouldn't want to swim offshore, since Boston Harbor's waters, while cleaner than in the past, are far from non-toxic – and they're freezing, to boot. However, the views of downtown and the harbor are spectacular, best appreciated along the walkway known as the "Sugar Bowl," which follows along a narrow peninsula that curls out into the water. Closer to the mainland, the island's lone snack bar, *Sullivan's*, is a local institution serving tasty portions of seafood and grilled fare at amazingly cheap prices.

Fort Independence

Fort Independence (Sat–Sun noon–3.30pm; free; Broadway **T**, then bus #9 or #11), a stout granite edifice just north of Castle Island, was one of the earliest redoubts in the Americas, originally established in 1634, though it has been rebuilt several times since. Today, what remains is a skeleton of its 1801 version, and its slate-gray walls aren't much to look at from the outside. However, the ranger-led weekend tours provide some decent history and folklore about the dank interior corridors. One such story recalls a prisoner held here in the early 1800s for killing another man in a duel. One night, the victim's friends supposedly broke into the prison and chained the assassin into an alcove, then built a brick wall around him and left him to die. A young lawyer in the area by the name of Edgar Allan Poe apparently heard the rumor and used it as the basis for his story, "The Cask of Amontillado."

Dorchester

Occupying the southeast corner of the city, **Dorchester** lies beneath South Boston. Originally built on the narrow neck of land that connected Boston to the mainland, it's now a fairly unlovely and uninteresting lower- and middle-class residential neighborhood. North Dorchester was from its earliest days a center of trade and remains a largely industrial area today. South Dorchester has seen more turbulence over the years: once a coveted spot for elite country homes, it followed the streetcar suburb pattern of the southern districts, and remained relatively affluent until after World War II, when the middle class left, property values plummeted, and crime and unemployment rose. Today, both parts of Dorchester are home to a broad ethnic mix, notably Irish, Haitians, Vietnamese, Caribbeans and African-Americans. Save for the **John F. Kennedy Museum and Library**, there's not much to see, and parts – especially in South Dorchester – are downright unsafe.

Dorchester Heights Monument

At the convergence of South Boston and Dorchester rises the incline of **Dorchester Heights** (Broadway **T** to #11 bus to G St stop), a neighborhood of three-story rowhouses whose northernmost point, Thomas Park, is crowned by a marble Georgian revival **monument** commemorating George Washington's bloodless purge of the Brits from Boston. After the Continental Army had held the British under siege in the city for just over a year, Washington wanted to put an end to the whole thing. On March 4, 1776, he amassed all the artillery he could get his hands on and placed it on the towering peak of Dorchester Heights, so the tired Redcoats could get a good look at the patriots' firepower. Intimidated, they swiftly left Boston – for good.

The park – generally empty and pristinely kept – still commands the same sweeping views of Boston and its southern communities that it did during the Revolutionary War. The best vista is from the top of the monument itself, though it's only open sporadically (July–Aug Wed 4–8pm, Sat & Sun 10am–4pm; free), and anyway is quite a bit out of the way from any other major points of interest.

John Fitzgerald Kennedy Library and Museum

As with all presidential museums, the **John Fitzgerald Kennedy Library and Museum**, at Columbia Point (daily 9am–5pm; $8; CityPass accepted; ☎929-4500 or 1-877/616-4599, ⓦwww.cs.umb.edu/jfklibrary; JFK/UMass **T**; free shuttle every twenty minutes), is faced with the difficult task of extolling a president and icon's virtues while maintaining a veneer of scholarly objectivity. It performs the task with mixed results; even so, the **museum** still stands out by providing a fascinating glimpse into the culture of a recent era, while being spectacularly situated in a stunning, curvilinear I.M. Pei-designed building – allegedly the architect's favorite commission – overlooking Boston Harbor. The **library**, meanwhile, is not open to the public, only to researchers with specific requests, and holds JFK's papers – some 8.4 million pages in all – from his curtailed term in the Oval Office. Oddly enough, the museum is also the repository for Ernest Hemingway's original manuscripts; Kennedy helped Hemingway's wife get the papers out of Cuba following her husband's 1961 suicide (call ☎929-4523 for an appointment to see them).

The main presentation at the museum opens with a well-done eighteen-minute film covering Kennedy's political career through the 1960 Democratic National Convention, peppered with soundbites from Kennedy himself. Much of the remaining displays cover the presidential campaign of 1960 and highlights of the truncated Kennedy administration against a backdrop of stylized recreations of his campaign headquarters, the CBS studio that hosted the first televised presidential debate, and the main White House corridor. The campaign exhibits are most interesting for their television and radio ads, which illustrate the squeaky-clean self-image America possessed at that time. Several features on JFK and the media unabashedly play up the contrast between Kennedy's telegenic charisma and Richard Nixon's jowly surliness, citing it as a key factor in JFK's victory over Tricky Dick. The section on the Kennedy administration is more serious, animated by a 22-minute film on the Cuban Missile Crisis that well evokes the tension of the event, if exaggerating Kennedy's heroics. Most sobering is the darkened hallway towards the end where a televised announcement of his assassination plays in a continuous loop. Lighter fare is on display in the Jackie O. exhibits, which trace her life from early debutante days to her status as First Lady-cum-popular icon.

The best part of the museum is actually outside of the exhibition chambers: a 115-foot-high **atrium** overlooking the harbor, with a gigantic American flag suspended above modest inscriptions bearing some of Kennedy's more memorable quotations – affecting enough to move even the most jaded JFK critic.

Roxbury

Roxbury has borne the brunt of being one of Boston's most maligned neighborhoods. Occupying most of south-central Boston below the South End and between Dorchester and Jamaica Plain, this once pastoral region was one of the city's most coveted addresses in the seventeenth and eighteenth centuries, when wealthy families built sumptuous country houses here. It wasn't really until the 1950s that the area hit hard times, and the urban blight has left its scars, despite an ongoing attempt to restore some of the impressive, if neglected, properties and attract former South Enders who've been pushed out by that neighborhood's sky-rocketing real-estate prices. While it is nowhere as dangerous as the rougher sections of bigger cities like LA, visitors still may feel unwelcome or unsafe in parts, especially at night. By day, the area holds some historical interest around **Dudley Square**, where a couple of African-American institutions have been preserved, but the main attraction here, especially if you have children in tow, is the **Franklin Park Zoo**, in yet another of Olmsted's green spaces.

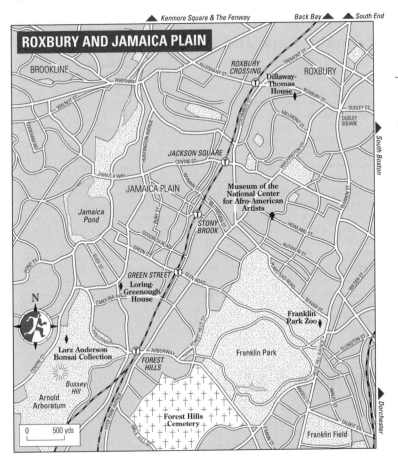

Kenmore Square & The Fenway ▲   Back Bay ▲   ▲ South End

ROXBURY AND JAMAICA PLAIN

BROOKLINE

ROXBURY CROSSING

Dillaway-Thomas House

ROXBURY

RIVERWAY

ALLEGHANY ST.

TREMONT ST.

ROXBURY ST.

DUDLEY ST.

DUDLEY SQUARE

WALNUT ST.

MILLMONT ST.

SNOWHAM RD.

HUNTINGTON AVENUE

WASHINGTON ST.

JACKSON SQUARE

CENTRE ST.

JAMAICA WAY

JAMAICA PLAIN

Museum of the National Center for Afro-American Artists

Jamaica Pond

BURR ST.

WYMAN ST.

BEETHOVEN ST.

HOWLAND ST.

STONY BROOK

GOODRICH ROAD

GREEN ST.

RUTHVEN ST.

POND ST.

ELIOT ST.

GREEN STREET

GLEN ROAD

Loring-Greenough House

N

CAROLINA AVE.

FOREST HILLS ST.

HALSTEAD ROAD

SEAVER ST.

WILDER ST.

Franklin Park Zoo

ARBORWAY

ELLINGTON ST.

BLUE HILL AVENUE

Larz Anderson Bonsai Collection

ARBORWAY

FOREST HILLS

Franklin Park

CENTRE ST.

HYDE PARK AVENUE

Bussey Hill

ANGELL ST.

WALK HILL ST.

WALES ST.

Arnold Arboretum

Forest Hills Cemetery

Franklin Field

TALBOT St.

E. MAIN ST.

South Boston ▶

Dorchester ▶

0   500 yds

Dudley Square and around

Roxbury's commercial center is **Dudley Square** – the intersection of Dudley and Washington streets – which is little more than the usual mix of shops and convenience stores. If you're in the area, you may want to check out the **Dillaway-Thomas House**, at 183 Roxbury St between Dudley Square and the Roxbury Crossing **T** stop (Wed–Fri 10am–4pm, Sat–Sun noon–5pm; donation requested), a structure built in 1750 as a parsonage and subsequently used as a fort in the Revolutionary War. Its first floor is remarkably well-preserved, featuring many details of its original construction, while the upstairs has rotating exhibits of African- and African-American-themed art; the best part, though, may be the serene apple orchard surrounding it.

Further south, the **Museum of the National Center for Afro-American Artists**, at 300 Walnut Ave (Tues–Sun 1–5pm; $4; ☎442-8614), housed in the Victorian Gothic "Oak Bend" mansion, has a decent collection of African-American visual art from throughout the twentieth century, highlighted by some richly textured woodcuts by Wilmer Jennings and Hale Woodruff, as well as Edward McCluney's *Nine American Masters*, depicting the likes of Toni Morrison, Alice Walker and jazz great Ella Fitzgerald.

Franklin Park and the zoo

The southernmost link in the Emerald Necklace, **Franklin Park** was one of Olmsted's proudest accomplishments when it was completed, due to the sheer size of the place, and its scale is indeed astounding – 527 acres of green space, with countless trails for hikers, bikers, and walkers leading through the hills and thickly forested areas. That's about it, though, as much of the park has unfortunately become overgrown from years of halfhearted upkeep. It's quite easy to get lost among all the greenery and forget that you're in the middle of a city, though this is perhaps not such a hot idea – the park borders some of Boston's more dangerous areas, and the place can feel quite threatening, especially at night.

The **Franklin Park Zoo**, on the far eastern edge of Franklin Park (April–Sept Mon–Fri 10am–5pm, Sat–Sun 10am–6pm; Oct–March daily 10am–4pm; $9.50, children $5; ☎442-2002, ⓦwww.zoonewengland.com; Forest Hills **T**) is much like any other zoo, and is really only a must-see if you're traveling with kids, who'll definitely get a kick out of the Children's Zoo, where they're allowed to pet and feed rhinos and the like. Adults may enjoy the decent array of exotic fauna, much of which is contained in the African Tropical Forest, an impressively recreated savanna that's the largest indoor open-space zoo design in North America, housing gorillas, monkeys and pygmy hippos. More fun is had at Bird's World, a charming relic from the days of Edwardian zoo design: there's a huge, ornate wrought-iron cage you can walk through while birds fly overhead.

Jamaica Plain

Diminutive **Jamaica Plain** – "JP" in local parlance – is one of Boston's more successfully integrated neighborhoods, with a good mix of students, immigrants, and working-class families crowded into its relatively cheap apartments. Located between Roxbury and the section of the Emerald Necklace known as the Muddy River Improvement, the area's activity centers around, appropriately, **Centre Street**, which holds some inventive, and remarkably inexpensive, cafés and restaurants (see p.167 and p.185). While you might call in at the historic estate just off the street or indulge at one of those eating establishments, the more likely bet is to head straight for Jamaica Plain's star attraction, the **Arnold Arboretum**, on its southwestern edge.

Loring-Greenough House

At Centre Street's foot stands the fusty **Loring-Greenough House**, 12 South St (June–Aug Tues 10am–noon, Sat–Sun noon–3pm, Sept–May Tues & Sat 10am–noon; $3 suggested donation; ☎524-3158, ⓦwww.lghouse.org; Forest Hills **T** or Back Bay **T** to bus #39), built in 1760 for Loyalist Commodore Joshua Loring and confiscated by colonial troops in 1775 for use as a Revolutionary War hospital. Restored to private use in 1780, the house was occupied by lawyer David Stoddard Greenough's family until 1926, when it was designated a historic site. The house's significance – as the last of JP's country estates from that period – does more for it than its refurbished chambers, whose highlights are unrelated exhibits of jeweled handbags and ornate calling-card cases collected by the women of the Tuesday Club, the organization that manages the house.

Arnold Arboretum

The 265-acre Harvard University-run **Arnold Arboretum**, at 125 Arborway (daily March–Oct dawn to dusk, Nov–Feb Mon–Fri dawn to dusk, Sat–Sun 10am–2pm; $1 donation requested; ☎524-1718, ⓦwww.arboretum .harvard.edu; Forest Hills **T**), is the most spectacular link in the Emerald Necklace and the southern districts' only must-see sight. Its collection of over 14,000 trees, vines, shrubs and flowers has benefited from more than 100 years of both careful grooming and ample funding, and is now one of the finest in North America. The plants are arranged along a series of paths populated by runners and dog-walkers as well as serious botanists, though it certainly doesn't require any expert knowledge to enjoy the grounds.

The array of Asian species – considered one of the largest and most diverse outside Asia – is highlighted by the **Larz Anderson Bonsai Collection**, brilliantly concentrated along the Chinese Path walkway at the center of the park. Although the staff does an impressive job of keeping the grounds looking fabulous year-round, it's best to visit in spring, when crabapples, lilacs and magnolias complement the greenery with dazzling chromatic schemes. "Lilac Sunday," the third Sunday in May (see "Festivals and events," p.228), sees the Arboretum at its most vibrant (and busiest), when its collection of lilacs – the second largest in the US – is in full bloom. One of the best ways to appreciate the scope of the place is to make your way to the top of 198-foot **Bussey Hill** in the Arboretum's center, where you can overlook the grounds in their impressive entirety, and, on a clear day, catch a great view of downtown Boston besides.

Cambridge

J ust across the Charles River from Boston, **CAMBRIDGE** has the feel of an overgrown college town. Highlighted by two of the most illustrious institutions of higher learning in the country, it's altogether more unbuttoned and laidback than its big city counterpart, and populated by a younger and more bohemian type of resident, for the most part. Those

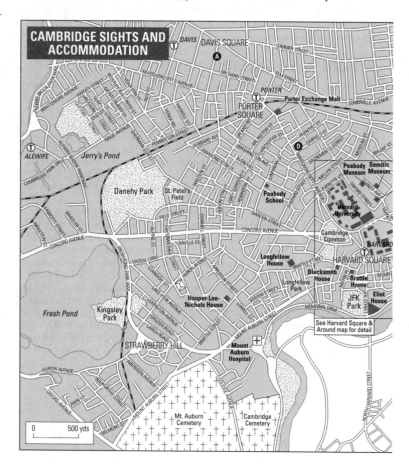

denizens, from clean-cut college students and grungy punks to vendors purveying braided handbags and street artists performing magic tricks, manage to support a buzzing streetlife and café culture that can either be seen as a refreshing change from provincial Boston, or just a continuation of it. Because for many Cantabridgians there need not be life past the Charles: everything they need is here.

No different from central Boston, a walk down Cambridge's colonial-era brick sidewalks and narrow, crooked roads, takes you past plaques and monuments honoring literati and revolutionaries who lived and worked in the area – some hailing from as early as the seventeenth century. There's the congestion, diversity and idiosyncratic neighborhoods typical of most urban centers. And as in any modern city, Cambridge has its own share of starched, standoffish business-people, a growing homeless population, and numerous meeting points where busloads of visitors get dropped off for a quick poke around. Nevertheless, it manages – perhaps even better than Boston itself – an exhilarating mix of colonial past and urban present; the extensive range of residents and activities, and the sheer energy that pervades its classrooms and coffeehouses make Cambridge an essential stopover while traveling in the area.

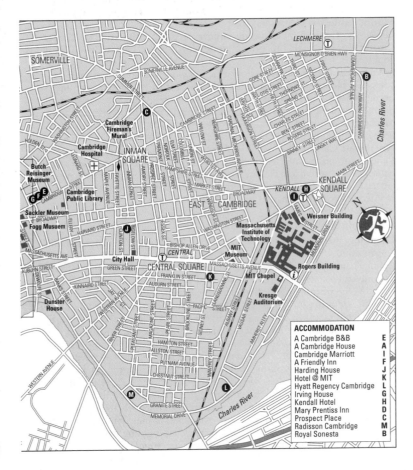

ACCOMMODATION

A Cambridge B&B	E
A Cambridge House	A
Cambridge Marriott	I
A Friendly Inn	F
Harding House	J
Hotel @ MIT	K
Hyatt Regency Cambridge	L
Irving House	G
Kendall Hotel	H
Mary Prentiss Inn	D
Prospect Place	C
Radisson Cambridge	M
Royal Sonesta	B

Geographically, Cambridge resembles a bow tie, with Harvard Square forming the knot. On its southern border is the sinuous Charles River, with Boston on the opposite bank, while the concave northern side is shared with the large, mostly residential town of **Somerville**, popular with locals for its restaurant and café scene centering on bohemian **Davis Square**. Cambridge proper, meanwhile, is loosely organized around a series of squares – actually confluences of streets that are the focus of each area's commercial activity. By far the most important of these is **Harvard Square**, which radiates out from the **T** stop along Massachusetts Avenue, JFK Street and Brattle Street. Roughly coterminous with Harvard Square is **Harvard University**; together, these two areas make up the cultural and academic heart of Cambridge. This is where people converge to check out Ivy League academia, historical monuments, a lively coffeehouse-and-bookstore scene, and a disgruntled counterculture. Its total area – only a single square mile – is small in comparison with the entirety of Cambridge, but the density of attractions here make it one part of town not to be missed.

West from Harvard is **Old Cambridge**, the clean, impeccably kept colonial heart of the city, and easily accessible from Harvard Square; sights here include impressive mansions – most notably the **Longfellow House** – and peaceful **Mount Auburn Cemetery**. East from here, on the other side of the University, **Central** and **Inman squares** represent the core of **Central Cambridge**, a neighborhood far more down-to-earth than its collegiate counterpart. It's no coincidence that this working-class atmosphere continues in **East Cambridge**, as well – both areas grew up around industry rather than academia. However, East Cambridge draws most of its modern-day interest from the **Massachusetts Institute of Technology (MIT)**, one of the world's premier science and research institutions. Home to peculiar architecture and an excellent museum, MIT spreads out below **Kendall Square**, which itself is home to a cluster of stalwart high-tech companies. Finally, above Harvard, **Northwest Cambridge** is an ill-defined corner of the city, a catchall term for some of the places not identified with its more happening districts – and as such is easily overlooked. Despite some good shopping and decent restaurants, especially along **Huron Avenue** and around **Porter Square**, the area is more of interest to residents than to travelers.

Some history

Cambridge began inauspiciously in 1630, when a group of English immigrants from Charlestown founded **New Towne** village on the narrow, swampy banks of the Charles River. These Puritans hoped New Towne would become an ideal religious community; to that end, they founded a college in 1636 for the purpose of training clergy. Two years later, the college took its name in honor of a local minister, **John Harvard**, who bequeathed his library and half his estate to the nascent institution. New Towne was eventually renamed Cambridge in honor of the English university where many of its figureheads were educated, and became one of the largest publishing centers in the New World after the arrival of the printing press in the seventeenth century. Its university and printing industry established Cambridge as an important center of intellectual activity and political thought, a status that became entrenched in the city over the course of the United States' turbulent early history – particularly during the late eighteenth century when the population was sharply divided between the many artisan and farmer sympathizers of the revolution and the moneyed Tory minority. When fighting began, the Tories were driven from their mansions on modern-day Brattle Street (then called

"Tory Row"), and their place was taken by Cambridge intelligentsia and prominent revolutionaries.

The area remained unincorporated until 1846, when the Massachusetts Legislature granted a city charter linking Old Cambridge (the Harvard Square area) and industrial East Cambridge as a single municipality. Initially, there was friction between these two very different parts of Cambridge; in 1855, citizens from each area unsuccessfully petitioned for the two regions to be granted separate civic status. The failure of these efforts was followed by a thaw in relations which has resulted in a more cohesive community, though each area retains a distinctive character. The late nineteenth and early twentieth centuries brought substantial growth to the town. A large immigrant population was drawn to opportunity in the industrial and commercial sectors of East Cambridge, while academics increasingly sought out Harvard, whose reputation continued to swell, and the Massachusetts Institute of Technology, which moved here from Boston in 1916. By the 1960s, Cambridge had earned the name "Moscow on the Charles" due to its unabashedly Communist character; today, leftist politics still rule the roost, though Communism lives on mostly via tongue-in-cheek bar names. Whatever its political leanings, the fact that half of Cambridge's near-100,000 residents are university affiliates ensures its legacy as one of America's intellectual strongholds.

Harvard Square and around

The Harvard **T** station marks Cambridge's epicenter, opening up onto **Harvard Square**, where a moody youth brigade stews in the shadow of the Harvard Yard buildings. A small **tourism kiosk** run by the Cambridge Tourism Office (daily 9am–5pm; ☎441-2884 or 1-800/862-5678, ⍟www.cambridge-usa.com) faces the station exit, but more of the action is in the adjacent sunken area known as **The Pit**, a triage center for fashion victims of alternative culture. Disgruntled teens spend entire days sitting here admiring each other's green hair and body piercings while the homeless (and some of the teens) hustle for change and other handouts. This is also the focal point of the **street music scene**, where folk diva Tracy Chapman (a graduate from Tufts University, in nearby Somerville) and country maven Bonnie Raitt (a Radcliffe alumna) both got their starts. The square reaches its most frenetic state on Friday and Saturday nights and Sunday afternoons, when all the elements converge – crowds mill about, evangelical demonstrators engage in shouting matches with angry youths, and magicians, acrobats and bands perform on every corner.

Old Burying Ground

Facing Harvard Square to the north along Massachusetts Avenue is one of Cambridge's first cemeteries, the **Old Burying Ground**, whose style and grounds have scarcely changed since the seventeenth century. You're supposed to apply to the sexton of nearby **Christ Church** for entry, but if the gate at the path beside the simple, graywashed eighteenth-century church is open (as it frequently is), you can enter so long as you're respectful of the grounds. The epitaphs have an archaic ring to them ("Here lyes..."), and the stone grave markers are adorned in a style blending Puritan austerity and medieval superstition: inscriptions praise the simple piety of the staunchly Christian deceased,

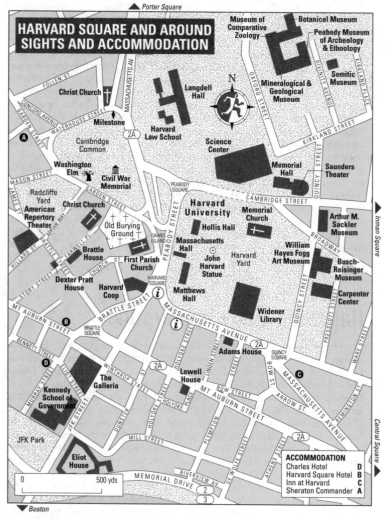

HARVARD SQUARE AND AROUND SIGHTS AND ACCOMMODATION

▲ Porter Square

Museum of Comparative Zoology
Botanical Museum
Peabody Museum of Archeology & Ethnology
Semitic Museum
Mineralogical & Geological Museum
Langdell Hall
Christ Church
Milestone
Harvard Law School
Science Center
Cambridge Common
Washington Elm
Civil War Memorial
Memorial Hall
Saunders Theater
Radcliffe Yard
American Repertory Theater
Christ Church
Old Burying Ground
Harvard University
Memorial Church
Arthur M. Sackler Museum
Hollis Hall
Brattle House
Massachusetts Hall
John Harvard Statue
Harvard Yard
William Hayes Fogg Art Museum
Busch-Reisinger Museum
First Parish Church
Dexter Pratt House
Harvard Coop
Matthews Hall
Widener Library
Carpenter Center
Adams House
Lowell House
The Galleria
Kennedy School of Government
JFK Park
Eliot House

▶ Inman Square
▶ Central Square

0   500 yds

MEMORIAL DRIVE

▼ Boston

ACCOMMODATION
Charles Hotel   **D**
Harvard Square Hotel   **B**
Inn at Harvard   **C**
Sheraton Commander   **A**

but are surrounded by death's-heads carved to ward off evil spirits. Its most famous occupants include several of Harvard's first presidents as well as two black veterans of the Revolutionary War, Cato Stedman and Neptune Frost. Be sure to check out the **milestone** at the northeast corner of the cemetery, found just inside the gate, whose two-and-a-half-centuries-old inscription is still readily visible. Originally set to mark the then-daunting distance of eight miles to Boston, the letters A.I. identify the stone's maker, Abraham Ireland.

Dawes Island

A triangular traffic island squeezed into the intersection of Massachusetts Avenue, Garden Street and Peabody Street, **Dawes Island** is anything but bucolic – the wedge of concrete serves as Harvard Square's central bus stop.

What import it has as a tourist attraction stems from its namesake, the patriot who rode to alert residents that the British were marching to Lexington and Concord on April 19, 1775 – the *other* patriot, that is, William Dawes. While Longfellow opted to commemorate Paul Revere's midnight ride instead – as have most history classes – the citizens of Cambridge must have appreciated poor Dawes' contribution just as much. Bronze hoofmarks in the sidewalk mark the event, and several placards provide information on the history of the Harvard Square/Old Cambridge area.

Cambridge Common

Cambridge Common, a trapezoidal patch of green located between Massachusetts Avenue, Garden Street and Waterhouse Street, has been a site for recreation and community events since Cambridge's earliest settlers first used it as a cow pasture. Tourists flock to the common for its historical interest, but Cantabridgians congregate in its wide green spaces for Frisbee and sunbathing – although after dusk it can be an altogether lonelier, and somewhat dodgier, place.

Early Harvard commencements took place here, as did public debates and training exercises for the local militia. You can retrace a portion of the old **Charlestown–Watertown path**, along which the British Redcoats beat a sheepish retreat to Watertown during the Revolutionary War, and which still transects the park from east to west. A broad range of **statuary** dots the southeast corner of the park, and you can't miss the towering monument to Lincoln and other Civil War dead, which all but overshadows the recently added tableau of two emaciated figures nearby, wrought as an unsettling memorial to the Irish Potato Famine.

The most prominent feature on the common, however, is the revered **Washington Elm**, under which it's claimed George Washington took command of the Continental Army. The elm is at the southern side of the park, almost facing the intersection of Garden Street and Appian Way, and is accompanied by a predictable wealth of commemorative objects: a cannon captured from the British when they evacuated Boston, a statue of Washington standing in the shade of the beloved tree, and monuments to two Polish army captains hired to lead revolutionary forces – excessive rewards, really, for mercenaries. What the memorials don't tell you is that the city of Cambridge cut down the original Washington Elm in 1946 when it began to obstruct traffic; it stood at the common's southwest corner, near the intersection of Mason and Garden streets. The present tree is only the offspring of that tree, raised from one of its branches. To further confuse the issue, the Daughters of the American Revolution erected a monument commemorating the south*east* corner of the park as the spot where Washington did his historic thing. And recently, American historians have adduced evidence strongly suggesting that Washington never commissioned the troops on the common at all, but rather in Wadsworth House at Harvard Yard.

Radcliffe Yard

Just across Garden Street from Cambridge Common is a less crowded park, **Radcliffe Yard**, originally the center of Radcliffe College, established in 1878 to give women access to (then exclusively male) Harvard. The two colleges merged in the 1970s, and since then Radcliffe has functioned primarily as a resource center for women in higher education. The yard itself is a picturesque, impeccably preserved quadrangle; enclosed by brick buildings and Ionic columns, it's dotted with fountains and pathways, making it a great place for a summer picnic or stroll.

JFK Street

The stretch of JFK Street below Harvard Square holds more of the city's many public spaces, certainly the least of which is **Winthrop Square**, site of the original New Towne marketplace and since converted into a lackluster park. Cross the park and walk down Winthrop Street to the right to get a sense of the sloping topography and narrow street design of early Cambridge. Just to the right of the nightclub *House of Blues* (see review p.196) is a **stone wall** that was built along the original shoreline of the Charles River.

John F. Kennedy Park, located where JFK Street meets Memorial Drive, was only finished in the late 1980s, making it an infant among Harvard Square's venerable spots. Though certainly not the first pious shrine to Boston's favorite modern son, this one is cleaner and more spacious than most other parks in the area. The **memorial** to Kennedy in its center is worth a look for its unusual lack of grandeur; it's a low, pink-granite pyramid surrounded by a moat, covered constantly but imperceptibly by a thin film of flowing water.

Harvard Yard and the university

The transition from Harvard Square to **Harvard Yard** – the proper center of the university – is brief and dramatic: in a matter of only several feet, the buzz of car traffic and urban life gives way to grassy lawns and towering oaks, pervaded by an aura of Ivy League intellectualism. The atmosphere is more mythological than real, however, as the yard's narrow, haphazard footpaths are constantly plied by preoccupied students and numerous camera-clicking tour groups, who often make the place seem more like an amusement park than a staid university campus. You can join the hullabaloo by taking a free 45-minute guided tour from the Holyoke Center, 1350 Massachusetts Ave (June–Aug Mon–Sat 10am, 11.15am, 2pm & 3.15pm, Sun 1.30pm & 3pm; Sept–May Mon–Fri 10am & 2pm, Sat 2pm; ⓦwww.news.harvard.edu/guide), where you can also pick up maps and brochures detailing everything Harvard-related.

The Old Yard

The most common entrance to Harvard Yard is the one directly across from Harvard Square proper, which leads by **Massachusetts Hall** (holding the office of the university president) to the **Old Yard**, a large, rectangular area dating from 1636, when it was created as a grazing field for university livestock. In front of stark, symmetrical, slate-gray **University Hall** is the yard's trademark icon, the **John Harvard statue**, source of the oft-told story of the "three lies" (it misdates the college's founding; erroneously identifies John Harvard as the college's founder; and isn't really a likeness of the man at all). While it's a popular spot for visitors to take pictures, male college students prize the statue as a prime spot to urinate in public; anyone managing to pull off the feat is granted a certain honorary status among students on campus – as a result, there are now about twenty surveillance cameras trained on the site, acting as a deterrent.

Along the northwest border of the yard is stout **Hollis Hall**, the dormitory where Henry David Thoreau lived as an undergraduate. The architectural contrast between modest Hollis, which dates from 1763, and its grandiose southern neighbor, **Matthews Hall**, built around a hundred years later, mirrors Harvard's transition from a quiet training ground for ministers to a wealthy, cosmopolitan university. The **indentations** in Hollis' front steps also hold some historical interest: students used to warm their rooms by heating cannonballs; come time to leave their quarters for the summer, they would dispose of the cannonballs by dropping them from their windows rather than having to carry them down the stairs. Harvard's first chapel, the charming 1744 **Holden Chapel** to the rear, is also worth a quick peek for its attractive Georgian architecture and provincial blue and white pediment.

The New Yard

To the east of the Old Yard lie the grander buildings of the Tercentenary Theatre, colloquially known as the **New Yard**, where a vast set of steps leads up to the enormous pillars of **Widener Library**. Named after Harvard grad and *Titanic* victim Harry Elkins Widener, whose mother paid for the project, it's the center of the largest private library collection in the US, with a first folio of Shakespeare and a Gutenberg Bible among its holdings – you'll need Harvard student ID to see them. At the opposite side of the New Yard is **Memorial Church** (℡495-5508, ⓦwww.memorialchurch.harvard.edu), whose narrow, white spire strikes a balancing note to the heavy pillared front of Widener; its 172-foot-high steeple, topped by a medieval pennant-shaped **weathervane**, is a classic postcard image of Harvard Yard. Inside the church, the nave bears the names of alumni who've died at war; the organ at the rear is a much fancier affair, adorned with gilded carvings of starfish, kelp, cod, and crab.

Harvard Science Center

The immense structure facing the New Yard is Harvard's **Science Center**. The big lecture halls on the first floor are the locations of Harvard's most popular classes; one celebrity professor who taught here was the late evolutionary biologist Stephen Jay Gould. A popular myth has it that the center was designed to look like a camera, since one of its main benefactors was Polaroid magnate Edwin Land, though any likeness is purely accidental.

Harvard Law School

Up Massachusetts Avenue, on the east side of Cambridge Common, lies the main quad of the famed **Harvard Law School**, focusing on the stern gray pillars of **Langdell Hall**, an imposing edifice on its western border, whose entrance bears the inscription "*Non sub homine, sed sub deo et lege*" ("Not under man, but under God and law"). You can practically smell the stress in the air inside the **Harvard Law Library**, officially reserved for Harvard students, though visitor privileges can be applied for at the front desk – not that it's worth the trouble, anyway, unless you fancy reviewing jurisprudence on your trip.

Memorial Hall and the Carpenter Center

The rest of the campus lies east of the Science Center, starting with the pointed arches and flying buttresses of **Memorial Hall**, built to commemorate the

Harvard students who died during the Civil War. While it resembles a church, right down to its central vaulted **narthex**, which is bathed in filtered sunlight through Tiffany and LaFarge stained-glass windows, the space actually serves as **Sanders Theater**, undoubtedly Harvard's most impressive public lecture space; it's worth attending a lecture here simply to experience the grandeur.

The conspicuously modern **Carpenter Center** is hard to miss as you continue past Memorial Hall and look down Quincy Street: a slab of slate-gray granite standing out amidst Harvard's ever-present brick motif. Completed in 1963 as a center for the study of visual art at Harvard, the Carpenter Center is the only building in America designed by modernist French architect Le Corbusier (known for Zurich's eponymous Centre Le Corbusier and avant-garde furniture design), and its jarring difference from its surroundings has drawn a great deal of criticism from staunch Harvard traditionalists. Still, it's a striking and reasonably functional space; be sure to traverse its trademark feature, a **walkway** that leads through the middle of the building, meant to reflect the path worn by students on the lot on which the center was constructed. The modest **Sert Gallery**, on the third floor (Mon–Sat 10am–5pm, Sun 1–5pm; free; no phone, ⓦwww.artmuseums.harvard.edu/sert), puts on rotating contemporary art exhibits culled from Harvard's collections, while the lower floors of the building frequently display student art exhibits.

Harvard University art museums

Harvard's three art **museums** (Mon–Sat 10am–5pm, Sun 1–5pm; $6.50; free Sat 10am–noon; ☎495-9400; ⓦwww.artmuseums.harvard.edu) have benefited from years of scholarly attention and donors' financial generosity. Largely underappreciated and underattended by most visitors, not to mention the students themselves, the collections are easily some of the finest in New England; certainly the Fogg Art Museum has the most important collection of Picassos around. Note that a ticket to one buys you entry to the others.

William Hayes Fogg Art Museum

Housed on two floors surrounding a lovely mock sixteenth-century Italian Renaissance courtyard, the **William Hayes Fogg Art Museum**, at 32 Quincy St, showcases the highlights of Harvard's substantial collection of Western art. Much of the first floor is devoted to **medieval** and **Renaissance** material, mainly religious art with the usual complement of suffering Christs, most prominent in the far room to the right, below a marvelous circa-1540 oak ceiling carved with scrolls and arabesques. This part of the collection is best for a series of capitals salvaged from the French cathedral of Moutiers-Saint-Jean, which combine a Romanesque predilection for classical design with medieval didactic narrative. Additional first-floor chambers are devoted to **portraiture** of the seventeenth and eighteenth centuries, featuring two Rubens, a Rembrandt, and three Poussins, whose startling *Hannibal Crossing the Alps*, depicts the great Carthaginian instructing his troops from atop a massive tusked elephant. The remainder is rather stale, though the work of local John Singleton Copley figures prominently.

The second floor includes spaces for rotating exhibits, as well as smaller rooms displaying the museum's well-chosen **Impressionist**, **Post-Impressionist**, and **Modernist** works. There's an especially strong showing from the late-nineteenth-century French contingent of Dégas, Monet, Manet, Pissarro and Cézanne. You'll also see Picasso's *Mother and Child*, famously exemplary of his blue period, a sickly *Self-Portrait, dedicated to Paul Gauguin* by Van Gogh, and

Toulouse-Lautrec's queasy *The Hangover (Suzanne Valadon)*. But it's the focus on American counterparts to European late-nineteenth- and early-twentieth-century artists that truly distinguishes the collection, from the fine range of John Singer Sargent portraits, his solitary *The Breakfast Table* among them, to an ethereal Whistler *Nocturne* in blue and silver tints. Modernism is represented by, among others, Pollock's narrow beige and black *No. 2*, and Sheeler's outstanding *Upper Deck*, a representation of technology that ingeniously combines realism with abstraction. Fine examples of lesser-known nineteenth-century sensualist works are also displayed throughout the museum; look for Rodin's downright sexy *Eternal Idol* marble, and Gustave Moreau's highly eroticized *Apparition*.

Busch-Reisinger Museum

Secreted away at the rear of the Fogg's second floor is the entrance to Werner Otto Hall, home of the rich – though somewhat jarring – collection of the **Busch-Reisinger Museum**. Despite its small size, it's one of the finest collections of German Expressionists and Bauhaus works in the world. Its six rooms contain *fin de siècle* art, including Klimt's *Pear Tree*, a dappled meditation on the natural environment, and several Bauhaus standouts like Feininger's angular *Bird Cloud* and Moholy-Nagy's *Light-Space Modulator* – a quirky sculpture-machine set in motion for ten-minutes just once a week (Wed 1.45pm) due to its fragility. The gallery is strongest in Expressionist portraiture, notably, Kirchner's sardonic *Self-Portrait with a Cat* and Beckmann's garish *The Actors*, a narcissistic triptych.

Arthur M. Sackler Museum

Right out of the Fogg and dead ahead is the Arthur M. Sackler Building, 485 Broadway, three floors of which comprise the **Sackler Museum**, dedicated to the art of **classical**, **Asian** and **Islamic** cultures. The museum's holdings have far outgrown its available space, which is why the first floor is devoted to rotating exhibits based on permanent collection holdings. Islamic and Asian art are the themes of the second floor, featuring illustrations from Muslim texts, Chinese landscapes from the past several centuries, and an outstanding collection of Japanese woodblock prints. The fourth floor is best known for its excellent array of sensuous **Buddhist sculptures** from ancient China, India and Southeast Asia; one of them is housed in an ornate gilt and bronze portable shrine. You'll also see a strong display of classical work – standing out from the usual Greek vases and sculpture are intelligent studies on the **coins** of Alexander the Great and **seals** from ancient Babylonia.

Harvard Museum of Natural History

North past the Sackler Museum, Divinity Avenue holds another series of museums, the bulk of which are grouped together in a consortium called the **Harvard Museum of Natural History** (ⓦ www.hmnh.harvard.edu), which showcase objects from the natural world in tandem with cultural artifacts discovered on professor-led digs. The result is a pretty specialized collection of academic odds and sods; still, even the most dispassionate observer will find something of interest here, especially so in the **Peabody Museum of Archeology and Ethnology** and the **Botanical Museum**, which, in certain cases, succeed at rendering the arcane almost enthralling. The **Mineralogical and Geological Museum**, on the other hand, along with the **Museum of**

Comparative Zoology, are less compelling – though all four, at least, can be seen on one ticket.

Peabody Museum of Archeology and Ethnology

The most prominent of Harvard's natural history museums, the **Peabody Museum of Archeology and Ethnology**, 11 Divinity Ave (Mon–Sat 9am–5pm, Sun 1–5pm; $5, free Sat 9am–noon; ⓦwww.peabody.harvard.edu), displays materials culled from Harvard's anthropological and archeological expeditions. The strength of the museum lies in its collection of pieces from Mesoamerica, ranging from digs in the pueblos of the southwestern United States to artifacts from Incan civilizations. The ground floor anthropological material centers mainly on indigenous cultures of North America, with a detailed presentation on the Ju/wa bushmen of the Kalahari desert, colorful Katcina dolls crafted by Arizona Hopi for their children, and stupendous examples of Northwest Coast ceremonial masks with pronounced bird beaks. The displays are extensive and informative, covering the history, art, traditions and lifestyles of native peoples from around the world – though the wax dummies in traditional garb and the miniature dioramas can't help but seem hokey and out of place.

Mineralogical and Geological Museum

A second-floor passageway connects the Peabody with Harvard's **Mineralogical and Geological Museum** (Mon–Sat 9am–5pm, Sun 1–5pm; $5, free Sat 9am–noon; ⓦwww.peabody.harvard.edu/museum_mineral.html), the thrust of whose collection is, basically, a bunch of rocks with a stunning 1600-pound amethyst-encrusted cavity serving as their centerpiece. As such, if you don't know much about geology, this probably won't do too much for you, as the only easily accessible display (to a layperson, anyway) deals with birthstones. On the other hand, it's reputed to be one of the world's finest mineral collections, and most of the gems are aesthetically as well as academically interesting.

Botanical Museum

Right next door, and similarly narrow in scope, is the **Botanical Museum**, at 26 Oxford St (Mon–Sat 9am–5pm, Sun 1–5pm; $5, free Sat 9am–noon; ⓦwww.huh.harvard.edu/collections/botanical.htm), also connected by walkway to the former two. You may think this collection is only of interest to botanists, and much of it may well be, but it's definitely worth a pass to take in the stunning **Ware Collection of Glass Models of Plants**. This project began in 1887 and terminated almost fifty years later in 1936, leaving the museum with an absolutely unique and visually stunning collection of flower models constructed to the last detail, entirely from glass, by a father and son team from Dresden, Germany. It's a spectacle that must be seen to be believed.

Museum of Comparative Zoology

Housed in the same building as the Botanical Museum, but lacking a knock-out attraction like the Ware Collection, the **Museum of Comparative Zoology** (Mon–Sat 9am–5pm, Sun 1–5pm; $5, free Sat 9am–noon; ⓦwww.mcz.harvard.edu), is really just the tip of the iceberg of the university's collection of zoological materials. Most of the collection is inaccessible to visitors; what is consists of rote displays of stuffed dead animals with some fascinating amber-preserved insects and impressive fossils thrown in.

Harvard Semitic Museum

Facing the Peabody is the **Harvard Semitic Museum**, at 6 Divinity Ave (Mon–Fri 10am–4pm, Sun 1–4pm; free; ⓦwww.fas.harvard.edu/~semitic), whose informative, if somewhat unfocused, displays chronicle Harvard's century-old excavations in the Near East. Pieces range from Egyptian tombs to Babylonian cuneiform, and include a particularly appealing collection of tiny stone-cut votive figurines. What distinguishes the collection, though, is its focus on the process and methodology of the digs, with concomitant examples of charts, infrared devices and dusting tools, in addition to their results.

Harvard houses

Harvard's fancy upperclassmen residences, most of which are nested in the quad east of JFK Street and south of Massachusetts Ave, are a visible – and sometimes ostentatious – reminder of the university's elite past. Nearest the Yard, at 46 Plympton St, **Adams House** has the most rebellious history of the lot, having been used as a revolutionary prison for General "Gentleman Johnny" Burgoyne, and later serving as a speak-easy during Prohibition. Just south of Adams juts the graceful, blue-topped bell tower of **Lowell House**, at 2 Holyoke Place, which boasts one of Harvard's most beautiful courtyards, surrounded by a compound of sober brick dormitories and fastidiously manicured grounds. Further southwest, along the banks of the Charles, rises the purple spire of **Eliot House**, at 101 Dunster St, a community that remains a bastion of social privilege, counting David Rockefeller and Leonard Bernstein among its illustrious alumni. To the east, at 945 Memorial Drive, lies **Dunster House**, whose red Georgian tower top is a favorite subject of Cambridge's tourist brochures; the clock tower is modeled after Christchurch College's Big Tom in Oxford. Alongside Adams, Dunster has long been considered a center for radical culture – at least by Cambridge's very proper standards.

Old Cambridge: upper Brattle Street

After the outbreak of the American Revolution, Cambridge's bourgeois majority ran the Tories out of town, leaving their sumptuous houses to be used as the quarters of the Continental Army. What was then called Tory Row is modern-day **Brattle Street**, the main drag of the **Old Cambridge** district. Extending west from Eliot Street and Harvard Square, Brattle runs through a tree-lined neighborhood of expansive, impeccably kept lawns foregrounding stately mansions, many of which have been labeled with explanatory blue oval plaques commemorating their onetime owners.

Brattle House and Farwell Place

The first of several noteworthy residences, the **Brattle House**, at no. 42, fails to reflect the unabashedly extravagant lifestyle of its former resident, William Brattle. It doesn't appear nearly as grand as it once did, dwarfed as it is by surrounding office buildings, nor is it open to the public – no great loss since it now only houses offices. Down the street and to the right, tiny **Farwell Place** features several modest Federal-style houses dating to the early nineteenth century and is the best (and only remaining) example of the square's residential character before it became a teeming center of activity. The recently restored house at no. 17 is one of the best examples of the genre; it now houses Christ Church's thrift shop (Tues & Thurs 10am–4pm, Sat 11.30am–2.30pm; ☎492-3335).

Dexter Pratt House

A sign on the corner of Brattle and Story streets marks the site of a tree that once stood near the **Dexter Pratt House**, at 56 Brattle St, home of the village blacksmith celebrated by Longfellow in a popular poem that began, "Under a spreading chestnut tree / The village smithy stands, / The smith a mighty man is he, / With large and sinewy hands; / And the muscles of his brawny arms / Are strong as iron bands." In 1876, the chestnut was cut down, despite Longfellow's vigorous opposition, because it was spreading into the path of passing traffic. The city of Cambridge fashioned a chair out of the felled tree, presented it to Longfellow as a birthday present, who then composed a mawkish poem about the whole affair ("From My Easy Chair"), and all was forgiven. These days the house has a more humdrum role as home to the Hi-Rise Bread Company, producers of some of the finest baked treats in greater Boston – which may be the most exciting thing about the place. Beyond the Pratt House, at the intersection of **Mason** and **Brattle streets**, the advent of a tree-lined neighborhood of elite mansions signals the edge of Old Cambridge proper.

Longfellow House

One house you can visit is the recently renovated **Longfellow House** at 105 Brattle St (May–Oct; Wed–Sun 10am–4.30pm, tours hourly 10.30–11.30am & 1–4pm; $3; ☎876-4491, Ⓦwww.nps.gov/long; Harvard **T**). Erected for Royalist John Vassal in 1759, who promptly vacated it on the eve of the Revolutionary War, and inhabited by George Washington during the war itself – it was used as his headquarters during the siege of Boston – it later became home to the poet Henry Wadsworth Longfellow, who moved in as a boarder in 1843. When he married the wealthy Fanny Appleton, her father purchased the house for them as a wedding gift, and Longfellow lived here until his death in 1882.

Preserved to recall the decorating sensibilities of his era, the result is a solid, if somewhat strenuously presented, example of Brattle Street's opulence during the nineteenth century. The halls and walls are festooned with Longfellow's furniture and art collection, including etchings of fellow writers like Ralph Waldo Emerson and Nathaniel Hawthorne. Most surprising is the wealth of nineteenth-century pieces from the Far East amassed by Longfellow's renegade son, Charlie, on his world travels; four of his Japanese screens are included, the best of which, a two-panel example depicting geishas in spring and winter costumes, is in an upstairs bedroom. His other son, Ernie, stayed at home, trying – and failing – to make a name for himself as a landscape painter; a number of his unremarkable works adorn the walls of the house.

Hooper-Lee-Nichols House

The second of the Brattle Street mansions open to the public is the bluewashed **Hooper-Lee-Nichols House** at no. 159 (Tues & Thurs 2–5pm, tours every

△ Harvard University

hour; $5; @www.cambridgehistory.org), half a mile west of the Longfellow House. While a bit out-of-the-way, the house – one of the area's oldest residences – does give an intimate sense of colonial Cambridge life. It's particularly unusual for its various architectural incarnations: it began as a stout, post-medieval farmhouse, and underwent various renovations until it became the Georgian mansion it is today. Rooms have been predictably restored with period writing tables, canopy beds and rag dolls, but knowledgeable tour guides spice things up a bit, opening secret panels to reveal centuries-old wallpaper and original foundations. Its sporadic opening hours don't lend themselves to impromptu visits; you'll also have to knock vigorously on the front door to gain entry.

Mount Auburn Cemetery

On past the Hooper-Lee-Nichols House, at the intersection of Brattle and Mount Auburn streets, is the **Mount Auburn Cemetery**, whose 170 acres of grounds are more like a beautifully kept municipal park than a necropolis, with as many joggers as there are mourners. The best way to get a sense of the cemetery's scope is to ascend the **tower** that lies smack in its center atop a grassy bluff – from here, you can see not only the entire grounds but, on a clear day, all of downtown Boston and its environs. Of course, like most cemeteries in the Boston area, Mount Auburn also has its share of deceased luminaries, most notably Winslow Homer and Isabella Stewart Gardner; ask the folks in the main office for a map of famous graves if you're interested.

Central Square

Central Square, as you might expect, is located roughly in the geographical center of Cambridge, and is appropriately the city's civic center as well, home to its most important government buildings. It's an interesting mix of cultural and industrial Cambridge, a working-class area with an ethnically diverse population and little of the hype that surrounds other parts of town. There's nothing much to see, but it's a good place to shop and eat, and is home to some of the best nightlife in Cambridge. Indeed, you'll find substantially more activity here after dark, especially along Massachusetts Avenue, as denizens flock to hear live music at *Middle East* or head upstairs to lounge at *The Enormous Room* (see reviews p.196 and p.191). The Gothic quarters of **City Hall**, at 795 Massachusetts Ave (Mon–Fri 8.30am–5pm), house Cambridge's municipal bureaucracy and act as an occasional venue for town meetings or public events, but little else stands out here.

Inman Square

Overshadowed by Cambridge's busier districts, **Inman Square** marks a quiet stretch directly north of Central Square that's centered around the confluence of Cambridge, Beacon and Prospect streets. There's little of interest here, either – just a pleasant, mostly residential neighborhood where much of

Cambridge's working-class, Portuguese-speaking population resides. What does make Inman worth a visit, though, along with its ethnic markets, is its broad range of excellent restaurants, where you can enjoy some of Cambridge's finest food without breaking the bank. Most of the action happens on the square's main drag, Cambridge Street, which finds the *East Coast Grill* just down the street from the popular *1369 Coffee House* (see reviews p.186 and p.167). If you're in the area, check out Inman's lone landmark, the charmingly inexpert **Cambridge Firemen's Mural**, at the corner of Cambridge and Antrim streets, a work of public art commissioned to honor local men in red.

East Cambridge and Kendall Square

East Cambridge is split into two main areas of activity, though neither has especially much to recommend it unless you're into checking out the corporate headquarters of numerous biotech and software companies that survived the dotcom bust. In the northernmost region, there's the CambridgeSide Galleria (see "Shopping," p.214), a gargantuan shopping multiplex where mall rats mingle in the neon-lit food court. Further inland and adjacent to MIT, **Kendall Square** grew from the ashes of the post-industrial desolation of East Cambridge in the 1960s and 1970s to become a glittering testament to the economic revival that sparked Massachusetts in the 1980s. Technology and its profits built the square, and it shows. By day, Kendall bustles with tech students and programmers lunching in chic eateries; at night, the business crowd goes home and the place becomes largely deserted. The exception to this is the Kendall Square Cinema, which draws large crowds to see some of the best art and second-run movies in the area (see "Performing arts and film," p.202).

Massachusetts Institute of Technology

Occupying more than 150 acres alongside the Charles, the **Massachusetts Institute of Technology** (**MIT**) provides an intellectual counterweight to the otherwise working-class character of East Cambridge. Originally established in Allston (see p.113) in 1865, MIT moved to this more auspicious campus across the river in 1916 and has since risen to international prominence as a major center for theoretical and practical research in the sciences. Both NASA and the Department of Defense pour funds into MIT in exchange for research and development assistance from the university's best minds.

Architecturally speaking, the campus buildings and geography reflect the quirky, nerdy character of the institute, emphasizing function and peppering it with a peculiar notion of form. Everything is obsessively numbered and coded: you can, for example, go to 1-290 (the Rogers Building) for a lecture in 1.050 (Solid Mechanics), which gets you closer to a minor in 1 (Civil and Environmental Engineering).

The Rogers Building

Behind the massive pillars that guard the entrance of MIT's main building, the **Rogers Building**, at 77 Massachusetts Ave, you'll find a labyrinth of corridors – known to Techies as the **Infinite Corridor** – through which students can traverse the entire east campus without ever going outside. Atop the Rogers Building is MIT's best-known architectural icon, a massive gilt hemisphere called the **Great Dome**. Just inside the entrance to Rogers, you'll find the **MIT Information Center** (Mon–Fri 9am–5pm), which dispenses free campus maps and advice.

The Kresge Auditorium and MIT Chapel

MIT has drawn the attention of some of the major architects of the twentieth century, who have used the university's progressiveness as a testing ground for some of their more experimental works. Two of these are located in the courtyard across Massachusetts Avenue from the Rogers Building. The **Kresge Auditorium**, designed by Finnish architect Eero Saarinen, features an impressive rounded roof – though its real claim to fame is that it amazingly rests on three, rather than four, corners; Saarinen designed the structure over breakfast, using his grapefruit as a model. In the same courtyard is the red-brick **MIT Chapel**, also the work of Saarinen, and shaped like a stocky cylinder with an abstract sculpture crafted from paper-thin metals serving as a rather unconventional spire; inside, a delicate metal screen scatters light patterns across the floor. A couple of blocks back towards Kendall Square, the I.M. Pei-designed **Weisner Building** hosts the **List Visual Art Center** (Tues–Sun noon–6pm; free), which displays student works; heavily influenced by science and relying on a great deal of computer design, they're often more technologically impressive than visually appealing.

MIT Museum

Of much greater interest than the Art Center is the **MIT Museum**, near Central Square at 265 Massachusetts Ave (Tues–Fri 10am–5pm, Sat–Sun noon–5pm; $5; ☏253-4444, ⊛web.mit.edu/museum). The museum has several permanent displays, of which the holography exhibit, a collection of seriously cool eye-trickery, and the Metafield Maze, a virtual reality labyrinth projected onto the floor, are both sure to delight. Another chamber hosts Mind and Hand, a dry retrospective on 150 years of MIT; the highlight is a small retrospective on some of the pranks ("hacks") pulled by Techies, which details how the madcap funsters wreaked havoc at the annual Harvard–Yale football game, for one, by landing a massive weather balloon in the middle of the gridiron.

Northwest Cambridge and Somerville

Northwest Cambridge, off any university-oriented or colonial heritage sightseeing circuit, has more mundane charms on offer. If the amorphous area has a center, it's **Porter Square**, located a mile north of Harvard Square along Massachusetts Avenue. The walk from Harvard will take you past some of

Cambridge's most chic lounges and boutiques, *Temple Bar* and *Audubon* among them (see reviews p.194 and p.191), while Porter Square itself is hard to miss – look for the forty-foot red kinetic **sculpture** right outside the subway stop. Just before this gargantuan mobile is the **Porter Exchange**, a mall of mostly unimpressive shops, save for an obscure hallway lined with tiny Japanese food outlets – cramped bar-style restaurants where the food is so authentic you'll have to point to the menu to order, unless, of course, you speak Japanese.

Strawberry Hill

In the lowest corner of Northwest Cambridge, just to the east of the Fresh Pond reservoir, slopes the gentle grade of **Strawberry Hill**, whose main street, **Huron Avenue**, runs up and around it. This slice of upper-middle-class suburbia is serene and arboreal, one with a charming array of apothecaries and specialty shops. Formaggio Kitchen, at no. 244, has some of the best cheeses in town, and the bookshelves at Bryn Mawr Book Shop, 373 Huron Ave, still open onto the street (see reviews p.212 and p.209). Places like these make for a lovely promenade, but needn't be major stops on your itinerary – the area is predominantly local, and there are no sights to speak of.

Davis Square

Beyond Porter Square, sleepy **SOMERVILLE**'s recent "discovery" by young residents is reflected in latter-day gentrification to the area's central plaza, **Davis Square**, a former working-class stronghold. You're unlikely to make it this far out, however, unless you're angling to jump on the scenic **Minuteman Bike Trail**, which begins nearby, at the Alewife **T** stop, and continues through Arlington and Lexington to Bedford (☎ 542-BIKE; ⓦ www.massbike.org). Still, if you've got the time to spare, the square itself is a fun place to kick around for an afternoon. Homey coffee shops like *Someday* (see review p.170) face the square's central plaza which, on weekends, is typically occupied by folksy musicians and street performers; there's little else to see besides.

Out of the city

There's enough of interest in Boston itself to keep you going for several days at the very least. However, the city lies at the center of a region concentrated with historic sights, and there's plenty to see and do within a relatively short distance. Perhaps the best inland day-trip you can make within a 25-mile radius of Boston is to the revolutionary battlegrounds of **Lexington** and **Concord**, but the city also makes an excellent base for visiting the numerous quaint and historic towns that line the North Shore of the Massachusetts coast. For many, the notorious witch sights of **Salem** make that the first place of interest – and there's much more there besides, notably to do with its prosperous days as a major port. Nearby **Marblehead** is pretty enough to merit a wander, too, if lacking any real must-sees; after a short stop there, you can continue on to somewhat more rustic **Gloucester** and **Rockport**, worthwhile if you have the time and are captivated by the faded glories of the New England fishing trade. Route 1 is the quickest way up the coast, though coastal Route 1A is more scenic. Buses run up this direction as well, operated both by the MBTA and by independent tour companies (see p.25) as does the MBTA commuter rail, with trains leaving regularly from Boston's North Station, on the Orange and Green lines.

On the South Shore, the 1627 Pilgrim village of **Plymouth** is the main tourist draw, with recreations of Pilgrim settlements and the vessel that brought them here, the *Mayflower II*. In summer a ferry from Boston puts **Provincetown**, the exuberant old fishing village at the tip of Cape Cod, within easy reach; its beaches and happening streetlife scene are among the best in the region.

Lexington and Concord

The sedate towns of **Lexington** and **Concord**, almost always mentioned in the same breath, trade on their notoriety as the locations of the first armed confrontation with the British. Today, though, Lexington is mostly suburban, while Concord, five miles east, is even sleepier, though it has a bit more character. Most of Concord and Lexington's historical quarters have been incorporated into the **Minute Man National Park**, which takes in the Lexington Battle Green, North Bridge and much of Battle Road, the route the British followed on their retreat from Concord back to Boston. These notorious battles are evoked in a piecemeal but relentless fashion throughout the park, with scale models, remnant musketry and the odd preserved bullet hole. The Old Manse and The Wayside, two rambling old Concord houses with bookish pasts, are also situated on the grounds, while some other literary sights, such as **Walden Pond** in Concord, are just beyond its boundaries.

Lexington

The main thing to see in **LEXINGTON** is the grassy **Battle Green**, where the American flag flies 24 hours a day. The land serves as Lexington's town common and is fronted by Henry Kitson's famous statue of *The Minute Man*. This musket-bearing figure of Captain John Parker, which dates from 1900, stands on boulders dislodged from the stone walls behind which the colonial militia fired at their British opponents on April 19, 1775.

On the eastern periphery of the green, the **visitor's center** (daily: April–Oct 9am–5pm, Nov–Mar 9am–4pm; free; ☎781/862-7753, ⦿www.nps.gov/mima) has a diorama that shows the detail of the battle and a host of revolutionary regalia belonging to both sides. Facing the green, the **Buckman Tavern** (mid-March to Nov Mon–Sat 10am–5pm, Sun 1–5pm; 30–45min guided tour; $5; ☎781/862-5598), an eighteenth-century bar and hostelry that served as the Minute Mens headquarters while awaiting news of British incursion, looks like your typical pub, right down to the seven-foot-wide fireplace and lengthy tap bar on the first floor. The tour includes a visit to the spare, upper chambers, but the only bonafide revolutionary tidbit is the hole from a British bullet that's been preserved in an inner door near the tap room.

A couple of blocks north, at 36 Hancock St, a plaque affixed to the brown, two-story **Hancock-Clarke House** (mid-March to late Oct Mon–Sat 9am–5pm, Sun 1–5pm; 30–45min guided tour; $5; ☎781/862-1703) solemnly reminds that this is where "Samuel Adams and John Hancock were sleeping when aroused by Paul Revere"; the latter was the grandson of Reverend John Hancock, the man for whom the house was built in 1698. Exhibits on the free-admission first floor include the drum on which William Diamond beat the signal for the Minute Men to converge and the pistols that British Major John Pitcairn lost on the retreat from Concord. Less interesting is the small wooden **Munroe Tavern**, somewhat removed from the town center at 1332 Massachusetts Ave (mid-March to late Oct Mon–Sat 9am–5pm, Sun 1–5pm; 30–45min guided tour; $5; ☎781/862-2016), which served as a field hospital for British soldiers, though only for a mere hour and a half. If you intend to visit all three sights, you'll save a bit by getting a combination ticket ($10), available at any of the three.

If you're looking to have a **meal**, you might want to try *Via Lago*, at 1845 Massachusetts Ave (☎781/861-6174), a casual counter-service spot that's good on fresh, tasty pastas, sandwiches and salads; or, you can head to *Vinny Testa's*, 20 Waltham St (☎781/860-5200), for heaping portions of reliable Italian fare like fennel sausage lasagna and spaghetti bolognese.

Concord

One of the few sizeable inland towns of New England at the time of the Revolution, **CONCORD**, a fifteen-minute drive west of Lexington, and a forty-minute train ride ($4 one way) from Boston's North Station, retains a pleasant country atmosphere despite its reputation as just another wealthy western suburb. Trains arrive at Concord Station, about half a mile from the city center, and within walking distance of the rambling **Colonial Inn**, near the corner of Main and Monument streets. An old hostelry with a traditional dining room and a tavern that served as a makeshift revolutionary hospital dur-

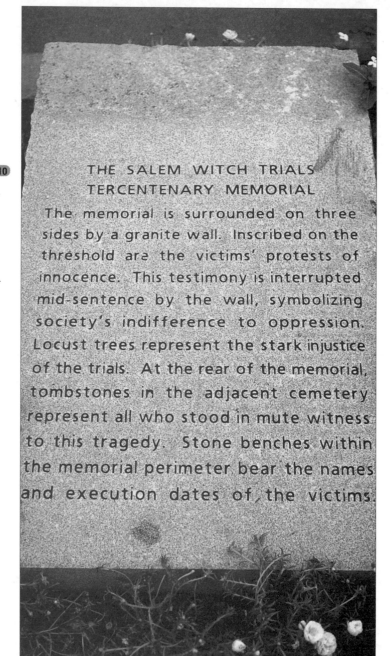

THE SALEM WITCH TRIALS
TERCENTENARY MEMORIAL

The memorial is surrounded on three sides by a granite wall. Inscribed on the threshold are the victims' protests of innocence. This testimony is interrupted mid-sentence by the wall, symbolizing society's indifference to oppression. Locust trees represent the stark injustice of the trials. At the rear of the memorial, tombstones in the adjacent cemetery represent all who stood in mute witness to this tragedy. Stone benches within the memorial perimeter bear the names and execution dates of the victims.

△ Witch Trials Memorial, Salem

ing the war, the inn is also a good place to stop for a pint or a hearty lunch.

From the top of **Hill Burying Ground** to the west, you can survey Concord, as did Pitcairn when the Americans amassed on the far side of North Bridge. A few blocks behind it on Route 62 is **Sleepy Hollow Cemetery** – though not the one of headless horsemen fame that is located far from here in the Hudson River Valley. You will, however, find eminent Concord literati Emerson, Hawthorne, Thoreau and Louisa May Alcott buried atop the grave-yard's "Author's Ridge," as signs clearly indicate.

North Bridge and Old Manse

The most hyped spot in Concord is **North Bridge**, site of the first effective armed resistance to British rule in America. If you take the traditional approach from Monument Street, you'll be following the route the British took. Just before crossing the bridge, an inscription on the mass grave of some British regulars reads, "They came 3000 miles and died to keep the past upon its throne." The bridge itself, however, looks a bit too well-preserved to provoke much sentiment, and no wonder: it's actually a 1954 replica of yet another replica of the original structure.

A stone's throw from North Bridge is the gray-clapboard **Old Manse**, at 269 Monument St (mid-April to Oct Mon–Sat 10am–5pm, Sun noon–5pm; $7; ☎978/369-3909), built for Ralph Waldo Emerson's grandfather, the Reverend William Emerson, in 1770. The younger Emerson lived here on and off, and this was where, in 1834, he penned *Nature*, the book that signaled the begin-ning of the Transcendentalist movement. Of the numerous rooms in the house, all with period furnishings intact, the most interesting is the small upstairs study, where Nathaniel Hawthorne, a resident of the house in the early 1840s, wrote *Mosses from an Old Manse*, a rather obscure book that gave the place its name. Hawthorne passed three happy years here shortly after getting married to his wife Sophia, who, following a miscarriage, used her diamond wedding ring to etch the words "Man's accidents are God's purposes" into a window pane in the study. On the first floor, look for the framed swath of original English-made wallpaper with the British "paper tax" mark stamped on the back.

The Wayside and Concord Museum

Also worth a visit is **The Wayside**, east of the town center at 455 Lexington Rd (April–Oct Tues–Sun 10am–5.30pm; $4; ☎978/369-6975), a 300-year-old yellow wooden house that's another literary landmark, once home to both the Alcotts and Hawthornes, though at different times. Louisa May Alcott's girl-hood experiences here formed the basis for *Little Women* (though she actually penned *Little Women* next door at the Orchard House, where the family lived from 1858 to 1867 and her father, Bronson, founded his School of Philosophy). Among the antique furnishings, the most unusual is the slanted writing desk at which Hawthorne toiled standing up, in the fourth floor "tower" he added on for that purpose. If you don't feel like taking a guided tour, you can stop in at the small but very well-presented **museum** (free) at the admissions area for a brief overview.

Just down the road at no. 200, the excellent **Concord Museum** (Jan–March Mon–Sat 11am–4pm, Sun 1–4pm; April–Dec Mon–Sat 9am–5pm, Sun noon–5pm; $7; ☎978/369-9763, ⓦwww.concordmuseum.org), located on the site of Emerson's apple orchard, has more than a dozen galleries displaying period furnishings from eighteenth- and nineteenth-century Concord, including a sizeable collection of Thoreau's personal effects, such as the bed from his Walden Pond hut (see below). More interesting, however, are the Revolutionary War artifacts throughout, such as one of the signal lanterns hung from the Old North Church in Boston, to warn of the British march.

When hunger strikes, you can try the *Cheese Shop*, at 29 Walden St (☎978/369-5778), a great place to stop for deluxe picnic fixings from pate and jellies to, of course, all manner of cheeses. If you favor a sit-down meal, head to *Walden Grille*, 24 Walden St (☎978/371-2233), for baby shrimp quesadillas, lamb salad or crab-cake sandwiches in a refurbished nineteenth-century firehouse.

Walden Pond

Though the tranquility that Thoreau sought and savored at **Walden Pond**, just two miles south of Concord proper off Route 126 (daily dawn–dusk; $5 parking fee; ☎978/369-3254), is for the most part gone – thanks mainly to the masses of tourists who pour in to retrace his footsteps – the place itself has remained much the same since the author's famed two-year exercise in self-sufficiency began in 1845. "I did not feel crowded or confined in the least," he wrote of his life in the simple log cabin; and, though his semi-fictionalized account of the experience might have you believing otherwise, Thoreau hardly roughed it, taking regular walks into town to stock up on amenities and receiving frequent visitors at his single-room hut.

The reconstructed cabin, complete with a journal open on its rustic desk, is situated near the parking lot (you'll have to content yourself with peering through the windows), while the site of the original structure, closer to the shores of the pond, is marked out with stones. The pond itself, which spans about a quarter-mile across (and is only half a mile long), is quite the popular swimming hole. The water looks best at dawn, when the pond still "throws off its nightly clothing of mist"; late-risers should plan an off-season visit to maximize their transcendental experience of it all.

Salem

SALEM, an unpretentious city just sixteen miles, and a twenty- to thirty-minute train ride from Boston's North Station ($3 one way), is the most intriguing destination on the North Shore, standing out from the other provincial towns that line the coast if only because of its peculiar history. This is where Puritan self-righteousness reached its apogee in the horrific **witch trials** of 1692, and the place uses the stigma to its tourist advantage by hyping up the correlating spookiness, especially around Halloween. Less known were the many years it spent as a flourishing seaport, and, the remnants from this era only add to the unsettling aura, with abandoned wharves, rows of stately sea captains' homes and an astounding display of their riches at the Peabody Essex Museum. Ironically, Salem's dark legacy has proven to be its salvation, leading to a major sprucing-up of its touristy core.

The Town

Today, the 1.7-mile **Salem Heritage Trail**, modeled after Boston's, red-brick and all, links the town's principal historic sights, the majority of which are tied

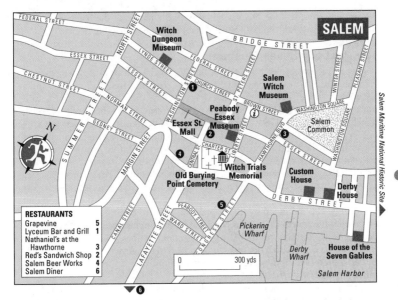

RESTAURANTS

Grapevine	5
Lyceum Bar and Grill	1
Nathaniel's at the Hawthorne	3
Red's Sandwich Shop	2
Salem Beer Works	4
Salem Diner	6

to the town's gloomy witch-hanging days. In an even more ironic twist of history, a sizeable and highly visible contingent of **Wiccans** now live proudly in modern Salem. These latter-day sorceresses are more than willing to accept modest fees for their fortune-telling services, despite their New Age spirituality; keep in mind they're as much a part of the tourist industry as everything else in Salem. To pick up **information** on the trail and various sights about town, head to the helpful Salem National Visitor's Center, at 2 New Liberty St (daily 9am–5pm; ☎978/740-1650, ⊛www.salemweb.com); it also serves as the trail's unofficial starting point.

Salem's witch sights

The hokey **Salem Witch Museum**, at 19¹/₂ Washington Square (daily: July–Aug 10am–7pm; Sept–June 10am–5pm; $6; ☎978/744-1692 or 1-800/544-1692, ⊛www.salemwitchmuseum.com), provides some entertaining orientation on the witch hysteria – though it's only a sound-and-light show that makes ample use of wax figures to depict the events of 1692, housed in a suitably spooky one-time Romanesque church. Right in front of the museum is the imposing statue of a caped **Roger Conant**, founder of the town's original 1626 Puritan settlement, when it was still known as Naumkeag.

More evocative is the **Witch Dungeon Museum**, on the west side of town at 16 Lynde St (April–Nov daily 10am–5pm; $6; ☎978/741-3570, ⊛www.witchdungeon.com), which occupies a nineteenth-century clapboard church and treats visitors to farcical re-enactments of key witch trial-related events. Upstairs, it's the trial of Sarah Good – a pipe-smoking beggar woman falsely accused of witchcraft – based on actual court transcripts; after the show, actors escort visitors below ground to a re-created dungeon with prison cells no bigger than telephone booths. Dank and supremely eerie, it's not hard to believe claims that the place is haunted.

On a less sensationalistic note, the **Witch Trials Memorial**, wedged into a corner of the **Old Burying Point Cemetery** at Charter and Liberty streets, is a simple series of stone blocks etched with the names of the hanged. One of the witch judges, John Hathorne, also happens to be buried here.

The Peabody Essex Museum

Right up Liberty Street from the Witch Memorial is a mix of red-brick and glass buildings that comprise the **Peabody Essex Museum**, at East India Square on the Essex Street Mall (April–Oct Mon–Sat 10am–5pm, Sun noon–5pm; Nov–March Tues–Sat 10am–5pm, Sun noon–5pm; $10; ☎978/745-9500 or 1-800/745-4054, ⓦwww.pem.org), the oldest continuously operating museum in the US. Currently undergoing a major facelift and expansion at the hands of Canadian architect Moishe Safdie, whose trademark use of atrium entranceways will be in evidence once the structure is complete in June 2003, the museum's vast space incorporates more than thirty galleries displaying art and artifacts from around the world, illustrating Salem's past importance as a major point of interaction and trade between the Eastern and Western worlds. Founded by ship captains in 1799 to exhibit their exotic items obtained while overseas, the museum also boasts the biggest collection of nautical paintings in the world. Other galleries hold Chinese and Japanese export art, Asian, Oceanic, and African ethnological artifacts, American decorative arts and, in a preserved house that the museum administers, court documents from the Salem Witch Trials.

Currently, the first floor is home to the core museum displays, with creatively curated whaling exhibits that feature not only the requisite scrimshaw but Ambrose Garneray's famous 1835 painting, *Attacking the Right Whale*, and the gaping lower jaw of a sperm whale. Upstairs highlights include a cavernous central gallery with the fanciful figureheads from now-demolished Salem ships hung from the walls and the reconstructed salon from America's first yacht, *Cleopatra's Barge*, which took to the seas in 1816. The collections are likely to be considerably reorganized after a planned three-month closure in early 2003, so be sure to pick up a new floor plan at the admissions desk.

Salem Maritime National Historic Site

Little of Salem's original waterfront remains, although the 2000-foot-long **Derby Wharf** is still standing, fronted by the imposing Federalist-style **Custom House** at its head. These two, and ten other mainly residential buildings once belonging to sea captains and craftsmen, comprise the **Salem Maritime National Historic Site**, which maintains a **visitor's center** at 174 Derby St (daily 9am–5pm; ☎978/740-1650, ⓦwww.nps.gov/sama). The Custom House is where Nathaniel Hawthorne worked as chief executive officer for three years, a stint which he later described as "slavery." The office-like interior is rather bland, as is the warehouse in the rear, with displays of tea chests and such. Park rangers (guides, really) also give free tours of the adjacent **Derby House** (daily 9am–5pm), whose millionaire owner had it built here, overlooking the harbor, to more closely monitor his shipping empire. Next door, the **West India Goods Store** sells goods like sugar and molasses, and nautical knick-knacks like fishhooks common to Salem's nineteenth-century shops, including "gunpowder tea," a tightly-rolled, high-grade Chinese green tea.

House of the Seven Gables

The most famous sight in the waterfront area is undoubtedly the **House of the Seven Gables**, at 54 Turner St (daily: July–Oct 10am–7pm; Nov–June 10am–5pm; closed Jan; $10; ☎978/744-0991, ⓦwww.7gables.org), a rambling old mansion by the sea that served as inspiration for Hawthorne's eponymous novel. Forever the "rusty wooden house with seven acutely peaked gables" that Hawthorne described, this 1688 three-story house has some other notable features, such as the bricked-off "Secret Stairway" that leads to a small room. The house was inhabited in the 1840s by Susan Ingersoll, a cousin of Hawthorne whom he often visited. The author's birthplace, a small undistinguished house built before 1750, has been moved to the grounds, which also feature a wishing well amidst lovely surrounding gardens.

Eating and drinking

Grapevine 26 Congress St ☎978/745-9335. Top-notch bistro with exotic dishes like Cambodian mussels, roasted red snapper with Thai sauce, and good vegetarian options.

Lyceum Bar and Grill 43 Church St ☎978/745-7665. Popular spot for Yankee cooking with modern updates like dill-infused clam chowder and lobster stuffed with shrimp, scallions, ginger and bread crumbs.

Nathaniel's at the Hawthorne 18 Washington Square ☎978/744-4080. Upscale comfort food including roasted scrod and grilled pork tenderloin.

Red's Sandwich Shop 15 Central St ☎978/745-3527. Hearty breakfast and brunch fare served in a stone house built in 1700.

Salem Beer Works 278 Derby St ☎978/745-2337. You can try microbrews or nouveau pub food – like boneless chicken wings and smoked salmon – at this glossy brewery.

Salem Diner 70 Loring Ave ☎978/741-7918. Basic diner fare in an original Sterling Streamliner diner car.

Marblehead

The maritime town of **MARBLEHEAD**, about a thirty-minute drive northeast of Boston, is a town of winding streets lined with small but well-preserved private sea captains' homes that lead down to its harbor, which makes for a decent respite from Salem's witch-related sights. Once the domain of Revolutionary War heroes – it was Marblehead boatmen who rowed Washington's assault force across the Delaware River to attack Trenton – it's now mainly home to Boston commuters. One thing that hasn't changed over the years is the town's dramatic setting on a series of rocky ledges overlooking the wide natural harbor, which makes it one of the East Coast's biggest **yachting centers**. The annual Race Week takes place the last week of July.

Settled in 1629, Marblehead has largely escaped commercialism thanks to its occupants' affluence and, oddly, a severe shortage of parking. The latter should not deter you from visiting, however, as this is one of the most picturesque ports in New England. You can get a good look at it from **Fort Sewall**, which juts into the harbor at the end of Front Street; these are the remnants of fortifications the British originally built in 1644, which later protected the *USS Constitution* in the War of 1812. Closer to the center of town is **Old Burial Hill**, which holds the graves of more than six hundred Revolutionary War soldiers and has similarly sweeping views. **Abbot Hall**, on Washington Street (Mon, Tues, Thurs & Fri 8am–5pm, Wed 7.30am–7pm, Sat 9am–6pm, Sun 11am–6pm), an attractive 1876 town hall which can be seen from far out at sea, houses Archibald Willard's famous patriotic painting *The Spirit of '76*, painted for the Philadelphia Centennial Exposition of 1876, and the 1684 town deed signed by Nanapashemet Indians.

Given Marblehead's waterfront location, seafood headlines the town's few dining options. If you're looking for a **snack**, try *Flynnie's at the Beach*, on

Devereaux Beach (summers only), for inexpensive fish and chips. Alternatively, *The Landing*, 81 Front St, serves fresh seafood in a room overlooking the harbor; you can also tuck into a steak at *The Barnacle*, 141 Front St, while sitting on an outdoor terrace overlooking the water.

Gloucester

Founded in 1623, **GLOUCESTER**, just forty miles north of Boston up Route 1 to 127, is the oldest fishing and trading port in Massachusetts – though years of overfishing the once cod-rich waters have robbed the town of any aura of affluence it may have had in the past. Indeed, what little notoriety remains stems from the tragedy of the *Andrea Gale*, a local fishing boat caught, and lost, in the worst storm in (recorded) history, when three simultaneous storms merged off the coast in October 1991 and produced 100-foot-high waves; her story is told in Sebastian Junger's *The Perfect Storm* (see "Books", p.246). The fate of all the sailors (some 100,000 total) who have perished offshore is commemorated by a 1923 bronze statue, *Man at the Wheel*, overlooking the harbor. There's little contemporary goings-on besides, as the once-ballyhooed **Rocky Neck Art Colony**, for instance, is not much of a colony anymore, though a number of local artists do show their work in area galleries. Unfortunately, most of these are undistinguished, and others are downright tacky.

Gloucester's only really compelling attraction is found a short drive south along the rocky coast of Route 127: the imposing **Hammond Castle Museum**, at 80 Hesperus Ave (June–Aug daily 10am–5pm; Sept–May weekends only 10am–3pm; $8; ☎978/283-7673, ⓦwww.hammondcastle.org), whose builder, the eccentric financier and amateur inventor John Hays Hammond Jr, wanted to bring medieval European relics back to the US. The austere fortress, which overlooks the ocean from the spot that inspired Longfellow's poem *The Wreck of the Hesperus*, is loaded with treasures from armor and tapestries to, strangely enough, an elaborately carved wooden facade of a fifteenth-century French bakery, and the partially crushed skull of one of Columbus' shipmates. The ultimate flight-of-fancy, however, is the 30,000-gallon pool whose contents can be changed from fresh to salt water at the switch of a lever – Hammond allegedly liked to dive into it from his balcony.

Should you fancy a **meal**, stop by the *Blackburn Tavern*, at 2 Main St (☎978/282-1919) for the usual pub grub; the cozy *Home Port Café*, at 2A Pond Rd (☎978-281-6200, closed Sat & Sun 8am–noon), for Portuguese and American fare; or sit seaside at *The Studio*, 51 Rocky Neck Ave (☎978/283-4123), for steak or fresh seafood.

Rockport

ROCKPORT, about five miles north of Gloucester, is a coastal hamlet that's more self-consciously quaint than its southern neighbor – though only oppressively so on summer weekends, when it becomes tourist central. Its main drag is a thin peninsula called **Bearskin Neck**, lined with old salt-box fishermen's cottages transformed into art galleries and restaurants. The Neck rises as it reaches the sea, and there's a nice view of the rocky harbor from the end of it. Otherwise, aside from some decent antique shopping and strolling around **Dock Square** at the town's center, there isn't much doing here.

Inside the aptly named **Paper House** (daily April–Oct 10am–5pm), a few miles north of here in the small residential neighborhood of **Pigeon Cove**, everything is made of paper, from chairs and a piano (keys excepted) to a desk made from copies of the *Christian Science Monitor*. It's the end result of a twenty-year project undertaken in 1922 by a local mechanical engineer who "always resented the daily waste of newspaper." You'll have to decide for yourself if you think he's helped the cause.

For **food**, the *Greenery Restaurant*, at 15 Dock Square (℡978/546-9593), has a pleasant atmosphere, with a light seafood and vegetarian menu. More upscale is *My Place by the Sea*, on Bearskin Neck (℡978/546-9667), which has a stupendous seaside setting to match its delicious lobster. If you want wine with your meal, you'll have to bring your own, however, as there's none sold here; Rockport is a "dry town."

Plymouth

Though the South Shore makes a clean sweep of the coast from suburban Quincy to the former whaling port of New Bedford, really the only place of interest is tiny **PLYMOUTH**, America's so-called "hometown," forty miles south of Boston. It's mostly given over to commemorating, in various degrees of taste and tack, the landing of the 102 Pilgrims here in December of 1620.

The proceedings start off with a solemn pseudo-Greek temple by the sea that encloses the otherwise nondescript **Plymouth Rock**, where the Pilgrims are said to have touched land. As is typical with most sites of this ilk, it is of symbolic importance only – they had already spent several weeks on Cape Cod before landing here. On the hill behind the venerable stone, the **Plymouth National Wax Museum**, at 15 Carver St (daily: March–May & Oct–Nov 9am–7pm; June–Sept 9am–9pm; closed Dec–Feb; $5; ℡508/746-6468), charges admission to its inadvertently kitsch sound-and-light tableaux of the early days of settlement. Down the street is the similarly unconvincing **Pilgrim Hall Museum**, at 75 Court St (Feb–Dec daily 9.30am–4.30pm; $5; ℡508/746-1620, ⓦwww.pilgrimhall.org), where you enter a room filled with furniture

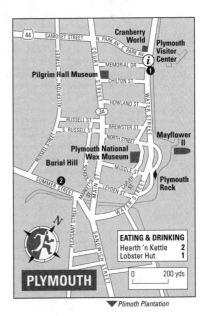

▼ *Plimoth Plantation*

which may or may not have come over on the *Mayflower*, along with numerous pairs of shoes which the Pilgrims may or may not have worn.

A more authentic attraction, and a better way to spend your time, is the newly restored replica of the *Mayflower*, called the **Mayflower II** (April–Nov daily 9am–5pm; $8; ☎508/746-1622, ⓦwww.plimoth.org), on the State Pier in Plymouth Harbor. Built in Britain by English craftsmen following the detailed and historically accurate plans of an American naval architect at MIT, the *Mayflower II* was ceremoniously docked in Plymouth in 1957 and given to America as a gesture of goodwill. You are free to wander the ship at leisure and there are trained staff members – in contemporary clothing – available to answer any questions.

Similar in approach and authenticity is the **Plimoth Plantation**, three miles south of town off Route 3 (April–Nov daily 9am–5pm; $20; ☎508/746-1622, ⓦwww.plimoth.org). Everything you see in the plantation, such as the Pilgrim Village of 1627 and the Wampanoag Indian Settlement, has been created using traditional techniques; even the farm animals were "backbred" to resemble their seventeenth-century counterparts. Again, actors dressed in period garb try to bring you back in time; depending on your level of resistance, it can be quite enjoyable. If you intend to see both the Plantation and the *Mayflower*, you'd do better to buy a combo ticket ($22) from the admissions desk.

A reasonably interesting way to pass time for free is at **Cranberry World**, at 225 Water St, just past the visitor's center on the north side of town (May–Nov daily 9.30am–5pm; ☎508/747-2350), a slick little museum sponsored by juice giant Ocean Spray. Exhibits show how the tart crimson berries are harvested from local bogs and processed; frequent tours end with free juice samples.

Massachusetts pilgrimage

The band of English **Pilgrims** that spurred Britain's attempt to colonize New England were way off course when their vessel, the *Mayflower*, arrived in Cape Cod harbor on November 21, 1620 – they had actually been aiming for the Hudson Valley, where the Virginia Company had granted them a parcel of land. Instead of re-charting their path, however, the 102 Church of England Separatists decided to claim for themselves the land they surveyed before them. The move prompted the 41 men aboard to draft and sign the **Mayflower Compact**, self-proclaimed as the "first written constitution in the world," which the group agreed to uphold with "all due submission and obedience"; the document became the foundation for all subsequent American governmental legalese.

After going ashore in **Provincetown**, the land party returned with reports of bleak and extreme conditions, and the lot sailed on to rocky shore a few miles west, where they disembarked during a brutal winter storm, on December 16, 1620. The party that came ashore christened the new land **Plymouth**, after their English starting point, and strove to establish a life free of the religious persecution they had known back home. In doing so, however, the Pilgrims encountered such harsh conditions that within the first year of their arrival, almost half of their number had died. Even so, when the *Mayflower* sailed once more for England the following spring, not a single Pilgrim returned with her.

Their lot changed for the better in the fall of 1621, when the harvest, which they had sewn with the help of resident **Wampanoag Indians**, a local Algonquin tribe, proved bountiful. To celebrate, the Pilgrims invited the natives to join them in a three-day feast that's considered the genesis of modern-day American holiday of **Thanksgiving**, a yearly November celebration decreed by Abraham Lincoln more than two centuries later, on October 3, 1863.

You can also slake your thirst at the *John Carver Inn*, at 25 Summer St (☎1-800/274-1620), which has a tavern and a **restaurant**, the *Hearth 'n Kettle*, that is an excellent setting for a very American meal or a drink; as far as other eating options go, the *Lobster Hut*, on the waterfront (☎508/746-2270), has good, reasonably priced seafood.

Provincetown

The brash fishing burgh of **PROVINCETOWN**, at the very tip of Cape Cod, is a popular summer destination for bohemians, artists and fun-seekers lured by the excellent beaches, art galleries and welcoming atmosphere. While it's become a major **gay** resort destination, complete with frequent festivals and theme weekends to match, P-town – as this coastal community of five thousand year-round inhabitants is commonly known – also has a drop of **Portuguese** culture to embellish it, after a smallish population of fishermen began settling here starting in the mid-1800s; their legacy is now celebrated in an annual June festival complete with music and Portuguese soup-tasting competitions. The appealing hamlet should not be missed by anyone, especially as it's just a few hours' ferry ride from Boston. For online information before your trip, visit ⓦ www.provincetown.com; gay men and lesbians can also check ⓦ www.gayprovincetown.com.

The Town and beaches

Provincetown's center is essentially two three-mile long streets connected by nearly forty tiny lanes of no more than two short blocks each, making for a

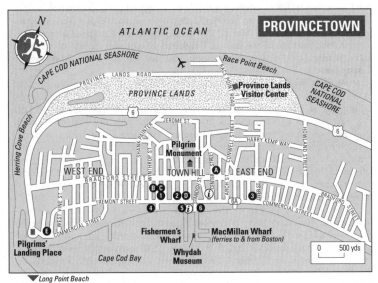

ACCOMMODATION				EATING			
Beaconlight Guesthouse	B	Secret Garden Inn	D	Bayside Betty's	4	Lobster Pot	6
Gifford House Inn & Dance Club	C	Sunset Inn	A	Chester	3	Portuguese Bakery	5
Land's End Inn	E			Front Street	2	Spiritus	1

pretty compact place that's easy to get around on foot. The first of these two main strips, the aptly named **Commercial Street**, is where the action is, loaded with restaurants, cafés, art galleries, and trendy shops. Jutting right into the middle of Provincetown Harbor, just off Commercial Street, **MacMillan Wharf** is busy as well, though with whale-watching boats, yachts, and colorful old Portuguese fishing vessels. It also houses the engaging **Whydah Museum**, at 16 Macmillan Wharf (June–Aug daily 10am–7pm; May & Sept–Oct daily 10am–5pm; Nov–Dec Sat & Sun 10am–5pm; $8; ☎508/487-8899, ⓦwww.whydah.com), which displays some of the bounty from the *Whydah*, a pirate ship commandeered by "Black Sam" Bellamy that shipwrecked off the coast of Wellfleet in April 1717. The collection ranges from odds-and-ends like silver shoe buckles and flintlock pistols to rare African gold jewellery attributed to West Africa's Akan people that was likely en-route to England, where it would have been melted to make guineas.

Two blocks north of the wharf, on Town Hill, is the 252-foot granite tower of the **Pilgrim Monument**, named for the Puritans who actually first landed near here before moving on to Plymouth. From the observation deck of the Florentine-style bell tower, accessible by stairs and ramps, the whole Cape (and sometimes Boston) can be seen (daily; July–Aug 9am–7pm; May–June & Sept–Nov 9am–4.15pm; $6; ☎508/487-1310, ⓦwww.pilgrim-monument .org). At the bottom of the hill on **Bradford Street**, the second of the two main roadways, is a bas-relief monument to the Pilgrims' **Mayflower Compact**.

In the quiet **West End** of P-Town, many of the weathered clapboard houses are decorated with colored blinds, white picket fences and wildflowers spilling out of every possible crevice. A modest bronze **plaque** on a boulder at the western end of Commercial Street commemorates the Pilgrim's actual landing place. West of town, along Route 6A, **Herring Cove Beach** is easily reached by bike and is justly famous for its sunsets, while at the Cape's northern tip, off Route 6, **Race Point Beach**, a wide strip of white sand backed by tall dunes, is the archetypal Cape Cod beach. It abuts the ethereal **Province Lands**, where vast sweeping moors and bushy dunes are threatened by a deadly sea, site of some 3000 known shipwrecks.

One of the best things to do around Provincetown is to take an organized, but unusual, tour: choose to either ramble about the dunes in a four-wheel-drive vehicle with **Art's Dune Tours**, at Commercial and Standish (April–Oct 10am–dusk; $12; ☎508/487-1950, ⓦwww.artsdunetours.com), or fly over them in a replica 1938 biplane ($60; ☎1-888/BIPLANE or 508/428-8732; advance reservations required). Twenty-minute flights take off from the Cape Cod Airport, near the intersection of Race Lane and Route 149; or, if you wish, you and two friends can also opt to board a Cessna (same phone; $69) instead.

Accommodation

P-Town's **accommodation** options run the gamut from full-scale resorts to motels, with a few B&Bs and rental villas rounding out the package. Provincetown Reservations (☎1-800/648-0364, ⓦwww.ptownres.com) and Intown Reservations (☎1-800/677-8696, ⓦwww.intownreservations.com) can usually rustle up lodgings at busy times. For accommodation price codes, see box on p.158 or on the inside front cover.

Beaconlight Guesthouse 12 Winthrop St ☎1-800/696 9603, ⓦwww.beaconlightguesthouse.com. Stylish ten-room guesthouse with individually appointed rooms, equipped with air conditioning, TV and VCR. ❸

Gifford House Inn & Dance Club 9–11 Carver St ☎1-800/434-0130, ⓦwww.giffordhouse.com. Popular gay resort with lobby piano bar, restaurant and dance floor; continental breakfast included in rates. ❷

Land's End Inn 22 Commercial St ☎1-800/276-7088, ⓦwww.landsendinn.com. Meticulously decorated rooms and suites, many with sweeping ocean views, in a fanciful turreted house; continental breakfast included. ❹

Secret Garden Inn 300a Commercial St ☎866/786-9646, ⓦwww.provincetown.com/secretgardeninn. Four quaint rooms in a house with a verandah, done up in country furnishings, and with modern touches like TVs and air conditioning; country breakfast included. ❸

Sunset Inn 142 Bradford St ☎508/487-9810, ⓦwww.sunsetinnptown.com. Clean, quiet rooms in an 1850 captain's house with double or queen beds and private or shared bath. ❷–❸

Eating

Provincetown **restaurants** range from the expected lobster-joints to creative Portuguese eateries. Many of them also do just fine for a **drink**, too.

Bayside Betty's 177 Commercial St ☎508/487-6566. Funky waterfront eatery with hearty breakfasts and seafood dinners; it's also a popular spot to grab a martini.

Chester 404 Commercial St ☎508/487-8200. Sophisticated pillared eatery with stellar New-American menu featuring dishes like wild mushroom risotto and seared sea scallops, plus a well-chosen wine list.

Front Street 230 Commercial St ☎508/487-9715. Popular Italian and Continental restaurant located in a Victorian house; menu changes weekly, but you might find dishes like potato-crusted salmon with raspberry butter, and chickpea and artichoke flan.

Lobster Pot 321 Commercial St ☎508/487-0842. Let the landmark neon lobster sign lead you to ultrafresh and affordable crustaceans.

Portuguese Bakery 299 Commercial St ☎508/487-1803. An excellent stop for baked goods, particularly the fried rabanada (similar to french toast).

Spiritus 190 Commercial St ☎508/487-2808. One of the cheapest places to fill up on fabulous pizza and gourmet coffee. Open late.

Drinking and nightlife

P-town's **nightlife** is heavily geared towards a gay clientele, resulting in ubiquitous tea dances, drag shows and video bars; some of them have terrific waterfront locations and terraces to match, making them ideal spots to sit out with a drink at sunset.

Boatslip 161 Commercial St ☎800/451-SLIP, ⓦwww.boatslipresort.com. The Sunday tea dances at this resort are legendary; you can either dance away on a long wooden deck overlooking the water, or cruise inside under a disco ball and flashing lights.

Crown and Anchor 247 Commercial St ☎508/487-1430, ⓦonlyatthecrown.com. A massive complex housing several bars, including *The Vault*, P-Town's only leather bar, *Wave*, a video-karaoke bar, and *Paramount*, a cabaret with nightly acts.

Pied Piper 193 Commercial St ☎508/487-1527, ⓦwww.thepied.com. Though predominantly a lesbian club (it's the oldest one in the country), the outdoor deck and inside dance floor at this trendy waterfront space attract men, too, for their longstanding After Tea T-Dance (Sun 6.30–9pm). Thurs is Classic Disco night; Friday and Saturday are house nights.

Steve's Alibi 291 Commercial St ☎508/487-2890, ⓦ www.stevesalibi.com. Campy bar with four daily drag shows (4pm, 7pm, 9pm & 11pm).

Listings

Listings

Accommodation

For such a popular travel destination, Boston has a surprisingly limited range of reasonably priced **accommodation**. Though there are still bargains to be found, prices at many formerly moderate hotels have inched into the expense-account range – you're looking at spending upwards of $200 just to stay the night during **high season**.

Your best bet to save money is to make your booking online: most hotels offer discounted rates on their websites, as do discount booking agencies like Orbitz. Additional discounts can often be had with an AAA membership, which usually knocks around ten percent off the rate. Your other option, if you don't mind braving the sharp East Coast winter, is to come in the **off season**, around November through April, when many hotels not only have more vacancies but also offer weekend package discounts. At any other time of year, be sure to make reservations well in advance. September (start of the school year) and May through June (graduation) are particularly busy months, due to the large student population here.

In response to the hotel crunch, some visitors turn to less-expensive **bed and breakfasts**, many of which are tucked into renovated brownstones in Back Bay; other good B&B choices are to be found outside the city center, in Brookline and Cambridge. Short-term **furnished apartments**, spread throughout the city, are another option, though most have two-week minimums. There are also a handful of decent **hostels** if you're looking for truly budget accommodation.

Throughout this chapter, hotels and B&Bs (not hostels, though; exact prices are given for these) are **price coded** using a system explained in the box on p.158, and, for quick reference, on the inside front cover as well. Keep in mind, though, that these price codes reflect what a double room in high season generally averages; in the off season you'll often be paying less than what's indicated in our reviews. Finally, all accommodations are **keyed** to the relevant **chapter map** in the Guide portion of this book; see the index for page numbers.

Hotels

Boston and Cambridge combined have an underwhelming fifty **hotels** or so between them, a shortage which helps, somewhat, to explain the exorbitant prices charged to stay in them.

While Boston hotels are not suited to every traveler's budget, they do cater to most tastes, and range from the usual assortment of chains to some excellent independently run hotels, the highest concentration of which – including some of the best – are in **Back Bay**. Most of the business hotels are located in or around the **Financial District**, and are not bad if you don't mind being away from the nightlife.

Accommodation price codes

The price codes given in the reviews in this chapter reflect the **average price for a standard double room in high season** (June to September, as well as around Christmas and other holidays), excluding **room tax**, which is 12.45 percent. Most B&Bs are exempt from this tax; if you're concerned about costs adding up, make sure to ask about this when booking your room.

❶ less than $75
❷ $75–100
❸ $100–130
❹ $130–165
❺ $165–200
❻ $200–250
❼ $250–300
❽ $300–350
❾ $350 and up

Modestly cheaper rates can be found at **Cambridge**'s hotels, though rates at these, too, go sky-high around college commencement and during the fall. Note that you'll save some money by booking your hotel on line; if calling, be sure to inquire about special packages when reserving a room. A handful of gay-friendly hotels, mostly located in the **South End** district, are listed on p.205.

Downtown

Boston Harbor Hotel 70 Rowes Wharf ☎439-7000 or 1-800/752-7077, ⓦwww.bhh.com; Aquarium T. Opulent accommodation in an atmosphere of studied corporate elegance. There's a health club, pool, gracious concierge staff, and rooms with harbor and city views; the former are substantially pricier. ❻–❼

Boston Marriott Long Wharf 296 State St ☎227-0800 or 1-888/236-2427, ⓦwww.marriott .com; Aquarium T. All the rooms here boast harbor views, but the stunning vaulted lobby is what really makes this *Marriott* stand out. The rooms themselves are standard business-class affairs, with the expected data port phone hook-ups, in-room movies, and generic furnishings. ❻–❼

Harborside Inn 185 State St ☎723-7500, ⓦwww.hagopianhotels.com; State T. This small hotel is housed in a renovated 1890s mercantile warehouse across from Quincy Market. The (relatively) reasonably priced rooms – with exposed brick, hardwood floors, and cherry furniture – are a welcome surprise for this part of town. ❺

Le Meridien 250 Franklin St ☎451-1900 or 1-800/543-4300, ⓦwww.lemeridien.com; State T. Located in the heart of the Financial District, this stern granite building is the former Federal Reserve Bank of Boston. The rooms are spacious and modern, with perks like high-speed Internet access, but the overall atmosphere is a bit stiff. ❺–❻

Marriott's Customs House 3 McKinley Sq ☎310-6300 or 1-888/236-2427, ⓦwww.marriott.com; Aquarium T. All the rooms at this downtown landmark-turned-hotel are high-end, one-bedroom suites with spectacular Boston Harbor and city views; there's also a great gym on the top floor. ❼

Millennium Bostonian Hotel Faneuil Hall Marketplace ☎523-3600 or 1-866/866-8086, ⓦwww.millenniumhotels.com; State T. Formerly known as the *Regal Bostonian*, this hotel has splendid quarters, some with fireplaces and en-suite balconies, located in the heart of downtown. The rooms and lobby are festooned with portraits of famous colonial-era figures. ❻–❼

Milner 78 Charles St South ☎426-6220 or 1-877/MILNERS, ⓦwww.milner-hotels.com; Boylston T. An uninspiring but affordable hotel convenient to the Theater District, Bay Village and the Public Garden. All room rates include a continental breakfast, served in a European-style nook in the lobby. ❹

Nine Zero Hotel 90 Tremont St ☎772-5800 or 1-800/434-7347, ⓦwww.ninezerohotel.com; Park St T. Executive-class hotel with polished quarters equipped with high-speed Internet access, CD players and VCRs, and cushy linens. ❾

Omni Parker House 60 School St ☎227-8600 or 1-800/843-6664, ⓦwww.omniparkerhouse.com; Park T. No one can compete with the *Omni Parker House* in the history department: it's the oldest continuously operating hotel in the US. Though the present building only dates from 1927, the lobby, decorated in dark oak with carved gilt moldings, recalls the splendor of the original nineteenth-century building that once housed it. The rooms are small, however, and a bit dowdy. ❻

Swissôtel 1 Avenue de Lafayette ☎451-2600 or 1-800/621-9200, ⓦwww.swissotel.com; **Downtown Crossing T.** Boston's *Swissôtel* is a plush if peculiarly located option – on the fringes of ragged Downtown Crossing, not the best place to be at night. There's no pedestrian access to the sleek sixteen-story tower; entry is via the parking garage. ❹–❺

Tremont House 275 Tremont St ☎426-1400 or 1-800/331-9998, ⓦwww.wyndham.com; **NE Medical Center T.** The opulent lobby of this 1925 hotel, the former national head-quarters of the Elks Lodge, somewhat compensates for its rather small rooms; and, if you want to be in the thick of the Theater District you can't do better. ❹–❺

XV Beacon 15 Beacon St ☎670-1500 or 1-877/XVBEACON, ⓦwww.xvbeacon.com; **Park St T.** Ultra-decadent boutique hotel across from the Boston Athenaeum, with 61 spectacular rooms equipped with marble bathrooms, in-room fax, high-speed internet, Kiehl toiletries, CD player, beautiful upholstry and working gas fireplaces; some rooms even have four-poster beds. All rates include access to your own chauffeured Mercedes for the length of your stay. ❽–❾

Charlestown

Constitution Inn YMCA 150 Second Ave ☎241-8400 or 1-800/495-9622, ⓦwww.constitutioninn.com. Despite its billing as a YMCA, this inn, which is easily connected to downtown by ferry, has 150 private rooms equipped with cable TV, air conditioning and private baths; there's also an on-site weight room, sauna and pool. Though predominantly servicing military personnel, civilians are more than welcome. ❷

Beacon Hill and the West End

Beacon Hill Hotel 25 Charles St ☎723-7575 or 1-888/959-BHHB, ⓦwww.beaconhillhotel.com; **Charles T.** A luxurious boutique hotel occupying two mid-1800s brownstones. Its twelve sleek chambers are decked out with flat-screen televisions, mahogany fireplaces, and louvered windows. ❻

Charles Street Inn 94 Charles St ☎314-8900, ⓦwww.charlesstreetinn.com; **Charles T.** Intimate nine-room inn with lavish rooms styled after the (presumed) tastes of various Boston luminaries; the Isabella Stewart Gardner room features a Rococco chandelier, while Oliver Wendell Holmes' chamber boasts a king-sized sleigh bed. All rooms come with working fireplaces, too. ❽–❾

Holiday Inn Select – Government Center 5 Blossom St ☎742-7630 or 1-800/HOLIDAY, ⓦwww.holiday-inn.com; **Bowdoin T.** Somewhat misleadingly named – located in the West End and more convenient to Beacon Hill than Government Center – this Holiday Inn-standard property has all the modern accoutrements, including a weight room and pool. ❺

The John Jeffries House 14 David G Mugar Way ☎367-1866, ⓦwww.johnjeffrieshouse.com; **Charles T.** Mid-scale, recently renovated hotel at the foot of Beacon Hill, with a cozy lounge for hotel guests, and all rooms done up in Victorian style, with cable TV and air conditioning; single-occupancy studios include kitchenettes. And, though it's wedged in between a busy highway and the local **T** stop, multipaned windows keep most of the sound out. ❷

The Shawmut Inn 280 Friend St ☎720-5544 or 1-800/350-7784, ⓦwww.shawmutinn.com; **North Station T.** Located in the old West End near the FleetCenter, this place has 66 comfortable, modern rooms, all of which come equipped with kitchenettes and include continental breakfast. Nothing special, but not bad at all for the price. ❹

Back Bay

Back Bay Hilton 40 Dalton St ☎236-1100 or 1-800/874-0663, ⓦwww.hilton.com; **Hynes T.** Though this chain hotel is fairly charmless, it does have good weekend packages, a fitness room and pool, as well as a guaranteed good American-style breakfast at the hotel's informal restaurant, *Boodle's* (see review p.182). It's actually a bit out of Back Bay, closer to the bohemian area of the Berklee College of Music than the shops of Newbury Street – a plus in some folks' eyes. ❺

Boston Park Plaza Hotel & Towers 64 Arlington St ☎426-2000 or 1-800/225-2008, ⓦwww.bostonparkplaza.com; **Arlington T.** The *Park Plaza* is practically its own neighborhood, housing the original *Legal Seafoods* restaurant (see review p.182) alongside three other eateries, plus offices for American, United and Delta airlines. Its old-school elegance and hospitality – plus its central location – make it stand out; the high-ceilinged rooms are comfortable, too. **6**

Charlesmark Hotel 655 Boylston St T247-1212, Wwww.thecharlesmark.com; Copley **T**. New, 33-room European-style hotel; while the rooms are on the small side, they compensate with cozy beechwood furnishings and modern accoutrements like in-room CD players, VCRs, and dataports. **5–6**

The Colonnade 120 Huntington Ave T424-7000 or 1-800/962-3030, Wwww.colonnadehotel.com; Prudential **T**. With its beige poured-concrete shell, the *Colonnade* is barely distinguishable from the Church of Christ buildings directly across the street. Still, there are spacious rooms (if at a price) and, in summer, a rooftop pool – the only one in Boston. **7**

Copley Square Hotel 47 Huntington Ave T536-9000 or 1-800/225-7062, Wwww.copleysquare-hotel.com; Copley **T**. Situated on the eastern fringe of Copley Square, this family-run, low-key hotel is popular with a European crowd. The rooms won't win any style awards, given their dowdy linens, but they're spacious enough and equipped with modern hook-ups, cable TV, coffeemakers, and the like. **6**

Eliot 370 Commonwealth Ave T267-1607 or 1-800/442-5468, Wwww.eliothotel.com; Hynes **T**. West Back Bay's answer to the *Ritz-Carlton*, this calm, plush, nine-floor suite hotel has sizeable rooms with kitchenettes and luxurious Italian marble baths; they also serve a nice breakfast downstairs. **6–9**

Fairmont Copley Plaza 138 St James Ave T267-5300 or 1-800/795-3906, Wwww.fairmont.com; Copley **T**. Built in 1912, the *Fairmont* has long boasted Boston's most elegant lobby, with its glittering chandeliers, mirrored walls and *trompe-l'oeil* sky. Most rooms are decorated in a French neo-Classical style; but even if you don't stay here, have a martini in the fabulous *Oak Bar* (see review p.190), with its high-coffered ceilings and mahogany chairs. **5–6**

Four Seasons 200 Boylston St T338-4400 or 1-800/332-3442, Wwww.fourseasons.com; Arlington **T**. The tops in city accommodation, with 288 large rooms – with amenities like high-speed Internet access and in-room fax – offering quiet, contemporary comfort. The penthouse-level health spa has an indoor pool that seems to float over the Public Garden, and the superlative *Aujourd'hui* restaurant (see review p.181) is housed here, too. **9**

The Lenox 710 Boylston St T536-5300 or 1-800/225-7676, Wwww.lenoxhotel.com; Copley **T**. Billed as Boston's version of the *Waldorf-Astoria* when its doors first opened in 1900, the *Lenox* – after a recent renovation – is still one of the most comfortably upscale hotels in the city, with 212 rooms featuring high ceilings, walk-in closets, and, in some, working fireplaces. **5–6**

Marriott at Copley Place Copley Place T236-5800 or 1-800/228-9290, F236-5885; Copley **T**. There's not a whole lot of character here (the *Marriott* downtown has loads more; see p.158) but it's modern, clean, and well-located, with an indoor pool. Ask about lower weekend rates that include full breakfast. **7**

Ritz-Carlton 15 Arlington St T536-5700 or 1-800/241-3333, Wwww.ritzcarlton.com; Arlington **T**. This is the *Ritz-Carlton* flagship, and even if the rooms are a bit cramped, the hotel retains a certain air of refinement (it *is* the *Ritz-Carlton*, after all). The one thing no one can complain about is the view of the Public Garden, available from the second-floor dining room or street-level *Ritz Bar*. **9**

Sheraton Boston Hotel 39 Dalton St T236-2000 or 1-800/325-3535, F617/236-1702; Hynes **T**. After a major renovation, the *Sheraton* is looking less like a chain and more like a Back Bay boutique. Featuring sleigh beds with pillow-top mattresses and an expanded in-room work area, the *Sheraton* mostly plays host to convention-goers; the Hynes Convention Center and Prudential Center are both connected to the hotel. **7**

Westin Copley Place T262-9600 or 1-800/228-3000, Wwww.westin.com; Copley **T**. Rooms are modern and spacious at this well-located hotel. Always hopping with convention-goers, it's a lively place to hole up in winter. Request a room facing the Charles River. **6**

Kenmore Square and the Fenway

The Buckminster 645 Beacon St T236-7050 or 1-800/727-2825, F617/262-0068; Kenmore **T**. Though renovated not so long ago, the 1905 *Buckminster* retains the feel of an old Boston hotel with its antique furnishings. Its Kenmore Square location also puts it within easy walking distance of Fenway Park and Boston University; great rates, too. **4**

Gryphon House 9 Bay State Rd T375-9003 or 1-877/375-9003, Wgryphonhouseboston.com; Kenmore **T**. This hotel-cum-B&B around the corner from Fenway has eight wonderfully appointed suites equipped with working gas fireplaces, cable TV, VCR, CD player, high-speed Internet connection, continental breakfast, and free parking (a big plus in Boston). You won't want to leave your room. ❹–❼

Cambridge

Cambridge Marriott 2 Cambridge Center ☎494-6600 or 1-800/228-9290, ⓦwww.marriott.com; Kendall **T**. Stately, well-appointed rooms with a minimum of pretension. Many have views of the river, while the rest look out onto industrial Kendall Square. Some weekend packages include a sumptuous brunch. ❹

Charles Hotel 1 Bennett St ☎864-1200 or 1-800/882-1818, ⓦwww.charleshotel.com; Harvard **T**. Clean, bright rooms – some overlooking the Charles – that have a good array of amenities: cable TV, three phones, minibar, Shaker furniture, and access to the

adjacent WellBridge Health Spa. There's also an excellent jazz club, *Regattabar*, and restaurant, *Henrietta's Table* on the premises – see p.196 and p.186 for reviews. ❺

Harvard Square Hotel 110 Mt Auburn St ☎864-5200 or 1-800/222-8733, ⓦwww.theinnatharvard.com; Harvard **T**. Sister hotel of the *Inn at Harvard* (see p.162), the rooms here aren't as elegant as its sibling's are, but they do have a pleasant enough oak-and-burgundy decor and amenities like mini-fridges; great location in the midst of Harvard Square. ❺–❻

Hotel @ MIT 20 Sidney St ☎577-0200 or 1-800/524-2538, ⓦwww.hotelatmit.com; Kendall Square **T**. Contemporary hotel anchoring an office tower near MIT, with a lobby festooned with AI robots created by the university's tech-savvy students; the modern rooms have nice touches like louvered window shades and muted color schemes, and come with high-speed Internet access. ❹

Hyatt Regency Cambridge 575 Memorial Drive ☎492-1234 or 1-800/233-1234,

△ Boston Harbor Hotel at Rowes Wharf

@www.cambridge.hyatt.com; Kendall **T**. Brick ziggurat-like riverside monolith, with luxurious rooms, pool, health club, and a patio with gazebo. Picturesque location on the Charles, but it's a hike from Cambridge's major points of interest. ❺–❻

Inn at Harvard 1201 Massachusetts Ave ☎491-2222 or 1-800/222-8733, @www.theinnatharvard.com; Harvard **T**. This carefully constructed hotel is designed to give the impression of old-school grandeur; plus it's so close to Harvard you can smell the ivy. Pleasant but rather small rooms. ❺–❻

Kendall Hotel 350 Main St ☎577-1300, @www.kendallhotel.com; Kendall Square **T**. This hotel near MIT occupies a former 1893 fire station. The 65 rooms are country-chic, with quilts and reproduction antiques; modern furnishings include high-speed Internet access. ❺–❻

Radisson Cambridge 777 Memorial Drive ☎492-7777 or 1-800/333-3333, @www.radisson.com; Central or Harvard **T**. The

business-class rooms at this chain hotel, located between Harvard and MIT, are nothing extraordinary, but many come with terrific views of the Charles and Back Bay; also, there's an indoor pool and gym. ❹

Royal Sonesta Cambridge Parkway ☎491-3600 or 1-800/SONESTA, @www.sonesta.com; Kendall Square **T**. Luxury quarters with good views of the downtown Boston skyline. The fancy rooms have big, sparkling bathrooms, and the vast lobby is festooned with strikingly bad art. ❻

Sheraton Commander 16 Garden St ☎547-4800 or 1-800/535-5007, @www.sheratoncommander .com; Harvard **T**. The hotel's name refers to George Washington, who, legend has it, took command of the Continental Army on nearby Cambridge Common. Rooms tend to be rather dark and small, though there are some cute frills, such as terrycloth robes, nightlights and even an umbrella service (should you have forgotton to pack yours). ❺

Bed and breakfasts

The **bed and breakfast** industry in Boston is thriving, for the most part because it is so difficult to find accommodation here for under $200 a night – and some B&Bs offer just that, at least in the off-season. On the other hand, many B&Bs cash in on the popularity of their old-world charm, meaning their prices may hover near those of the swankier hotels.

Some of the best B&Bs are outside the city, in either **Cambridge** or **Brookline**, though there are nice in-town options as well. You can make reservations directly with the places we've listed; there are also numerous B&B **agencies** that can do the booking for you, and find you a room in an unlisted house (see box below).

B&Bs and short-term accommodation

Rental agencies

Bed & Breakfast Agency of Boston 47 Commercial Wharf, Boston, MA 02110 ☎720-3540 or 1-800/248-9262, UK ☎ 0800/895 128, @www.boston-bnbagency.com. Can book you a room in a brownstone, a waterfront loft or even on a yacht.

Bed & Breakfast Associates Bay Colony Ltd PO Box 57166 Babson Park Branch, Boston, MA 02157 ☎781/647-4949 or 1-888/486-6018, @www.bnbboston.com. Features some real finds in Back Bay and the South End.

Bed & Breakfast Reservations PO Box 590264 Newtown Center, MA 02459 ☎964-1606 or 1-800/832-2632, ⊠332-8572, @www.bbreserve.com. Lists B&Bs in Greater Boston, North Shore and Cape Cod.

Boston Reservations/Boston Bed & Breakfast, Inc ☎332-4199, ⊠332-5751, @www.bostonreservations.com. Competitive rates at B&Bs as well as at leading hotels.

Greater Boston Hospitality PO Box 1142 Brookline, MA 02446 ☎277-5430, ⊠277-7170, @www.bostonbedandbreakfast.com. Rentals in homes, inns and condominiums.

Charlestown

Bed & Breakfast Afloat 28 Constitution Rd ☎241-9640, ⦿www.bostonharbor.com/bb.html; **Community College T.** Guests at this original B&B get to hole up on their own personal houseboat, sailboat or yacht, right in Boston Harbor; the fancier vessels come with DVD players and deck-top Jacuzzis. All come with continental breakfast and access to the marina pool. ❸–❾

Beacon Hill

Beacon Hill Bed & Breakfast 27 Brimmer St ☎523-7376; **Charles T.** Only two spacious rooms with fireplaces are available in this well-situated brick townhouse, built in 1869. There are sumptuous full breakfasts; two-night minimum stay, three on holiday weekends. ❻

Back Bay

463 Beacon Street Guest House 463 Beacon St ☎536-1302, ⦿www.463beacon.com; **Hynes T.** The good-sized rooms in this renovated brownstone, located in the heart of Back Bay, are available by the night, week, and month, and come equipped with kitchenettes, cable TV, and various hotel amenities (though no maid service); some have a/c, hardwood floors, and ornamental fireplaces. Ask for the top-floor room. ❶–❸
Copley House 239 W Newton St ☎236-8300 or 1-800/331-1318, ⦿www.bostonapartments.com; **Prudential T.** Furnished studios and one-bedroom apartments on an attractive edge of Back Bay, across from the Copley Plaza shopping center; rented by the week or month. ❽–❾
Copley Inn 19 Garrison St ☎236-0300 or 1-800/232-0306, ⦿www.copleyinn.com; **Prudential T.** Comfortable rooms with full kitchens, friendly staff and a great location make this an ideal place to stay in Back Bay. Get one night free with a week's stay. ❸
Newbury Guest House 261 Newbury St ☎437-7666, ⦿www.hagopianhotels.com; **Copley T.** Big Victorian brownstone that still fills up whenever there's a big convention in town, so be sure to call ahead. The 32 rooms range from cramped chambers with over-stuffed chairs to spacious bay-windowed quarters with hardwood floors and sleighbeds. Continental breakfast included. ❸–❺

The South End

82 Chandler Street 82 Chandler St ☎482-0408 or 1-888/482-0408, ⦿www.channel1.com /82chandler; **Back Bay T.** Basic rooms with minimal service in a restored, 1863 brownstone that sits on one of the most up-and-coming streets of the South End. Breakfast, when and if it's available, is served on the sunny top floor, where you'll also find the best room in the house. ❸–❹

Kenmore Square and the Fenway

Oasis Guest House 22 Edgerly Rd ☎267-2262, ⦿www.oasisgh.com; **Symphony T.** Sixteen comfortable, very affordable rooms, some with shared baths, in a renovated brownstone near Symphony Hall, with continental breakfast and nightly meet-and-greet soiree at 8pm – they supply the hors d'oeuvres, you bring the booze. ❷–❹

Brookline

Beacon Inn 1087 and 1750 Beacon St ☎566-0088 or 1-888/575-0088, ⦿www.beaconinn.com; **Hawes T.** Fireplaces in the lobbies and original woodwork contribute to the relaxed atmosphere in these two nineteenth-century brownstones, part of the same guest house. The rooms here would be well-suited to a country inn, with their patterned wallpaper, hardwood floors and window sconces; some have working fireplaces. ❸–❺
Beacon Townhouse Inn 1047 Beacon St ☎1-800/872-7211, ⦿www.beacontownhouseinn .com; **Saint Mary T.** National Register historic brownstone within walking distance of the Fenway and Boston University; the rooms are perfectly ordinary, but do come with private bath and cable TV; some have kitchenettes. ❸–❹
Brookline Manor Inn 32 Centre St ☎232-0003 or 1-800/535-5325, ☎734-5815, ⦿www.beaconmanorinn.com; **Coolidge Corner T.** This small guest house, with private and shared baths, is located on a pleasant stretch off Beacon Street; it's just a short subway ride from Kenmore Square. The same management also runs the *Beacon Townhouse Inn*. ❶–❸

Cambridge

A Cambridge B&B 1657 Cambridge St ☎868-7082 or 1-877/994-0844,

ⓦ www.cambridgebnb.com; Harvard **T**. This homey colonial revival house has three pleasant rooms outfitted with canopy beds, and a common room furnished with over-stuffed chairs and plenty of lace. Shared bath. **②**

A Cambridge House 2218 Massachusetts Ave ⓣ 491-6300 or 1-800/232-9989, ⓦ www .acambridgehouse.com; Davis **T**. A classy B&B with gorgeous rooms decked out in canopy beds and period pieces. There are full breakfasts plus evening wine-and-cheese in the parlor. It's a bit far out from any points of interest, but worth the trek. **③**–**⑦**

A Friendly Inn 1673 Cambridge St ⓣ 547-7851; Harvard **T**. A good deal, and just a few min-utes' walk from Harvard Square. The rooms are nothing special and the service doesn't exactly live up to the name, but there are private baths, cable TV and laundry service. **③**–**④**

Harding House 288 Harvard St ⓣ 876-2888, ⓦ www.irvinghouse.com; Harvard **T**. This cozy Victorian home has fourteen bright rooms

with hardwood floors, throw rugs, TVs and air conditioning; includes breakfast. Shared or private bath. **③**–**⑤**

Irving House 24 Irving St ⓣ 547-4600, ⓦ www.irvinghouse.com; Harvard **T**. A quaint option near Harvard Square sharing the same management as the *Harding House*, with laundry and kitchen facilities; both shared and private baths. **③**–**⑤**

Mary Prentiss Inn 6 Prentiss St ⓣ 661-2929, ⓦ www.maryprentissinn.com; Harvard **T**. Eighteen clean, comfortable rooms in an impressively refurbished mid-nineteenth-century Greek Revival building. Full break-fast and snacks are served in the living room, or, weather permitting, on a pleasant outdoor deck. **④**–**⑥**

Prospect Place 112 Prospect St ⓣ 864-7500 or 1-800/769-5303, ⓦ www.prospectpl.com; Central **T**. This Italianate edifice holds a restored parlor, along with nineteenth-century period antiques – including two grand pianos – and recently renovated, floral-decor rooms. **③**–**⑤**

Hostels

There are fairly limited **hostel** accommodations in Boston, and if you want to get in on them, you should definitely book ahead, especially in the summer-time.

Beantown Hostel 222 Friend St ⓣ 723-0800; North Station **T**. This former bowling alley, next door to the *Irish Embassy Youth Hostel* (see p.165), has several co-ed and single-sex dorm rooms, plus a comfy lounge with TV and Internet access. Curfew 1.45am. $22/dorm bed.

Berkeley Residence YWCA 40 Berkeley St ⓣ 375-2524, ⓦ www.ywcaboston.org/berkeley .html; Back Bay **T**. Clean and simple rooms (for women only) in a safe location – next door to a police station. All rates include breakfast; dinner is an additional $6.50. Singles are $50, doubles $70, and triples $75, plus a $2 membership fee.

Greater Boston YMCA 316 Huntington Ave ⓣ 927-8040, ⓦ www.ymcaboston.org; Symphony **T**. Good budget rooms, and access to the Y's health facilities (pool, weight room, etc). Singles are $45–65, but you can get a four-person room for $96. Co-ed facilities are available from late June until early September; the rest of the year it's men only. Ten days maximum stay.

HI–Back Bay Summer Hostel 519 Beacon St ⓣ 353-3294, ⓕ 424-6558, ⓦ www.usahostels.org; Kenmore **T**. This con-verted BU dorm has 63 beds, and a handful of basic single and double rooms. The perks, such as free linen service, self-serve laundry and TV room make it popular with visiting international students. Open mid-June to late August only. $24–54.

HI–Boston 12 Hemenway St ⓣ 536-1027, ⓕ 424-6558, ⓦ www.bostonhostel.org; Hynes **T**. Around the Back Bay–Fenway border, stan-dard dorm accommodation with three or four beds per room. Members $29, non-members $32.

HI–Fenway Summer Hostel 575 Commonwealth Ave ⓣ 267-8599, ⓕ 424-6588, ⓦ www.bostonhostel.org; Kenmore **T**. Another converted BU residence with private rooms and a handful of three-bed dorms with en-suite baths and air conditioning; there's also laundry and Internet access on-site. Open mid-May to late Aug. $35.

Irish Embassy Youth Hostel 232 Friend St

☎973-4841, ℻720-3998. **North Station T.**
Boston's only independent youth hostel is
above the *Irish Embassy* pub (see review
p.190) in the West End, and not far from

Faneuil Hall. The place can be noisy, but
prices include free admission to pub gigs
on most nights, and free barbecues on
Tuesday and Sunday. $22 / dorm bed.

Cafés, snacks and light meals

U
nlike Boston's accommodation options, its choices for quick bites are numerous. The city is packed with all manner of cafés, diners, delis and other places where you can warm up with a coffee, grab a hefty sandwich or salad, and generally keep yourself fueled-up in this city that demands much energy for walking about and exploring.

We've broken down the listings below into two categories: **cafés** and **breakfast, snacks and light meals**. Obviously there will be some crossover between the two, as most cafés offer more than just a good cup of coffee and a relaxing atmosphere. As well, you may find some of the spots offer full meals; however, we've tried to categorize more dinner-oriented options in Chapter 13, Restaurants.

Eating and drinking maps

Within this chapter, as well as Chapter 13, Restaurants, and Chapter 14, Drinking, you'll find maps where we've keyed the eating and drinking options for the major Boston neighborhoods. These maps can be found on the following pages:

Downtown	pp.168–169	Back Bay and the South End	p.183
The North End	p.171	Cambridge	pp.192–193
Beacon Hill	p.180		

Cafés

Boston's role as a university town is reflected in its well-established **café** scene. The toniest spots are those that line Back Bay's **Newbury Street**, where you pay as much for the fancy environs as for the quality of the coffee. Value is much better in the **North End**, whose Italian cafés serve excellent beverages and desserts, plus providing the liveliest atmosphere in town. The most laid-back cafés are across the river in **Cambridge**, catering to the large student population.

Downtown

Boston Coffee Exchange 101 Arch St
☎737-3199; Downtown Crossing **T.**
Cramped coffee shop with a good selection of pastries and sweets to nosh while sipping some of the best coffee in town – the decaf is so good, you'll be forgiven for thinking it's the real thing.

The North End

Caffé dello Sport 308 Hanover St ☏523-5063; **Haymarket T.** A continuous stream of Rai Uno soccer matches is broadcast from the ceiling-mounted TV sets, making for an agreeable din amongst a very local crowd. Opens very early.

Caffé Paradiso 255 Hanover St ☏742-1768; **Haymarket T.** Not much on atmosphere, but the pastries are, hands-down, the best in the North End, and their superb gelato is the only homemade stuff around.

Caffé Vittoria 296 Hanover St ☏227-7606; **Haymarket T.** A Boston institution, the *Vittoria's* atmospheric original section, with its dark wood paneling, pressed tin ceilings, murals of the Old Country and Sinatra-blaring Wurlitzer, is vintage North End. It's only open at night, though a street-level addition next door is open by day for excellent cappuccinos.

Beacon Hill

Panificio 144 Charles St ☏227-4340; **Charles T.** Fine cups o' joe, fresh tasty pastries (biscotti is the standout), and some of the best home-baked bread in the city.

Back Bay

Caffé Romano 33 Newbury St ☏266-0770; **Arlington T.** Affordable pastries, sandwiches and coffee drinks on the poshest block of Newbury Street. Those who require a dose of aesthetics will be gratified by the rotating installations of contemporary paintings.

The Other Side Cosmic Café 407 Newbury St ☏536-9477; **Hynes T.** This ultracasual spot on "the other side" of Massachusetts Avenue, cut off from the trendy part of Newbury Street, offers gourmet sandwiches, "creative green salads" and fresh juices. Local band videos and short art films are shown Monday nights; there's a jazz/ambient brunch on weekends.

Trident Booksellers & Café 338 Newbury St ☏267-8688; **Copley T.** A window seat at this bookstore café (see p.209 for bookstore review), perennially popular with the cool student set, is the ideal vantage point from which to observe the flood of young passersby outside.

The South End

Flour Bakery + Café 1595 Washington St ☏267-4300; **Back Bay T.** Quite possibly the best café in town, this stylish South End spot has a drool-worthy array of brioche au chocolat, old-fashioned sour cream coffee cake, gooey caramel nut tarts, rich cakes, savory sandwiches, homemade breads and thirst-quenching drinks. Choosing just one can be torture.

Garden of Eden Café 571 Tremont St ☏247-8377; **Back Bay T.** The doyen of the South End café scene has a prime streetside terrace, perfect espressos, and delectable morsels like orange- and pistachio-encrusted paté de canard and chocolate and raspberry mousse cakes. You can also stock up on outstanding cheeses and pastries from the adjoining gourmet shop.

Kenmore Square and the Fenway

Espresso Royale Caffe 736 Commonwealth Ave ☏277-8737; **Kenmore T.** Funky little coffeeshop serving traditional cups of java alongside original blends like a zesty orange cappuccino; the cheerful decor is enhanced by abstract wall paintings and cozy seats.

The southern districts

Coffee Cantata 605 Center St, Jamaica Plain ☏522-2223; **Heath St T.** Inviting local café with good coffee and delicious cupcakes, complemented by more substantial offerings like frittatas and asparagus ravioli.

JP Licks 659 Center St, Jamaica Plain ☏524-6740; **Heath St T.** Whatever your pleasure, be it luscious ice cream or hearty bagels, this funky Jersey cow-themed café is a fine place to indulge it.

Cambridge

1369 Coffee House 757 Massachusetts Ave ☏576-4600; **Central T.** The *1369* mixes earnest thirty-something leftists with youthful hipsters in a relaxed environment; your best bets are the standard array of caffeinated beverages and particularly exquisite desserts. A second location is at 1369 Cambridge St (☏576-1369; #69 bus).

Algiers 40 Brattle St ☏492-1557; **Harvard T.** A fashionable North African café popular with the artsy set. While the food is so-so and the service slow, there are few more atmos-

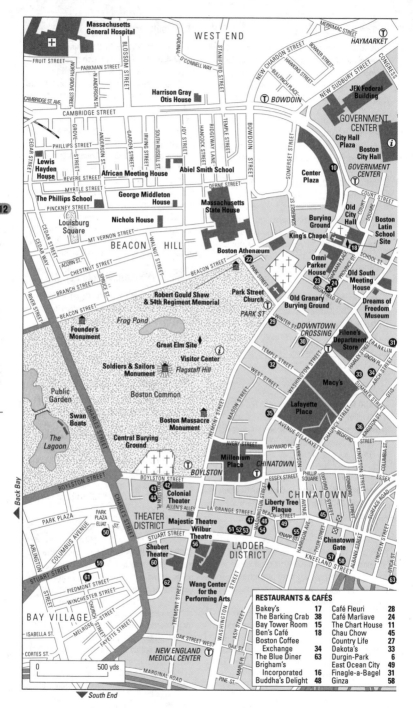

Massachusetts General Hospital

WEST END

HAYMARKET

FRUIT STREET

PARKMAN STREET

CAMBRIDGE ST. AVE.

Harrison Gray Otis House

T BOWDOIN

JFK Federal Building

CAMBRIDGE STREET

GOVERNMENT CENTER

City Hall Plaza

Boston City Hall

Lewis Hayden House

African Meeting House

Abiel Smith School

Center Plaza

10

GOVERNMENT CENTER T

The Phillips School

George Middleton House

Old City Hall

Boston Latin School Site

COURT STREET

Nichols House

Massachusetts State House

Burying Ground

King's Chapel

18

Louisburg Square

MT VERNON STREET

BEACON HILL

Boston Athenæum

22

Omni Parker House

23

Old South Meeting House

24

Robert Gould Shaw & 54th Regiment Memorial

Park Street Church

26

Dreams of Freedom Museum

PARK ST T

Old Granary Burying Ground

Founder's Monument

Frog Pond

29

WINTER ST. DOWNTOWN CROSSING

Filene's Department Store

31

Great Elm Site

30

Visitor Center

TEMPLE STREET

32

Soldiers & Sailors Monument

Flagstaff Hill

WEST STREET

WASHINGTON STREET

33

Macy's

34

Public Garden

Boston Common

Lafayette Place

35

36

Swan Boats

Boston Massacre Monument

AVENUE DELAFAYETTE

The Lagoon

Central Burying Ground

AVERY STREET

HAYWARD PL.

Millenium Place

CHINATOWN

BOYLSTON STREET

42

T BOYLSTON

43

44

Colonial Theater

ALLEN'S ALLEY

CHINATOWN

Liberty Tree Plaque

LA GRANGE STREET

45

THEATER DISTRICT

PARK PLAZA

50

Majestic Theatre Wilbur Theatre

47 48

49

51 52 53

54

55

Chinatown Gate

STUART STREET

LADDER DISTRICT

56

57 58

Shubert Theater

60

KNEELAND STREET

63

BAY VILLAGE

59

61

62

Wang Center for the Performing Arts

NEW ENGLAND MEDICAL CENTER T

0   500 yds

MARGINAL ROAD

South End

Back Bay

RESTAURANTS & CAFÉS			
Bakey's	**17**	Café Fleuri	**28**
The Barking Crab	**38**	Café Marliave	**24**
Bay Tower Room	**15**	The Chart House	**11**
Ben's Café	**18**	Chau Chow	**45**
Boston Coffee		Country Life	**27**
Exchange	**34**	Dakota's	**33**
The Blue Diner	**63**	Durgin-Park	**6**
Brigham's		East Ocean City	**49**
Incorporated	**16**	Finagle-a-Bagel	**31**
Buddha's Delight	**48**	Ginza	**58**

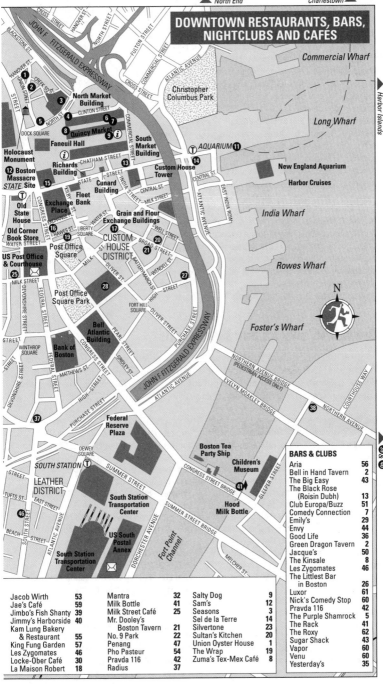

pheric spots in which to sip first-rate coffee.

Bookcellar Café 1971 Massachusetts Ave
℡864-9625; Porter **T**. Relaxed basement coffeehouse, with furnishings consisting primarily of a few old sofas and some folding chairs on the concrete floor – but the coffee is good – and cheap – and you can peruse the wide range of magazines and used books while you chill.

Café Pamplona 12 Bow St ℡547-2763; **Harvard T**. Eurochic hits its pretentious peak in this tiny basement café. The coffee is surprisingly average, and the waitstaff a bit snooty. On balmy evenings, the patio seating provides refuge from thick blue clouds of clove cigarette smoke.

Caffé Paradiso 1 Eliot St ℡868-3240; **Harvard T**. This glossy Italian café strikes a bright, comfortable contrast to the atmospheric dimness of most Harvard Square coffeehouses. The coffee is good (and reasonably priced); the service is swift, and the setting free of pretension.

Tealuxe 0 Brattle St ℡441-0077; **Harvard T**.

In a twist on the standard coffeehouse, what was once a curiosity shop called Loulou's Lost and Found has reincarnated itself as the only teahouse in Harvard Square. They manage to stock over 100 varieties of the stuff – loose and by the cup – though the place is smaller than a teacup. Art Deco trimmings help you "skip the java in flavor of tea" in style.

Diesel 257 Elm St ℡629-8717; **Davis T**. They take their caffeine seriously at this trendy, garage-like coffee shop where patrons get revved on High Octane (double shots), Vietnamese blends, or just plain black java. Purists might be disappointed to learn they do serve herbal teas, as well.

Someday Café 51 Davis Sq ℡623-3323; **Davis T**. This ultra laid-back café is as close an approximation to a university common room as you'll find outside of a university dormitory, mismatched sofas and resident couch potatoes included.

Breakfast, snacks and light meals

In most neighborhoods in Boston you won't have a problem finding somewhere to grab **breakfast**, a **snack** or a **light meal**, whether it's from a diner, deli or take-out stand. See also the pubs in Chapter 14, Drinking, and the cafés above, many of which offer food all day.

Downtown

Bakey's 45 Broad St ℡426-1710; **State T**. Easily recognized by its decorative sign depicting a man slumped over an ironing board, *Bakey's* was one of the first after-hours Irish pubs to surface in the Financial District. Though it can be pricey if you don't watch what you order ($9 for a turkey sandwich), it's a safe bet if you're caught hungry wandering around this part of town.

Brigham's Incorporated 50 Congress St ℡523-9822; **State T**. Wholesome *Brigham's* features burgers and "MegaMelt" sandwiches, plus an excellent soda fountain. Great ice cream, too; stick to basic ice cream flavors – chocolate chip, vanilla – and you'll be happiest.

Café Fleuri 250 Franklin St in *Le Meridien* ℡451-1900; State, Aquarium or Downtown Crossing **T**. Though this restaurant does standard upscale meals all day, it's mainly

worth checking out on Saturday afternoons (except summers), when its $18 all-you-can-eat Chocolate Bar Buffet entitles you to sample everything from chocolate Grand Marnier ravioli to chocolate croissant bread pudding. Truly decadent.

Finagle-a-Bagel 70 Franklin St ℡261-1900; **Downtown Crossing T**. A small Boston chain with more than fifteen varieties of bagels, from pumpkin raisin to triple chocolate chip, that are always served fresh. Has another location in Back Bay at 535 Boylston St (℡266-2500; Copley **T**).

Kam Lung Bakery and Restaurant 77 Harrison St ℡542-2229; **Chinatown T**. Tiny take-out joint that peddles dim sum, bakery treats (sweet rolls, sugary moon pies) and more exotic delicacies like pork buns and meat pies.

Milk Bottle 300 Congress St ℡482-3343; **South Station T**. This Boston landmark in front of the Children's Museum dishes out bagels and cream cheese, ice cream and coffee

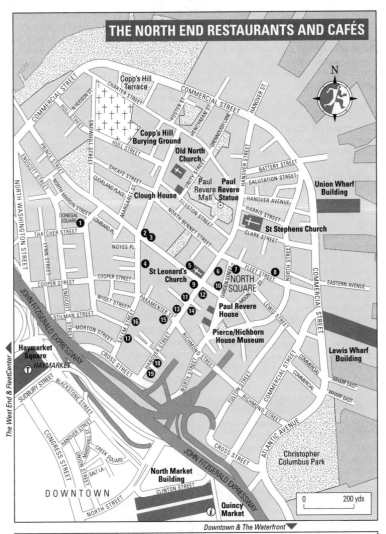

THE NORTH END RESTAURANTS AND CAFÉS

RESTAURANTS & CAFÉS							
Artu	10	Caffé Vittoria	11	Giacomo's	6	Pizzeria Regina	1
Assaggio	5	The Daily Catch	12	Il Panino	15	Prezza	8
Café Pompeii	13	Dolce Vita	19	Mama Maria	7	Rabia's	16
Caffé dello Sport	9	Ernesto's	17	Marcuccio's	4	Sage	2
Caffé Paradiso	18	Galleria Umberto	14	Monica's	3		

from its tiny kiosk window; patrons content themselves by sitting at nearby picnic tables.
Milk Street Café 50 Milk St ☎542-3663; State T; Post Office Square Park ☎350-7273; Downtown Crossing T. Kosher and quick are the key words at these two downtown eateries, popular with suits and vegetarians

for the large designer sandwiches and salads.
Sultan's Kitchen 72 Broad St ☎338-7819; Aquarium T. The best Turkish food in Boston, this lunch spot is favored by businessmen who queue up for the agreeably spicy Ottoman classics. Take a table in the

casual upstairs room and you'll feel a million miles away from nearby tourist-laden Quincy Market.

The Wrap 82 Water St ☎357-9013; **State T.** Sandwiches rolled in tortillas, fruit smoothies, and other lunchtime treats, all quick, easy and cheap.

The North End

Café Pompeii 280 Hanover St ☎227-1562; **Haymarket T.** Though you may not enjoy the garish murals or mediocre pizza, this is the only real late-night joint in the North End, open till 4am.

Ernesto's 69 Salem St ☎523-1373; **Haymarket T.** The cheap, oversized slices of thin-crust pizza served here can't be beat for a quick lunch.

Galleria Umberto 289 Hanover St ☎227-5709; **Haymarket T.** When a place is only open daily from 11am to 2pm, yet there's a line out the door during the limited hours of operation, you know something good is cooking. Here, that something is pizza, cut in greasy, delicious squares.

Rabia's 73 Salem St ☎227-6637; **Haymarket T.** The best thing about this small restaurant is the "Express Lunch" special: a heaped plate of pasta, chicken parmigiana or the like is yours to savor for a mere $5 from noon until 2pm daily.

Charlestown

Sorelle Bakery and Café 1 Monument Ave ☎242-2125 Phenomenal muffins and cookies, plus pasta salads and other lunch fare which you can enjoy on a delightful hidden patio.

Beacon Hill and the West End

Paramount 44 Charles St ☎720-1152; **Charles T.** The Hill's neighborhood diner serves Belgian waffles and frittatas to the brunch regulars by day, and decent American standards like hamburgers and meatloaf by night.

Ruby's Diner 280 Cambridge St ☎367-3224; **Charles T.** Very basic breakfast chow – eggs and such – done cheaply and well. Open all night Thurs–Sat.

Back Bay

29 Newbury 29 Newbury St ☎536-0290; **Arlington T.** A small upscale café/bar and eatery with good, if pricey, salads and the like. In warmer weather, the self-consciously hip crowd migrates to the sidewalk terrace. Don't miss the 29 Smooch, their signature dessert made with brownies and caramel ice cream. Open until 1.30am.

Armani Café 214 Newbury St ☎437-0909; **Copley T.** People-watching is the *mot du jour* at this fashionista hotspot where patrons seem to prefer wearing black and talking on their cellphones from behind dark sunglasses; the good contemporary Italian fare like saffron shrimp risotto and veal scaloppine shouldn't be overlooked, mind you.

Café de Paris 19 Arlington St ☎247-7121; **Arlington T.** The Parisian pretensions of this spot, where you order your sandwich off a wall menu or select a pre-prepared salad from the counter, are sort of a joke, though people still line up. If you want a pastry, ask for the freshest to avoid disappointment.

Café Jaffa 48 Gloucester St ☎536-0230; **Hynes T.** Boston's best falafel and other Middle Eastern staples are served in this cool, inviting space with polished wood floors.

Emack & Bolio's 290 Newbury St ☎247-8772; **Copley T.** Pint-sized ice-cream parlor named for a long-defunct rock band. Try a scoop each of Chocolate Moose and Vanilla Bean Speck in a chocolate-dipped waffle cone to get hooked.

Steve's Greek-American Cuisine 316 Newbury St ☎267-1817; **Hynes T.** Excellent Greek food makes this one of Boston's classic cheap eats. Steve's Greek Salad is a favorite among the Newbury Street lunch crowd, and the Grilled Chicken Sandwich could convert a vegetarian.

The South End

Bertucci's Brick Oven Pizzeria 43 Stanhope St ☎247-6161; **Back Bay T.** Though it may not be the best pizza in Boston, *Bertucci's* inexpensive slices more than do the trick; there's also great free garlic bread in this funky South End location.

Finale 1 Columbus Ave ☎423-3184; **Boylston or Arlington T.** Devilishly good desserts are the mainstay at this extremely cushy sweet-tooth emporium; the top-notch wines and cordials that go with them are pretty fine, too.

Geoffrey's 578 Tremont St ☎266-1122; **Back Bay T.** This cheerful, affordable eatery serves a nice range of salads and sand-

CAFÉS, SNACKS AND LIGHT MEALS | Breakfast, snacks and light meals

wiches from a menu that also includes more substantial fare like seven-vegetable couscous, asparagus mousse ravioli and huge portions of cake.

Mike's City Diner 1714 Washington St ☎ 267-9393; Back Bay T. Classic diner breakfasts and lunches – both greasy but good – in an out-of-the way setting in the South End.

Kenmore Square and the Fenway

Anna's Taqueria 1412 Beacon St ☎ 739-7300; Coolidge Corner T. Exceptional tacos, burritos and quesadillas are the only things on the menu at this bright, extremely cheap Mexican eatery – but they're so good branches had to be opened around the corner at 446 Harvard St (Coolidge Corner T) and in Cambridge at 8222 Somerville Ave (Porter T) to accommodate its legions of devotees.

Cambridge

C'est Bon 1432 Massachusetts Ave ☎ 661-0610; 110 Mt Auburn St ☎ 492-6465; Harvard T (both locations). Small, centrally located shop, in two branches, both of which serve up excellent coffee, fresh baked goods, and the best falafel in the area at inexpensive prices. Open late.

Darwin's Ltd 148 Mt Auburn St ☎ 354-5233; Harvard T. The rough-hewn exterior con-

ceals a delightful deli serving the best sandwiches on Harvard Square – wonderfully inventive combinations, such as roast beef, sprouts, and apple slices, served on freshly baked bread.

Herrell's Ice Cream 15 Dunster St ☎ 497-2179; Harvard T. Both the long lines and the profusion of "Best of Boston" awards that adorn the walls attest to the well-deserved popularity of this local ice-cream parlor. The chocolate pudding flavor is a particular delight, especially combined with "smooshins," such as Junior Mints or crushed Oreo cookies. Open until midnight.

Leo's Place 35 JFK St ☎ 354-9192; Harvard T. Possibly the best-kept secret in Cambridge, Leo's red-walled retro diner serves hearty breakfasts until late – and for next-to-nothing. A real find.

Porter Square Café and Diner 1933 Massachusetts Ave ☎ 354-3898; Porter T. This place manages to pull off the unlikely combination of coffeehouse and diner culture. It's best for good, cheap American breakfast fare: specials are served all day, and there's a make-your-own omelette option, too.

Toscanini's 1310 Massachusetts Ave ☎ 354-9350; Harvard T. An ever-changing ice-cream list includes original flavors like Khulfee, a concoction of pistachios, almonds, and cardamom.

CAFÉS, SNACKS AND LIGHT MEALS | Breakfast, snacks and light meals

Restaurants

H istorically, weather-beaten Yankees have tended to favor hot and hearty meals made from native ingredients without a lot of fuss. Today, though, while outsiders may see menu items like broiled scrod, clam chowder and Yankee pot roast as quintessentially New England, most Bostonians consider such dishes as little more than part of the tourist package.

Indeed, the city's current dining scene mirrors the diversity of Boston's population itself, with innovative restaurants taking root everywhere – most recently, in the South End, where French and fusion cuisine (in a fashionable setting, of course) are the catch of the day. Happily, too, there is no shortage of places to eat in Boston: the city is packed with bars and pubs that double as restaurants, cafés that serve full and affordable meals (for these, see p.166), plus plenty of higher-end, dinner-only options.

As for Boston's culinary landscape, there are ever-popular **Italian** restaurants – both traditional southern and fancier northern – that cluster in the **North End**, mainly on Hanover and Salem streets. The city's tiny **Chinatown** packs in not only a fair number of Chinese spots, but **Japanese**, **Vietnamese** and **Malaysian** too. Dim sum, where you choose selections from carts wheeled past your table, is especially big at lunchtime.

On the other end of the spectrum, Boston's trendiest restaurants, many serving voguish **New American** fusion cuisine, tend to cluster in **Back Bay** and the **South End**. Meanwhile, across the Charles, **Cambridge**'s eating options, mostly strung out along Massachusetts Avenue between Central, Harvard and Porter squares, run the gamut from budget Mexican eateries to high-end American cuisine. Funky (if slightly out-of-the-way) Inman Square, just below Cambridge's border with **Somerville**, has a few good spots as well, many of them specializing in contemporary twists on New England classics.

Below, we've divided our listings up by neighborhood; you'll also find a complete cross-referenced list by cuisine in the box beginning on p.176. Note that it's always a good idea to make reservations ahead of time, especially at the more upscale places.

Eating and drinking maps

Within this chapter, as well as Chapter 12, Cafés, snacks and light meals, and Chapter 14, Drinking, you'll find maps where we've keyed the eating and drinking options for the major Boston neighborhoods. These maps can be found on the following pages:

Downtown	pp.168–169	Back Bay and the South End	p.183
The North End	p.171	Cambridge	pp.192–193
Beacon Hill	p.180		

Downtown

The Barking Crab 88 Sleeper St (at the Northern Avenue Bridge) ☎426-CRAB; South Station **T**. This endearing seafood shack aims to please with its homey atmosphere, friendly service and unpretentious, inexpensive menu – centered around anything they can pull from the ocean and fry, sauté, marinate or grill. Located right on the Boston Harbor with a view of the city skyline.

Bay Tower Room 60 State St ☎723-1666; State **T**. Located on the 33rd floor of a downtown high-rise, the *Bay Tower* is notable mostly for its spectacular views of Boston Harbor. The food is less remarkable, but reliable upscale American cuisine nonetheless, such as filet mignon and the like.

Ben's Café 45 School St ☎227-3370; Government Center or Park **T**. This relaxed French eatery is situated in a French Second Empire building that for a hundred years served as Boston's City Hall. Ask for a table in "The Vault" and go with the prix fixe menu; otherwise head for its airy, hideaway bar, where the price of a drink includes free hors d'oeuvres. Upstairs is the more formal *La Maison Robert* (see p.177). Closed Sundays.

The Blue Diner 150 Kneeland St ☎695-0087; South Station **T**. Campy bar and restaurant with a rare feature among retro diners – genuinely good food. A popular spot for a late-night nosh, open till 4am on weekends.

Buddha's Delight 5 Beach St ☎451-2395; Chinatown **T**. Menu items fall between quotation marks since the "beef" and "chicken" here are actually made from tofu. While the ersatz meats of this vegetarian Vietnamese fare don't exactly taste like the real thing, they're still good. *Buddha's Delight Too* is at 404 Harvard St, Brookline (☎739-8830; Coolidge Corner **T**).

Café Marliave 10 Bosworth St ☎423-6340; Park **T**. This Italian-American hideaway is one of Boston's oldest restaurants. Visit for the first-rate ravioli and unmistakeably Bostonian ambience; located behind the *Omni Parker House Hotel*.

The Chart House 60 Long Wharf ☎227-1576; Aquarium **T**. Three-floor restaurant with rich food for the rich, though worth the price if you can afford it; the lobster and swordfish are particularly good. For a less highbrow experience, try eating on the first-floor – while you lose the view for which this chain

is also known, you'll also feel more casual.

Chau Chow 52 Beach St ☎426-6266; Chinatown **T**. One of the first Chinatown restaurants to specialize in seafood, and still one of the best. The setting is stripped-down so there's nothing to distract you from delicious salt-and-pepper shrimp or, if you're in a more adventurous mood, sea cucumber. The *Grand Chau Chow*, just across Beach Street, serves basically the same food at somewhat higher prices and with fancier accoutrements such as table-cloths and linen napkins.

Country Life 200 High St ☎951-2685; Aquarium **T**. An all-vegetarian buffet near the waterfront, whose cheap and quick meal options vary daily; call the menu hotline (☎951-2462) to find out what's cooking.

Dakota's 34 Summer St in the 101 Arch Street Building ☎737-1777; Downtown Crossing or Park **T**. Frequented mainly by office workers for lunch and pre-commute dinners, the clubby feel of this expansive American grill restaurant and great food make it the perfect place to dine after visiting nearby Filene's Basement. There are also very good salads, pasta dishes and Key Lime Pie.

Durgin-Park 340 Faneuil Hall Marketplace ☎227-2038; Government Center **T**. A Boston landmark in operation since 1827, *Durgin-Park* has a no-frills Yankee atmosphere and a somewhat surly waitstaff. That doesn't stop folks from coming for the sizable, pricey pot roast and roast beef dinners in the upstairs dining room. The downstairs raw bar is considerably livelier.

East Ocean City 25–29 Beach St ☎542-2504; Chinatown **T**. Another seafood specialist full of aquariums where you can greet your dinner before it appears on your plate. They have especially good soft-shell crabs.

Ginza 16 Hudson St ☎338-2261; Chinatown **T**. Open until 4am on weekends, *Ginza* is a popular after-hours spot serving perhaps the best sushi in the city. Any of the vast number of options goes well with a pitcher of warm house sake. There's another location in Brookline at 1002 Beacon St (☎566-9688; St. Marys **T**).

Jacob Wirth 31 Stuart St ☎338-8586; Arlington **T**. A German-themed Boston landmark, around since 1868; even if you don't like bratwurst washed down with a hearty lager, something is sure to please. A Boston must-visit.

American

Amrhein's	p.185
Audubon Circle	p.184
Back Bay Brewing Company	p.181
Bartley's Burger Cottage	p.185
Bay Tower Room	p.175
The Blue Cat Café	p.181
The Blue Diner	p.175
Bob the Chef	p.185
Boodles	p.182
Cambridge Common	p.186
Charlie's Kitchen	p.186
Claremont Café	p.184
Cottonwood Restaurant & Café	p.182
Dakota's	p.175
Durgin-Park	p.175
Grand Canal	p.181
Grill 23	p.182
Hamersley's Bistro	p.184
Henrietta's Table	p.186
House of Blues	p.186
The Hungry I	p.181
Locke-Ober Café	p.178
Mr Dooley's Boston Tavern	p.178
Redbones	p.187
The Rosebud Diner	p.187
Silvertone	p.178
Top of the Hub	p.184
Upstairs at the Pudding	p.187
Washington Square Tavern	p.185

Brazilian

Buteco	p.185

Chinese

Betty's Wok & Noodle Diner	p.181
Chau Chow	p.175
East Ocean City	p.175
King Fung Garden	p.177

French

Ambrosia	p.181
Aquitane	p.184
Aujourd'hui	p.181
Ben's Café	p.175
Central Kitchen	p.186
Chez Henri	p.186
Du Barry Restaurant Français	p.182
Hamersley's Bistro	p.184
L'Espalier	p.182
La Maison Robert	p.177
Les Zygomates	p.177
Mistral	p.184
No. 9 Park	p.178
On the Park	p.184
Radius	p.178
Sel de la Terre	p.178
Sonsie	p.182
Truc	p.184

German

Jacob Wirth	p.175

Indian

Bombay Café	p.182
Café of India	p.186
Diva	p.187
Kashmir	p.182
Rangoli	p.185
Tandoor House	p.186

Irish

Doyle's	p.185
Matt Murphy's	p.185

Italian

Artu	p.181
Assaggio	p.179
Bella Luna	p.185
Café Marliave	p.175
Dolce Vita	p.179
Giacomo's	p.179
Il Panino	p.179
Mama Maria	p.179
Marcuccio's	p.179
Monica's	p.179
No. 9 Park	p.178

Jae's Café 212 Stuart St ☎451-7788; Arlington T. The first floor of the Theater District location of this popular chain is a sushi bar and jazz room, while the third is a Korean barbecue where chefs slice and dice at your table. In between lies the main café, with an emphasis on Korean seafood, though you can also create your own noodle dish. Another location at 1281 Cambridge St, near Inman Square (☎497-8380; #69 bus).

Jimbo's Fish Shanty 245 Northern Ave ☎542-5600; South Station T. Operated by the proprietor's of *Jimmy's Harborside* (see below), serving basically the same food at lower prices in a more casual atmosphere – though without the picturesque views.
Jimmy's Harborside 242 Northern Ave ☎423-1000; South Station T. Totally tacky, but the harbor views and seafood are beyond reproach. House specialties include the

13

RESTAURANTS | Downtown

sizeable king lobsters and the Shore Dinners, a panoply of shellfish harvested along the New England seashore.

King Fung Garden 74 Kneeland St ☎357-5262; **Chinatown T.** The interior won't impress with its size or style, but the authentic Shangdong province food served here will. Inexpensive and delicious, the *King* is best on classics like pot stickers, scallion pancakes and (if you let them know ahead of time) Peking duck.

La Maison Robert 45 School St ☎227-3370; **Government Center or Park T.** Upstairs from *Ben's Café* (see p.175), this *haute-gamme* French restaurant matches its formal, white-tablecloth atmosphere with classic dishes like foie gras, lobster bisque and sole meunière.

Les Zygomates 129 South St ☎542-5108; **South Station T.** The name comes from the

French term for the facial muscles that make you smile. An eclectic crowd ranging from bankers to black-clad artistes gather for the inventive contemporary French cuisine and the prime selection of wines – more than a hundred international varieties.

Locke-Ober Café 3 Winter Place ☎542-1340; **Park T**. Don't be fooled by the name: *Locke-Ober Café* is very much a restaurant, and one of the most blueblooded in Boston. The fare consists of stuff like steak tartare and oysters on the half shell, while the setting is dark, ornate and stuffy. There's an archaic dress code, too – jacket and tie for men.

Mantra 52 Temple Place ☎542-8111; **Park St T**. A snazzy hookah den completes the over-the-top atmosphere at this chi-chi Indian-French restaurant, where you can dine on grilled filet mignon and caramelized sweet-breads, or treat yourself to a chocolate "degustation" – four rich, cocoa-infused desserts. All in all, a definite experience.

Mr Dooley's Boston Tavern 77 Broad St ☎338-5656; **State T**. One of the many Irish pubs downtown, though with a quieter and more atmospheric interior than the rest. Also known for its live music acts and Traditional Irish Breakfast Sundays – nice, especially since finding anything open around here on Sunday is a challenge.

No. 9 Park 9 Park St ☎742-9991; **Park St T**. Highly recommended restaurant with sedate green walls and plates busy with southern French and Italian entrées ranging from crispy duck with quince to squab pot-au-feu with croutons. A seven-course tasting menu ($85; with wine, $135) allows you to try almost everything.

Penang 685 Washington St ☎451-6373; **Chinatown T**. *Penang* takes its name from an island off the northwest coast of Malaysia. The painfully overdone interior is countered by consistently good food: try the *roti canai* appetizer or the copious yam pot dinner.

Pho Pasteur 682 Washington St and 8 Kneeland St ☎482-7467; **Chinatown T**. Two restaurants, both offering a multitude of variations on *pho*, a Vietnamese noodle dish. The Kneeland location serves only *pho*, while the one on Washington has other Vietnamese specialties as well – and it's all incredibly cheap.

Pravda 116 116 Boylston St ☎482-7799; **Arlington T**. Known more for its faux-hip scene than its Mediterranean-American entrées and reasonably priced tapas, *Pravda 116* also has a small dance club in the rear (see review p.189).

Radius 8 High St ☎426-1234; **South Station T**. Housed in a former bank, this ultramodern French restaurant tries to inject a dose of minimalist industrial chic to the cautious Financial District with über cool decor and innovative menu. New Yorker Michael Schlow's tasty *nouvelle cuisine* is complemented by an extensive wine list.

Salty Dog Faneuil Hall Marketplace ☎742-2094; **Government Center T**. It's worth braving the long waits here for the fresh seafood, such as the particularly good raw oysters, clams and generous lobster dinners, all best enjoyed in the outdoor dining area.

Sam's 100 City Hall Plaza ☎227-0022; **Government Center T**. Specializing in what they call "modern comfort food," *Sam's* fabulously fresh offerings range from scallops served with mashed potatoes and tropical salsa to pasta tossed with garlic, basil, chicken, green beans and (wait for it) grapes.

Seasons North and Blackstone sts (in the *Bostonian Hotel*) ☎523-4119; **Government Center or State T**. With inventive, truly excellent Modern American fare, such as stone crab with smoked corn minestrone, *Seasons* has a knack for attracting up-and-coming chefs before sending them on their way to culinary stardom.

Sel de la Terre 255 State St ☎720-1300; **Aquarium T**. The less-expensive sister to upscale *L'Espalier* (see review p.182) *Sel de la Terre* honors its name (salt of the earth) with rustic Provençal fare like hearty bouillabaisse, lamb and eggplant, and perhaps the best french fries in Boston. Conveniently, you can acquire the fixings for a waterfront picnic here, too, by calling ahead to order a hamper ($15, minus the basket), and picking it up on your way to the ferry.

Silvertone 69 Bromfield St ☎338-7887; **Downtown Crossing T**. Though cocktails are the big draw at this Downtown Crossing basement bar and eatery, its Caesar salads and roasted salmon with homemade potato chips are excellent and surprisingly inexpensive.

Union Oyster House 41 Union St ☎227-2750; **Government Center or State T**. The oldest continuously operating restaurant in America has two big claims to fame: French king

Louis-Philippe lived over the tavern during his youth, and, perhaps apocryphally, the toothpick was first used here. The food is good too: fresh, well-prepared seafood, plus one of Boston's best raw bars.

Zuma's Tex-Mex Café 7 N Market St ☎367-9114; State T. Tex-Mex is a long way from home in Boston, but *Zuma's* comes up with a close approximation, complemented by a garish interior and sassy waitstaff. Especially good are the fajitas, which come to your table billowing with smoke, and the salty, tangy margaritas.

The North End

Assaggio 29 Prince St ☎227-7380; Haymarket T. An extensive wine list allows *Assaggio* to stand on its own as a wine bar, but it's also reliable for classic Italian fare with contemporary touches. The main dining room, with its ceiling mural of the zodiac and steady stream of opera music, is calm and relaxing.

The Daily Catch 323 Hanover St ☎523-8567; Haymarket T; 261 Northern Ave ☎338-3093; South Station T. Ocean-fresh seafood, notably calamari and shellfish – Sicilian-style, with megadoses of garlic – draws big lines to this tiny storefront restaurant. The downtown location offers a solid alternative to the touristy Yankee scrod-and-chips thing.

Dolce Vita 237 Hanover St ☎720-0422; Haymarket T. Sit in the quiet upstairs dining room in this longstanding North End spot to savor their famous Ravioli Rose, in a tomato cream sauce. Don't come here if you're in a hurry, though – service can be very slow.

Giacomo's 355 Hanover St ☎523-9026; Haymarket T. This small eatery, with its menu written on a chalkboard attached to a brick wall, serves fresh, flavorful seafood and pasta specialties; try the pumpkin tortellini in sage butter sauce. There's a location in the South End as well at 431 Columbus Ave (☎536-5723; Back Bay T). Dinner only, closed Mondays.

Il Panino 11 Parmenter St ☎720-1336; Aquarium T. A bona-fide Boston best, with incredible pasta specials at lunch; a bit more formal by night.

Mama Maria 3 North Square ☎523-0077; Haymarket T. A favorite special-occasion restaurant, and considered by some to be the best the district has to offer; in any case

its location, on historic North Square, is as good a reason as any to come. The northern Italian fare is of consistently impeccable quality. Dinner only.

Marcuccio's 125 Salem St ☎723-1807; Haymarket T. Contemporary Italian food in a nice setting, with Pop Art updates of Renaissance masterpieces on the walls. The chef has a light, piquant touch that works particularly well with seafood dishes, risottos and salads. No credit cards; dinner only.

Monica's 67 Prince St ☎720-5472; Haymarket T. Some of the most intensely flavored Italian fare around, prepared and served by Monica's three sons, one of whom drew the cartoons plastered over the walls. They do a brisk takeout (sandwiches and such) at lunch, though the best dishes are reserved for dinner. Monica herself has a gourmet shop around the corner at 130 Salem St (see p.212).

Pizzeria Regina 111/2 Thatcher St ☎227-0765; Haymarket T. Visit *Regina* for tasty, cheap pizza, served in a neighborhood feed station where the wooden booths haven't budged since the 1940s. Vintage North End.

Prezza 24 Fleet St ☎227-1577; Haymarket T. New, minimalist Italian hotspot offering decadent dishes (though at a price) like sweet rock shrimp and risotto with shaved black truffles.

Sage 69 Prince St ☎248-8814; Haymarket T. Diminutive Italian restaurant that doesn't scrimp on flavor; the refreshing seasonal menu finds dishes like savory lemon and asparagus risotto and vegetable casseroles; perfect fodder for an intimate tête-à-tête.

Charlestown

Figs 67 Main St ☎242-2229; Community College T. This noisy, popular offshoot of *Olives* (see below) has excellent thin-crust pizzas, topped with such savory items as figs and prosciutto or caramelized onions and arugula. Another location at 42 Charles St in Beacon Hill (☎242-3447; Charles T).

Olives 10 City Square ☎242-1999; Community College T. *Olives* is consistently rated among Boston's best restaurants, and justifiably so. Chef Todd English turns out New Mediterranean food of unforgettable flavor in sizeable portions. No reservations save for parties of six or more; very expensive. Closed Sun and Mon.

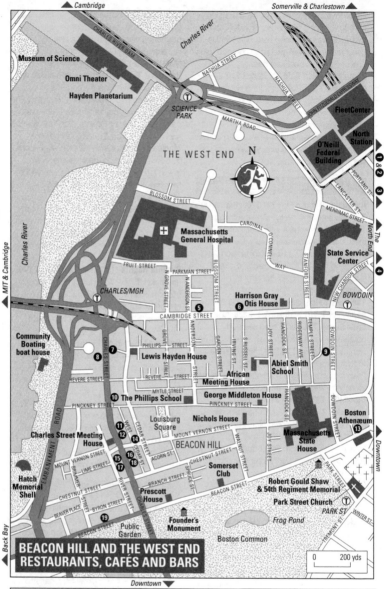

BEACON HILL AND THE WEST END
RESTAURANTS, CAFÉS AND BARS

0   200 yds

RESTAURANTS & CAFÉS

Artu	**10**	The Hungry I	**12**	Ristorante		21st Amendment	**9**	Irish Embassy	**2**
Beacon Hill Bistro	**18**	The King & I	**7**	Toscano	**16**	The Bull & Finch Pub	**19**	McGann's	**3**
The Federalist	**13**	Lala Rokh	**14**	Ruby's Diner	**5**	Fours	**1**	Sevens Ale House	**11**
Figs	**15**	Panificio	**8**			The Hill	**6**		
Grand Canal	**4**	Paramount	**17**						

BARS

Beacon Hill and the West End

Artu 89 Charles St ☎ 227-9023; Charles **T**.
Though squeezed into a tiny storefront on
Charles Street, *Artu* keeps things fresh,
flavorful and affordable. Authentic Italian
country cooking focused on soups,
risottos, roast meats and panini. The other
location in the North End (6 Prince St;
☎ 742-4336; North Station **T**) is larger, but
equally charming.

Beacon Hill Bistro 25 Charles St (in the *Beacon
Hill Hotel)* ☎ 723-1133; Charles **T**. Sleek New
American and French bistro with an upscale
neighborhood feel. Short ribs with prunes
share counter space with cod with capers
and tomatoes; breakfast is traditional
American.

Grand Canal 57 Canal St ☎ 523-1112; North
Station **T**. Atmospheric West End Irish pub
and restaurant with nineteenth-century
accoutrements, such as linen tablecloths
and a great mahogany bar with a mirror
behind. Relatively inexpensive lobster dinners as well as American comfort food.

The Federalist 15 Beacon St ☎ 670-1500; Park
St **T**. The lofty, chandeliered dining room
verges on sterile, but the seafood is anything but. The "Seafood Flight" – a citrus-
flavored sea urchin and shrimp concoction
– as well as the braised lobster and roasted
sea bass with truffles, are out of this world
(and so are the prices).

The Hungry I 71 Charles St ☎ 227-3524;
Charles **T**. Don't sweat the pricey menu and
hyped-up, romantic surroundings, because
the food here is delectable – classic
American fare with creative twists that
change nightly. If you're there on a night
featuring the signature venison with poivre
noir (black pepper), prepare for food
heaven.

The King & I 145 Charles St ☎ 227-3320;
Charles **T**. Excellent, inventive Thai with
bold, but not overbearing, flavors. The
"Shrimp in Love" is almost worth trying for
its name alone.

Lala Rokh 97 Mount Vernon St ☎ 720-5511;
Park **T**. Have the waitstaff help you with the
inscrutable menu at this exotically plush
Azerbaijani restaurant, where you can fill up
on the appetizers (such as roasted eggplant
kashk-e-bademjan) and exotic *torshi* (condiments) alone.

Ristorante Toscano 47 Charles St ☎ 723-4090;
Charles **T**. In the midst of the New Italian

craze, *Toscano* stayed traditional, and survived. It serves particularly good southern
Italian food, made with classic flair and
fresh ingredients.

Back Bay

Ambrosia 116 Huntington Ave ☎ 247-2400;
Prudential or Copley **T**. When you get the
craving for raw fish over noodles in a
flavored sea oil, or a crispy potato and
cararmelized butternut spring roll, this is the
place. The French Provençal-meets-Asian
fusion cuisine is inventively prepared in a
high-tech but accessible environment of
dazzling floral arrangements, hand-blown
crystal and intricate metalwork – most love
it, though the flavors don't always measure
up to the elaborate presentation. At lunch,
most salads, gourmet sandwiches and
other entrées are priced under $16.

Anago 65 Exeter St (in the *Lenox*) ☎ 266-6222;
Copley **T**. Comfort food like spit-roasted
pork and rotisserie chicken prepared with a
thoughtful and not overblown New
American accent; desserts include the likes
of coconut crème brûlée and ginger
poached pear dipped in chocolate.

Aujourd'hui 200 Boylston St (in the *Four
Seasons*) ☎ 338-4400 or 1-800/332-3442;
Arlington **T**. Near the top of everyone's list of
Boston's best restaurants, this is a good
place to splurge. Nibble roasted Maine lobster – accompanied by crabmeat wontons,
pineapple compote and fenugreek broth –
from antique china while enjoying the view
out over the Public Garden.

Back Bay Brewing Company 755 Boylston St
☎ 424-8300; Copley **T**. Of all the brewpubs in
Boston, this feels the least like a glorified
bar: the breakfast fare is every bit as good
as the inventive lunch and dinner offerings.
If you just want a brew, though, settle into
the comfortable second-floor lounge and
take your pick.

Betty's Wok & Noodle Diner 250 Huntington
Ave ☎ 424-1950; Symphony **T**. Mix and match
from a list of rice, noodles, sauces (from
Asian Pesto to Cuban Chipotle-Citrus),
vegetables and meats and, minutes later,
you'll be enjoying a piping-hot plateful of
tasty Chino-Latino food. Open everyday
until 11pm.

The Blue Cat Café 94 Massachusetts Ave
☎ 247-9922; Hynes **T**. This cavernous restau-
rant/bar has gone back to basics with a
rustic, exposed brick decor and tasty, all-

American staples like pizzas, pastas and steaks; popular with an after-work crowd, who guzzle martinis while nibbling down.

Bombay Café 175 Massachusetts Ave ☎247-0555; Hynes **T**. The chicken tikka and stuffed naan are good bets – as is anything with seafood – at this casual Indian restaurant.

Boodles 40 Dalton St (in the *Back Bay Hilton*) ☎236-1100 or 1-800/874-0663; Hynes **T**. English-style steakhouse serving the usual grill fare and some eighty microbrews to a predominantly older crowd of theater-goers. The food's not terribly adventurous, but certain standbys, like the Caesar salad and smoked clam chowder, are good, if unextraordinary.

Cactus Club 939 Boylston St ☎236-0200; Hynes **T**. Cavernous Tex-Mex restaurant with funky decor and surprisingly tasty nibbles (including great quesadillas); equally sought out for its popular bar.

Cottonwood Restaurant & Café 222 Berkeley St ☎247-2225; Arlington **T**. Creative, tasty Southwestern fare served in a bright setting on the first floor of the 22-story Houghton Mifflin Building. Locally (and justly) famous for its margaritas, this is one of Back Bay's best bets for lunch or Sunday brunch with a twist.

Du Barry Restaurant Français 159 Newbury St ☎262-2445; Copley **T**. A bastion of tradition on otherwise trendy Newbury Street, *Du Barry* is one of the few classic French restaurants in Boston. Nothing too inventive, just good, hearty staples like *boeuf bourguignon*, and a hidden terrace on which to enjoy your meal in warmer weather. The quiet bar is popular with locals.

Grill 23 161 Berkeley St ☎542-2225; Arlington **T**. This carnivore-fest is as clubby as Boston gets: the steaks are aged in-house, accompanied by myriad wines, and served amidst patrons who are encouraged to smoke ad nauseum – cigars too, no less.

Gyuhama 827 Boylston St ☎437-0188; Hynes **T**. A very noisy basement-level sushi bar, favored by many college students for late-night Japanese snacks. The nigiri sushi, spicy maki rolls and grilled shrimp – cooked at your table – are good bets for satisfying those late-night hunger pangs.

Kashmir 279 Newbury St ☎536-1695; Hynes **T**. The food and decor are equally inviting at Newbury Street's only Indian restaurant. Good choices include shrimp samosas, tandoori rack of lamb and vegetarian curries, all of which go well with the excellent naan bread.

Kaya 581 Boylston St ☎236-5858; Copley **T**. This is the place to go when the craving for Japanese-Korean food kicks in; try the teriyaki salmon or steaming shabu shabu beef (it means "swish swish").

Legal Seafoods 27 Park Square (in the *Park Plaza Hotel*) ☎426-4444; Arlington **T**; 100 Huntington Ave, Level Two Copley Place ☎266-7775; Copley **T**; 800 Boylston St, Prudential Center ☎266-6800; Prudential **T**; 5 Cambridge Center ☎864-3400; Kendall **T**. This local chain is probably the best-known seafood restaurant in America, and for many, it's the best, as well. Its trademark is freshness: the clam chowder, Boston scrod and lobster are all top quality. There are some New Asian offerings on the menu, too. Go early to avoid long lines, which can be expected no matter the location or day of the week.

L'Espalier 30 Gloucester St ☎262-3023; Hynes **T**. A ravishing French restaurant in a Back Bay brownstone. The food is first-rate, but the minimalist portions at lofty prices suggest that ambience is factored (generously) into your bill.

Miyako 279 Newbury St ☎236-0222; Copley **T**. Authenticity comes at a price at this Japanese standby, which has a popular terrace on Newbury Street, a sleek sushi bar inside and a minimalist decor of muted grays and bright floral arrangements.

Papa Razzi 271 Dartmouth St ☎536-9200; Copley **T**. Though this urbane, basement-level eatery doesn't look like a chain restaurant, it is – a fact reflected in the menu of standard-issue bruschetta, salads and pastas. It's all good, but for more authentic fare, head to the North End.

Skipjack's 199 Clarendon St ☎536-3500; Arlington **T**. Cool, South Beach-style decor and a bold menu distinguish this seafood spot from its rival, the always-busy *Legal Seafoods* – you're as likely to find fresh mahi mahi dipped in lemon and soy as fried scrod with tartar sauce. The Sunday jazz brunch is quite popular.

Sonsie 327 Newbury St ☎351-2500; Hynes **T**. The pretension factor is high at this scenester hangout, where the ultra-trendy meet over strange marriages of French and Asian food, such as miso clam soup with spring morels and tofu and grilled salmon with edible blossoms (yes, edible blossoms). Worth braving the scene if only for the hot

BACK BAY RESTAURANTS, CAFÉS AND BARS

RESTAURANTS

Ambrosia	36
Anago	26
Aujourd'hui	28
Back Bay Brewing Company	23
Betty's Wok & Noodle Diner	41
The Blue Cat Café	4
Bombay Café	35
Boodles	32
Cactus Club	20
Café Jaffa	28
Cottonwood Restaurant & Café	25
Du Barry Restaurant Français	10
Grill 23	9
Gyuhama	22
Kashmir	17
Kaya	14
L'Espalier	6
Legal Seafoods	30, 33 & 37
Miyako	18
Papa Razzi	30
Skipjack's	34
Stephanie's on Newbury	7
Steve's Greek-American Cuisine	24
Thai Basil	2
Top of the Hub	18
Turner Fisheries	29

CAFÉS

29 Newbury	12
Armani Café	16
Café de Paris	1
Caffè Romano	11
Emack & Bolio's	15
The Other Side Cosmic Café	3
Sonsie	5
Trident Booksellers & Café	13

BARS

Back Bay Brewing Company	38
BarCode	23
Bristol Lounge	19
Bukowski Tavern	28
Clery's Restaurant	27
Dad's	40
Daisy Buchanan's	21
Oak Bar	8
Whiskey Park	31
	33

Landmarks and streets:

Public Garden — Ducklings Statue, Swan Boats, George Washington Statue, Ether Memorial
Charles Street, Beacon Street, Marlborough Street, Commonwealth Avenue, Newbury Street, Boylston Street, Arlington Street, Berkeley Street, Clarendon Street, Dartmouth Street, Exeter Street, Fairfield Street, Gloucester Street, Hereford Street, Massachusetts Avenue, Huntington Avenue, Stuart Street, St James Avenue, Columbus Avenue, Stanhope Street, Dalton Street, St Cecilia Street, Belvidere Street, St Germain Street, Clearway Street, Garrison Street, West Newton Street, West Canton Street, Holyoke Street, Yarmouth Street, Cumberland Street, Chandler Street, Lawrence Street, Providence Street, Winchester Street, Park Plaza, Branch Street, Byron St, Beaver Place

Gibson House Museum, First Lutheran Church, Emmanuel Church of Boston, Arlington St. Church, Baylies Mansion, Ames-Webster Mansion, Church of the Covenant, Trinity Church, John Hancock Tower, First Baptist Church, Copley Square, Newbury Street Mural, New Old South Church, Boston Public Library, Copley Place, Tent City, Institute of Contemporary Art, Prudential Center, Hynes Convention Center, Christian Science Center, Reflecting Pool, Burrage Mansion, Oliver Ames Mansion, Stable Shops, Mapparium, Berklee College of Music, Christian Science Mother Church

Storrow Lagoon

N

0   200 yds

▲ Beacon Hill ▲ Cambridge ▲ Kenmore Square ▲ The South End

chocolate bread pudding.

Stephanie's on Newbury 190 Newbury St
☎ 236-0990; Copley **T**. Though they pride
themselves on their smoked salmon potato
pancake, what sets *Stephanie's* apart is
their sidewalk dining in the prime people-
watching territory of Newbury Street. Open
until midnight.

Thai Basil 132 Newbury St ☎ 424-8424;
Copley **T**. Excellent seafood, vegetarian and
pad thai dishes, plus a cool, soothing decor
in which to enjoy it; parties of six can get
the full experience by reserving an entire
bamboo-matted room.

Top of the Hub 800 Boylston St ☎ 536-1775;
Prudential **T**. There are several benefits of
dining atop the 50th floor of the Prudential
Tower, not the least of which is enjoying the
excellent city views. There's also surprisingly inventive New England fare and a big,
bright space in which to dine.

Turner Fisheries 10 Huntington Ave ☎ 424-
7425; Prudential **T**. The traditional New
England seafood at this cheerful spot –
scrod, Boston clam chowder, lobster
bisque – is as good as any in the city. Most
nights feature live jazz performances.

The South End

Aquitaine 569 Tremont St ☎ 424-8577; Back
Bay **T**. This swanky French brasserie is *the*
place to be and be seen; settle into a marvelous leather banquette, gape at the
astonishing array of wines, and feast on the
best steak frites and foie gras in town.

Claremont Café 535 Columbus Ave ☎ 247-
9001; Back Bay **T**. Diverse appetizers (like
cornmeal-fried oysters with jicama slaw),
imaginatively garnished entrées and particularly flavorful desserts, including a stellar
banana creme pie. Closed Mondays.

Delux Café 100 Chandler St ☎ 338-5258; Back
Bay **T**. The South End's cool spot of the
moment is this retro hideaway *boîte*. The
menu is loosely American fusion – but it
doesn't matter, as most go for the buzz
more than the food.

Franklin Café 278 Shawmut Ave ☎ 350-0010;
Back Bay **T**. Popular, upscale diner that's
earned local fame for tasty renditions of
Yankee comfort food like turkey meatloaf
with spicy fig sauce.

Hamersley's Bistro 553 Tremont St ☎ 423-
2700; Back Bay **T**. *Hamersley's* is widely
regarded as one of the best restaurants in

Boston, and with good cause. Every night
star chef (and owner) Gordon Hamersley
dons a baseball cap and takes to the open
kitchen, where he dishes out unusual – and
unforgettable – French-American fare that
changes with the seasons.

Mistral 221 Columbus Ave ☎ 867-9300;
Arlington **T**. Still one of *the* places to go in
Boston, *Mistral* serves pricey modern
Provençal food in a bright, airy space above
the Turnpike. Despite the raves, the food
doesn't live up to the cost. Dinner only.

On the Park One Union Park ☎ 426-0862;
Back Bay **T**. Its secluded setting on the
quiet south side of Union Park is as much
of a draw as the French bistro fare at this
neighborhood restaurant. The vegetarian
cassoulet is a winner, and there's an intimate brunch on weekends.

Pho Republique 1415 Washington St ☎ 262-
0005; Back Bay **T**. Funky Vietnamese restaurant that attracts a young, stylish clientele
who dine on hearty servings of *pho* and sip
divine lemongrass martinis; an in-house DJ
keeps patrons nodding their heads long
after their meal is done.

Truc 560 Tremont St ☎ 338-8070; Back Bay **T**.
That Julia Child was a regular (before she
left town in 2002) suggests the *hauteur* to
which this secluded French bistro aspires.
The limited menu doesn't disappoint, with
appetizers like warm mushroom salad and
entrées like crab-stuffed trout; ask for a
table in the romantic greenhouse room at
the back, to dine overlooking a charming
garden.

Kenmore Square and the Fenway

Audubon Circle 838 Beacon St ☎ 421-1910;
Kenmore **T**. The seemingly endless bar is
what grabs your attention first, but it's the
food that's worth staying for. Any of the
appetizers are good bets, as is anything
grilled – from burgers with chipotle ketchup
to tuna steak with banana salsa and fufu
(fried plantains mashed with coconut milk).
There's a limited selection of homemade
desserts, as well.

Brown Sugar 129 Jersey St ☎ 266-2928;
Kenmore **T**. Charming neighborhood restaurant near the Museum of Fine Arts, serving
Boston's best Thai food. Everything here is
wonderfully fresh, and some selections, like
the *gai garprow*, are superbly spicy. There
are ample vegetarian options, too.

Buteco 130 Jersey St ☎247-9508; **Kenmore T.**
The setting's not much, but the downright
tasty Brazilian home-cooking served at this
no-frills joint more than compensates. The
weekend *feijoada* – a sausage, dried beef
and black bean stew – is utterly authentic
and is often accompanied by a live Brazilian
band.

Allston-Brighton and Brookline

Ducky Wok 122–126 Harvard Ave, Allston-
Brighton ☎782-8868; **Harvard Ave T.** Popular
Chinese-Vietnamese restaurant where you
select your own fish from a giant tank. The
lemongrass chicken, stir-fried peapod
stems, and avocado smoothies (for dessert)
all stand out.
Matt Murphy's 14 Harvard St, Brookline ☎232-
0188; **Coolidge Corner T.** Authentic Irish comfort food such as warm potato and leek
soup with brown bread and rabbit pie with
Irish soda bread crust. The place is tiny,
and you may have to wait, but it's well
worth it.
Rangoli 129 Brighton Ave, Allston-Brighton
☎562-0200; **Harvard Ave T.** Inexpensive
southern Indian fare, favoring spicy vegetarian selections. Be sure to try the *dosa*:
sourdough pancakes rolled like giant cannoli around a variety of savory fillings.
Washington Square Tavern 714 Washington
St, Brookline ☎232-8989; **Washington Square T.**
Cozy, off-the-beaten-path restaurant/bar
with an eclectic fusion menu that turns out
inventive meals like pork tenderloin with fig
glaze and sweet potatoes. Just hanging out
and absorbing the vibe at the bar is worthwhile, too.
Wonder Bar 186 Harvard Ave, Allston-Brighton
☎351-2665; **Harvard Ave T.** Popular late-night
twenty- and early thirtysomething hangout
that scores points with its clay pot concoc-
tions and tapas snacks, though it really
comes alive after dark. The strict dress
code (no tennis shoes, ripped jeans or hats)
is a bit over-the-top for the neighborhood,
however.

The southern districts

Amrheins 80 W Broadway, South Boston ☎268-
6189; **Broadway T.** A Southie landmark and a
favorite of local politicians for generations.
The good-ole' American comfort food won't
dazzle your palate, but it's reasonably
priced and you get a lot of it.

Bella Luna 405 Centre St, Jamaica Plain ☎524-
6060; **Green St T.** *Nouvelle* pizza with a funky
array of fresh toppings (you can order from
their list of combinations or design your
own) in a festive space. Jazz brunch on
Sunday mornings and live entertainment on
most weekends.
Bob the Chef 604 Columbus Ave, Roxbury
☎536-6204; **Mass Ave T.** The best soul food
in New England. Good chitlins, black-eyed
peas and collard greens – and don't miss
the "glori-fried chicken," the house
specialty. Live jazz on weekends.
Doyle's 3484 Washington St, Jamaica Plain
☎524-2345; **Green St T.** Excellent, inexpensive Irish pub-restaurant, with fish-and-
chips, rack of lamb, burgers, clam
chowder, and good beers on tap. A
friendly neighborhood place that's equally
good for a drink or brunch.

Cambridge

Bartley's Burger Cottage 1246 Massachusetts
Ave ☎354-6559; **Harvard T.** The walls here
are decorated with references to political
humor and pop culture, while the names of
the dishes on the menu poke fun at celebri-
ties of the hour. The food itself is loaded
with cholesterol, but a burger and "frappé"
(milkshake) here is a definite experience.
Blue Room 1 Kendall Sq ☎494-9034; **Kendall
T.** Unpretentious restaurant with superlative
grilled fusion; tuna steak and braised lamb
are common, but what accompanies them
– cumin and basmati yogurt or tomatillos –
isn't. Menu changes with what's available,
so the food is always fresh and innovative.
Boca Grande 1728 Massachusetts Ave ☎354-
7400; **Porter T.** Somewhere in between a
restaurant and a taco stand, crowded *Boca*
vends delectable, if not quite authentic,
Mexican fare at incredibly low prices – no
entrée is above $5. The overstuffed burritos
are excellent meals in themselves.
Border Café 32 Church St ☎864-6100; **Harvard
T.** Cambridge's most popular Tex-Mex
place is pretty good, though not nearly
enough to justify the massive crowds that
form on weekend nights. The margaritas
are salty and strong, and the moderately
priced food is so pungent you'll carry its
aroma with you for hours afterward.
Café of India 52 Brattle St ☎661-0683; **Harvard
T.** This inexpensive Indian spot stands out
primarily because of its uplifting, woody

interior; in summer, the facade is removed for semi-alfresco dining. Its best dishes are tried-and-true Indian standards – chicken tikka, saag paneer, and particularly light, delectable naan bread.

Cambridge Common 1667 Massachusetts Ave ☎547-1228; Harvard or Porter **T**. Half bar, half restaurant, *Cambridge Common* is a popular after-work place for young professionals and graduate students. The "Ultimate Nachos" appetizer could stand as a meal on its own. A downstairs music venue, the *Lizard Lounge* (see review p.196), has decent rock and jazz acts almost nightly.

Central Kitchen 567 Massachusetts Ave ☎491-5599; Central **T**. Hip Central Square bistro with a delightful chalkboard menu offering French classics (moules frites) and New American twists (grilled octopus with shaved fennel) in an intimate, stylish setting.

Charlie's Kitchen 10 Eliot St ☎492-9646; Harvard **T**. Marvelously atmospheric townie hangout in the heart of Harvard Square, with red vinyl booths, sassy waitresses with beehive hairdos, and greasy diner food. Try the cheap but filling Double Cheeseburger Special.

Chez Henri 1 Shepard St ☎354-8980; Harvard or Porter **T**. Does paying more at a fancy restaurant actually mean you'll get a vastly superior meal? At *Chez Henri*, the answer is an emphatic yes. If you can get a table (no reservations, and the weekend wait tops one hour even late at night), you'll enjoy what may well be Cambridge's finest cuisine. Chef Paul O'Connell's experiment in fusion brings Modern French together with Cuban influences, best sampled in the light salads and excellent Cuban crab cake appetizers, and the chicken asado that follows.

East Coast Grill 1271 Cambridge St ☎491-6568; Harvard or Central Square **T**. A festive and funky atmosphere in which to enjoy fresh seafood (there is a raw bar tucked into one corner) and Caribbean side dishes such as grilled avocado, pineapple salsa and fried plaintains. The Sunday serve-yourself Bloody Mary bar is reason enough to visit.

Harvest 44 Brattle St ☎868-2255; Harvard **T**. Upscale, white-tableclothed Harvard Square institution with an oft-changing menu of rich New American cuisine; the smashing outdoor courtyard is another fine feature.

Henrietta's Table 1 Bennett St (in the *Charles Hotel*) ☎661-5005; Harvard **T**. One of the only restaurants in Cambridge that serves classic New England fare. Rich entrées such as roasted duck or pork chops work well with side dishes of wilted greens or mashed potatoes – although some would say a trip to *Henrietta's* is wasted if it's not for their famous brunch, served every Sunday from noon to 3pm; it costs $35 per person but allows unlimited access to a cornucopia of farm-fresh treats from around New England.

House of Blues 96 Winthrop St ☎491-2583; Harvard **T**. The desultory waitstaff at the original *House of Blues* serves up mediocre Southern food – like jambalaya and ribs – in a decor carefully manufactured to effect a casual roadhouse look. The real reason to come here is for the big-name blues and rock acts at the upstairs venue (see review p.196).

Iruña 56 JFK St ☎868-5633; Harvard **T**. Located in a diminutive, unassuming spot in an alley off JFK Street, this fairly uncrowded spot serves authentic Spanish fare. Lunch specials are incredibly cheap, including paella and a rich *arroz con pollo*; dinner is more expensive but equally good.

Pho Pasteur 35 Dunster St, in the *Garage* ☎864-4100; Harvard **T**. This more upscale Harvard Square incarnation of the successful Chinatown string of Vietnamese joints (see p.178) serves a variety of filling and delicious *pho* noodle soups beginning at $7. The spring rolls are another treat.

Siam Garden 451/2 Mt Auburn St ☎354-1718; Harvard **T**. Tasty and cheap Thai food in an atmosphere that tries really hard to invoke images of the exotic East.

Tandoor House 569 Massachusetts Ave ☎661-9001; Central **T**. Consistently at the top of the list of Cambridge's many fine Indian restaurants, *Tandoor* has excellent chicken saag and a great mushroom bhaji. Definitely the best Indian spot outside Harvard Square – and perhaps in the whole city.

Trattoria Pulcinella 147 Huron Ave ☎491-6336; Porter **T**. A creative menu blends fresh ingredients with Continental flair. The eggplant-stuffed ravioli with a tomato basil garlic sauce is a must, as is the perfectly decadent tiramisu. Waitstaff is unusually attentive without being intrusive.

Upstairs at the Pudding 10 Holyoke St ☎864-1933; Harvard **T**. The dining room was converted from what was originally the eating area for Harvard's ultra-elite Hasty Pudding Club – and the attitude lingers on. The food is excellent, though, falling somewhere in between New American and Old Colonial, with results like duckling salad with Roquefort flan, and pork chops served with a creamy polenta sauce. Even old standards like the porterhouse steak get a twist – the mashed potatoes on the side are jazzed up with goat cheese. Advance reservations are essential.

Somerville

Dalí 415 Washington St ☎661-3254; Harvard T. Waitresses dance the flamenco at this upscale tapas restaurant, which features live, energetic Spanish music, excellent sangria, a good wine list and superlative tapas. Order the Spanish white asparagus, farm trout with red wine sauce, and the braised rabbit in sweet-and-sour sauce; your taste buds will thank you.

Diva 246 Elm St ☎629-4963; Davis T. This trendy Davis Square spot isn't your typical Indian restaurant: the space is stylishly modern and cushy, the entrées pricey ($12–16), and the mix of northern and southern dishes unusually mild, spice-wise.

Gargoyles on the Square 215 Elm St ☎776-5300; Davis T. The classiest joint in Davis Square combines contemporary American with a touch of French; look for house-smoked ostrich, duck confit risotto, grilled venison, and outstanding service.

Redbones 55 Chester St ☎628-2200; Davis T. All styles of American barbecue are represented in huge portions here, accompanied by delectable sides such as collard greens and Cajun "dirty rice." After eating, you won't likely have room for dessert – but if you do, the pecan pie is top-notch. Long lines at dinner, so arrive early. No cards.

The Rosebud Diner 381 Summer St ☎666-6015; Davis T. Authentic diner car with red vinyl booths, pink neon sign and chrome detail, that serves the expected burgers, fries and Boston Creme Pie along with more contemporary favorites like pasta, grilled chicken and veggie burgers.

14

Drinking

espite – or, perhaps, because of – the lingering Puritan ethic that pervades Boston, people here tend to **drink** more than they do in the rest of the country, with the consequence that few American cities offer as many bars per capita in which to knock back a few beers. Before you start planning a big night out, however, it's worth pointing out that drinking in Boston is not without its headaches – and we don't just mean the morning after.

While the number of watering holes in Boston is high, the range of options is not, and most stop serving alcohol at 2am. Another sticking point is that the city's university culture means the US drinking-age minimum of 21 is strictly enforced; even if you're obviously of-age, you'll still be required to show at least one form of valid photo identification, either in the form of a driver's license or passport, to gain entrance to any place serving drinks. Finally, as the T shuts down at 12.30am, it can be difficult to find a taxi due to the mass exodus of drinkers when the bars let out at 2am.

As for types of places, it's not surprising that, given the city's Irish heritage, **pubs** make up the majority of Boston's drinking establishments. Especially high concentrations of these are found in the **West End**, **Cambridge**, and **downtown** around Quincy Market; many are unextraordinary, but several are the real deal, drawing as many Irish expats as they do Irish-American locals.

More upscale are the **bars** and **lounges** of **Back Bay**, especially those along Newbury and Boylston streets, which offer as much scenester attitude as atmosphere. Some of the most popular bars in this area are actually adjuncts of restaurants and hotels; still others cater to the city's gay population (see Chapter 17, Gay & lesbian Boston, for the best).

The rest of the city's neighborhood bars, pick-up joints and yuppie hotspots are differentiated by their crowds: **Beacon Hill** tends to be older and stuffier; **downtown**, mainly around Quincy Market and the Theater District, draws a healthy mix of tourists, business people and sporty types; while **Kenmore Square** and **Cambridge** are mainly student-oriented, with a clientele sporting a generic uniform of khakis, university logo t-shirts and ball caps.

Eating and drinking maps

Within this chapter, as well as Chapter 12, Cafés, snacks and light meals, and Chapter 13, Restaurants, you'll find maps where we've keyed the eating and drinking options for the major Boston neighborhoods. These maps can be found on the following pages:

Downtown	pp.168–169	Back Bay and the South End	p.183
The North End	p.171	Cambridge	pp.192–193
Beacon Hill	p.180		

Bell in Hand Tavern 45 Union St ☎227-2098; State or Government Center **T**. The oldest continuously operating tavern in Boston draws a fairly exuberant mix of tourists and young professionals.

The Black Rose (Roisin Dubh) 160 State St ☎742-2286; State **T**. Down-home Irish pub specializing in imported beers from the Emerald Isle: Harp, Murphy's and – especially – Guinness all flow freely. Things get pretty boisterous in here on weekends.

Emily's 48 Winter St ☎423-3649; Park **T**. Red-velvet curtains and floor-to-ceiling mirrors give this downtown spot as much style as any place in Back Bay, but without the accompanying attitude. On weeknights it's mellow, while on weekends a DJ spins Top 40 mixes to overenthusiastic (or overserved) dancers.

Good Life 28 Kingston St ☎451-2622; Downtown Crossing **T**. This trendy, swanky bar generates quite a buzz, due as much to its potent martinis as its 1970s decor, which features wicked groovy orange vinyl walls; also serves standard bar food, including "east of" Buffalo wings.

Green Dragon Tavern 11 Marshall St ☎367-0055; Government Center **T**. Another tavern that dates to the colonial era, this was a popular meeting place for patriots during the Revolution. There's a standard selection of tap beers, a raw bar and a full menu rife with twee historical humor ("One if by land, two if by seafood").

The Kinsale 2 Center Plaza ☎742-5577; Government Center **T**. Shipped brick by brick from Ireland to its current location in the shadow of Government Plaza, this outrageously popular Irish pub is as authentic as it gets; the menu even lists beer-battered fish and hot pastrami on a "bulkie" (Boston slang for a sandwich bun).

Les Zygomates 129 South St ☎542-5108; South Station **T**. Also reviewed in the Restaurants chapter (p.177), this elegant wine bar has a wide and exceptional selection of varietals. Neophytes might want to get their palates wet at the weekly wine-tasting sessions (Tues 6–8pm; $25).

The Littlest Bar in Boston 47 Province St ☎523-9766; Downtown Crossing **T**. The tiny size of this place – it's only allowed 38 people in its cramped quarters at any given time – is part of the charm, as are the quality pints of Guinness and free music by bands crammed into an alcove – perhaps also the littlest performance space in Boston.

Pravda 116 116 Boylston St ☎482-7799; Boylston **T**. Red curtains, plush seating, and back-lit walls are a fittingly decadent backdrop to the whopping 116 varieties of vodka on tap (whence the digits in the bar's name). Unfortunately, you won't find any mysterious-looking Russians sipping the spirits; the crowd is more suited to an Abercrombie & Fitch catalog.

The Purple Shamrock 1 Union St ☎227-2060; State or Government Center **T**. A lively watering hole that draws a broad cross-section of folks, the *Shamrock* has one of Boston's better straight singles scenes. It gets very crowded on weekends.

The Rack 24 Clinton St ☎725-1051; Government Center **T**. Well-dressed twenty- and thirtysomethings convene at this pool hall to dine, smoke cigars, drink a bewildering variety of cocktails and, of course, shoot a rack or two. While there are 35 pool tables and a fair share of wannabe hustlers, about half the crowd shows up just to see and be seen.

Charlestown

Warren Tavern 2 Pleasant St ☎241-8142; Community College **T**. An atmospheric place to enjoy a drink, and the oldest standing structure in Charlestown. The *Warren* also has a generous menu of good tavern food.

Beacon Hill and the West End

21st Amendment 148 Bowdoin St ☎227-7100; Bowdoin **T**. This dimly lit, down-home watering hole, which gets its name from the amendment that repealed Prohibition, is a favorite haunt of legislators from the adjacent State House and students from nearby Suffolk University.

The Bull & Finch Pub 84 Beacon St ☎227-9605; Arlington **T**. If you don't already know, and if the conspicuous banners outside don't tip you off, this is the bar that served as the inspiration for the TV show *Cheers*. If you've gotta go, be warned – it's packed with camera-toting tourists, the inside bears little resemblance to the NBC set, and the food, though cutely named (eNORMous burgers), is pricey and mediocre. Plus, it's almost certain that nobody will know your name.

Fours 166 Canal St ☎720-4455; North Station **T.** The classiest of the West End's sports bars, with an army of TVs to broadcast games from around the globe, as well as paraphernalia from the Celtics, Bruins and other local teams.

The Hill 228 Cambridge St ☎742-6192; Charles **T.** The only centrally located bar in Beacon Hill, this classic yuppie hangout attracts suits who like to tip back a lot of pricey imported beer; there's often a long line to get in on weekend nights.

Irish Embassy 234 Friend St ☎742-6618; North Station **T.** Up in the West End, this is one of the city's most authentic Irish (rather than Irish-American) pubs, with the crowd to match. Live Irish entertainment most nights, plus broadcasts of Irish soccer matches.

McGann's 197 Portland St ☎227-4059; North Station **T.** Similar to the nearby *Irish Embassy* (see above), but with a more upmarket, restauranty feel. There are British eats like shepherd's pie and pan-seared calf's liver if you're in the mood.

Sevens Ale House 77 Charles St ☎523-9074; Charles **T.** While the tourists pack into the *Bull & Finch*, you can drop by this cozy wood-paneled joint to watch the game or shoot darts in an authentic Boston neighborhood bar. Wide selection of draft beers, plus daily specials, substantial food and a relaxed feel.

Back Bay and the South End

33 33 Stanhope ☎572-3311; Back Bay **T.** Sashay through the discreetly labeled doors and head straight down the smoked-glass stairwell to find this restaurant-lounge's intimate basement club. Decked out in a curious pastiche of wire netting and puffy, mushroom-cap footstools, this place is popular with a thirtysomething set who tap their feet to deep house.

Back Bay Brewing Company 755 Boylston St ☎424-8300; Copley **T.** Despite the name, this is actually more a restaurant than bar – but the second-floor lounge is one of the city's most inviting spaces to drink a tasty draft. See restaurant review p.181.

BarCode 955 Boylston ☎421-1818; Hynes **T.** The sign above the door is hardly legible – it's a series of bars and numbers resembling the symbol scanned into cash regis-

ters at checkout – but there's no gimmickry to the fashionable bar inside, which draws a crowd of well-dressed Euros and yuppies who typically skip the food (the place is technically a restaurant) in favor of sipping Cosmopolitans.

Bristol Lounge 200 Boylston St ☎351-2053; Arlington **T.** A posh lobby-side lounge in the *Four Seasons* where the desserts are as popular as the drinks.

Bukowski Tavern 50 Dalton St ☎437-9999; Hynes **T.** Arguably Boston's best dive bar, this parking garage watering hole has views over the Mass Pike and such a vast beer selection that a homemade "wheel of indecision" is spun by waitstaff when patrons can't decide what to drink. Excellent rock 'n' roll jukebox, plus regular poetry and fiction readings, too.

Clery's Restaurant 113 Dartmouth St ☎262-9874; Back Bay **T.** Despite a name change (known, until recently as *The Claddaugh*), and a renovation, this Irish-flavored bar and restaurant on the northern edge of the South End remains lackluster in the food department while consistently packing in a lively drinking clientele; head downstairs to the sofa-strewn lounge area and cozy up with a pint by the fire.

Dad's 911 Boylston St ☎296-3237; Hynes **T.** Dim lights and scantily clad barmaids make this a fairly un-Back Bay watering hole – all the more so given it's actually set in an old-school diner. Down that $6 martini and prepare to cruise.

Daisy Buchanan's 240A Newbury St ☎247-8516; Copley **T.** A real-life beer commercial: young guys wearing baseball caps eye up scantily clad gals, watch professional sports on TV, and contribute nightly to the bar's pervasive smell of booze.

Oak Bar 138 St. James Ave (in the *Fairmont Copley Plaza*) ☎267-5300; Copley **T.** Rich wood paneling, high ceilings, swirling cigar smoke and excellent martinis make this one of the more genteel Back Bay spots to drink.

Whiskey Park 64 Arlington St (in the *Park Plaza*) ☎542-1482; Arlington **T.** Owned by Randy Gerber (aka Mr Cindy Crawford), this lounge's chic chocolate-brown leather chair design was conceived by Michael Czysz, the guy behind Lenny Kravitz's swinging Miami pad. The prices match the celebrity name-dropping, but there's hardly a better place in town to grab a cocktail.

Kenmore Square and the Fenway

An Tua Nua 835 Beacon St ☎262-2121; Kenmore **T**. A very popular BU pub that's a great spot to catch a Sox game and a pint by day, as a few more drinks and some dancing by night (see p.197 for nightlife reviews). Also offers good (though standard) bar food, plus a great view of Beacon Street.

Audubon Circle 838 Beacon St ☎421-1910; Kenmore **T**. Sleek, modern bar where a well-dressed crowd gathers for cocktails and fancy bar food (see restaurant review p.184) before and after Sox games at nearby Fenway Park.

Bill's Bar 5 1/2 Lansdowne St ☎421-9678; Kenmore **T**. A fairly relaxed and homey Lansdowne Street spot, with lots of beer, lots of TV and occasional live music – in which case expect a cover charge of $5.

Boston Beer Works 61 Brookline Ave ☎536-2337; Kenmore **T**. A brewery located right by Fenway Park, *Boston Beer Works* is a popular place for the Red Sox faithful to warm up before games and drown their sorrows after. Their signature ale is the Boston Red, but the seasonal brews are also worth a taste. Decent food, too.

Copperfield's/Down Under 98 Brookline Ave ☎247-8605; Kenmore **T**. Two adjoining bars, though the difference between them is minimal: both offer cheap drafts and pool, and are frequented by a raucous collegiate crowd. Cover of $5 on weekends to see loud bands.

The southern districts

Brendan Behan 378 Centre St, Jamaica Plain ☎522-5386; Jackson Square **T**. The godfather of Boston's Irish pubs, this dimly lit institution has the usual friendly staff all week long, as well as live music and free buffets available on most weekends.

James's Gate 5–11 McBride St, Jamaica Plain ☎983-2000; Forest Hills **T**. Beat Boston's harsh winter by sipping Guinness by the blazing fireplace in this cozy pub, or by trying the hearty fare in the restaurant in back. Traditional Irish music on Sundays, open mic on Thursdays.

Cambridge

B-Side Lounge 92 Hampshire St ☎354-0766; Central **T**. Cantabridgians flock to this

tarted-up dive bar to partake of its extensive drinks list and quirky bar food (hard-boiled eggs, anyone?). The en-suite kitchen's tasty soul food offerings are none too shabby either, making this the kind of place where a quick stop for an after-work drink often winds up leading to dinner, too.

The Cellar 991 Massachusetts Ave ☎876-2580; Harvard **T**. Two floors, each with a bar, filled with a regular crowd of Harvard faculty members, older students, and other locals imbibing fine beers and killer Long Island iced teas.

The Druid 1357 Cambridge St ☎497-0965; #69 bus. Twee Inman Square bar featuring an old Celtic motif, with murals of druid priests and ever-present pints of Guinness; blessedly free of the college scene.

Enormous Room 577 Massachusetts Ave (no phone); Central **T**. Walking into this comfy lounge tucked above *Central Kitchen* (see p.186 for review) is tantamount to entering an opium den minus the pipe smokers. Sundry good-looking types primp and pose on thick-piled futon mattresses and deep leather sofas, while deep house is piped in over the soundsystem.

The Field 20 Prospect St ☎354-7345; Central **T**. Although *The Field* is located between Harvard and MIT, this Irish pub attracts an eclectic non-college crowd. Play pool or darts while you sip one of several varieties of tap beers.

Grafton Street 1280 Massachusetts Ave ☎497-0400; Harvard **T**. Authentic, cozy Irish atmosphere, in which an older, well-dressed set enjoys smooth drafts and equally good food.

Grendel's Den 89 Winthrop St ☎491-1160; Harvard **T**. A favorite spot of locals and grad students for drinking ale, these dark, conspiratorial environs have a fantastic happy-hour special, with big plates of appetizers (fried calamari, nachos) for just $1.50 each.

Hong Kong 1236 Massachusetts Ave ☎864-5311; Harvard **T**. The bizarre homemade "Scorpion," a boozy concoction served in a dragon boat and loaded with ample straws for communal sharing, makes this bland restaurant-bar definitely worth a visit – once.

Miracle of Science 321 Massachusetts Ave ☎868-2866; Central **T** or #1 bus. Surprisingly hip despite its status as an MIT hangout. There's noir decor and a trendy crowd of well-dressed professionals; can get quite crowded on weekend nights.

People's Republik 880 Massachusetts Ave ☎492-8632; Central or Harvard **T**. Smack dab between MIT and Harvard, and attracting a good mix of technocrats and potential world-leaders as a result, this Marxist-styled bar takes its Communist propaganda seriously – on the walls, anyway; the range of tap offerings is positively democratic.

Plough & Stars 912 Massachusetts Ave ☎441-3455; Central or Harvard **T**. Off-the-beaten-path neighborhood hideaway that's very much worth the trek, whether for its animated cribbage games, live UK and European soccer broadcasts, quality pub grub or its nightly live music. Sunday nights sometimes find the Ray Corvair Trio providing a soundscape of surf, strip and spy

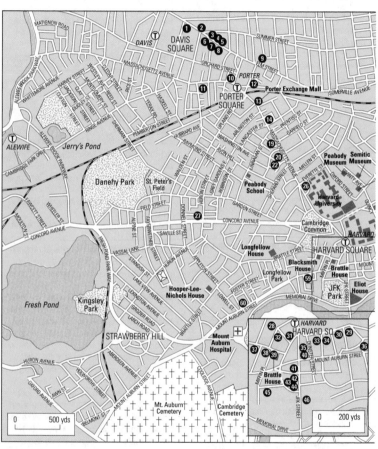

RESTAURANTS AND CAFÉS

1369 Coffeehouse	18 & 48	Cambridge Common	26	Gargoyles on		Redbones	8
Algiers	39	C'est Bon	33	the Square	4	The Rosebud Diner	5
Anna's Taqueria	12	Central Kitchen	51	Harvest	37	Siam Garden	60
Bartley's Burger		Charlie's Kitchen	43	Henrietta's Table	45	Someday Café	6
Cottage	30	Chez Henri	22	Herrell's Ice Cream	35	Tandoor House	50
Blue Room	24	Cottonwood Restaurant		House of Blues	42	Tealuxe	31
Boca Grande	19	& Café	13	Iruña	46	Toscanini's	30
Bookcellar Café	14	Dalí	15	Legal Seafoods	25	Trattoria Pulcinella	27
Border Café	28	Darwin's Ltd	59	Leo's Place	44	Upstairs at	
Café of India	38	Diesel	3	Pho Pasteur	40	the Pudding	34
Café Pamplona	36	Diva	7	Porter Square Café			
Caffé Paradiso	43	East Coast Grill	16	& Diner	10		

music as patrons smoke, drink and rub elbows in the cramped space.

Rialto 1 Bennett St ☎ 661-5050; Harvard T.
The bar adjunct to the posh restaurant of the same name caters to a wealthy crowd that matches the plush atmosphere. Dress semi-formal and be prepared to pay big-time for the drinks and cocktails, which are, admittedly, excellent.

Shay's 58 JFK St ☎ 864-9161; Harvard T.
Relaxed contrast to the crowded and sweaty student-oriented sports bars of Harvard Square. Unwind with grad students over wine and quality beer.

Temple Bar 1688 Massachusetts Ave ☎ 547-5055; Harvard or Porter T. Cambridge's stand-out scenester bar attracts a chi-chi crowd to its smart digs outfitted with attractive

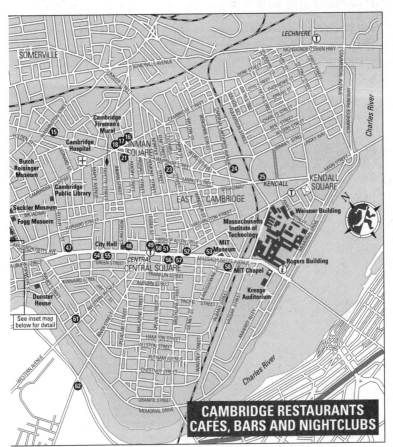

CAMBRIDGE RESTAURANTS CAFÉS, BARS AND NIGHTCLUBS

BARS AND NIGHTCLUBS

B-Side Lounge	23	Grendel's Den	41	Paradise	58	Shay's	46
The Burren	2	Hong Kong	30	People's		T.T. the Bear's	56
The Cellar	47	House of Blues	42	Republik	55	Temple Bar	20
Club Passim	32	Johnny D's	1	Plough & Stars	54	Thirsty Scholar	
The Druid	17	Lizard Lounge	26	Regattabar	45	Pub	9
Enormous Room	51	ManRay	57	Rialto	45	Tir Na Nog	11
The Field	49	Middle East	56	Ryles	21	Wally's Café	52
Grafton Street	29	Miracle of Science	53	Scullers	62	Western Front	61

touches like fancy floral arrangements and arty Martini Rosso advertising posters.

Somerville

The Burren 247 Elm St ☎ 776-6896; Davis **T**. Busy student bar, with the expected baseball caps and cargo pants, whose overflowing crowds spill out onto its outdoor terrace, which is a prime spot for Davis Square people-watching.

Thirsty Scholar Pub 70 Beacon St ☎ 497-2294; Harvard **T**. One of the coziest bars around, *Thirsty*'s warm red-brick and burnished wood interior is matched by a smiling waitstaff and down-home comfort food like shepherd's pie and baked beans. Bring a book to read, or listen up while distinguished writers opine from their own at the bar's oft-hosted readings.

Tir na Nog 366A Somerville Ave ☎ 628-4300; Washington Square **T**. Tiny, wonderful pub with a marvelously homey feel, thanks to bookcase-lined walls and friendly barstaff who pour terrific pints behind a gleaming mahogany bar.

Nightlife

n recent years Boston's **nightlife** has received something of a wake-up call, although for a major American city, its scene still feels small, and is geared primarily to a buttoned-down college crowd; you'll find that even at the wildest venues, locals tend to sport the reserved preppy look characteristic of Boston's universities.

A few stylish clubs have sprung up in places such as **Downtown Crossing**, that were previously mere ghost towns by night. Though the city is by no means a 24-hour one, these new hotspots have breathed a bit of fresh air into a scene that once lived in the shadow of the city's so-called highbrow culture. Elsewhere, the same old clubs reinvent themselves every few years in the hopes of catching up with current trends.

Live music plays a huge role in the city's nightlife arena, with bars and clubs catering to a young crowd, especially around Kenmore and Harvard squares, where you're as likely to hear a squalling rock band as a mellow DJ. Boston has spawned its share of enormous **rock** acts, from the ever-enduring Aerosmith to a smattering of post-punk and indie groups such as the Pixies and Sebadoh. There is a bit less in the way of **jazz** and **blues**, but you can usually find something cheap and to your liking almost any day of the week. If you're interested in hearing classical or opera, check Chapter 16, Performing arts and film.

For **club and music listings**, check Thursday's *Boston Globe* "Calendar," the *Boston Phoenix*, the *Improper Bostonian* and *Stuff@night*. You'll also find a number of websites helpful for up-to-date listings; for details on these, see p.20.

Live music

The strength of Boston's **live music** is in the intimacy of its smaller venues, though superstar acts make the city a regular stop on their world tours as well. Two of the biggest **concert halls** are far out of town: the Tweeter Center, south of the city in Mansfield (☎508/339-2333, ⓦwww.tweetercenter. com), and the Worcester Centrum, an hour or so west in Worcester (☎508/755-6800, ⓦwww.centrumcentre.com).

On a more human scale, plenty of **alternative venues** serve up everything from name bands to obscure new acts; if all else fails, there's always street music at "the Pit" in Harvard Square (p.125), where you're bound to hear some free amateur acts – whether you like it or not.

Rock venues

FleetBoston Pavilion Fan Pier, Northern Ave ☎728-1600, ⓦwww.fleetbostonpavilion.com; South Station **T**. Concerts by well-known performers from Mel Tormé to the Gipsy Kings are held here during the summer under a huge white tent at Boston Harbor's edge.

FleetCenter 50 Causeway St ☎624-1750, ⓦwww.fleetcenter.com; **North Station T.** This arena, up in the West End, attracts many of the big-name acts that pass through New England – usually at a hefty price.

Lizard Lounge 1667 Massachusetts Ave, Cambridge ☎547-0759; **Harvard or Porter T.** The downstairs portion of the *Cambridge Common* restaurant (see review p.186), a favorite among local students, featuring rock and jazz acts almost nightly for a fairly nominal cover charge.

Middle East 472 Massachusetts Ave, Cambridge ☎864-3278, ⓦwww.mideastclub.com; **Central T.** Local and regional bands of every sort – salsa to ska and mambo to hardcore – stop in regularly at this Cambridge institution. Bigger acts are hosted downstairs; smaller ones ply their stuff in a tiny upstairs space. A third venue, the "Corner" has free shows every night, with belly dancing every Wednesday. The attached restaurant has decent – you guessed it – Middle Eastern food.

Orpheum Theater Hamilton Place ☎679-0810; **Park or Downtown Crossing T.** Once an old-school movie house, the *Orpheum* is now a venue for big-name music acts. The small space means you're closer to the action, but it sells out quickly and the cramped seating discourages dancing.

Paradise Rock Club 967 Commonwealth Ave ☎562-8800; **Kenmore T.** Usually a dance club (see *M-LXXX*, p.198), but occasionally hosts mid-level music shows. Crazy decor and pricey drinks, but it rarely sells out and the acoustics are quite good.

T.T. the Bear's 10 Brookline St, Cambridge ☎492-2327; **Central T.** A downmarket version of the *Middle East*, with less popular acts in a space with a gritty intimacy its neighbor lacks. All kinds of bands appear, mostly punk, rock and electronica.

Jazz, blues and folk venues

Club Passim 47 Palmer St, Cambridge ☎492-7679, ⓦwww.clubpassim.com; **Harvard T.** Folkie hangout in Harvard Square where Joan Baez and Suzanne Vega got their starts. World music and spoken word performances in windowed basement setting.

House of Blues 96 Winthrop St, Cambridge ☎491-2583, ⓦwww.hob.com; **Harvard T.** The first in the corporate monolith spawned by the same evil geniuses that started the Hard Rock Café conglomerate. The faux-roadhouse decor and stiff, middle-class patrons are painfully inauthentic, but the *House* still features top blues acts.

Johnny D's 17 Holland St, Somerville ☎776-2004, ⓦwww.johnnyds.com; **Davis T.** A mixed bag with talent ranging from the sublime to the ordinary. Acts include garage bands, progressive jazz sextets, traditional blues artists, and some uncategorizables.

Regattabar 1 Bennett St, Cambridge ☎661-5000; **Harvard T.** This place draws top jazz acts, though, as its location in the swish *Charles Hotel* suggests, the atmosphere (and clientele) is decidedly sedate. Dress nicely and prepare to pay at least $10 cover; it's sometimes necessary to purchase tickets ahead of time.

Ryles 212 Hampshire St, Cambridge ☎876-9330, ⓦwww.rylesjazz.com; **Central T.** Two levels of live music – swing and salsa upstairs, and smooth jazz and blues downstairs.

Scullers 400 Soldiers Field Rd, Cambridge ☎783-0090, ⓦwww.scullersjazz.com; **Harvard T.** Upscale jazz club in the *DoubleTree Guest Suites* draws five-star acts, including some of the stars of the contemporary jazz scene. Hop in a taxi to get here, as the walk along the river at night can be dodgy.

Wally's Café 427 Massachusetts Ave, Roxbury ☎424-1408, ⓦwww.wallyscafe.com. **Massachusetts T.** This refreshingly unhewn bar is Boston's oldest jazz joint, and its A-list jazz (Tues–Thurs & Fri–Sat), blues (Mon) and fusion (Sun) shows draw a vibrant crowd. It gets pretty packed on weekends, but that's part of the experience. No cover.

Western Front 343 Western Ave, Cambridge ☎492-7772; **Central T.** The *Front* puts on rollicking jazz, blues and reggae shows for a dance-crazy audience. Drinks are cheap, and the Jamaican food served on weekends is delectably authentic.

Yesterday's 533 Washington St ☎350-5555; **Downtown Crossing T.** Located on the fringe of Downtown Crossing near a cluster of abandoned grand old theaters, this traditional pub showcases live jazz (Wed), blues (Thurs–Fri), and swing (Sun); Saturday nights are more likely to find rock 'n' roll bringing down the house.

Nightclubs

Boston's **nightclubs** are mostly clustered in downtown's Theater District and around Kenmore Square – Tremont Street in the former and Lansdowne Street in the latter being the centers of activity – with a few prominent ones in Back Bay and the South End. Many of the venues in those two neighborhoods are **gay clubs**, often the most happening places in town; for a complete listing see Chapter 17, Gay and lesbian Boston.

The music at these clubs changes almost nightly, so to keep apprised of what's on, check the individual club websites, the "Calendar" section in Thursday's *Boston Globe*, or the listings in the weekly *Boston Phoenix*. **Cover charges** are generally in the $5–15 range, though sometimes there's no cover at all. Boston's venues tend to be easily entered – no New York style selection at the door – though there is a tendency for bouncers to frown upon sneakers and jeans in favor of collared shirts and dress pants. On weekends, clubs can be overrun with suburban yuppies; come on a weeknight for the most authentic local scene.

Downtown, Back Bay and the South End

Aria 246 Tremont St ☎ 338-7080, ⓦ www .ariaboston.com; Boylston **T**. This cushy, upscale club in the basement of the Wilbur Theater is as close as Boston gets to the velvet-rope attitude of New York clubs. The emphasis is more on lounging around in plush seats and posing for the well-dressed Euro crowd than dancing to house music, an activity relegated to a small dance floor.

The Big Easy One Boylston Place ☎ 351-7000, ⓦ www.alleyboston.com; Boylston **T**. Bar and jazz club with a New Orleans theme and a mix of live acts and DJs; open Thursday to Saturday night only. Cover $5–8.

Club Europa/Buzz 67 Stuart St ☎ 267-8969, ⓦ www.buzzboston.com; Boylston **T**. On the edge of the Theater District, this is one of Boston's better dance clubs. Most of the action is on the third floor; the second tends to be louder and more crowded. On Saturday night the club becomes "Buzz," long the most plugged-in gay disco in Boston.

Envy 25 Boylston Place ☎ 542-3689; Boylston **T**. The musical menu at this small, casual (but no baseball caps or sneakers, please) club ranges from classic alternative to Top 40 and high energy house, depending on which DJ happens to be on duty.

The Roxy 279 Tremont St ☎ 338-7699, ⓦ www.roxyboston.com; Boylston **T**. Located in the former grand ballroom of the *Tremont House* hotel, this Theater District club is a magnet for Eurotrash, who brave the most byzantine admission process – long queues, even in winter, and lots of doors – to gyrate to loud house, techno and salsa music.

Sugar Shack One Boylston Place ☎ 351-2510, ⓦ www.alleyboston.com; Boylston **T**. This perennial favorite with the collegiate set features a decor of fake broken windows and drinks with names like Raspberry Truffle. Dance to hip-hop, R&B and Top 40 at this cheesy club, and discover what college guys look like without their baseball caps on the sweaty dance floor.

Venu 100 Warrenton St ☎ 338-8061, ⓦ www.venuboston.com; Boylston **T**. The city's ultimate Euro hotspot, this slick Theater District club gives you opulent eye candy for your hefty ($15) cover charge: Art Deco stylings, beautiful patrons and dark house music on a laser-lit dance floor.

Kenmore Square and the Fenway

An Tua Nua 835 Beacon St ☎ 262-2121; Kenmore **T**. Despite its Gaelic name ("the new beginning"), this popular neighborhood hangout is just as much dance bar as it is Irish pub. Thursday's hip-hop nights get especially crowded with BU and Northeastern undergrads, who sweat it out on the dance-floor or check each other out from the many ringside seats.

Avalon 15 Lansdowne St ☎ 262-2424, ⓦ www.avalonboston.com; Kenmore **T**. *Avalon's* 1500-person capacity makes it the biggest dance club in Boston, and any weekend night the place is positively jamming, often to the tracks laid down by out-of-town talent like Paul Oakenfold and John Digweed. The cavernous central floor is flanked on either side by bars. Sunday is gay night.

Axis 13 Lansdowne St ☏262-2437, ⓦwww.axisboston.com; Kenmore **T**. Adjacent to *Avalon* but with more techno and trance leanings. On certain nights, the two clubs open their doors to each other, forming one megaclub; check current listings.

Bill's Bar 5 1/2 Lansdowne St ☏421-9678; Kenmore **T**. This fairly relaxed Lansdowne Street spot packs it in for its hip-hop nights (Tues & Sat) and nightly live music shows; covers range from $5 to $15, depending on who's in the house.

Karma 9 Lansdowne St ☏421-9595, ⓦwww.karmaclub.com; Kenmore **T**. This multi-room, faux-hip Top 40 dance club aspires with limited success to a futuristic Hindu temple decor. Cover $8–10; under 21s allowed.

M-LXXX (M-80) 967 Commonwealth Ave ☏562-8800, ⓦwww.m80.com; Boston University **T**. Boston's substantial pack of international students dances here to redubbed mainstream hits and foreign disco beats. Everyone's dressed to the nines and able to afford the exorbitant prices for drinks; there's also a $10 cover. Open Wed, Fri and Sat.

The Modern 36 Lansdowne St ☏351-2581; Kenmore **T**. Although *Mama Kin* once resided here, the *Modern* bears little resemblance to the legendary rock palace co-owned by Aerosmith. The plush forest-green velvet chairs, relaxed lounge atmosphere and variety of DJ nights make it hard to believe grungy bands once cut their teeth here.

Sophia's 1270 Boylston St ☏354-7001, ⓦwww.sophiaboston.com; Kenmore **T**. Lively dance club with a Latin beat. There's a roof to cool off on, drop-in salsa lessons (Thurs––Sat), plus a stylish downstairs restaurant serving Spanish tapas and full meals. A strictly enforced dress code (no blue jeans or sneakers) keeps the crowd looking posh; when there's a cover, it's $5–10.

Comedy central

Boston's **comedy clubs** can be a pleasant alternative to the club scene, especially when you factor in the lack of dress code and the top-notch comics who often headline as part of a cross-country tour.

Comedy Connection, 245 Quincy Market (☏248-9700, ⓦwww.comedyconnectionboston.com; Government **T**), is a high caliber venue attracting both local and national acts; Thursday nights are popular with the college crowd as Frank Santos, the "R-Rated Hypnotist" takes the stage.

The city's only improv venue, the **Improv Asylum Theater**, 216 Hanover St (☏263-6887, ⓦwww.improvasylum.com; North Station **T**) often brings the house down with off-the-cuff sketches based on audience cues. Boston's comedy mainstay, **Nick's Comedy Stop**, 100 Warrenton St (☏482-0930; Boylston **T**), has brought in national acts including the likes of Jay Leno and Jerry Seinfeld, during its twenty-year tenure. In all cases, book your tickets ($10–40) ahead of time, as shows often sell out.

16

Performing arts and film

B oston's cultural scene is famously vibrant, and many of the city's artistic institutions are second to none in the US. Foremost among these is the Boston Symphony Orchestra, which gave its first concert on October 22, 1881. Indeed, Boston is arguably at its best in the **classical music** department, and there are many smaller but internationally known chamber and choral music groups – from the Boston Symphony Chamber Players to the Handel & Hayden Society – to shore up its reputation. The Boston Ballet is also considered world-class, though it's probably best known in Boston itself for its annual holiday production of *The Nutcracker* with audience numbers ranking it as the most attended **ballet** in the world.

The **theater** here is quite active, too, even if it is a shadow of its 1920s heyday, when more than forty playhouses were crammed into the **Theater District** (for more on the history and legacy of those days, see p.52). Boston remains a try-out city for Broadway productions, however, and smaller companies have an increasingly high visibility; it's a real treat to see a play or musical at one of the opulent old theaters such as the Colonial or Emerson Majestic. For current productions, check the listings in the *Boston Globe's* Thursday "Calendar" section, the *Boston Phoenix* or the *Improper Bostonian*.

The **film** scene is dominated by the Sony conglomerate, which runs several cinema multiplexes featuring major first-run movies. For foreign, independent, classic or cult cinema, you'll have to look mainly to other municipalities – Cambridge is best in this respect, though Brookline and Somerville also have their own art-movie and rerun houses.

Classical music

Boston prides itself on being a sophisticated city of high culture, and nowhere does that show up more than in its proliferation of **orchestras** and **choral groups** and the venues that house them. This is helped in no small part by the presence of four of the foremost music academies in the nation: the Peabody Conservatory, the New England Conservatory, the Berklee College of Music, and the Longy School of Music, across the river in Cambridge.

Performance venues

**Berklee Performance Center 136
Massachusetts Ave** ℡747-2261 for scheduling
information or ℡931-2000 for tickets,
ⓦwww.berkleebpc.com; **Symphony T.** Berklee
College of Music's main performance
center, known for its quality contemporary
repertoire.

**Isabella Stewart Gardner Museum 280 The
Fenway** ℡278-5150,
ⓦwww.gardnermuseum.org; **Museum T.**
Chamber and classical concerts, including
many debuts, are held regularly at 1.30pm
on weekends Sept–May in the museum's
decadent Tapestry Room. The $18 ticket
price includes museum admission.

Jordan Hall 30 Gainsborough St ℡536-2412,
ⓦwww.newenglandconservatory.edu; **Symphony
T.** The impressive concert hall of the New
England Conservatory, just one block west
from Symphony Hall, is the venue for many
chamber music performances, as well as
those by the Boston Philharmonic (℡868-
6696).

Museum of Fine Arts 465 Huntington Ave
℡369-3770/3306, ⓦwww.mfa.org; **Museum T.**
During the summer, the MFA's jazz, folk and
world music "Concerts in the Courtyard"
take place each Wednesday at 7.30pm; a
variety of indoor performances are also
scheduled for the rest of the year.

Symphony Hall 301 Massachusetts Ave ℡266-
1492 for concert information, ℡638-9289 or 1-
888/266-1200 for tickets, ⓦwww.bso.org;
Symphony T. This is the regal, acoustically
perfect venue for the Boston Symphony
Orchestra; the famous Boston Pops concerts happen in May and June; in July and
August, the BSO retreats to Tanglewood, in
the Berkshires.

**Tsai Performance Center 685 Commonwealth
Ave** ℡353-TSAI for event information or ℡353-
8725 for box office, ⓦwww.bu.edu/tsai; **Boston
University T.** Improbably tucked into Boston
University's School of Management, this
mid-sized hall is a frequent venue for
chamber music performances, prominent
lecturers, and plays; events are often affili-
ated with BU and either free or very inexpensive.

Chamber music ensembles

Boston has a formidable range of
chamber music groups, many affili-
ated with the local universities.
Except where otherwise noted, the
companies perform at various venues;
check the usual listings sources for
concert information, or call the
groups directly.

Alea III and Boston Musica Viva ℡353-3340
(Alea III) and ℡354-6910, ⓦwww.bmv.org
(Boston Musica Viva). Two regulars at BU's
Tsai Performance Center.

Boston Baroque ℡484-9200, ⓦwww
.bostonbaroque.org. One of the country's
oldest Baroque orchestras is now a
resident ensemble at BU.

Boston Camerata ℡262-2092, ⓦwww
.bostoncamerata.com. Regular performances
of choral and chamber concerts, from
medieval to early American, at various
locations in and around Boston.

Boston Chamber Music Society ℡349-0086,
ⓦwww.bostonchambermusic.org. This society
has soloists of international renown who
perform in Jordan Hall (Fridays) and the
Sanders Theater at Harvard (Sundays).

Boston Symphony Chamber Players ℡638-
9289 or 1-888/266-1200, ⓦwww.bso.org. The
only permanent chamber group sponsored
by a major symphony orchestra and made
up of its members; they perform at Jordan
Hall.

The Cantata Singers & Ensemble ℡267-
6502, ⓦwww.cantatasingers.org. Boston's
premier choral group, which also performs
at Jordan Hall.

Handel & Hayden Society ℡266-3605,
ⓦwww.handelandhaydn.org. Performing
chamber and choral music since 1815,
these distinguished artists can be heard at
Symphony Hall.

Pro Arte Chamber Orchestra ℡661-7067,
ⓦwww.proarte.org. Cooperatively run
chamber orchestra in which musicians have
full control. Sunday afternoon concerts in
Harvard's Sanders Theater.

Dance

The city's longest-running **dance** company is the **Boston Ballet** (☎695-6950 or 1-800/447-7400, ⓦwww.bostonballet.org), with an unparalleled reputation in America and beyond; their biggest blockbuster, the yearly performance of the *The Nutcracker*, has an audience attendance of more than 140,000. The troupe performs at the Wang Center, 270 Tremont St (☎482-9393 or 1-800/447-7400, ⓦwww.wangcenter.org; Boylston **T**); see overleaf for more details.

In addition, smaller but still prominent troupes, like **World Music** (ⓦwww.worldmusic.org), put on music and dance performances that are a bit less traditional and staid, in venues like the Berklee (see opposite), the Shubert (see below) and the Orpheum Theater (p.196).

Theater

It's quite possible to pay dearly for a night at the **theater**. Tickets to the bigger shows range from $25 to $75 depending on the seat, and there is, of course, the potential of a pre- or post-theater meal (see p.175 for restaurants in the Theater District). Your best option is to pay a visit to **BosTix** (☎482-BTIX) – a half-price, day-of-show ticket booth with two outlets; in Copley Square, at the corner of Dartmouth and Boylston streets, and Faneuil Hall, by Abercrombie & Fitch (☎482-2849; Mon–Sat 10am–6pm, Sun 11am–4pm) – tickets go on sale at 11am, and only cash is accepted.

Full-price tickets can be had via **Ticketmaster** (☎931-2000, ⓦwww.ticketmaster.com) or by contacting the individual theater directly in advance of the performance. The **smaller venues** tend to showcase more offbeat and affordable productions; shows can be under $10 – though you shouldn't bank on that.

Major venues

American Repertory Theater 64 Brattle St, at the Loeb Drama Center, Cambridge ☎547-8300, ⓦwww.amrep.org; Harvard **T**. Excellent theater near Harvard Square known for staging plays by big names like Shaw and Wilde as well as postmodern heavyweights like Ionesco and Stoppard.

Charles Playhouse 74 Warrenton St ☎426-6912, ⓦwww.broadwayinboston.com; Boylston **T**. The Charles has two stages, one of which is more or less the permanent home of *Shear Madness*, a participatory, comic murder mystery that's now become the longest-running non-musical in American theater (ⓦwww.shearmadness.com; $34). The other stage hosts somewhat edgier material.

Colonial Theatre 106 Boylston St ☎426-9366, ⓦwww.broadwayinboston.com; Boylston **T**. Built in 1900 and since refurbished, this is the glittering *grande dame* of Boston theaters, known primarily for its Broadway-scale productions.

Emerson Majestic Theatre 219 Tremont St ☎824-8725, ⓦwww.maj.org; Boylston **T**. Emerson College, a communications and arts school, took stewardship of this 1903 Beaux Arts beauty in 1983. The lavish venue, with soaring Rococo ceiling and Neoclassical friezes, is set to reopen in 2003 following renovations in honor of its centennial, and resume hosting productions of the Emerson Stage company and the Boston Lyric Opera.

Huntington Theatre Company 264 Huntington Ave ☎266-8488, ⓦwww.bu.edu/huntington; Symphony **T**. Productions here range from the classic to the contemporary, but they are consistently well staged at this small playhouse, the official theater of Boston University.

Shubert Theatre 265 Tremont St ☎482-9393 or 800/447-7400, ⓦwww.wangcenter.org; Boylston **T**. Stars from Sir Laurence Olivier to Kathleen Turner have played the city's "Little Princess" at some point in their careers. Recent renovations have restored the 1680-seat theater to its prettier early

1900s appearance to boot, with white walls and gold leaf accents replacing the previous gaudy brown tones.

Wang Center for the Performing Arts
270 Tremont St ☎ 482-9393 or 800/447-7400, ⊛ www.wangcenter.org; Boylston **T**. The biggest performance center in Boston opened in 1925 as the Metropolitan Theater, a movie house of palatial proportions – its original Italian marble, gold leaf ornamentation, crystal chandeliers and 3800 seats all remain. The Boston Ballet (see p.201) is headquartered here; when their season ends, Broadway musicals often take center stage.

Wilbur Theatre 246 Tremont St ☎ 423-4008, ⊛ www.broadwayinboston.com; Boylston **T**. *A Streetcar Named Desire*, starring Marlon Brando and Jessica Tandy, debuted in this small Colonial Revival theater before going to Broadway, and the Wilbur has been working on trying to live up to that production ever since. In winter, avoid the seats toward the back, where the loud, old heating system may leave you straining to hear.

Smaller venues

Boston Center for the Arts 539 Tremont St ☎ 426-2787, ⊛ www.bcaonline.org. Back Bay **T**. Several theater troupes – many experimental – stage productions at the BCA, which incorporates a series of small venues on a single South End property. One of these is the Cyclorama Building, originally built to house a monumental painting called *The Battle of Gettysburg* (see p.98).

Hasty Pudding Theatre 12 Holyoke St, Cambridge ☎ 495-5205, ⊛ www.hastypudding.org. Harvard **T**. Harvard University's Hasty Pudding Theatricals troupe, one of the country's oldest, mounts one show per year (usually a musical comedy; Feb & March) at its eponymous theater, then hits the road, after which the Cambridge Theatre Company moves in.

Institute of Contemporary Art Theatre 955 Boylston St ☎ 927-6620, ⊛ www.icaboston.org; Hynes **T**. Count on the unconventional at the theater of the ICA, Boston's leading venue for all things postmodern and cutting-edge.

Lyric Stage 140 Clarendon St ☎ 437-7172, ⊛ www.lyricstage.com; Copley **T**. Both premieres and modern adaptations of classic and lesser-known American plays are held at this small theater within the big YWCA building.

Film

In Boston, as in any other large American city, it's easy enough to catch general release **films** – the usual listings sources carry all the details you need. If you're looking for out-of-the-ordinary film fare, however, you'll have to venture out a bit from the center. Whatever you're going to see, admission will cost you about $8, though matinees before 6pm can be considerably cheaper. You can call ☎ 333-FILM for automated film listings.

Brattle Theater 40 Brattle St, Cambridge ☎ 876-6837, ⊛ www.brattlefilm.org; Harvard **T**. An historic basement indie cinema that pleasantly looks its age. They have thematic film series plus occasional author appearances and readings.

Coolidge Corner Moviehouse 290 Harvard St, Brookline ☎ 734-2500, ⊛ www.coolidge.org; Coolidge Corner **T**. Film buffs flock to this classic theater for foreign and independent movies. The interior has balconies and is adorned with Art Deco murals.

Harvard Film Archive Carpenter Center, 24 Quincy St, Cambridge ☎ 495-4700, ⊛ www.harvardfilmarchive.org; Harvard **T**.

A mixed bag of artsy, foreign, and experimental films are shown here at the Film Archive.

Kendall Square Cinema One Kendall Square, East Cambridge ☎ 494-9800, ⊛ www.landmarktheatres.com; Kendall **T**. All the neon decoration, cramped seating, and small screens of your average multiplex, but this one has the area's widest selection of first-rate foreign and independent films. It's actually located on Binney St near Cardinal Medieros Ave.

Museum of Fine Arts Theater 465 Huntington Ave ☎ 267-9300, ⊛ ww.mfa.org/film; Museum **T**. Offbeat art films and documentaries, mostly by locals, and often accompanied by lectures from the filmmaker. Also hosts several showcases like the Boston Jewish Film Festival and the Boston French Film Festival. **Somerville Theatre 55 Davis Square, Somerville** ☎ 625-5700, ⓦ www.somervilletheatreonline.com; Davis **T**. Wacky home for camp, classic, cult,

independent, foreign and first-run pictures. Also doubles as a venue for live music. It's way out there – in more ways than one – past Cambridge, but well worth the trip. **Sony Nickelodeon 606 Commonwealth Ave** ☎ 424-1500; Kenmore **T**. Originally an art-flick place, now taken over by the Sony group; it shows the better of the first-run features.

Gay and lesbian Boston

For a town with a Puritan heritage and long-entrenched Blue Laws, it may come as some surprise that Boston happens to be one of the more gay-friendly cities on the East Coast. Much of the action centers around the **South End**, a largely residential neighborhood whose gay businesses (primarily restaurants and cafés) are concentrated on a short stretch of Tremont Street above Union Park. There's a sense of community here not found elsewhere in Boston – the occasional gay pride flag flies openly, and same-sex couples sit together on their stoops to enjoy summer nights along with the rest of the diverse neighborhood.

Adjacent to the South End, on the other side of Arlington Street, is tiny **Bay Village**, a smaller gay enclave with a couple of good bars and clubs. Largely leftist **Cambridge**, at least around Harvard Square, is also gay-friendly, with a few established gay nights to show for it, while **Jamaica Plain**, a neighborhood south of Boston, is quietly establishing itself as a lesbian-friendly community.

Although the city's **gay nightlife** does range from leathermen at the *Ramrod* to cocktail-swilling guppies at *Club Café*, it remains small and fairly concentrated; the lesbian club scene, meanwhile, despite gaining more of a foothold in recent years, is still vastly under-represented in comparison.

In the summer, the **Charles River Esplanade** between Dartmouth and Fairfield streets, at the northern perimeter of Back Bay, is a popular spot for cruising. Footbridges lead from the end of both streets over Storrow Drive to a narrow urban beach alongside the river. You can't swim in the Charles, but it's more than acceptable to sun yourself in a bathing suit here. The area can get a bit dodgy at night, though, as can the rest of the Esplanade.

Information and resources

Boston's two free **gay newspapers** are *in newsweekly* (Ⓦ www.innewsweekly .com) and *Bay Windows* (Ⓦ www.baywindows. com). The latter is one of two good sources of **club information**, the other being the gay-friendly alternative paper *The Boston Phoenix*. All can be found in various venues and bookstores, notably We Think the World of You, 540 Tremont St; Glad Day Bookstore, 673 Boylston St; and New Words, 186 Hampshire St. The latter two's vestibules also have gay and lesbian community **bulletin boards**, with postings for apartment rentals, club happenings and so forth.

Online, check out ⓦwww.butchdykeboy.com, a thorough resource for the lesbian community, with local message boards, event listings, columns and more. Link Pink, at ⓦwww.linkpink.com, is the definitive "pink pages" for businesses, hotels, shops and services catering the New England GBLT community. There's also The List, ⓦwww.queeragenda.org – sign up to receive free weekly emails about upcoming gay and lesbian events in the Boston area.

Other **resources** for the gay community include the Gay and Lesbian Helpline (☏267-9001), a general information source; the AIDS Action Hotline (☏1-800/235-2331 or 536-7773); and Fenway Community Health Center, 7 Haviland St (☏267-0900 or 1-888/242-0900, ⓦwww.fenwayhealth.org), which offers HIV testing during the week.

If you need to hit the **gym** while on vacation, head to gay-friendly Metropolitan Health Club, 209 Columbus Ave (☏536-3006; $30). To book your trip to or from Boston, the Travel Alternatives Group (☏1-800/464-2987, ⓦwww.gaytravelnews.com) will route your call to your nearest gay-friendly **travel agent**.

Accommodation

All of Boston's **accommodations** are gay-friendly but none endorse a strict gay-only clientele policy. That said, you're likely to find more gay visitors than straight ones sleeping in at the city's few gay-run hotels, which usually attract a good mix of gay, lesbian and gay-positive guests. Most are situated in **Back Bay** and the **South End**, putting you within walking distance of the city's best gay bars and cafés; a quieter option in **Jamaica Plain** may appeal to members of the lesbian community, given its proximity to dyke-friendly spots like the *Midway Café*. You can either book a spot yourself, or save some money by going through Citywide Reservations (☏267-7424 or 1-800/468-3593, ⓦwww.cityres.com), a **discount reservation agency** with a Boston-area hotel category devoted to "celebrating diversity."

463 Beacon Street Guest House 463 Beacon St ☏536-1302, ⓦwww.463beacon.com; Hynes **T**. The good-sized rooms in this renovated brownstone, in the heart of Back Bay, are available by the night, week and month, and come equipped with kitchenettes, cable TV and various hotel amenities (though no maid service); some have air conditioning, hardwood floors and ornamental fireplaces. Ask for the top-floor room. ❶–❸

Chandler Inn 26 Chandler St ☏482-3450 or 1-800/842-3450, ⓦwww.chandlerinn.com; Back Bay **T**. Small, comfortable 56-room European-style hotel above the popular *Fritz* bar (see p.206); perks like satellite TV, in-room Internet hook-up and continental breakfasts are included in the rates. ❸

Oasis Guest House 22 Edgerly Rd ☏267-2262, ⓦwww.oasisgh.com; Symphony **T**. Sixteen comfortable, very affordable rooms, some with shared baths, in a renovated brownstone near Symphony Hall, with continental breakfast and nightly get-together at 8pm – they supply the hors d'oeuvres, you bring the booze. ❷–❹

Taylor House 50 Burroughs St, Jamaica Plain ☏888/228-2956, ⓦwww.taylorhouse.com; Green Street **T**. This delightful B&B is a bit out of the way, but its three charming rooms, tucked away on the second floor of an 1855 Italianate house, include queen-sized beds, TV with VCR, Internet access, continental breakfast and two friendly golden retrievers. ❸–❹

Bars, clubs and cafés

Only one **club** in Boston maintains its gay banner seven days a week, the long-standing *Vapor* (formerly *Chaps*); to pick up the slack, some of Boston's more popular clubs designate one or two nights a week as gay nights. The best ones, Campus at *ManRay* (Thurs), *Buzz* (Sat), and *Avalon* (Sun) draw a good mix; see Chapter 15, Nightlife, for further details on nightclub venues.

Friday night's Circuit Girl party at *Club Europa* is the hottest lesbian night around. For those night owls who haven't gotten their fill of dancing after the clubs close, ask around for an invite to Boston's hush-hush, after-hours private party, Rise, at 306 Stuart St; the member's-only stomping ground for gays and straights only gets going at 2am.

Buzz 51 Stuart St ☎267-8669, ⓦwww .buzzboston.com; **New England Medical T**. Resident DJs Michael Sheehan and MaryAlice lay down dance and house tracks at this two-floor dance club where the drinks are poured by pumped and shirtless bartenders. $10 cover charge.

Circuit Girl 67 Stuart St, ⓦwww.circuitgirl.com; **New England Medical T**. This four-year old Friday night lesbian soirée packs the house with DJs spinning current dance, house, Latin and R&B in one room; there's a lounge and pool tables, too.

Club Café 209 Columbus Ave ☎536-0966, ⓦwww.clubcafe.com; **Back Bay T**. This combination restaurant/video bar popular among South End guppies has two back lounges, *Moonshine* and *Satellite*, showing the latest videos and making a wide selection of martinis with fey names like Pouty Princess and Dirty Birdie.

Eagle 520 Tremont St ☎542-4494; **Back Bay T**. Neighborhood bar whose eagle-bedecked interior has the looks of a biker hangout, and attracts an outgoing crowd that gets busiest around last call. A live DJ spins house and Top 40 on the weekends; his recorded sessions are played back on weeknights.

Francesca's Espresso Bar 565 Tremont St ☎482-9026; **Back Bay T**. A great place to check out the Tremont Street crowd passing by the plate-glass windows, this coffee shop gets packed in the evenings before clubs open, with a largely gay clientele caffeinating itself for a night out.

Fritz 26 Chandler St ☎482-4428; **Back Bay T**. South End sports bar below *Chandler Inn* (see review p.205) often likened to the gay version of *Cheers*, thanks to its mix of casually attired locals and visitors, plus convivial staff.

Jacque's 79 Broadway ☎338-7472; **Boylston T**. *Priscilla, Queen of the Desert* invades New England at this drag dream where past-it divas lip-synch *I Love the Nightlife* while youngsters explore gender issues and transvestite/transexual prostitutes peddle their wares. Showtime is 10.30pm Tues–Sun.

Luxor 69 Church St ☎423-6969; **Arlington T**. Not as popular as it once was, but still a good place to drink and cruise, either in the upstairs gay video bar with a modern finish or downstairs at the sports bar.

Machine 1254 Boylston St ☎266-2986; **Kenmore T**. A favorite with the gay crowd on Fridays and Saturdays when the club's large dance floor and top-notch music has the place pumping. The pool tables and bar near the dance floor let you take a breather and soak up the scene. Sundays attract a lesbian crowd as Mix Mistress gets on the decks for Trix.

ManRay 21 Brookline St, Cambridge ☎864-0400, ⓦwww.manrayclub.com; **Central T**. One massive space with five bars, two dance floors, and four very different theme nights. Campus (Thurs) is relatively wholesome, with J Crew types and plenty of straights. The scene is altogether different on Fridays, when a fetish-and-bondage fest, replete with leather and dominatrixes galore, takes over.

Midway Café 3496 Washington St, Jamaica Plain, ⓦwww.dykenight.com; **Green Street T**. Neighborhood hangout with a popular Thursday dyke night; there's free pool 8–10pm, $2 drink specials 9–10.30pm, and dancing till 2am.

Paradise 180 Massachusetts Ave, Cambridge ☎494-0700, ⓦwww.paradisecambridge.com; **Central T**. Upstairs, male dancers (almost) bare it all; those who want to keep some clothes on stay downstairs where a smallish dance floor rocks out to Top 40 tunes.

Ramrod 1254 Boylston St ☏266-2986, ⓦwww.ramrodboston.com; Kenmore T. This Fenway meat market attracts a pretty hungry crowd with its strictly enforced Levi/leather dress code (Fri & Sat) – no shirts or cologne allowed. Not quite as hardcore as it sounds, as it's directly upstairs from the harmless *Machine* (opposite)

Ryles 212 Hampshire St, Cambridge ☏628-0288, ⓦwww.nestovipers.org; Central T. The last Sunday of the month brings The Amazon Slam to *Ryles*; it's a poetry slam and dance hosted by the crew from *Nest of Vipers*, an online lesbian magazine. Words start flying at 8pm, and the music gets going at 10pm. Cover $8.

Vapor 100 Warrenton St ☏695-9500; Arlington T. Returning visitors will recognize this hot spot for the 19-and-up set as the former home of *Chaps*. Aside from a few renovations, little has changed in the weekly repertoire which starts off with the relatively laidback Piano Bar (Mon) and Oldies (Tues) nights, and heats up from Wednesday to the weekend with Latino (Wed), Mocha (Thurs) and House (Fri & Sat). The usual Tea Dance still prevails Sun at 6pm. Cover $3–8.

Shopping

hough Boston has its share of chain stores and typical mall fare, there are plenty of unusual and funky places to **shop** here. The city is perhaps best loved for its bookstores, having established a reputation as a literary haven and academic center; on a more modern – and fashionable – note it has also become known for its small, exclusive boutiques that feature the work of local designers.

No matter what you're looking for, though, Boston is an extremely pleasant place to shop for it, with unique, high-quality stores clustered on atmospheric avenues like Charles Street, in Beacon Hill, and Newbury Street, in Back Bay. The former has a dense concentration of **antique shops**, while the latter is an eight-block stretch that starts off trendily, with all manner of clothes and crafts, then begins to cater to more of a student population as it moves west past Exeter Street; beyond this point, **record stores** and **novelty shops** take over, a theme continued out to Kenmore Square. This span also has its fair share of big **bookstores** – though the best are clustered in and around Harvard Square, across the Charles River in Cambridge.

Otherwise, most of the action takes place in various downtown quarters, first and foremost at the **Faneuil Hall Marketplace**. This area has become more commercialized over the years, but there's still enough homespun boutiques, plus the many food stalls of **Quincy Market**, to make a trip here worthwhile. To the south, **Downtown Crossing**, at Washington and Summer streets, is centered on **Filene's Basement**, a bargain-hunter's delight for marked-down brand-name clothing. Stores are generally open 9.30 or 10am to 6 or 7pm Monday through Saturday (sometimes later on Tuesday and Wednesday) and on Sunday from noon to 6pm.

Antiques

Abodeon 1731 Massachusetts Ave, Cambridge ☎497-0137; Porter **T**. A terrific trove of classic twentieth-century design, with furniture by top modern designers as well as assorted new bric-a-brac, at prices below those you might find in LA or New York.

Cunha, St John and Vining 131 Charles St
℡720-7808, Charles T. Tucked away on the
first floor of a recessed building, this shop
is easy to miss, but inside is a varied array
of Continental antiques – eighteenth- and
nineteenth-century English, Italian and
French, plus nineteenth-century Chinese
formal pieces.
Judith Dowling Asian Art 133 Charles St
℡523-5211; Charles T. A first-rate selection
of Asian pieces from all periods, though at
prices that encourage browsing rather than
buying.
Marcoz Antiques 177 Newbury St ℡262-0780;
Arlington T. An atmospheric antiques boutique with French, English and American
furniture and accessories.
Twentieth Century Limited 73 Charles St
℡742-1031; Charles T. Antique pieces from
the early twentieth century, with a focus on
American Art Deco and works from the
Roaring Twenties; good costume jewelry, too.

Bookstores

Boston has a rich history as a literary city, enhanced by its numerous universities as well as the many traces of authors and publishing houses that have at
one time called the town home. This legacy is well reflected in the quality and
diversity of **bookstores** found both in Boston and neighboring Cambridge.
For books with a Boston connection, check out pp.246–250 in Contexts.

New

Barnes & Noble Downtown Crossing ℡426-
5502; Downtown Crossing T; 660 Beacon St
℡267-8484; Kenmore T. Two large outposts
of the national bookstore chain, with decent
newsstands and good selections of bargain
books and calendars. The one on Beacon
Street is topped off by the neon Citgo sign
(see p.101).
Brookline Booksmith 279 Harvard St, Brookline
℡566-6660, ꊱwww.brooklinebooksmith.com;
Coolidge Corner T. With its hardwood floors
and friendly staff, this cozy shop doesn't
have a particular strength, but its friendly
staff makes it perfect for browsing; holds a
good author reading series, too.
Harvard Book Store 1256 Massachusetts Ave,
Cambridge ℡661-1515, ꊱwww.harvard.com;
Harvard T. Three huge rooms of new books
upstairs, with a basement for used volumes
and remainders downstairs. Academic and
critical work in the humanities and social
sciences dominate, with a healthy dose of
fiction thrown in.
MIT Press Bookstore 292 Main St, Cambridge
℡253-5249, ꊱwww.mitpress.mit.edu
/bookstore; Kendall Square T. Lots of fascinating science and tech stuff, much of it
surprisingly accessible, and racks of discounted and remaindered books as well.
Trident Booksellers & Café 338 Newbury St
℡267-8688; Copley T. A preferred lair of
Back Bay's New Agers. If the aroma of one
too many essential oils doesn't deter you,

buy an obscure magazine and have a flip-
through over coffee in the café (see p.167).
WordsWorth Books 30 Brattle St ℡354-5201,
ꊱwww.wordsworth.com; Harvard T. Discount
bookstore with up to forty percent off most
titles; also hosts regular readings by well-
known authors.

Used

Brattle Book Shop 9 West St ℡542-0210,
ꊱwww.brattlebookshop.com; Downtown
Crossing T. In these fairly dingy digs is one
of the oldest antiquarian bookstores in the
country. Three levels, with a good selection
of yellowing travel guides on the second.
Bryn Mawr Book 373 Huron Ave ℡661-1770;
Porter T. This neighborhood bookstore vends
used titles in a friendly, relaxed Cambridge
setting. Weather permitting, there are sidewalk displays for pedestrian browsers.
House of Sarah 1309 Cambridge St ℡547-
3447; Central T. A wacky Inman Square spot
in which to peruse used fiction and scholarly work – sit in one of the chunky red
couches and look up at the various stuffed
creatures hanging from the ceiling. You may
find a 25¢ copy of a Danielle Steele novel
or some remaindered Foucault, and there is
often coffee and snacks, compliments of
the proprietors.

Travel

Boston Globe Store 1 School St ℡367-4000;
Park T. Small shop in the historic Old

Corner Bookstore building with New England travel guidebooks, Internet access, and lots of stuff emblazoned with the *Boston Globe* logo.

Globe Corner Bookstore 28 Church St, Cambridge ☎497-6277, ⓦ www.globecorner.com; Harvard **T**. These travel specialists are well wstocked with maps, travel literature and guidebooks, with an especially strong New England section.

Willowbee & Kent 519 Boylston St ☎437-6700; Copley **T**. The first floor of this roomy store has a good range of travel guidebooks and gear; the second is given over to a travel agency.

Gay and lesbian

Glad Day Bookshop 673 Boylston St ☎267-3010; Copley **T**. This second-floor gay bookstore is easily recognized from the sidewalk by the big rainbow flag in the window. A good selection of reasonably priced books, cards and adult reading material, plus a vast community bulletin board at the entrance.

We Think the World of You 540 Tremont St ☎423-1965, ⓦ www.wethinktheworldofyou.com; Back Bay **T**. With its cool music and good selection of international magazines, this bright, upscale South End gay bookstore invites lingering.

Specialty

Grolier Poetry Bookstore 6 Plympton St, Cambridge ☎547-4648; Harvard **T**. Diminutive store specializing in in-print poetry. With 14,000 volumes of verse, it has gained an international following among poets and their fans, and it hosts frequent readings.

Kate's Mystery Bookstore 2211 Massachusetts Ave ☎491-2660, ⓦ www.katesmysterybooks.com; Davis **T**. Mystery-only bookstore selling both old and new titles; you'll know the place from the faux gravestones in the front yard.

Lucy Parsons Center 549 Columbus Ave ☎267-6272, ⓦ www.tao.ca/~lucyparsons; Mass Ave **T**. The radical left lives on in this shrine to socialism, with a particular bent toward women's issues, labor issues and radical economics. They also have plenty of free pamphlets on local demonstrations, and occasional readings and lectures.

Nini's Corner/Out of Town News Harvard Square, Cambridge; Harvard **T**. These two good, old-fashioned newsstands lie directly across from each other in the heart of Harvard Square. Few published magazines cannot be found at one of these two spots.

Schoenhof's 76A Mount Auburn St, Cambridge ☎547-8855, ⓦ www.schoenhofs.com; Harvard **T**. Well-stocked foreign language bookstore that's sure to have that volume of Proust you're looking for, as well as any children's books you might want.

Clothes

It's unlikely you'd consider Boston a center for cutting-edge fashions, more the type of place to buy tweedy suits and conservative wear; still, there's enough variety among local designers to make browsing a fun way to pass the time. Newbury Street is your most likely target.

Designer stores

Alan Bilzerian 34 Newbury St ☎536-1001; Arlington **T**. Tri-level store with international haute couture from Jean-Paul Gaultier and Comme des Garçons alongside the owner's own label. Menswear and accessories occupy the first floor and womenswear the second; clubwear roosts in a small basement section.

Allston Beat 348 Newbury St ☎421-9555, ⓦ www.allstonbeat.com; Hynes **T**. This small but dense fashion den may exceed the vinyl per square foot limit – cutting-edge designer wear, ogled by teenagers too young to afford it and others too old to wear it.

Gypsy Moon 1780 Massachusetts Ave ☎876-7095; Porter **T**. For the well-dressed Wiccan, eccentric women's wear sold by a staff that can help you look your best at the next coven meeting.

House of Culture 286 Newbury St ☎236-1090; Copley **T**. Even if you're not in the market for local designer Patrick Petty's trendy creations, nip into his suave shop to browse around and pick up flyers on club happenings.

Jasmine/Sola 344 Newbury St ☎867-4636, ⓦwww.jasminesola.com; Arlington **T**; Harvard Square ☎354-6043; Harvard **T**. Trendy shop retailing streetwear labels like Miss Sixty, Diesel, Juicy Couture and Bloom, as well as shoes and accessories; menswear shop at the Harvard location.

J. Press 82 Mt Auburn St ☎547-9886; Harvard **T**. Old Harvard lives on in J. Press' sober collection of high-quality men's suits; rates are mid-level ($400–1000 per suit) for the store's genteel clientele.

Louis, Boston 234 Berkeley St ☎262-6100, ⓦwww.louisboston.com; Arlington **T**. Occupying a stately, freestanding building from 1863 that once housed Boston's Museum of Natural History (which became the Museum of Science), this is Boston's classiest and most expensive clothes emporium. Though mostly geared toward men, the top floor is reserved for designer womenswear.

Riccardi 116 Newbury St ☎266-3158. Arlington **T**. This, the hippest designer schmatta shop in Boston, could hold its own just fine in Paris or New York. A few of the labels on parade are Dolce & Gabbana, Romeo Gigli and Jean-Paul Gaultier.

Serenella 134 Newbury St ☎266-5568; Arlington **T**. High-end women's boutique selling Euro labels like Pucci and Balenciaga to a well-heeled clientele.

Suzanne 81 Newbury St ☎266-4146; Arlington **T**. Women's special occasion apparel by leading international designers such as Montana and Thierry Mugler.

Wish 49 Charles St ☎227-4441, ⓦwww.wishstyle.com; Charles **T**. This gem of a boutique offers pretty dresses and ensembles by Nanette Lepore, Theory and Velvet that'll put you in good stead for either a Nantucket getaway or a Sunday stroll on Charles Street.

Chain stores

Burberry 2 Newbury St ☎236-1000; Arlington **T**. The famously conservative British clothier seems right at home in its four-story Newbury Street digs, across from the *Ritz-*

Carlton. Excellent quality stuff; pricey, too.

Patagonia 346 Newbury St ☎424-1776; Hynes **T**. Patagonia invented the soft, synthetic fleece called "Synchilla," and there's still no better way to fend off a Boston winter than in a jacket or vest lined with the colorful stuff.

Used and thrift

Bobby from Boston 19 Thayer St ☎423-9299; NE Medical or Broadway **T**. Long adored by local rockers and movie wardrobe professionals, Bobby's South End loft is, hands-down, the best place to find men's vintage clothing from the 1920s through the 1960s.

The Closet Upstairs 223 Newbury St ☎267-5757, ⓦwww.theclosetupstairs.com; Copley **T**. The most atmospheric of Newbury Street's numerous retro clothes stores, this over-sized second-floor closet is stuffed with everything from silly hats to designer shoes.

Dollar-a-Pound 200 Broadway, Cambridge ☎876-5230, ⓦwww.dollarapound.com; Kendall **T**. Warehouse full of bins crammed with used togs. If you have the time to sift through the leftovers of twentieth-century fashion, you'll happen upon some great bargains – all at the rate of $1.50 per pound of clothing. And on Fridays, it's even reduced to 50¢/pound.

Mass Army & Navy Store 895 Boylston St ☎267-1559; Hynes **T**. You can stock up on camouflage and combat boots at this military surplus store, and there's also a good and inexpensive range of (mostly men's) pants, shirts and shoes worth inspecting.

Oona's 1210 Massachusetts Ave, Cambridge ☎491-2654; Harvard **T**. Since 1972, Oona's has been the place to find vintage "experienced clothing" – in this case kimonos, flapper dresses, leather jackets and various accessories.

Second Time Around 176 Newbury St ☎247-3504, ⓦwww.secondtimearound.net; Arlington **T**; 8 Eliot St ☎491-7185; Harvard **T**. Great prices on barely worn, albeit conservative, clothing, predominantly from Banana Republic, the Gap, Anne Taylor and Abercrombie & Fitch.

Crafts

Beadworks 349 Newbury St ☎247-7227, ⓦwww.beadworksboston.com; Hynes **T**. With so many kinds of beads, it's a good thing

the sales staff can assist you in creating a "distinctly personal adornment."

The Cambridge Artists' Cooperative

59A Church St ☎868-4434, ⓦwww.cambridgeartistscoop.com; Harvard T. Three floors fill this Harvard Square shop with all kinds of crafts, from woodcarvings and glass sculptures to wearable art and beaded bags.

Rugg Road Paper Co. 105 Charles St ☎742-0002; Charles T. They've got fancy paper products of all kinds, including lovely cards, stationery and wrapping paper.

Simon Pearce 115 Newbury St ☎450-8388 or 1-877/452-7763, ⓦwww.simonpearce.com; Arlington T. Hand-blown glassware from this Irish-born, Vermont-based craftsman.

Food and drink

Look no further than the North End for all manner of tasty pastry; for gourmet-style take-home eats, Cambridge is especially strong in variety.

Bakeries

Bova's Bakery 76 Prince St ☎523-5601; Haymarket T. An all-night bakery in the North End, vending delights like plain and chocolate cannolis, oven-fresh cakes and whoopie pies; famously cheap, too, with most items around $5.

LMNOP Bakery 79 Park Plaza ☎338-4220; Arlington T. Purveyor of bread to neighboring restaurants, this hideaway is the best gourmet bakery in Boston. Besides those breads, pastries and cookies, they also have great sandwiches and pasta specials at lunchtime.

Maria's Pastry Shop 46 Cross St ☎523-1196 or 1-888/688-2889; North Station T. The place doesn't look like much but *Maria's* has the best Neapolitan treats in town; her custard-filled *sfogliatelle* and *ossa di morti* (bones of the dead) cookies are to die for.

Mike's Pastry 300 Hanover St ☎742-3050; Haymarket T. The famed North End bakery is one part Italian and two parts American, meaning in addition to cannoli and tiramisu, you'll find counters full of brownies and cookies. The homemade ice cream is not to be missed, either – but expect to wait in line for it.

Panini 406 Washington St ☎666-2770; #86 bus. Baguettes and bruschetta, desserts and danishes – Panini offers a diverse array of baked goods, all created on the premises. So popular it's hard to find a place to sit on weekends.

Rosie's Bakery 243 Hampshire St ☎491-9488, ⓦwww.rosiesbakery.com; #69 bus. This bakery features the richest, most decadent desserts in Cambridge. Their specialty is a fudge brownie called the "Chocolate Orgasm" (though the less provocatively named lemon squares are just as good).

Gourmet food and wine shops

Barsamian's 1030 Massachusetts Ave, Cambridge ☎661-9300; Harvard or Central T. Gourmet meats, cheeses, coffee and bread, plus a great range of desserts – including the best tart in Cambridge.

Dairy Fresh Candies 57 Salem St ☎742-2639 or 1-800/336-5536, ⓦwww.dairyfreshcandies.com; North Station T. Mouth-watering array of confections from chocolates and hard candies to dried fruits and nuts; the perfect pick-me ups for a Little Italy stroll.

Cardullo's 6 Brattle St, Cambridge ☎491-8888, ⓦwww.cardullos.com; Harvard T. Gourmet products from just about anywhere are available at this well-stocked Harvard Square store; if nothing else, be sure to stop in for a sample.

Formaggio Kitchen 244 Huron Ave, Cambridge ☎354-4750, ⓦwww.formaggiokitchen.com; Harvard Square T; 268 Shawmut Ave, ☎350-6996; Back Bay T. Although regarded as one of the best cheese shops in Boston, the gourmet meats, salads, sandwiches and baked goods here are also worth sampling.

Monica's Salumeria 130 Salem St ☎742-4101; Haymarket T. Lots of imported Italian cheeses, cooked meats, cookies and pastas.

Polcari's Coffee 105 Salem St ☎227-0786; Haymarket T. Old and fusty, but brimming with coffees, as well as every spice you could think of. Worth going inside for the aroma alone.

Salumeria Italiana 151 Richmond St ☎523-8743 or 1-800/400-5916, ⓦwww.salumeriaitaliana.com; North Station T. Arguably the best Italian grocer this side of Rome, this salumeria stocks only the finest cheeses, meats, balsamic vinegars and more.

Savenor's 160 Charles St ☎ 723-6328; **Charles T.** Known for its meats, this small gourmet food shop in Beacon Hill also has a better-than-average produce selection, in addition to prepared foods – ideal for taking to the nearby Charles River Esplanade for an impromptu picnic.

See Sun Co. 19 Harrison St ☎ 426-0954; **Chinatown T.** The most accessible of Chinatown's markets, has all the basics – like huge bags of rice and a dizzying range of See Sun soy sauces, as well as more exotic delicacies like duck's feet.

V. Cirace & Sons 173 North St ☎ 227-3193; **North Station T.** A great liquor store, with the expected range of Italian wines – it's in the North End, after all – and much more.

Health food

Bread & Circus 15 Westland Ave ☎ 375-1010; **Symphony T.** The Boston branch of this New England whole foods chain, near Symphony Hall, has all the alternative food-stuffs you'd expect, plus one of Boston's best salad bars.

Nature Food Centers GNC 545 Boylston St ☎ 536-1226; **Copley T.** If you're looking for vitamin-enriched fruit juices, organic pro-duce and other healthful items, this small store in Copley Square is bound to have it.

Galleries

Dozens of Boston's major **art galleries** can be found on Newbury Street; most are generally browser-friendly. South Street, in downtown's so-called Leather District, tends to feature the most contemporary work, as does the SoWa district in the South End.

Alianza 154 Newbury St ☎ 262-2385; **Arlington T.** An artsy American crafts gallery whose strength is creative ceramics, glass work and jewelry, with funky sculptural clocks and picture frames as well.

Arden Gallery 129 Newbury St ☎ 247-0610; **Arlington T.** Arden's focus is on abstrac-tionist contemporary paintings, vivid exam-ples of which are displayed in the oversized second-story bowfront window.

Barbara Krakow Gallery 10 Newbury St, 5th floor ☎ 262-4490, ⊕ www.barbarakrakowgallery .com; **Arlington T.** This A-list multimedia gallery attracts the hottest artists from New York City and around the globe; Kiki Smith and Annette Lemieux are but two of the blockbuster artists that have shown here in recent years.

Bernard Toale Gallery 450 Harrison St ☎ 482-2477; **Back Bay T.** Curator Bernard Toale offi-cially sanctified the new SoWa district when he moved his Newbury Street gallery here in 1998; his new space shows painting, photography, drawing, sculpture, video and prints.

Clifford-Smith Gallery 450 Harrison St, 3rd floor ☎ 695-0255, ⊕ www.cliffordsmithgallery .com; **Back Bay T.** Hip gallery with large-scale multimedia installations, and some photog-raphy.

Galerie Europeenne 123 Newbury St ☎ 859-7062; **Arlington T.** Always something inter-esting on display: contemporary, figurative and abstract painting, all by living European artists.

Gallery NAGA 67 Newbury St ☎ 267-9060, ⊕ www.gallerynaga.com; **Arlington T.** Contemporary painting, sculpture, studio furniture and photography from Boston and New England artists, located in the Gothic Revival Church of the Covenant.

International Poster Gallery 205 Newbury St ☎ 375-0076, ⊕ www.internationalposter.com; **Copley T.** More than 6000 posters on dis-play from 1895 through World War II.

Nielsen Gallery 179 Newbury St ☎ 266-4835, ⊕ www.nielsongallery.com; **Copley T.** Back Bay's oldest gallery puts the accent on con-temporary painting and drawing, and occa-sionally, sculpture.

The Society of Arts and Crafts 175 Newbury St ☎ 266-1810, ⊕ www.societyofcrafts.org; **Arlington T.** The oldest non-profit crafts group in America has two floors here. The first is its commercial outpost, with a wide range of ceramics, glass and jewelry. The second floor is reserved for themed (and free) special exhibitions.

Malls and department stores

The major **malls** quite obviously cobble together all your needs in one convenient location; none here particularly stand out save perhaps the marketplace at Faneuil Hall, for atmosphere alone. For **department stores**, the most idiosyncratic is Filene's Basement, in Downtown Crossing.

Malls

CambridgeSide Galleria 100 Cambridgeside Place ☎621-8666, ⓦ www.cambridgesidegalleria .com; Kendall **T**. Not too different from any other large American shopping mall. The haze of neon and packs of teens can be exhausting, but there's no similarly dense and convenient conglomeration of shops in Cambridge.

Copley Place 100 Huntington Ave ☎375-4400, ⓦ www.shopcopleyplace.com; Copley **T**. This ambitious, upscale office-retail-residential complex features more than a hundred stores and an eleven-screen multiplex. The best of the shops are a Rizzoli bookshop, a Neiman Marcus department store, the gift shop for the Museum of Fine Arts, and the Artful Hand Gallery, representing solely American artists; the rest is pretty generic.

Faneuil Hall Marketplace Faneuil Hall ☎523-1300, ⓦ www.faneuilhallmarketplace .com; Government Center **T**. The city's most famous market, with a hundred or so shops, plus next door's Quincy Market. It's a bit tourist-oriented, but still worth a trip (see p.50).

The Heritage on the Garden 300 Boylston St ☎423-0002; Arlington **T**. Not so much a mall as a very upscale mixed-use complex across from the Public Garden that consists of condos, restaurants and boutiques. The latter include Arche Shoes, Escada, Sonia Rykiel and the St John boutiques Villeroy Boch and Hermés.

The Shops at Prudential Center 800 Boylston St ☎267-1002; Prudential **T**. This conglomeration of a hundred or so mid-market shops is heavily patronized by local residents and conventioneers from the adjacent Hynes Convention Center, who seem to genuinely enjoy buying commemorative t-shirts and ties from the center-atrium pushcarts.

Department stores

Filene's 426 Washington St ☎357-2100, ⓦ www.filenes.com; Downtown Crossing **T**. The merchandise inside downtown Boston's oldest department store is standard issue; the stunning 1912 Beaux Arts facade is not. You'll have better luck downstairs, in Filene's Basement.

Filene's Basement 426 Washington St ☎542-2011, ⓦ www.filenesbasement.com; Downtown Crossing **T**. Established in 1908, Filene's Basement is a separate business from Filene's; the discounted merchandise comes here not only from upstairs, but from other big-name department stores and a few Boston boutiques. The markdown system works like this: after 14 days, merchandise is discounted 25 percent, after 21 days, 50 percent and after 28 days, 75 percent. Anything that lasts more than 35 days goes to charity. Be warned: dressing rooms are communal.

The Harvard Coop 1400 Massachusetts Ave ☎499-2000, ⓦ www.thecoop.com; Harvard **T**. Harvard's local department store, with a wide selection of fairly expensive insignia clothing and the like.

Lord & Taylor 760 Boylston St ☎262-6000, ⓦ www.lordandtaylor.com; Copley **T**. This human-scale department store is an excellent place to stock up on high-end basics, from sweaters and suits to jewelry and cosmetics.

Macy's East 450 Washington St ☎357-3000, ⓦ www.macys.com; Downtown Crossing **T**. Much the generic urban department store, with all the basics covered, including a better-than-average cosmetics section and a men's department that outshines that of next-door neighbor Filene's.

Neiman Marcus 5 Copley Place ☎536-3660, ⓦ www.neimanmarcus.com; Copley **T**. Part of a Texas chain, Neiman's is the most luxurious of Boston's department stores, with prices to match. Three levels, with an impressive menswear collection on the first.

Music

Boston Beat 279 Newbury St ☎247-2428, ⓦwww.bostonbeat.com; Hynes **T**. A first-floor store stocking lots of independent dance and techno labels.

Cheapo 645 Massachusetts Ave ☎354-4455, ⓦwww.cheaporecords.com; Central **T**. Narrow, two-story Cambridge shop stuffed with bargains on just about every genre of used music. Slogging through the dense collection will produce considerable discoveries.

Disc Diggers 401 Highland Ave, Somerville ☎776-7560; Davis **T**. The largest selection of used CDs in New England, though higher in quantity than quality. Forgotten albums by one-hit wonders abound.

Looney Tunes 1106 Boylston St ☎247-2238; Back Bay **T**; 1001 Massachusetts Ave ☎876-5624; Harvard **T**. Rare classical and jazz CDs are the strength at this extremely cramped music store; the sidewalk bargain cassette bin usually yields some good finds, too.

Newbury Comics 332 Newbury St ☎236-4930, ⓦwww.newbury.com; Hynes **T**. Boston's biggest alternative record store carries lots of independent labels you won't find at the national chains, along with a substantial array of vinyl, posters, zines and kitschy t-shirts. It's also a good place to pick up flyers on local club happenings.

Nuggets 486 Commonwealth Ave ☎536-0679, ⓦwww.nuggetsrecords.com; Kenmore **T**. American jazz, rock and R&B are the strong suits at this venerable new and used record store.

Pipeline 257 Washington St ☎591-0590; #63 **bus**. This alluringly bizarre store defies categorization. Mainly used CDs and vinyl, particularly deep on indie and imports. Also new music, kitsch Americana, and videos of the Russ Meyer film ilk.

Planet Records 54B JFK St ☎492-0693, ⓦwww.planet-records.com; Harvard **T**; 536 Commonwealth Ave ☎353-0693; Kenmore **T**. To buy that old Duran Duran or Styx LP missing from your collection – or to sell one you've listened to a tad too much – head to this basement secondhand music shop in Harvard Square. Buys and sells CDs, too.

Satellite 49 Massachusetts Ave ☎536-5482, ⓦwww.satelliterecords.com; Hynes **T**. This storefront hideaway has a great selection of imported techno and trance, in both CD and vinyl format.

Skippy White's 538 Massachusetts Ave ☎491-3345; Central **T**. Excellent collection of jazz, blues, R&B, gospel, funk and hip-hop. Hum a few bars and the knowledgeable salesfolk will guide you to the right section.

Smash City Records 304 Newbury St ☎536-0216, ⓦwww.velvetcityrecords.com; Arlington **T**. Aside from its velvet Elvis collection, what distinguishes this record store from the others is its massive stock of vinyl for $1; there's even a free bin.

Stereo Jack's 1686 Massachusetts Ave ☎497-9447, ⓦwww.stereojacks.com; Porter **T**. Jazz and blues specialists – mostly used, but with some new stuff, too. CDs, tapes and vinyl.

Tower Records 1249 Boylston St ☎247-5900, ⓦwww.towerrecords.com; Hynes **T**. Typically vast representative of this music superstore chain, with a standard selection of popular music, as well as jazz, classical, world beat and the like, in a large warehouse space.

Twisted Village 12 Eliot St ☎354-6898, ⓦwww.twistedvillage.com; Harvard **T**. A really weird mix of fringe styles, among them avant-garde, beat, spoken word and psychedelic rock.

Specialty shops

Aunt Sadie's 18 Union Park St ☎357-7117; Back Bay **T**. General store-themed South End shop with delightfully campy items like vintage Hawaiian postcards and fun, scented candles with original odors like beach (coconut oil) and amusement park (popcorn).

Black Ink 101 Charles St ☎723-3883; Charles **T**; 5 Brattle St, Cambridge ☎497-1221; Harvard **T**. Eclectic assortment of things you don't

really need but are cool anyway: rubber stamps, a smattering of clothes, amusing refrigerator magnets and a wide assortment of vintage postcards.

Fi-Dough 103 Charles St ☎723-3266, ⓦwww.fidough.com; Charles **T**. Terrific neighborhood gourmet dog food shop and salon – stop in for a gift for the furry one you left back home, or bring your pet with you to nosh on free samples.

Fresh 121 Newbury St ☎421-1212; Arlington **T.** Pear Chocolate and Fig Apricot are only two varieties of the several sweet-sounding soaps you will find in this chic bath and body store. They carry over three hundred varieties of French milled soaps, lotions, oils and makeup, packaged so exquisitely you won't want to open them.

Fresh Eggs 58 Clarendon St ☎247-8150; Back Bay **T.** Small boutique featuring exceptionally stylish home furnishings and tchotchkes from pillow cases to bookends; conveniently, most of it is small enough to carry home in your bag.

Justin Tyme Emporium 91 River St, Cambridge ☎491-1088; Central **T.** Justin's is all about pop culture artifacts, featuring boffo American detritus like lava lamps, Donny and Marie Osmond pin-ups, and campy t-shirts with iron-ons.

Kitty House 223 Newbury St ☎262-0362, ⊛www.kittyhouse.net; Arlington **T.** Pretty much every Hello Kitty product ever made can be found at this small basement store devoted to the Japanese collectible. Kind of scary.

Koo de Kir 34 Charles St ☎723-8111, ⊛www.koodekir.com; Charles **T.** Their motto, "Ars longa, vita brevis," reflects their sales philosophy – to make even the most everyday objects artistic and beautiful. For a pretty penny, you can buy such beautified *objets* here.

Leavitt and Pierce 1316 Massachusetts Ave, Cambridge ☎547-0576; Harvard **T.** Old-school tobacconists that have been around almost as long as Harvard. An outstanding selection of cigars, imported cigarettes and smoking paraphernalia (lighters, rolling papers, ashtrays), plus an upstairs smoking loft right out of the carefree past.

The London Harness Company 60 Franklin St ☎542-9234, ⊛www.londonharness.com; Downtown Crossing **T.** Chiefly known for its high-quality luggage, this atmospheric shop reeks of traditional Boston – indeed, Ben Franklin used to shop here. They also vend a wide array of items like chess sets, clocks, candlesticks and inlaid decorative boxes.

Loulou's Lost & Found 121 Newbury St ☎859-8593; Arlington **T.** They say Loulou scours the globe in search of such essentials as tableware embossed with French cruise ship logos and silverware from long-gone five-star restaurants. A fine place to indulge your inner Martha Stewart.

Marquis 73 Berkeley St ☎426-2120; Back Bay **T.** Proffering a wide range of leather items and hardcore sexual paraphernalia, this South End shop leaves little to the imagination.

Matsu 259 Newbury St ☎266-9707; Copley **T.** A hip little shop featuring a medium-sized range of sleek Japanese clothing, knick-knacks (desk clocks, stationery, funky pens) and contemporary home decor items.

Million-Year Picnic 99 Mt Auburn St, Cambridge ☎492-6763; Harvard **T.** For the comic obsessive. Japanese anime and Superman, Tank Girl and Dilbert. Stronger on current stuff than old material. The staff has encyclopedic knowledge, and is tolerant of browsers.

Sherman's 26 Province St ☎482-9610; Downtown Crossing **T.** Forget those over-priced travel boutiques in the malls; this cavernous Downtown Crossing emporium stocks not only an impressive range of luggage but just about every travel gadget imaginable.

Union Shop 356 Boylston St ☎536-5651, ⊛www.weiu.org; Arlington **T.** The retail out-post of this long-established private social services organization features quality handmade household knick-knacks, toys, wrapping paper, stationery and a range of antiques.

19

Sports and outdoor activities

Bostonians have an acute love-hate relationship with their professional **sports** teams, obsessing over the four major franchises – baseball's Red Sox, football's Patriots, basketball's Celtics, and hockey's Bruins – with evangelical fervor. After years of watching their teams narrowly miss championship bids (with the exception of the Patriots' last-second 2002 Super Bowl win, and, of course, the Celtics' storied run in the 1980s) hope for a good post-season is extended cautiously here.

Boston's sports fans have an admirable tenacity, following their teams closely through good seasons and bad; indeed, supporters seem to love bemoaning their teams' woes nearly as much as they do celebrating their victories. This lively, vocal fan base makes attending a game a great way to get a feel for the city, though fans of an opposing team who might be inclined to root against Boston, be warned: you're in store for censure from the local faithful.

While the Patriots' **Foxboro Stadium** is located out of town and has little to recommend it, the new **FleetCenter**, where the Celtics and Bruins play, is at least conveniently accessible by **T**, even if it lacks the history of the classic Boston Garden that was demolished some years back. For fans of baseball, there is no more essential pilgrimage than the one to the Red Sox' idiosyncratic Fenway Park, accessed by the Green Line's Kendall **T**.

Boston isn't a city where **participatory sports** thrive particularly well, due mostly to the area's often dreary weather. There are, however, more than a number of good areas for jogging, biking, rollerblading and the like, especially around the Esplanade, not to mention the possibility of getting out on the water that surrounds the city. The **Metropolitan District Commisson** (**MDC**), 20 Somerset St (℡727-5114 extension 501, Ⓦwww.state.ma.us/mdc), oversees most facilities.

Baseball

The Boston **Red Sox** have tormented fans with an uncanny ability to choke late in the season: they haven't won a World Series since 1918, although they've come extremely close on several occasions (see p.104). In more recent years, they lost some of their faithful by not re-signing longtime players Roger Clemens and Mo Vaughn (currently with the Yankees and the Mets, respectively); however, superstars like Pedro Martinez and Nomar Garciaparra have more than compensated, and have attracted a more diverse fan base, especially Dominicans, who revel in Martinez' pitching mastery. The pair have helped the Red Sox stay very competitive; too bad for the team that it shares a division with hated rivals the New York Yankees, who have dominated not just the division, but the sport, for the best part of the last decade (indeed, century, really).

Even when the the Red Sox aren't performing so well, it's worth going to a game just to see **Fenway Park**, at 24 Yawkey Way, one of America's sports treasures. Dating from 1912, it's the oldest baseball stadium in the country, much more intimate than most, and one of bizarre dimensions, best represented by the abnormally tall (37-foot) left-field wall, dubbed the "Green Monster." Grandstand tickets can cost upwards of $44, but bleacher seats are closer to $20 and put you amid the raucous fans; there are few better ways to spend a Sunday summer afternoon in Boston. The stadium is near the Kenmore **T** stop; for ticket information, call ☎482-4SOX or visit ⓦwww.redsox .com. The season runs from April through September, with playoffs in October.

Basketball

While Boston's other sports franchises may have a reputation for falling just short of victory, basketball's **Celtics** have won sixteen NBA championships – more than any other professional sports teams except baseball's New York Yankees and hockey's Montréal Canadiens. But while they enjoyed dynastic success in the 1960s and 1980s, when they played on the buckling parquet floors of the beloved Boston Garden, the Celts fell on hard times in the 1990s; it's hoped that their making the 2002 Eastern Conference finals under coach Jim O'Brien foretells a new era.

Today, they play in the sleek if soulless **FleetCenter**, 150 Causeway St (☎624-1000, ⓦwww.nba.com/ celtics), located near the North Station **T** stop in the West End. Most tickets are pricey – good seats run between $50 and $95 – but you can sometimes snag some in the rafters for as little as $10; for those, show up in front of the stadium on game day and hope for the best. The season begins in late October, and continues all the way through June, playoffs included.

Football

For years, the New England **Patriots** were saddled with the nickname "Patsies," and generally considered to be a laughing stock. However, all that changed in 2002 when coach Bill Belichick, wonderkind quarterback Tom Brady and kicker Adam Vinatieri – whose last-second 48-yard field goal won the game – finally brought the coveted Super Bowl trophy home to New England.

Even before they won the Super Bowl, going to a game wasn't a reasonable goal unless you had connections or were willing to pay a scalper upwards of $100 – tickets sell out far in advance. If you can get your hands on a pair the old-fashioned way, expect to pay $49–99 a head. The stadium is located in distant Foxboro, just north of the Massachusetts–

Rhode Island border (for information, call ☎1-800/543-1776; for tickets, dial ☎931-2222 or visit Ⓦwww .patriots.com). Better to drop by a sports bar on a Sunday afternoon during the fall season (Sept–Dec); the best ones are located in the West End (see reviews p.189).

Ice hockey

Until a few years ago, ice hockey's Boston **Bruins** were a consistently successful franchise, at one point running up a streak of 26 straight winning seasons – the longest in professional sports, including appearances in the Stanley Cup finals on two occasions, 1988 and 1990, both of which they barely lost. A series of retirements, injuries, and bad luck turned things around fast, and in the 1996–97 year they posted the worst record in the National Hockey League.

Venue and tickets

The team has bounced back, though, and is again exciting to watch. You can catch the Bruins at the **FleetCenter**, 150 Causeway St (North Station **T**; ☎624-1000, Ⓦwww.bostonbruins .com), where tickets are expensive ($20–77), especially if a good opponent is in town. The long regular season begins in October and continues, with playoffs, into June.

College hockey

A cheap equally entertaining alternative to the Bruins is **college hockey**. The biggest event is the "Beanpot," an annual competition that takes place on the first two Mondays in February, in which the four big local teams – the **Boston University Terriers**, who play at Walter Brown Arena, 285 Babcock St (☎353-3838, Ⓦwww .bu.edu/athletics); the **Harvard Crimson**, at Bright Hockey Center, N Harvard St, Allston (☎495-2211 or 1-877/GO-HARVARD, Ⓦwww.fas .harvard.edu/~athletic); the **Boston College Eagles**, at the Conte Forum, Chestnut Hill (☎552-GoBC, Ⓦbceagles.ocsn.com); and the **Northeastern Huskies**, at Matthews Arena, St Botolph St (☎373-GoNU, Ⓦwww .gonu.com) – compete for city bragging rights. BU tends to dominate the Beanpot, and is consistently at the top of the national rankings, though BC and Harvard are generally competitive as well. Beanpot tickets ($15–25; ☎931-2000) are hard to come by, but regular-season seats go for around $5; the games are quite fun.

Running, rollerblading and cycling

On the rare days that Boston is visited by pleasant weather, residents take full advantage of it, turning up in droves to engage in **outdoor activities**. The most popular of these are **running**, **rollerblading** and **cycling**, and they all pretty much take place along the banks of the Charles River, where the **Esplanade** provides eighteen miles of well-kept, picturesque trails stretching from the Museum of Science all the way down to Watertown and Newton.

On the Cambridge side of the Charles is **Memorial Drive**, closed off to traffic between Western Avenue and Eliot Bridge (May to mid-Nov Sun 11am–7pm); it's a prime place for blading and tanning. **Rollerblades** are available for rent at the Beacon Hill Skate Shop, 135 S Charles St (☎482-7400; Charles **T**), or Blades, Boards and Skates, 349 Newbury St (☎437-6300; Hynes **T**), for about $15 per day; the InLine Club of Boston (☎781/932-5457, Ⓦwww.sk8net.com) organizes community skates and other in-line events.

Two of the most popular **bike trails** in the area are the Dr Paul Dudley

△ Gametime at the FleetCenter

White Bike Path (really just another name for the Esplanade loop) and the Minuteman Bikeway, which runs 10.5 miles from Alewife **T** station on the Red Line in Cambridge through Lexington to Bedford. The MDC has information about these trails, as does the Massachusetts Bicycle Coalition, 44 Bromfield St, room 207 (☎542-2453, ⓦwww.massbikeboston.org), and 214A Broadway, Cambridge (☎491-7433), which also sells a Boston bike map ($4.25). The Charles River Wheelmen (☎332-8546 or 325-BIKE for a recorded listing of rides, ⓦwww.crw.org) organize regular, and usually free, bike tours on weekends from April through November. You can rent bikes (starting around $25 a day for a hybrid model) at Community Bicycle Supply, 496 Tremont St (☎542-8623, ⓦwww.communitybicycle.com; Copley **T**); Back Bay Bicycles, 333 Newbury St (☎247-2336, ⓦwww.backbaybicycles.com; Hynes **T**); or at Wheelworks Bicycle Workshop, 259 Massachusetts Ave, Cambridge (☎876-6555; Central **T**), which also does repairs. You can take your bike on the T's Red, Orange and Blue lines (Mon–Fri 10am–2pm & 7pm–close, Sat & Sun all day), except on Patriots' Day, St Patrick's Day, Independence Day, and from 8.30–11pm whenever there's a Red Sox game or an event at the FleetCenter. MBTA buses and the Green Line do not allow bicycles on board at any time. When taking your bicycle on the subway, always follow the conductor's directions.

Ice skating

The MDC operates several **ice-skating rinks** in the Boston area between mid-November and mid-March, of which the best-kept and most convenient to downtown is the **Steriti Memorial Rink**, at 550 Commercial St (☎523-9327) in the North End. When it's cold enough, the lagoon in the Public Garden offers free skating, while the **Frog Pond** in Boston Common (Mon 10am–5pm, Tues–Thurs & Sun 10am–9pm, Fri–Sat 10am–10pm; $3; ☎635-4505; Park St **T**) charges for the sport but does rent skates on-site (adults $5, children $3). To find out dates and times and keep tabs on skating conditions throughout the city, call the MDC skating hotline (☎72-SKATE).

Watersports

The image of white sails dotting the Charles River Basin and Boston Harbor may be inviting; alas, you'll be stuck watching them from shore unless you have recognized **sailing** credentials or are willing to take a class. Should you have the former, present them to the Boston Harbor Sailing Club on Rowes Wharf (☎720-0049, ⓦwww.bostonharborsailing.com; Aquarium **T**) and you can rent yourself a variety of boats from a daysailer ($25/hr–$75/day) to a cruiser ($139/hr–$417/day).

Classes are available through a number of outfits, the best being Community Boating (April–Oct; two-day visitor's pass $50; ☎523-1038) and Piers Park Sailing Center, 95 Marginal St (April–Oct; $25; ☎561-677, ⓦwww.piersparksailing.org; Maverick **T**), which does a three-hour intro course for newbies that includes water time. Children sailors get the best deal of all, though, through Community Boating (see Chapter 20, Kids' Boston).

Possibly an easier way to get on the water is renting a **canoe** or **kayak** from the Charles River Canoe and Kayak Center, Sailor's Rd (May–Oct Fri 1pm–dusk, Sat–Sun 10am–dusk; ☎462-2513, ⓦwww.ski-paddle.com;

Harvard **T**), which maintains a green-roofed kiosk 200 yards from the Eliot Bridge on the Boston side of the Charles. Equipment is rented by the day or hour (canoes $11–44; kayaks $12–56); lessons are also available, but certainly not required.

Fitness centers

If you're staying at a hotel without a gym and are in need of a workout, a number of **health clubs** and **fitness centers** offer one-time daily memberships for out-of-towners. The Beacon Hill Athletic Clubs (Ⓦ www. beaconhillathleticclubs.com) with locations at 261 Friend St (Ⓣ 720-2422; North Station **T**) and 3 Hancock St (Ⓣ 367-2422; Park St **T**), frequently offers free day passes through its website or else sells them at the gym for $15, the same price as the City Gym and Aerobic Center, at 542 Commonwealth Ave (Ⓣ 536-4008; Hynes **T**). The Boston Athletic Club, 653 Summer St (Ⓣ 269-4300, Ⓦ www.bostonathleticclub.com; Downtown Crossing **T**), charges $25 a day for full use of their facilities, which include a sauna and pool, on presentation of your hotel key.

Otherwise, women can pay $12 to take advantage of Boston Fitness for Women, 27 School St (Ⓣ 523-3098; Government Center **T**), a gym with a relaxed female-only environment. Both sexes can practice their downward dogs at the drop-in **yoga** classes led by Baron Baptiste Power Yoga Institute (Ⓣ 661-YOGA, Ⓦ www.baronbaptiste.com); its two locations – 139 Columbus Ave, Boston ($12; Back Bay **T**) and 2000 Massachusetts Ave, Cambridge ($10; Porter **T**) – also rent mats ($1).

Bowling

Boston's variation on tenpin bowling is **candlepin bowling**, in which the ball is smaller, the pins narrower and lighter, and you have three rather than two chances to knock the pins down. It's somewhat of a local institution, and popular with all types of recreational bowlers to boot, as it's difficult to be very bad or very good at candlepins – Boston's serious bowlers stick to the tenpin variety.

The best candlepin spot is the Ryan Family Amusement Center, 82 Lansdowne St (Mon, Wed, Thurs & Sun noon–11pm, Tues 9am–11pm, Fri–Sat noon–midnight; Ⓣ 267-8495, Ⓦ www.ryanfamily.com; Kenmore **T**), while Lanes and Games, 195 Concord Turnpike out in Somerville (daily 9am–midnight; Ⓣ 876-5533, Ⓦ www.lanesgames.com; Alewife **T**), is a good spot for both tenpin and candlepin bowling.

Paintball

Among all the miscellaneous forms of sports(like) entertainment in the city, perhaps the oddest (and most fun, if you're into this type of thing) is **paintball** – a kind of simulated warfare where you shoot paintballs rather than bullets (and they do sting) at members of the opposing team, all while scampering around an area full of bunkers and obstacles. The proceedings take place in an old North End warehouse at **Boston Paintball**, 131 Beverly St, sixth floor (reservations Ⓣ 742-6612; $39; North Station **T**).

Pool

There are plenty of places to shoot **pool** in the Boston area, and not just of the divey variety you'll invariably find in some of the city's more down-and-out bars. One of the best is *Boston Billiard Club*, 126 Brookline Ave (☎536-7665; Kenmore **T**), a classy and serious pool hall that also has a nice bar. *Flat Top Johnny's*, at One Kendall Square in Cambridge (☎494-9565; Kendall **T**), draws a diverse young clientele to its smoky environment; and there's also *The Rack* at 24 Clinton St across from Faneuil Hall (☎725-1051; Government Center **T**), a slick joint that draws as many well-heeled yuppies as it does ardent pool players.

Kids' Boston

O ne of the best aspects of **traveling with kids** in Boston is the feeling that you're conducting an ongoing history lesson; while that may grow a bit tiresome for teens, younger children tend to eat up the Colonial-period costumes, cannons and the like. Various points on the Freedom Trail are, of course, best for this, though getting out of the city to Lexington and Concord (see Chapter 10, Out of the city) will point you along a similar path.

The city's **parks**, notably Boston Common, Franklin Park and the Public Garden – where you can ride the Swan Boats in the lagoon – make nice settings for an afternoon with the children, too. The best outdoor option, however, may be a Red Sox game at Fenway Park, as the country's oldest baseball stadium is easily reached by **T** and games here are affordable (see p.217). **Harbor cruises** are also a fairly popular and unique way to see Boston – as is ascending to the tops of various city skyscrapers. There are as well a number of **museums** aimed at the younger set, most of them located along one waterfront or another.

Museums and sights

Though kids might not have **historical attractions** at the top of their list of favorite places, most of Boston's major **museums** manage to make the city's history palatable to youngsters. This is especially true at the new **Dreams of Freedom Museum**, a hands-on look at the trials and tribulations of becoming an American citizen (see p.49). More history is on display at the *USS Constitution*, the old warship moored in the Charlestown Navy Yard (see p.69), and the **USS Constitution Museum**, where a video game on the top floor allows kids to test their battle skills.

The **Children's Museum, the Museum of Science** and the **MIT Museum** (p.56, p.82 & p.138, respectively) are three other obvious places to let the little ones loose for a while; all provide a lot of interactive fun that's as easy for adults to get lost in as it is children. For animal sightings, the **Franklin Park Zoo** and **the New England Aquarium** (p.120 & p.55, respectively) can't be beat. Finally, views from the dizzying heights of the Back Bay's **Prudential Center** (p.91) are always sure to thrill.

Activities

For a different kind of education, America's oldest public boating set-up, Community Boating, 21 Embankment Rd (☎523-1038, ⓦwww.community

-boating.org), between the Hatch Shell and Longfellow Bridge, offers youngsters aged 10 to 18 the cheapest **sailing lessons** around, for just $1. For that, the kids get summer-long access to the boathouse and are taught the ropes in a number of one- to five-day classes, including kayaking and windsurfing.

If that seems like too much work, your children can learn things sitting down at the **Charles Hayden Planetarium** (adults $8, children $6; ☎723-2500, ⓦwww.mos.com; Science Park **T**), which projects documentaries about the solar system onto its domed ceiling (as well as frivolous laser shows set to the music of Britney Spears); it will help prepare them for the Museum of Science's **Gilliland Observatory**, which opens its roof and points its telescopes heavenwards every Friday night (8.30–10pm; free; ☎589-0267 extension 1; Science Park **T**).

Another evening that makes learning fun is the Museum of Fine Arts' free Family Night Out (July–Aug Wed 5.30–8.30pm; ☎267-9300, ⓦwww.mfa.org; Museum **T**), which offers **drawing classes** and **readings** in a number of galleries; check the website or call the museum directly for additional goings-on during the school year.

Shops

If and when the history starts to wear thin, there's always the failsafe of Boston's **malls** to divert the kids' attention (see p.214). To combine history with your shopping, you could head to Faneuil Hall and Quincy Market; indeed, the latter holds a **chocolate store** sure to please the Chocolate Dipper (☎439-0190; Government Center **T**), where strawberries, pineapple slices, cookies, brownies and more get a quick bath in dark or milk chocolate. Red pops, warheads and other delightful candies can be had at Irving's Toy and Candy Shop, 371 Harvard St, Brookline (☎566-9327; Coolidge Crossing **T**). If the kids are screaming for **ice cream**, load them up with homemade scoops of maple cream and cookie dough at *Herrell's*, 15 Dunster St (☎497-2179; Harvard **T**), while you indulge in boozy flavors like peach schnapps and Kentucky bourbon.

Kids' tours

Boston is a great place for kids to see on a **tour**, in part due to the atypical means of public transportation: mostly trolleys and ships. Of the latter, the best options are Boston Harbor Cruises (☎227-4321, ⓦwww.bostonharborcruises.com; see p.55) and Boston Duck Tours (☎723-3825, ⓦwww.bostonducktours.com; see p.25). You can also take a ride on the schooner *Liberty* (June–Sept noon, 3pm & 6pm; adults $30, children $18; ☎742-0333, ⓦwww.libertyfleet.com), which departs from Long Wharf and sails for two hours around Boston's Harbor Islands (see p.57).

The New England Aquarium offers three- to five-hour whale-watching excursions into the harbor (June–Sept daily 9.30am & 2.30pm; adults $27, children $17; ☎973-5277, ⓦwww.neaq.org), as does Boston Harbor Cruises. One tour designed specifically for kids is Boston by Little Feet (May–Oct Mon & Sat 10am, Sun 2pm; $6; ☎367-2345 or 367-3766 for recorded info, ⓦwww.bostonbyfoot.com; State St **T**), which is a one-hour Freedom Trail walk for ages 6 to 12. Tours begin in front of the statue of Samuel Adams at Faneuil Hall and include a free map and kids' *Explorer's Guide*. Another fun way to see the Freedom Trail is with the Freedom Trail Players (July–Aug Sat & Sun 11am & 1pm; $12 adults, children $6; ☎227-8800, ⓦwww.thefreedomtrail.org), a troupe in Colonial garb that acts out Revolutionary historiana along the trail; tours last ninety minutes.

Few kids can resist FAO Schwarz, 440 Boylston St (☎262-5900; Arlington **T**), and whether or not you're turned off by **toys**, the huge bronze teddy bear plunked on the sidewalk in front of this colorful emporium is worth a glance. Inside is a two-level childrens' paradise of huge stuffed animals, a Barbie boutique, the latest home video games and many other useless but fun pieces of molded plastic.

There's no shortage of **bookstores** catering to children in Boston either; the Children's Book Shop, 237 Washington St (☎734-7323, 🅦users.erols.com /childrensbookshop; Coolidge Crossing **T**), and Curious George Goes to Wordsworth, 1 JFK St (☎498-0062 or 1-800/899-2202, 🅦curiousg.com; Harvard **T**), are sure to have the latest titles, and others you didn't know existed. Near the latter is an excellent **novelty** store, Animal, Vegetable, Mineral, at 2400 Massachusetts Ave (☎547-2404; Porter **T**), with gold fish bowls full of plastic dinosaurs, rubber eyeballs and the like.

Theater and puppet shows

If you want to get the tots some (kindergarten) culture, try the Boston Children's Theatre, 321 Columbus Ave (☎424-6634, 🅦www.bostonchildrenstheatre.org), where productions of kids' classics are performed at the C. Walsh Theater, on the Beacon Hill campus of Suffolk University. Otherwise, head out to Brookline for the Puppet Showplace Theater, 32 Station St (Sept–June Sat–Sun 1pm & 3pm; July–Aug Wed–Thurs 10.30am & 1pm; ☎731-6400, 🅦www.puppetshowplace.org); tickets are $8 a head – big or small.

Festivals and events

t's always good to know ahead of time what **festivals** or **annual events** are scheduled to coincide with your trip to Boston – though even if you don't plan it, there's likely to be some sort of parade, public celebration or seasonal shindig going on. For detailed information, call the Boston Convention and Visitors Bureau (℡1-888/SEE-BOSTON; Ⓦwww.bostonusa.com). For a look at public holidays in Boston, see the "Opening hours and public holidays" section of Basics.

The schedule below picks out some of the more fun and notable events happening throughout the year, and is certainly not meant to be exhaustive. If you are seeking out specific highlights, note that a few nationwide events more or less reach their apotheosis here, such as St Patrick's Day in March and Independence Day in July; top only-in-Boston happenings include the Head of the Charles Regatta, in August, and the Boston Tea Party Re-enactment, in December.

January

First Night The New Year's celebration does begin on New Year's Eve but continues on for the first few days of the year; see events under December, below.

Chinese New Year Dragon parades and firecrackers punctuate the festivities throughout Chinatown. It can fall in February, too, depending on the Chinese lunar calendar. ℡426-6500 or 1-888/SEE-BOSTON.

February

The Beanpot First two Mondays. Popular college hockey tournament, played between Boston University, Harvard, Boston College, and Northeastern. ℡624-1000; see p.219 for more details.

March

St Patrick's Day Parade and Festival March 17. Boston's substantial Irish-American community, along with much of the rest of the city, turns out for this parade through South Boston (see Chapter 8, The southern districts), which culminates in Irish folk music, dance and food at Faneuil Hall. This also happens to be "Evacuation Day," or the anniversary of the day that George Washington drove the British out of Boston during the Revolutionary War, which gives Bostonians another historical excuse to party. ℡536-4100.
New England Spring Flower Show Winter-weary Bostonians turn out in droves to gawk at hothouse greenery in this week-

long horticultural fest, which takes place down in Dorchester's Bayside Expo Center either the second or third week in March. ☎536-9280, ⊛www.masshort.org.

April

Patriot's Day Third Monday. A celebration and re-creation of Paul Revere's (and William Dawes') famous ride from the North End to Lexington that alerted locals that the British army had been deployed against the rebel threat. ☎536-4100.

Boston Marathon Third Monday. Runners from all over the world gather for this 26.2-mile affair, one of America's premier athletic events. It crosses all over Boston, ending in Back Bay's Copley Square. ☎236-1652, ⊛www.bostonmarathon.org.

May

Dulcimer Festival First weekend. In Cambridge, workshops and performances by experts of both mountain and hammer dulcimers are held. ☎547-6789, ⊛www.jonweinberg.com/dulcifest.
Greater Boston Kite Festival Mid-May. Franklin Park gets taken over by kite-lovers during

this celebration, which features kite-making, flying clinics and music. ☎635-4505.
Lilac Sunday Third Sunday. You can view more than three hundred lilac varieties in full bloom at the Arnold Arboretum during this early summer institution. ☎524-1718, ⊛www.arboretum.harvard.edu.

June

Boston Dairy Festival First week. Cows and other animals are brought back to Boston Common to graze. There's also an event here known as the "Scooper Bowl," which, for a modest donation of around $5, allows you unlimited samples of Boston's best ice creams.
Dragon Boat Festival Variable weekend early in the month. A colorful Chinese festival whose highlight, dragon boat racing on the Charles River, is accompanied by the thundering sound of Taiko drums. ☎426-6500 ext 778, ⊛www.bostondragonboat.org.
Bunker Hill Weekend Sunday nearest June 17. In Charlestown, the highlight of this three-day festival is the parade celebrating the Battle of

Bunker Hill (even though the bout was actually lost by the Americans). ☎242-5601.
Boston Early Music Festival Every odd-numbered year. This huge, week-long Renaissance fair – with a strong music theme – puts on concerts, costumes shows and exhibitions throughout town. ☎661-1812, ⊛www.bemf.org.
Boston Globe Jazz Festival Mid- to late June. The city's leading newspaper sponsors a week-long series of jazz events at various venues; some are free, though shows by big names can be pricey. ☎929-2000 or 1-800/SEE-BOSTON, ⊛bostonglobe.com/promotions/jazzfest.

July

Harborfest Late June–weekend nearest July 4. Harborfest hosts a series of concerts on the waterfront – mostly jazz, blues and rock. On the July 4th weekend there's the highly competitive "Chowderfest," and tons of fireworks. ☎227-1528; ⊛www.harborfest.com.
Boston Pops Concert and Fireworks July 4.

The Boston Pops' wildly popular annual evening concert in the Hatch Shell is followed by thirty minutes of flashy pyrotechnics; people sometimes line up at dawn in order to get good seats. ☎266-1492.
Reading of the Declaration of Independence July 4. Pretend it's July 4th – 1776, that is –

by attending the annual reading of the nation's founding document from the Balcony of Old State House.
USS Constitution Turn-Around July 4. Old

Ironsides pulls up anchor and sails out (briefly) into the Boston harbor in this annual turnaround and salute to the country's independence.

August

August Moon Festival Near the end of the month. During this festival, Chinatown's merchants and restaurateurs hawk their wares on the street amid dragon parades and firecrackers. ☎536-4100.
Italian Festas Last two weekends in August,

Features music, dancing and games throughout the North End; during parades, statues of the Virgin Mary are borne through the streets as locals pin dollar bills to the floats.

September

Arts Festival of Boston Around Labor Day weekend. Boston is transformed into a giant gallery, with five days of exhibits, arts and crafts pavilions, fashion shows, evening galas, receptions and outdoor musical performances at various locations. ☎451-ARTS for specific locations, times and, when applicable, entrance fees.
Cambridge River Festival Mid-September. Memorial Drive is closed off from JFK Street to Western Avenue for music shows,

dancing and eclectic food offerings, all along the Charles River. ☎349-4380.
Boston Film Festival Two weeks in early to mid-September. Boston theaters screen independent films, with frequent discussions by directors and screenwriters. ☎1-888/SEE-BOSTON.
Boston Blues Festival Late–September. The Boston Blues Festival brings blues to the shores of the Charles River for two cool, "my-baby-done-left-me" days.

October

Columbus Day Parade Second Monday. Kicked off by a ceremony at City Hall at 1pm, the raucous, Italian-flavored parade continues into the heart of the North End.
Head of the Charles Regatta Next-to-last weekend. Hordes of college students descend on the banks of the Charles River between Central and Harvard squares, ostensibly to watch the crew races, but really more to pal around with their cronies and get loaded. ☎868-6200, ⊛www.hocr.org.

Oktoberfest Early October. The usual beer, sauerkraut and live entertainment in Harvard Square, done Boston style – meaning the hops-fueled shenanigans end at 6pm. ☎491-3434, ⊛www.harvardsquare.com.
Salem Haunted Happenings / Halloween Two weeks up to and including the 31st. This festival of witch-related kitsch – seances and the like – end fittingly with the Halloween celebrations. ☎1-800/777-6848, ⊛ www.salemweb.com.

Open studios

Each fall, the **Boston Open Studios Coalition** arranges for local artists to showcase their paintings, pottery, photographs and other works of art to the public, on a neighborhood by neighborhood basis. Exhibitors include the United South End Artists (☎267-8862), the Jamaica Plain Artists (☎524-3816), ACT Roxbury (☎445-1061 extension 222), the Mission Hill Art Association (☎427-7399) and the Fort Point Channel Arts Community (☎423-4299). Check newspapers for listings.

November

Thanksgiving Last Thursday. In Plymouth, they commemorate the first Thanksgiving ever with tours of old houses and traditional feasts. Information ☎1-800/USA-1620, reservations ☎508/746-1622.

Annual Lighting Ceremony Late November. Faneuil Hall Marketplace kickstarts the holiday season with the annual lighting of some 300,000 festive bulbs at Faneuil Hall Marketplace.

December

Boston Tea Party Re-enactment Sunday nearest Dec 16. A lusty re-enactment of the march from Old South Meeting House to the harbor, and the subsequent tea-dumping that helped spark the American Revolution. ☎338-1773.
First Night December 31–January 2. A family-friendly festival to ring in the New Year, fea-

turing parades, ice sculptures, art shows, plays and music throughout downtown and Back Bay, culminating in a spectacular fireworks display over Boston Harbor. A button, granting admission to all events, tends to run around $15. ☎542-1399, ⓦwww.firstnight.org.

Directory

Airlines American and United have offices in the *Park Plaza Hotel* (in addition to one at Logan Airport); the British Airways office is across from the Government Center **T** station. International flights arrive and depart from Logan airport's Terminal E; domestic flights typically arrive and depart from Terminal C, with the exception of American Airlines and US Airways, which use Terminal B. For airline contact information, see Basics p.11.

Babysitting Try Nanny Poppins ($9–15/hr; ☏979/927-1811, ⊚www.nannypoppins.com).

Banks and ATMs Fleet Financial Group and the Bank of Boston together make up the biggest bank – Fleet Boston – with branches and ATMs throughout the city (☏1-800/841-4000, ⊚www.fleet.com). Citizens Bank also has branches scattered about town (☏1-800/922-9999, ⊚www.citizensbank.com). See "Costs, money and banks," p.26, for more.

Bicycles A copy of *Boston's Bike Map* ($4.25; ☏1-800/358-6013, ⊚www.bikemaps.com) will help you find all the trails and bike-friendly roads in the area; it's also available at Cambridge's Globe Corner Bookstore, 28 Church St (☏497-6277, ⊚www.globecorner.com; Harvard **T**). For information on rentals, along with the best spots to bike, see both Basics (p.24) and Sports, fitness and outdoor activities (p.219).

Car rentals Local branches: Avis, 3 Center Plaza (☏534-1400 or 1-800/331-1212, ⊚www.avis.com), 1 Bennett St, Cambridge (☏534-1430), and Logan Airport (☏561-3500); Enterprise, 800 Boylston St (☏262-9215 or 1-800/RENT-A-CAR, ⊚www.enterprise.com); Thrifty, 125 Summer St (☏330-5011 or 1-800/367-2277, ⊚www.thrifty.com) and Logan Airport

(☏634-7350). For nationwide information, see p.24 in Basics.

Consulates Canada, 3 Copley Place, suite 400 (☏262-3760, ⊚www.can-am.gc.ca/boston); France, 31 St James Ave (☏542-7374, ⊚www.franceboston.org); Germany, 3 Copley Place (☏536-4414, ⊚www.germany-info.org); Ireland, 535 Boylston St (☏267-9330); Japan, 600 Atlantic Ave (☏973-9772, ⊚www.embjapan.org/boston); UK, 1 Memorial Dr, suite 1600, Cambridge (☏245-4500, ⊚www.britain-info.org).

Emergencies Dial ☏911 for emergency assistance.

Exchange There are currency exchange counters at Logan Airport's Terminal E (International). In the city, there's Thomas Cook, 399 Boylston St (☏1-800/287-7362; Arlington **T**), and American Express, 39 JFK St (☏868-2600; Harvard **T**).

Film and photography Moto Photo has one-hour developing services and locations in the Financial District, 101 Summer St (☏423-6848); Back Bay, 657 Boylston St (☏266-6560); and Harvard Square, 36 JFK St, Cambridge (☏497-0731).

Health Inn-House Doctor, 839 Beacon St, Suite B (☏267-9407 or 859-1776; ⊚www.inn-housedoctor.net) makes 24hr house calls; rates are $150–250; prescriptions cost extra.

Internet Harvard's Holyoke Center, 1350 Massachusetts Ave; MIT's Rogers Building, 77 Massachusetts Ave and the Boston Public Library, 700 Boylston St, have free ten-to-fifteen minute Internet access.

Laundry Back Bay Laundry Emporium, 409A Marlborough St (daily 7.30am–11pm, last wash at 9pm; ☏236-4552), is a good, clean bet; drop-off service is 80¢ per pound.

Parking lots The cheapest downtown options are Center Plaza Garage, at the corner of Cambridge and New Sudbury streets ($9/hr–$25/max; ☏742-7807) and Garage at Post Office Square ($3.50/30min–$29/max; ☏423-1430).

Pharmacies The CVS drugstore chain has locations all over the city, though not all have pharmacies. For those, try the branches at 155–157 Charles St, in Beacon Hill (open 24 hours; ☏227-0437, pharmacy ☏523-1028), and 35 White St, in Cambridge's Porter Square (open 24 hours, ☏876-4037, pharmacy ☏876-5519).

Police Dial ☏911 for emergencies; for non-emergency situations, contact the Boston Police, headquartered at 154 Berkeley St, in Back Bay (☏343-4200).

Public toilets There aren't too many of these around. The cleanest ones are in the visitors' center on the fourth floor of the City Hall building in Government Center, and in the National Park Service visitors' center across from the Old State House. If desperate, you can always try ducking into a restaurant, bar, or hotel; of the latter, the *Fairmont Copley Plaza* is tops.

Taxis Boston Cab ☏536-5010; Cambridge Taxi ☏868-9690; Checker Taxi ☏536-7000; City Water Taxi ☏422-0392; Metro Cab ☏242-8000; Town Taxi ☏536–5000. If you lose something in a taxi, call ☏536-TAXI.

Telephones Local calls made from payphones cost 35¢; all local numbers are ten digits long, starting with the area code (☏617 in Boston, except where specified

otherwise) + the seven-digit number.

Time Boston is on Eastern Standard Time (five hours behind Greenwich Mean Time). Daylight Savings Time runs from April to October.

Tourist offices Boston National Historical Park, 15 State St (☏242-5642, ☻www.nps.gov/bost); Boston Parks and Recreation, 1010 Massachusetts Ave (☏635-4505, ☻www.cityofboston.com/parks); Cambridge Office of Tourism, 4 Brattle St (☏441-2884 or 1-800/862-5678, ☻www.cambridge-usa.org); Greater Boston Convention & Visitors Bureau, 2 Copley Place, suite 105 (☏1-888/SEE-BOSTON, ☻www.boston-usa.com); Massachusetts Office of Travel and Tourism, 100 Cambridge St, 13th floor (☏727-3201 or 1-800/447-MASS, ☻www.mass-vacation.com).

Travel agents Council Travel (☻www.counciltravel.com), 273 Newbury St (☏266-1926; Arlington **T**) and 12 Eliot St, 2nd floor, Cambridge (☏497-1497; Harvard **T**), specializes in student and youth travel; American Express Travel, 170 Federal Street, 1st floor (☏439-4400; Downtown Crossing **T**) and 39 JFK St, Cambridge (☏868-2600; Harvard **T**) provides general travel services including currency exchange.

Wire transfers Western Union has agents at multiple locations including Store Apple Three, 144 Tremont St (☏375-8021) and Stop and Shop, 181 Cambridge St (☏742-6094).

Contexts

Contexts

A brief history of Boston

Boston has been an important city since its Colonial days, even if it's been usurped in East Coast pre-eminence by New York and Washington as the centuries have gone by. Numerous crucial and decisive events, especially as they related to America's struggle for independence, have taken place here; it's also been fertile ground for various intellectual, literary and religious movements throughout the years. What follows is a very short overview of the city's development, with an emphasis on the key happenings and figures behind them; for a more in-depth look, check out some of the volumes listed in "Books," p.246.

Early exploration and founding

The first indications of explorers "discovering" the Boston area are the journal entries of **Giovanni da Verrazano** and **Estevan Gomez**, who – in 1524 and 1525, respectively – passed by Massachusetts Bay while traveling the coast of North America. The first permanent European settlement in the Boston area was undertaken by a group of 102 British colonists, around half of them Separatists – better known now as **Pilgrims** – chased out of England for having disassociated themselves entirely from the Anglican Church.

They had tried to settle in Holland, but the Dutch didn't want them either, so they boarded the ship *Mayflower* to try the forbidding, rugged coast of North America, where they landed in 1620 near Plymouth Bay – after a short stopover at the tip of Cape Cod – and founded Plimoth Plantation. Within the first decade, one of them, a disillusioned scholarly loner by the name of **William Blackstone**, began searching for land on which to make a new start; he found it on a peninsula at the mouth of the Charles River known as Shawmut by the local Indians. Blackstone thus became Boston's first white settler, living at the foot of modern-day Beacon Hill with a few hundred books and a Brahma bull.

In 1630, close to one thousand **Puritans**, led by **John Winthrop**, settled just across the river to create **Charlestown**, named after the king of England. Unlike the Pilgrims, the Puritans didn't necessarily plan to disconnect themselves completely from the Anglican Church, but merely hoped to purify themselves by avoiding what they considered to be its showy excesses. Blackstone eventually lured them to his side of the river with the promise of a better water supply, then sold them the entire Shawmut Peninsula, keeping only six acres for himself. The Puritans subsequently renamed the area after the town in England from which many of their company hailed: **Boston**.

The colonial period

Early Bostonians enjoyed almost total political autonomy from England and created a remarkably democratic system of government, whose primary body was the **town meeting**, in which white male church members debated over and voted on all kind of matters. This liberal approach was counterbalanced, however, by religious intolerance: four Quakers and Baptists were hanged for their non-Puritan beliefs between 1649 and 1651.

As well during these times, Boston and neighboring Cambridge were making great strides in culture and education: **Boston Latin**, the (not yet) nation's first secondary school, was established in 1635; **Harvard**, its first university, a year later; and the first **printing press** in America was set up in Cambridge in 1639, where the *Bay Psalm Book*, *New England Primer*, and freeman's oath of loyalty to Massachusetts were among the first published works.

With the restoration of the British monarchy in 1660, the crown tried to exert more control over the increasingly prosperous and free-thinking Massachusetts Bay Colony, appointing a series of governors, notably the despotic Sir **Edmund Andros**, who was chased from the colony by locals in 1689, only to be reinstalled by the monarchy the following year. Britain's relentless mercantilist policies, designed to increase the nation's monopolistic hold on .the new colonies, resulted in a decrease in trade that both plunged Boston into a depression and fanned the anti-British resentment which would eventually reach a boiling point during the mid-1700s. The **Molasses Act** of 1733, for example, taxed all sugar purchased outside the British Empire, dealing a stiff economic blow to the colonies, who were dependent upon foreign sources for their sugar supply.

The American Revolution

At the outset of the 1760s, governor Francis Bernard informed the colonists that their success was a result of "their subjugation to Great Britain," before green-lighting the **Writs of Assistance**, which gave British soldiers the right to enter colonists' shops and homes to search for evidence of their avoiding duties. The colonists reacted with outrage at this violation of their civil liberties, and a young Boston lawyer named **James Otis** persuaded a panel of judges headed by lieutenant governor Thomas Hutchinson to repeal the acts. After listening to his four-hour oration, many were convinced that revolution was justified, including future US president **John Adams**, who wrote of Otis' speech: "Then and there the child Liberty was born."

Nevertheless, in 1765 the British introduced the **Stamp Act**, which required stamps to be placed on all published material (the revenue on the stamps would go to the Imperial coffers), and the **Quartering Act**, which stipulated that colonists had to house British soldiers on demand. These acts galvanized the opposition to the English government, a resistance based in Boston, where a group of revolutionary firebrands headed by **Samuel Adams** and known as the "Sons of Liberty" teamed up with more level-headed folks like **John Hancock** and John Adams to organize protest marches and petition the king to repeal the offending legislation. Though Parliament repealed the Stamp Act, in 1766 it issued the **Declaratory Acts**, which asserted the Crown's right to bind the colonists by any legislation it saw fit, and, in 1767, with the **Townshend Acts**, which prescribed more tariffs on imports to the North American colonies. This was followed by a troop increase in Boston; by 1768, there was one British soldier in the city for every four colonists.

The tension erupted on March 5, 1770, when a group of British soldiers fired into a crowd of townspeople who'd been taunting them. The **Boston Massacre**, as it came to be known, was hardly a massacre – only five people were killed, and the accused soldiers were actually defended in court by John Adams and Josiah

Quincy – but the occupying troops were forced to relocate to **Castle Island**, at the tip of South Boston. The coming crisis was postponed for a few years following the Massacre, until December 16, 1773, when Samuel Adams led a mob from the Old South Meeting House to Boston Harbor as part of a protest against a British tax on imported tea. A segment of the crowd boarded the brig *Beaver* and two other ships and dumped their entire cargo overboard, the so-called **Boston Tea Party**; Parliament responded by closing the port of Boston and passing the **Coercive Acts**, which deprived Massachusetts of any self-government. England also sent in more troops and cut off the Dorchester Neck, the only land entrance to Boston. Soon after, the colonies convened the first **Continental Congress** in Philadelphia, with the idea of creating an independent government.

Two months after the province of Massachusetts was declared to be in a state of rebellion by the British government, the "shot heard 'round the world" was fired at Lexington on April 18, 1775, when a group of American militiamen skirmished with a company of British regulars; they lost that fight, but defeated the Redcoats in a subsequent incident at Concord Bridge, and the **Revolutionary War** had begun. The British troops left in Boston were held under siege, and the city itself was largely evacuated by its citizens.

The first major engagement of the war was the **Battle of Bunker Hill**, in which the British stormed what was actually Breed's Hill, in Charlestown, on three separate occasions before finally dislodging American battlements. Despite the loss, the conflict, in which the outnumbered Americans suffered fewer casualties than the British, bolstered the patriots' spirits and confidence.

George Washington took over the Continental troops in a ceremony on Cambridge Common on July 2, 1775; however, his first major coup didn't even require bloodshed. On March 16, 1776, under cover of darkness, Washington ordered much of the troops' heavy artillery to be moved to the top of Dorchester Heights, in view of the Redcoats. The British awoke to see battlements sufficient to destroy their entire fleet of warships; on March 17, they evacuated the city, never to return.

This was largely the end of Boston's involvement in the war; the focus soon turned inland and southward. After the Americans won the Battle of Saratoga in 1778, the French joined the war as their allies; on October 19, 1781, Cornwallis surrendered to Washington at Yorktown. Two years later, the **United States of America** became an independent nation with 1783's **Treaty of Paris**.

Economic swings and the Athens of America

Boston quickly emerged from the damage wrought by British occupation. By 1790, the economy was already booming, due primarily to the maritime industry. A merchant elite – popularly known as the "cod millionaires" – developed and settled on the sunny south slope of Beacon Hill. These were the original Boston **Brahmins** – though that name would not be coined until seventy years later – infamous for their stuffed-shirt elitism and fiscal conservatism. Indeed, the **trust fund** was invented in Boston at this time as a way for families to protect their fortunes over the course of generations.

The outset of the nineteenth century was less auspicious. Severe restrictions on international trade, notably Jefferson's **Embargo Act** in 1807, plunged the port of Boston into recession. When the War of 1812 began, pro-British Bostonian Federalists derided the conflict as "Mr. Madison's War" and, as such, met in Hartford in 1814 with party members from around New England to consider seceding from the Union – a measure that was wisely, though narrowly, rejected. America's victory in the war shamed Bostonians back into their patriotic ways, and they reacted to further trade restrictions by developing manufacturing industries; the city soon became prominent in **textiles** and **shoe production**.

This industrial revival and subsequent economic growth shook the region from its recession. By 1820, Boston's population had grown to 43,000 – more than double its total from the census of 1790. The city stood at the forefront of American intellectual and political life, as well, earning Boston the moniker "Athens of America."

One of these intellectual movements had its roots back in the late eighteenth century, when a controversial sect of Christianity known as **Unitarianism** – premised on the rational study of the Bible, voluntary ethical behavior, and (in Boston only) a rejection of the idea of a Holy Trinity – became the city's dominant religion (and one still practiced at King's Chapel), led by Reverend **Ellery Channing**. His teachings were the basis for **transcendentalism**, a philosophy propounded in the writings of Ralph Waldo Emerson and premised on the idea that there existed an entity known as the "over-soul," to which man and nature existed in identical relation. Emerson's theory, emphasizing intuitive (*a priori*) knowledge – particularly in contemplation of nature – was put into practice by his fellow Harvard alumnus, **Henry David Thoreau**, who, in 1845, took to the woods just northwest of the city at **Walden Pond** in an attempt to "live deliberately."

Boston was also a center of literary activity at this time: historical novels by **Nathaniel Hawthorne**, such as *The Scarlet Letter*, tweaked the sensibilities and mores of New England society, and poet **Henry Wadsworth Longfellow** gained international renown during his tenure at Harvard. For more on these developments throughout the nineteenth century, see "Literary Boston in the 1800s," p.244.

This intellectual flowering was complemented by a variety of social movements. Foremost among them was the **abolitionist movement**, spearheaded by the fiery **William Lloyd Garrison**, who, besides speechmaking, published the anti-slavery newspaper *The Liberator*. Beacon Hill resident **Harriet Beecher Stowe**'s seminal 1852 novel, *Uncle Tom's Cabin*, turned the sentiments of much of the nation against slavery. Other Bostonians who made key contributions to social issues were **Horace Mann**, who reformed public education; **Dorothea Dix**, an advocate of improved care for the mentally ill; **Margaret Fuller**, one of America's first feminists and as well the editor of *The Dial*, a journal founded by Emerson; and **William James**, a Harvard professor who pioneered new methods in psychology, coining the phrase "stream of consciousness."

Social transformation and decline

The success of Boston's maritime and manufacturing industries attracted a great deal of immigrants; the **Irish**, especially, poured in following Ireland's Potato Famine of the 1840s. By 1860, the city was marked by massive social divide, with overcrowded slums abutting beautiful mansions. The elite that had ruled for the first half of the century tried to ensure that the lower classes were kept in place: "No Irish Need Apply" notices accompanied job listings throughout Boston. Denied entry into "polite" society, the lower classes conspired to grab power in another way: the popular vote.

To the chagrin of Boston's WASP elite, **Hugh O'Brien** was elected mayor in 1885. His three-term stay in office was followed by that of John "Honey Fitz" Fitzgerald, and in the 1920s, the long reign of **James Michael Curley** began. Curley was to serve several terms as mayor, and one each as governor and congressional representative. These men enjoyed tremendous popularity among their supporters, despite the fact that their tenures were often characterized by rampant corruption: Curley was elected to his last term in office while serving time in a Federal prison for fraud. Still, while these mayors increased the visibility and political clout of otherwise disenfranchised ethnic groups, they did little to improve the lot of their constituents, which was steadily worsening – along with the city's economy.

Following the Civil War, competition with the railroads crippled the shipping industry, and with it, Boston's prosperous waterfront. Soon after, the manufacturing industry as well felt the impact of bigger, more efficient factories in the rest of the nation. The shoe and textile industries had largely disappeared by the 1920s; many companies had started to **move south**, where costs were much lower, and industrial production statewide fell by more than $1 billion during that decade. The **Great Depression** of the 1930s made a bad state of affairs even worse, as there were few natural resources the city provided that could keep it as an economic powerhouse.

On the heels of the depression, **World War II** turned Boston's moribund shipbuilding industry around almost overnight, but this economic upturn still wasn't enough to prevent a massive exodus from the urban center.

The 1950s to the 1980s

In the 1950s, a more long-lasting turnaround began under the mayoral leadership of **John Collins**, who undertook a massive plan to reshape the face of Boston. Many of the city's oldest neighborhoods and landmarks were razed, though it's questionable whether these changes beautified the city. Still, the project created jobs and economic growth, while making the downtown area more attractive to businesses and residents. By the end of the 1960s, a steady economic resurgence had begun. Peripheral areas of Boston, however, did not share in this prosperity. Collins' program paid little attention to the poverty that afflicted outlying areas, particularly the city's southern districts, or to the city's growing **racial tensions**. The demographic redistribution that followed the "white flight" of the 1940s and 1950s made Boston one of the most racially segregated cities in America by the mid-1970s: Charlestown's population was almost entirely white, while Roxbury was almost entirely black.

Along with other cities nationwide, Boston was ordered by the US Supreme Court to implement **busing** – sending students from one neighborhood to another and vice-versa in an attempt to achieve racial balance. More than two hundred area schools were involved, and not all reacted kindly: many Charlestown parents, for their part, staged hostile demonstrations and boycotted the public school system, which was especially embarrassing for Boston considering its history of racial tolerance. City officials finally scrapped their plan for desegregation after only a few years. The racial scars it left began to heal, thanks, in part, to the policies of **Ray Flynn**, Boston's mayor during the upbeat 1980s, helping to make the decade one of the city's healthiest in recent memory, both economically and socially.

The 1990s into the twenty-first century

That resurgence spilled over into the 1990s, a decade that saw the job market explode and rents spiral upward in reaction to it. The increase in housing prices was aided as well by the 1996 state vote to abolish **rent control** in the city, a decision that pushed much of the lower-paid working class out to neighborhoods like **Roxbury**, and kick-started a condominium boom, especially in the **South End**, that radically transformed the neighborhood from near slums into the trendy hotspot it is today. In any case, it seems that anyone who can afford a posh apartment these days works for some biotech company – Boston's strength in this market spared most of its citizens from the dotcom crash that injured other major US cities' economies.

Indeed, the city has had little in the way of strife in the last decade – the most notable hubbub occurred in 2002, when the archdiocese of the local Catholic church, the Church of the Holy Cross, found itself at the center of a **sex abuse scandal** that prompted calls for an overhaul of the procedures concerning the handling of errant priests. While reforms remained undecided on as of press time, the protesters that took up residency in front of the church doors during the heat of the scandal quieted down in short order, and the church quickly returned to business as usual – though with a tarnished reputation.

Most major changes to Boston in recent years have been superficial, as the city has dedicated its efforts to improving the city's infrastructure and public spaces. The most obvious of these civic-minded programs is downtown's **Big Dig** project, which, at over $1.6 billion per mile, is the most expensive highway construction project in US history; it's also potentially the most protracted, given it's not due to terminate before 2005, or fourteen years after the first jackhammer sounded in Charlestown.

In the interim, the **cleanup of Boston Harbor** has had a great effect in reclaiming abandoned beaches and reinvigorating species of long disappeared fauna, many of which are making their homes on the Boston **Harbor Islands**, a group of idyllic offshore isles originally used as defense posts, but declared a national park in 1996 and subsequently opened to the public, accessible via regular ferries from Long Wharf.

By the end of the twentieth century, the city's positive economic growth endowed a number of cultural institutions with funds to spruce up their digs; two of Boston's most intriguing libraries – the staid **Boston Athenæum** and the unusual **Mary Eddy Baker Library** – both reopened to the public in 2002, following substantial renovations. The most significant facelift however, is taking place at the **Museum of Fine Arts**, where a recently inaugurated multi-million-dollar expansion project is slated for partial completion by 2007. Ironically, the one institution that continues to be denied a monetary infusion is one that's been most touted for radical transformation: **Fenway Park**, the home of the Boston Red Sox and the country's oldest ballpark, continues to pack baseball fans into its bleacher seats despite the ongoing promise (or threat, depending on your outlook) of a new stadium.

Architecture and urban planning

The land to which William Blackstone invited John Winthrop and his Puritans in 1630 bore almost no resemblance to the contemporary city of Boston. It was virtually an island, spanning a mere 785 acres, surrounded on all sides by murky swamps and connected to the mainland only by a narrow isthmus, "the Neck," that was almost entirely submerged at high tide. It was also very hilly: three peaks formed its geological backbone and gave it the name that Puritans used before they chose Boston – the Trimountain – echoed today in the name of downtown's Tremont Street.

Colonial development

The first century and a half of Boston's existence saw this sleepy Puritan village slowly expand into one of the biggest shipping centers in the North American colonies. Narrow, crooked footpaths became busy commercial boulevards, though they retained their sinuous design, and the pasture land of **Boston Common** became the place for public gatherings. By the end of the eighteenth century, Boston was faced with the dilemma of how to accommodate its growing population and thriving industry on a tiny geographical center; part of the answer was to create more land. This had been accomplished in Boston's early years almost accidentally, by means of a process known as **wharving out**. Owners of shoreside properties with wharves found that rocks and debris collected around the pilings, until eventually the wharves were on dry land, necessitating the building of more wharves further out to sea. In this way, Boston's shoreline moved slowly but inexorably outward.

Post-revolution development

Boston's first great building boom began in earnest following the American Revolution. Harrison Gray Otis' company, the **Mount Vernon Proprietors**, razed Boston's three peaks to create tracts for new townhouses. The land from the tops of these hills was placed where Boston Common and the Charles River met to form a swamp, extending the shoreline out even farther to create what is now known as "the flat of the hill." Leftover land was used to fill some of the city's other coves and ponds, most significantly Mill Pond, near present-day North End. The completion of the Mount Vernon Proprietors' plans made the resulting area, **Beacon Hill**, the uncontested site for Boston's wealthy and elite to build their ideal home – as such, it holds the best examples of American architecture of the late eighteenth and early nineteenth centuries, ranging in styles from Georgian to early Victorian.

This period also ushered in the first purely American architectural movement, the **Federal style**. Prime examples of its flat, dressed-down facades are prevalent in townhouses throughout downtown and in Beacon Hill. **Charles Bulfinch** was its leading practitioner; his most famous work was the 1797 gold-domed **Massachusetts State House** looming over Boston Common, a prototype for state capitols to come. For more information on Bulfinch, see the box on p.76.

The expansion of the city

Boston continued to grow throughout the 1800s. Mayor **Josiah Quincy** oversaw the construction of a large marketplace, **Quincy Market**, behind the overcrowded Faneuil Hall building. These three oblong Greek Revival buildings pushed the Boston waterfront back several hundred yards, and the new surface area was used as the site for a symbol of Boston's maritime prosperity, the **US Custom House**. While Boston had codes prohibiting overly tall buildings, the Federal Government was not obligated to obey them, and the Custom House building, completed in 1847, rose a then-impressive sixteen stories.

Meanwhile, the city was trying to create enough land to match the demand for housing, in part by transforming its swampy backwaters into useable property. **Back Bay**, for example, was originally just that: a marsh along the banks of the Charles. In 1814, however, Boston began to dam the Charles, filling the resulting area with debris. When the project was completed in 1883, Back Bay quickly became one of Boston's choicest addresses, drawing some prominent families from their dwellings on Beacon Hill. The layout followed a highly ordered French model of city planning: gridded streets, with those running perpendicular to the Charles arranged alphabetically. The district's main boulevard, **Commonwealth Avenue**, surrounded a strip of greenery that terminated to the east in the **Public Garden**, a lush park completed by George Meachum in 1859, with ponds, statuary, weeping willows and winding pathways that is the jewel of Back Bay, if not all Boston.

As if this weren't enough, Back Bay's **Copley Square** was also the site of numerous high-minded civic institutions built in the mid- and late 1800s, foremost among which were H.H. Richardson's Romanesque **Trinity Church** and the **Public Library**, a High Victorian creation of Charles McKim, of the noted firm McKim, Mead and White. But the most impressive accomplishment of the century was certainly Frederick Law Olmsted's **Emerald Necklace**, a system of parks that connected Boston Common, the Public Garden, and the Commonwealth Avenue Mall to his own creations a bit further afield, such as the **Back Bay Fens**, **Arnold Arboretum**, and **Franklin Park**.

While Boston's civic expansion made life better for its upper classes, the middle and lower classes were crammed into the tiny downtown area. The city's solution was to annex the surrounding districts, beginning with **South Boston** in 1807 and ending with **Charlestown** in 1873 – with the exception of **Brookline**, which remained a separate entity. Toward the end of the century, Boston's growing middle class moved to these surrounding areas, particularly the southern districts, which soon became known as the "streetcar suburbs." These areas, once the site of summer estates for the wealthy, were built over with one of Boston's least attractive architectural motifs: the **three-decker**. Also known as the "triple-decker," these clapboard rowhouses held a family on each floor – models of unattractive efficiency.

Modernization and preservation

New construction waned with the economic decline of the early 1900s, reaching its lowest point during the **Great Depression**. The streetcar suburbs were hardest hit – the white middle class migrated to Boston's nearby towns in the 1940s and 1950s, and the southern districts became run-down, low-rent areas. Urban renewal began in the late 1950s, with the idea of creating a visibly modern city, and while it provided Boston with an economic shot in the arm, the drastic changes erased some of the city's most distinctive architectural features. The porn halls and dive bars of **Scollay Square** were demolished to make way for the dull gray bureaucracy complexes of Government Center, while the **West End**, once one of Boston's liveliest ethnic neighborhoods, was flattened and covered over with high-rise office buildings. Worst of all, the new elevated **John F. Fitzgerald Expressway** (I-93) tore through downtown, cutting off the North End and waterfront from the rest of the city. At least this concrete eyesore – thanks to the Big Dig – will soon be where it belongs: underground.

Following this period, the fury of displaced and disgruntled residents forced planners to create structures that either reused or integrated extant features of the city. The **John Hancock Tower**, designed by I.M. Pei and completed in 1975, originally outraged preservationists, as this Copley Square high-rise was being built right by some of the city's most treasured cultural landmarks; however, the tower managed a delicate balance – while it rises sixty stories smack in the middle of Back Bay, its narrow wedge shape renders it quite unobtrusive, and its mirrored walls literally reflect its stately surroundings. Quincy Market was also redeveloped and, by 1978, what had been a decaying, nearly defunct series of fishmongering stalls was transformed into a thriving tourist attraction. Subsequent development has, for the most part, kept up this theme, preserving the city's four thousand acres – and most crucially its downtown – as a virtual library of American architecture.

Literary Boston in the 1800s

America's literary center has not always been New York; indeed, for much of the nineteenth century, Boston wore that mantle, and since then – largely due to the lingering effects of those sixty or so years – it has managed to retain a somewhat bookish reputation despite no longer having the influence it once did on American publishing.

Puritanism and religious influence

The origins for that period actually go back to colonial times and the establishment of Puritanism. **John Winthrop** and his fellow colonists who settled here had a vision of a theocratic, utopian "City on a Hill." The Puritans were erudite and fairly well-off intellectuals, but religion always came first, even when writing: in fact, Winthrop himself penned *A Model of Christian Charity* while crossing the Atlantic. Religious **sermons** were the real literature of the day – those and the now-forgotten explorations of Reverend **Cotton Mather** such as *The Wonders of the Invisible World*, a look at the supernatural that helped foment the Salem Witch Trials.

In the years leading up to the Revolutionary War, Bostonians began to pour their energy into a different kind of sermon – that of anti-British sentiment, such as rants in radical newspapers like the *Boston Gazette*. Post revolution, the stifling atmosphere of Puritanism remained to some extent – the city's first theater, for example, built in 1794, had to be billed as a "school of virtue" in order to remain open. But writers began to shake off Puritan restraints and explore their new-found freedom; in certain instances, they drew upon the repressiveness of the religion as a source of inspiration.

The transcendentalist movement

Ironically enough, Boston's deliverance from parochialism began in the country-side, specifically Concord, scene of the first battle of the Revolutionary War. The **transcendentalist movement** of the 1830s and 1840s, spearheaded by **Ralph Waldo Emerson**, was born of a passion for rural life, intellectual freedom and belief in intuitive knowledge and experience as a way to enhance the relationship between man, nature and the "over-soul." The free thinking the movement unleashed put local writers at the vanguard of American literary expression; articles by Emerson, **Henry David Thoreau**, **Louisa May Alcott**, **Bronson Alcott** (Louisa's father), and other members of the Concord coterie filled the pages of *The Dial*, the transcendentalist literary review, founded by Emerson around 1840 and edited by **Margaret Fuller**. Fuller, an early feminist, also wrote essays prodigiously; while Alcott penned the classic *Little Women*, and Thoreau authored his famous study in solitude, *Walden*. Meanwhile, a writer by the name of **Nathaniel Hawthorne**, known mainly for short stories like "Young Goodman Brown," published *The Scarlet Letter*, in 1850, a true schism with the past that examined the effects of the repressive Puritan lifestyle and legacy.

The abolitionist movement and literary salons

The abolitionist movement also helped push Boston into the literary limelight. Slavery had been outlawed in Massachusetts since 1783, and Boston attracted the likes of activist **William Lloyd Garrison**, who published his firebrand newspaper, *The Liberator*, in a small office downtown beginning in 1831. Years later, in 1852, **Harriet Beecher Stowe**'s slave narrative *Uncle Tom's Cabin* hit the printing press in Boston and sold more than 300,000 copies in its first year of publication. It, perhaps more than anything else, turned national public opinion against slavery, despite that its writer was a New Englander with little firsthand knowledge of the South or the slave trade.

Another Bostonian involved with the abolitionist cause was **John Greenleaf Whittier**, who also happened to be among the founding members of Emerson's famed "**Saturday Club**," the name given to a series of informal literary gatherings that took place at the *Parker House Hotel* beginning in 1855. **Oliver Wendell Holmes** and poet **Henry Wadsworth Longfellow** were among the moneyed regulars at these salons, which metamorphosed two years later into *The Atlantic Monthly*, from its inception a respected, if staid, literary and political journal. One of its more accomplished editors, **William Dean Howells**, wrote *The Rise of Silas Lapham*, in 1878, a novel on the culture of commerce that set the stage for American Realism. Around the same time, more literary salons were being held at the **Old Corner Bookstore**, down the street from the Parker House, where leading publisher **Ticknor & Fields** had their headquarters. Regulars included not only the likes of Emerson and Longfellow, but visiting British authors like William Thackeray and Charles Dickens, who were not only published by the house as well, but also friends with its charismatic leader, Jamie T. Fields. Meanwhile, Longfellow was well on his way to becoming America's most popular poet, writing "The Midnight Ride of Paul Revere," among much other verse, while a professor at Harvard University.

The end of an era

In the last burst of Boston's literary high tide, sometimes resident **Henry James** recorded the sedate lives of the moneyed – and miserable – elite in his books *Watch and Ward* (1871) and *The Bostonians* (1886). His renunciation of hedonism was well-suited to the stifling atmosphere of Brahmin Boston, where well-appointed homes were heavily curtained so as to avoid exposure to sunlight; however, his look at the emerging battle of the sexes was in fact fueled by the liberty-loving principles of Emerson and colleagues in Concord thirty years before.

The fact that Boston's literary society was largely a members-only club contributed to its eventual undoing. **Edgar Allen Poe** slammed his hometown as "Frogpondium," in reference to the Saturday Club-style chumminess of its literati. Provincialism reared its head in the Watch & Ward Society, which as late as 1878 instigated boycotts of books and plays it deemed out of the bounds of common decency, spawning the phrase "**Banned in Boston**." To many observers, Howells' departure from *The Atlantic Monthly* in 1885 to write for *Harper's* in New York signaled the end of Boston's literary golden age.

Books

In the reviews below, publishers are listed in the format US/UK, unless the title is only available in one country, in which case the country has been specified. Highly recommended titles are signified by ⊡. Out of print titles are indicated by o/p.

History and biography

Cleveland Amory *The Proper Bostonians* (Parnassus Imprints US). First published in 1947, this surprisingly upbeat volume remains the definitive social history of Boston's old-money aristocracy.

Jack Beatty *The Rascal King: The Life and Times of James Michael Curley, 1874–1958* (Addison Wesley o/p). A thick and thoroughly researched biography of the charismatic Boston mayor and Bay State governor, valuable too for its depiction of big city politics in America.

David Hackett Fischer *Paul Revere's Ride* (University of Massachusetts Press/Oxford University Press). An exhaustive account of the patriot's legendary ride to Lexington, related as a historical narrative.

Jonathan Harr *A Civil Action* (Vintage Books US). The story of eight families in the community of Woburn, just north of Boston, who took a major chemical company to court in 1981, after a spate of leukemia cases raised suspicion about the purity of the area's water supply; made into a movie starring John Travolta in 1998.

Sebastian Junger *The Perfect Storm* (HarperCollins US). A nail-biting account of the fate of the *Andrea Gail*, a six-man swordfishing boat from Gloucester caught in the worst storm in recorded history; later turned into a movie starring George Clooney in 2000.

⊡ **Jonathan Kozol** *Death at an Early Age: The Destruction of the*

Hearts and Minds of Negro Children in the Boston Public Schools (Penguin US). Winner of the National Book Award, this is an intense portrait of prejudice and corruption in Boston's 1964 educational system.

⊡ **J. Anthony Lukas** *Common Ground: A Turbulent Decade in the Lives of Three American Families* (Vintage US). A Pulitzer Prize-winning account of three Boston families – one Irish-American, one black, one white middle class – against the backdrop of the 1974 race riots sparked by court-ordered busing to desegregate public schools.

Michael Patrick MacDonald *All Souls: A Family Story from Southie* (Beacon Press US). A moving memoir of growing up in South Boston in the 1970s among the sometimes life-threatening racial, ethnic, class, and political tensions of the time.

⊡ **Louis Menand** *Metaphysical Club* (Farrar, Strauss & Giroux US). Arguably the most engaging study of Boston heavyweights Oliver Wendell Holmes, William James, Charles Sanders Pierce and John Dewey ever written, this Pulitzer Prize-winning biography links the foursome through a short-lived 1872 Cambridge salon (the book's title), and extols the effect of their pragmatic idealism on American intellectual thought.

Mary Beth Norton *In the Devil's Snare: The Salem Witchcraft Crisis of 1692* (Knopf US). Analysis of the witchcraft accusations and executions in and around Salem in 1692; collecting newly available trial evidence, correspondence and papers, Norton argues that the crisis must be understood in the context of the horrors of the Second Indian War, which was being waged at the time in the area around Salem.

Douglass Shand-Tucci *The Art of Scandal: The Life and Times of Isabella Stewart Gardner* (HarperCollins US). Astute biography of this doyenne of Boston society, who served as the inspiration for Isabel Archer in Henry James' *Portrait of a Lady*. The book includes evocative photos of Fenway Courtyard in Gardner's Venetian-style palace – which is now the Gardner Museum.

Dan Shaughnessy *The Curse of the Bambino* (Penguin US). Shaughnessy, a Boston sportswriter, gives an entertaining look at the Red Sox' "curse" – no championships since 1918 – that began after they sold Babe Ruth to the Yankees. His *At Fenway: Dispatches from Red Sox Nation* (Crown Publishing US) is another memoir of a Red Sox fan.

Hiller B. Zobel *The Boston Massacre* (W.W. Norton US). A painstaking account of the circumstances that precipitated one of the most highly propagandized pre-revolution events – the slaying of five Bostonians outside the Old State House.

Travel and specific guides

Charles Bahne *The Complete Guide to Boston's Freedom Trail* (Newtowne Publishing US). Unlike most souvenir guides of the Freedom Trail, which have lots of pictures but little substance, this one is chock full of engaging historical tidbits on the stories behind the sights.

John Harris *Historic Walks in Old Boston* (Globe Pequot US). In most cases, you'll be walking in the footsteps of long-gone luminaries, but Harris infuses his accounts with enough lively history to keep things moving along at an interesting clip.

Walt Kelley *What They Never Told You About Boston (Or What They Did Were Lies)* (Down East Books US). Who would have guessed that in 1632, Puritans passed the world's first law against smoking in public? This slim book is full of such engaging Boston trivia.

★ **Thomas H. O'Connor** *Boston A to Z* (Harvard University Press US). This terrific, often irreverent, guide to the Hub will give you the lowdown on local hotshots from John Adams to "Honey Fitz," institutions like the Holy Cross Cathedral and the L Street Bathhouse and local lore on everything from baked beans to the Steaming Kettle.

Architecture, urban planning and photography

★ **Philip Bergen** *Old Boston in Early Photographs 1850–1918* (Dover Publications US). Fascinating stuff, including a photographic record of Back Bay's transition from swampland to swanky residential neighborhood.

Robert Campbell and Peter Vanderwarker *Cityscapes of Boston: An American City Through Time* (Houghton Mifflin US). An informative pictorial tome with some excellent photos of old and new Boston.

Mona Domosh *Invented Cities: The Creation of Landscape in Nineteenth Century New York and Boston* (Yale University Press US). Intriguing historical account of how these very different cities were shaped according to the values, beliefs and fears of the people and society who built them.

Matthew W. Granade and Joshua H. Simon (eds) *50 Successful*

Harvard Application Essays (St Martin's Press US). Just in case you want to know who they actually let into this hallowed university anyhow.

Jane Holtz Kay *Lost Boston* (Houghton Mifflin US). A photographic essay of long-gone architectural treasures.

Lawrence W. Kennedy *Planning the City Upon a Hill: Boston Since 1630* (University of Massachusetts Press US). This is the book to have if you want to delve deeper into how Boston's distinct neighborhoods took shape over the centuries.

Alex Krieger, David Cobb, Amy Turner and Norman B. Leventhal (eds) *Mapping Boston* (MIT Press US). Irresistible to any map-lover, this thoughtfully compiled book combines essays with all manner of historical maps to help trace Boston's conception and development.

Barbara Moore and Gail Weesner *Back Bay: A Living Portrait* (Centry Hill Press US). If you're dying to know what Back Bay's brownstones look – and looked – like inside, this book of hard-to-find photos is for you. They do a similar book on Beacon Hill.

★ **Susan and Michael Southworth** *AIA Guide to Boston* (Globe Pequot US). The definitive guide to Boston architecture, organized by neighborhood. City landmarks and dozens of notable buildings are given exhaustive but readable coverage.

Walter Muir Whitehill *Boston: A Topographical History* (Harvard University Press US). How Boston went from a tiny seaport on the Shawmut Peninsula to the city it is today, with detailed descriptions of the city's many land reclaiming projects.

Fiction

Margaret Atwood *The Handmaid's Tale* (Anchor Books US). Cambridge's Ivy League setting inspired the mythical Republic of Gilead, the post-nuclear fallout backdrop for this harrowing tale about women whose lives' purpose is solely the reproduction of children.

James Carroll *The City Below* (Houghton Mifflin US). Gripping historical novel of later-twentieth-century Boston, centered on two Irish brothers from Charlestown.

Michael Crichton *A Case of Need* (Signet US). Written long before Crichton conceived of "ER" or even *Jurassic Park*, and under a pseudonym to boot, this gripping whodunnit opens with a woman nearly bleeding to death on the operating table of a Boston hospital; she goes on to accuse her physician of attempted murder, and finds a trusty colleague trying to get at the truth of the affair.

Nathaniel Hawthorne *The Scarlet Letter* (Signet Classic US). Puritan Boston comes to life, in all its mirthless repressiveness, starring the adulterous Hester Prynne.

William Dean Howells *The Rise of Silas Lapham* (Viking Press US). This 1878 novel was the forerunner to American Realism. Howells' less-than-enthralling tale of a well-off Vermont businessman's failed entry into Boston's old-moneyed Brahmin caste gives a good early portrait of a uniquely American hero: the self-made man.

Henry James *The Bostonians* (Viking Press US). James' soporific satire traces the relationship of Olive Chancellor and Verena Tarrant, two fictional feminists in the 1870s.

★ **Dennis Lehane** *Darkness Take My Hand* (Avon Books US). Perhaps the best in Lehane's Boston-set mystery series; two private investigators tackle a serial killer, the Boston Mafia, and their Dorchester upbringing in this atmospheric thriller.

Michael Lowenthal *The Same Embrace* (Plume US). A young man comes out to his Jewish, Bostonian parents after his twin brother disowns him for his homosexuality; courageous and complex.

John Marquand *The Late George Appley* (Buccaneer Books US o/p). Winner of the 1937 Pulitzer Prize, this novel satirizes a New England gentry on the wane.

Carole Maso *Defiance* (Plume US). A Harvard professor sits on death row after having murdered a pair of her own star students, in this fragmentary, moving confessional.

Arthur Miller *The Crucible* (Penguin US). This compelling play about the 1692 Salem witch trials is peppered with quotes from actual court transcripts and loaded with appropriate levels of hysteria and fervor – a must for witch fanatics everywhere.

Sue Miller *While I Was Gone* (Ballantine US). An emotional psychodrama centered on a middle-aged woman who spends time under an assumed name in a Cambridge commune, while on the run from her husband.

Susan Minot *Folly* (Washington Square Press US). This obvious nod to Edith Wharton's *Age of Innocence* is set in 1917 Boston instead of New York, and details the proclivities of the Brahmin era, in which women

were expected to marry well, and the heartbreak that ensues from making the wrong choice.

Edwin O'Connor *The Last Hurrah* (Little, Brown US o/p). Fictionalized account of Boston mayor James Michael Curley, starring a 1950s corrupt politician; the book was so popular that the bar at the *Omni Parker House Hotel* was named after it.

Sylvia Plath *The Bell Jar* (Harper Perennial USA). Angst-ridden, dark, cynical – everything a teenaged girl wants out of a book. The second half of this brilliant (if disturbing) autobiographical novel about Esther Greenwood's mental breakdown is set in the Boston suburbs, where she ends up institutionalized.

George Santayana *The Last Puritan* (MIT Press US). The philosopher's brilliant "memoir in the form of a novel," set around Boston, chronicles the short life and education of protagonist Oliver Alden coming to grips with Puritanism.

Erich Segal *Love Story* (Avon US). This sappy story about the love affair between Oliver Barrett IV, a successful Harvard student born with a silver spoon in his mouth, and Jenny Cavilleri, a Radcliffe music student who's had to struggle for everything, has the uncanny ability to captivate even the most jaded reader; made into a movie in 1970.

Boston on film

Boston has served as the setting for surprisingly few major **films** despite its historic importance in shaping US culture. Here are a baker's dozen of titles to start with if you want to see how it's shown up thus far.

Two Sisters from Boston (Henry Koster, 1946)

Walk East on Beacon (Alfred L. Werker, 1952)

The Actress (George Cukor, 1953)

The Boston Strangler (Richard Fleischer, 1968)

Love Story (Arthur Hiller, 1970)

Between the Lines (Joan Micklin Silver, 1977)

Starting Over (Alan J. Pakula, 1979)

The Bostonians (James Ivory, 1984)

Tough Guys Don't Dance (Norman Mailer, 1987)

Good Will Hunting (Gus Van Sant, 1997)

A Civil Action (Steve Zaillian, 1998)

Next Stop Wonderland (Ben Anderson, 1998)

Legally Blonde (Robert Luketic, 2001)

Jean Stafford *Boston Adventure* (Harcourt Brace US). Narrated by a poverty-stricken young girl who gets taken in by a wealthy elderly woman, this long – but rewarding – novel portrays upper-class Boston in all its magnificence and malevolence.

★ **David Foster Wallace** *Infinite Jest* (Little, Brown US). Sprawling magnum opus concerning a video that eliminates all viewers' desire to do anything but watch said video. Many of the book's best passages take place at Enfield, a fictional tennis academy set outside Boston; another plot line involves a Canadian terrorist separatist cell in Cambridge.

William F. Weld *Mackerel by Moonlight* (Pocket Books US). The former federal prosecutor and governor of Massachusetts turns his hand to writing, in this uneven – though not unworthy – political mystery.

Local accent and jargon

Boston has a **language** all its own, plus a truly unmistakeable regional accent. One of Boston's most recognizable cultural idiosyncrasies is its strain of American English, distinguished by a tendency to drop one's "r"s, as on the ubiquitous t-shirts that exhort you to "Pahk the cah in Havvid Yahd" ("Park the car in Harvard Yard"). Listen, too, for the greeting "How why ya?" ("How are you?") or the genial assent, "shuah" ("Sure").

These lost "r"s crop up elsewhere, usually when words that end in "a" are followed by words that begin in a vowel – as in "I've got no idear about that." When the nasal "a" (as in "cat") is not followed by an "r", it can take on a soft, almost British tenor: "after" becomes "ahfta." And the "aw" sound (as in "body") is inverted, like "wa": "god" becomes "gwad."

If in doubt, the surest way to fit in with the locals is to use the word "wicked" as an adverb at every opportunity: "Joo guys see the Celts game lahst night? Theah gonna be wicked wasome this yeah!" What follows is a glossary of sorts for proper terms, slang and jargon in and around Boston.

Terms and acronyms

BC Boston College

Beantown Nickname for Boston – a reference to the local specialty, Boston baked beans – that no one uses any longer.

The Big Dig The ongoing project to put the elevated highway I-93 underground.

Brahmin An old-money Beacon Hill aristocrat.

Brownstone Originally a nineteenth-century terraced house with a facade of brown stone; now, any row- or townhouse.

BU Boston University.

Bubbler Water fountain.

C-Town Nickname for Charlestown.

The Cape Shorthand for Cape Cod.

The Central Artery The stretch of I-93 that runs through downtown, separating the North End and the waterfront from the rest of the city.

Colonial Style of Neoclassical architecture popular in the seventeenth and eighteenth centuries.

Combat Zone/Ladder District The once-busy strip of Washington Street designated for adult entertainment, just north of Chinatown. Recently renamed the Ladder District, after the area's

street grid's resemblance to a multi-runged ladder.

Comm Ave Commonwealth Avenue.

Dot Ave Dorchester Avenue.

Federal Hybrid of French and Roman architecture popular in the late eighteenth and early nineteenth centuries.

Frappe Milkshake (meaning milk, ice cream and syrup) – the "e" is silent. Order a *milkshake* in Boston and you'll likely get milk flavored with syrup – distinctly devoid of ice cream.

Georgian Architectural style popular during the late Colonial period; highly ornamental and rigidly symmetrical.

Greek Revival Style of architecture that mimicked that of classical Greece. Popular for banks and larger houses in the early nineteenth century.

Grinder A sandwich made of deli meats, cheese and condiments on a long roll or bun.

Hamburg Ground beef *sans* bun. Add an "–er" at the end for the classic American sandwich.

Hub Like Beantown, a nickname for Boston not really used anymore.

JP Jamaica Plain.

Mass Ave Massachusetts Avenue.

MBTA (Massachusetts Bay Transportation Authority) The agency in charge of all public transit – buses, subways, commuter trains and ferries.

MGH Massachusetts General Hospital; also, "Mass General."

Packie Liquor store (many signs say "Package Store").

The Pike The Massachusetts Turnpike (I-90); also, "Mass Pike."

P-town Provincetown.

Scrod Somewhat of a distasteful generic name for cod or haddock. Almost always served breaded and sold cheap.

Southie South Boston.

Spa An independently owned convenience store – not a pampering salon.

The T Catch-all for Boston's subway system.

Three-decker Three-story house, with each floor a separate apartment. Also called a "triple-decker."

Townie Originally a term for residents of Charlestown, it now refers to wicked long-term residents of Boston and its outlying suburbs, most readily identified by their heavy accents.

Victorian Style of architecture from the mid- to late 1800s that is highly eclectic and ornamental.

Wicked The definitive word in the Bostonian patois, still used to intensify adjectives, as in "wicked good."

Boston people

ADAMS Samuel (1722–1803). A standard-bearer for the Revolution, Adams's patriotic pursuits included founding the "Sons of Liberty" in 1765, creating the Committee of Correspondence – basically a hype machine for the revolutionary cause – in 1772, and leading the Boston Tea Party a year later. And yes, he brewed beer, too.

ALCOTT Bronson (1799–1888). Perpetually penniless father of writer Louisa May, Alcott launched a series of progressive though short-lived elementary-type schools in Boston, most notably the Temple School. He also spearheaded the failed utopian community of Fruitlands, outside Boston, in 1843.

ALCOTT Louisa May (1832–1888). Author of *Little Women* and other works that drew on her close-knit family, who lived in and around Boston. While a Civil War nurse, she was treated with mercury for a fever, beginning a painfully long demise that ended just a day after her father's funeral.

ATTUCKS Crispus (1723?–1770). Ex-slave who was killed in the Boston Massacre of 1770, the only one of the five slain to be remembered by history and the only one who was black.

BELL Alexander Graham (1847–1922). Scottish-born professor who moved to Boston in the 1870s and invented the telephone in a Boston University laboratory.

BLACKSTONE William (1595–1675). English reverend who was the first European settler on the Shawmut Peninsula, now Boston.

BOYLSTON Zabdiel (1679–1766). Boston doctor who invented a smallpox inoculation first used during the plague of 1721–1722. To allay fears about his cure, Boylston inoculated his son first.

BULFINCH Charles (1763–1844). Boston's leading architect of the Federalist style, he designed the State House and many townhouses on Beacon Hill that can still be seen today.

BULGER James "Whitey" (1935–). Reportedly on the lam in Ireland, the wayward brother of the president of the University of Massachusetts is one of America's most wanted mobsters; his name keeps coming up in the press in connection with long missing persons who have recently turned up dead.

CHILD Julia (1912–). Cookbook author, famed for simplifying French cuisine for the middle American dinner table, who calls Cambridge her home.

COPLEY John Singleton (1738–1815). A painter best known for his portraits of prominent Colonial-era Bostonians, Copley relocated to London in 1775.

CURLEY James Michael (1874–1958). Four-time Democratic mayor of Boston, this charismatic – and corrupt – Irish-American politician ruled for 35 years, also serving as a Massachusetts congressman and governor.

EDDY Mary Baker (1821–1910). The founder of Christian Science, a church with its world headquarters in Boston. Healed of an injury while reading a section of the New Testament in 1866, she was inspired to write *Science and Health*, the original Christian Science textbook.

EMERSON Ralph Waldo (1803–1882). Literary giant and renowned lecturer whose essay "Nature," penned in Concord, signaled the birth of transcendentalism.

FANEUIL Peter (1700–1743).
Wealthy merchant of French
Huguenot origin who donated the
eponymous town hall to the town of
Boston in 1742.

FIELDS James T. (1817–1881).
Partner in the local publishing firm
Ticknor & Fields, he helped persuade Nathaniel Hawthorne to pub-
lish *The Scarlet Letter*.

FRANKLIN Benjamin
(1706–1790). American statesman
and inventor born and raised in
Boston, he apprenticed to his brother, publisher of the independent-
minded *New England Gazette* newspaper, before settling in Philadelphia.

FULLER Margaret (1810–1850).
Literary critic who was the editor of
The Dial, the transcendentalist jour-
nal of the 1840s.

GARDNER Isabella Stewart
(1840–1919). This socialite and art
collector, described once as a "millionaire Bohemienne," enjoyed
shocking Boston's high society with
antics such as having John Singer
Sargent paint a low-neckline portrait
of her and, reputedly, walking her
pet lions down Tremont Street.

GARRISON William Lloyd
(1805–1879). Abolitionist who at 23
made his first public address in favor
of emancipation, in Boston's Park
Street Church. Also the publisher of
The Liberator, an anti-slavery newspaper.

HANCOCK John (1737–1793).
Wealthy Colonial-era merchant and
Declaration of Independence signatory who helped finance the early
revolutionary campaign; after the
war he served as the first governor
of the Commonwealth of
Massachusetts.

HOLMES Oliver Wendell
(1809–1894). Doctor, author and
pundit, Holmes coined the phrase
"Boston Brahmins," describing
Beacon Hill aristocrats, in a series of
Atlantic Monthly articles entitled
"Autocrat of the Breakfast Table."

HOMER Winslow (1836–1910).
Boston-born, self-taught naturalist
painter best known for his water-
colors of New England seascapes.

KENNEDY Edward M. (1932–).
Brother of JFK and longtime liberal
Massachusetts Democratic senator.

KENNEDY John F. (1917–1963)
The youngest president to be elected, and the first Catholic one,
Kennedy was born just outside
Boston proper in Brookline. He
served as Boston congressman and
Massachusetts senator before gaining
executive office in 1960. He was
assassinated on November 22, 1963.

LOWELL Robert (1917–1977).
Pulitzer Prize-winning Boston-born
poet whose most famous collection,
For the Union Dead, was inspired by
Robert Gould Shaw and the 54th
Massachusetts Regiment statue on
the Beacon Street promenade.

MATHER Cotton (1663–1728).
Puritan minister who entered Harvard
College at the age of 12, and proceed-
ed to pen many esoteric books,
including the 1300-page *Magnalia
Christi Americana*, which traced the
ecclesiastical history of America.

MATHER Increase (1639–1723).
Father of Cotton Mather, this minister secured a new royal charter for
the Massachusetts Bay Colony in
1692 and served some time as president of Harvard College.

MENINO Thomas (1942–).
Boston's current mayor and the first
one of Italian descent.

QUINCY Josiah (1772–1864).
Popular mayor of Boston in the
1820s who cleaned up Beacon Hill
of prostitution and stopped development of the land that would become
the Public Garden.

REVERE Paul (1735–1818).
Silversmith and principal rider for
Boston's Committee of Public
Safety, he made his midnight ride to
Lexington and Concord to warn the
rebels that the British were coming,
an event immortalized in an 1863
Longfellow poem of questionable
accuracy.

RICHARDSON Henry Hobson (1838–1886). Architect noted for his oversized Romanesque Revival works such as Trinity Church. **STUART Gilbert** (1755–1828). Early American painter who made his mark with a series of portraits of George Washington – one of which is replicated on the US one-dollar bill.

Index

+ small print

Index

Map entries are in color

INDEX

INDEX

Twenty Years of Rough Guides

In the summer of 1981, Mark Ellingham, Rough Guides' founder, knocked out the first guide on a typewriter, with a group of friends. Mark had been travelling in Greece after university, and couldn't find a guidebook that really answered his needs. There were heavyweight cultural guides on the one hand – good on museums and classical sites but not on beaches and tavernas – and on the other hand student manuals that were so caught up with how to save money that they lost sight of the country's significance beyond its role as a place for a cool vacation. None of the guides began to address Greece as a country, with its natural and human environment, its politics and its contemporary life.

Having no urgent reason to return home, Mark decided to write his own guide. It was a guide to Greece that tried to combine some erudition and insight with a thoroughly practical approach to travelers' needs. Scrupulously researched listings of places to stay, eat and drink were matched by careful attention to detail on everything from Homer to Greek music, from classical sites to national parks and from nude beaches to monasteries. Back in London, Mark and his friends got their Rough Guide accepted by a farsighted commissioning editor at the publisher Routledge and it came out in 1982.

The Rough Guide to Greece was a student scheme that became a publishing phenomenon. The immediate success of the book – shortlisted for the Thomas Cook award – spawned a series that rapidly covered dozens of countries. The Rough Guides found a ready market among backpackers and budget travelers, but soon acquired a much broader readership that included older and less impecunious visitors. Readers relished the guides' wit and inquisitiveness as much as the enthusiastic, critical approach that acknowledges everyone wants value for money – but not at any price.

Rough Guides soon began supplementing the "rougher" information – the hostel and low-budget listings – with the kind of detail that independent-minded travelers on any budget might expect. These days, the guides – distributed worldwide by the Penguin group – include recommendations spanning the range from shoestring to luxury, and cover more than 200 destinations around the globe. Our growing team of authors, many of whom come to Rough Guides initially as outstandingly good letter-writers telling us about their travels, are spread all over the world, particularly in Europe, the USA and Australia. As well as the travel guides, Rough Guides publishes a series of dictionary phrasebooks covering two dozen major languages, an acclaimed series of music guides running the gamut from Classical to World Music, a series of music CDs in association with World Music Network, and a range of reference books on topics as diverse as the Internet, Pregnancy and Unexplained Phenomena. Visit **www.roughguides.com** to see what's cooking.

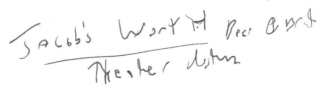

Rough Guide credits

Text editor: Hunter Slaton
Series editor: Mark Ellingham
Editorial: Martin Dunford, Jonathan Buckley, Kate Berens, Ann-Marie Shaw, Helena Smith, Olivia Swift, Ruth Blackmore, Geoff Howard, Claire Saunders, Gavin Thomas, Alexander Mark Rogers, Polly Thomas, Joe Staines, Richard Lim, Duncan Clark, Peter Buckley, Lucy Ratcliffe, Clifton Wilkinson, Alison Murchie, Matthew Teller, Andrew Dickson, Fran Sandham, Sally Schafer (UK); Andrew Rosenberg, Yuki Takagaki, Richard Koss, Chris Barsanti (US)
Production: Susanne Hillen, Andy Hilliard, Link Hall, Helen Prior, Julia Bovis, Michelle Draycott, Katie Pringle, Zoë Nobes, Rachel Holmes, Andy Turner, Dan May

Cartography: Maxine Repath, Melissa Baker, Ed Wright, Katie Lloyd-Jones
Cover art direction: Louise Boulton
Picture research: Sharon Martins, Mark Thomas
Online: Kelly Martinez, Anja Mutic-Blessing, Jennifer Gold, Audra Epstein, Suzanne Welles, Cree Lawson (US)
Finance: John Fisher, Gary Singh, Edward Downey, Mark Hall, Tim Bill
Marketing & Publicity: Richard Trillo, Niki Smith, David Wearn, Chloë Roberts, Demelza Dallow, Claire Southern (UK); Simon Carloss, David Wechsler, Megan Kennedy (US)
Administration: Julie Sanderson, Karoline Densley

Publishing information

This third edition published March 2003 by **Rough Guides Ltd**, 80 Strand, London WC2R ORL Penguin Putnam, Inc., 375 Hudson Street, NY 10014, USA
Distributed by the Penguin Group
Penguin Books Ltd, 80 Strand, London WC2R ORL
Penguin Putnam, Inc., 375 Hudson Street, NY 10014, USA
Penguin Books Australia Ltd, 487 Maroondah Highway, PO Box 257, Ringwood, Victoria 3134, Australia
Penguin Books Canada Ltd, 10 Alcorn Avenue, Toronto, Ontario, Canada M4V 1E4
Penguin Books (NZ) Ltd, 182–190 Wairau Road, Auckland 10, New Zealand
Typeset in Bembo and Helvetica to an original design by Henry Iles.

Printed in Italy by LegoPrint S.p.A

© David Fagundes and Anthony Grant 2003

272pp includes index
A catalogue record for this book is available from the British Library

ISBN 1-84353-044-9

Help us update

We've gone to a lot of effort to ensure that the third edition of **The Rough Guide to Boston** is accurate and up-to-date. However, things change – places get "discovered", opening hours are notoriously fickle, restaurants and rooms raise prices or lower standards. If you feel we've got it wrong or left something out, we'd like to know, and if you can remember the address, the price, the time, the phone number, so much the better.

We'll credit all contributions, and send a copy of the next edition (or any other Rough Guide if you prefer) for the best letters. Everyone who writes to us and isn't already a subscriber will receive a copy of our full-color thrice-yearly newsletter. Please mark letters: **"Rough Guide Boston Update"** and send to: Rough Guides, 80 Strand, London WC2R ORL, or Rough Guides, 4th Floor, 345 Hudson St, New York, NY 10014. Or send an email to: **mail@roughguides.co.uk** or **mail@roughguides.com**

Acknowledgements

Arabella Bowen Thanks to Megan Brumby and Aaron Ritzenberg for sharing their flat with me (and introducing me to the Boston Celtics); Nancy Civetta, Sarah Leaf-Herrmann, Chris Haynes and Martha Sullivan for foodie-guidance; Michele Topor for her excellent tour of North End salumerias and enotecas; and Aimee O'Brien formerly of the Greater Boston Convention and Visitors Bureau, for getting me city-wide access. Above all, thanks are due to my Rough Guide editor, Hunter Slaton, who managed to whip the book (and the maps) into wicked good shape.

Thanks, also, to Link Hall for the smooth layout; Katie Lloyd-Jones for fine cartography work; Jo Mead for detailed proofreading; Stephen Lipuma for cheerful photo research; Louise Boulton for the book's cover; Zoë Nobes for inside cover matter; Helen Prior, Julia Bovis and Michelle Draycott for their skillful managing of the project; and Andrew Rosenberg for his excellent editorial guidance (and music-talk).

SMALL PRINT

Photo Credits

Cover credits

front small top picture Sailing boat, Charles River © Robert Harding

front small lower picture Harvard University © Alamy

back top picture Charles River © Robert Harding

back lower picture State House © Getty Images

Color introduction

Faneuil Hall © Tibor Bognar / Network Aspen

Old State House and Ames Building © Samuel Laundon

Citgo Sign © Steve Dunwell

George Washington Statue © Steve Edson

Lobster © Getty Images

Rollerbladers on bridge © Steve Lupowski

Harvard Square street performer © Fay photo.com

Big Dig crane © Margot Balboni

Marlborough Street townhouses © Steve Edson

Trinity Church reflected in Hancock Tower © David Paler

Things not to miss

1 Massachusetts State House © 2002 PictureQuest.com

2 Ware Collection of Glass Models of Plants © courtesy of Boston's Botanical Museum

3 Isabella Stewart Gardner Museum © courtesy of Isabella Stewart Gardner Museum

4 Beacon Hill street sign © picture-gallery.com

5 Baseball game at Fenway © ALLSPORT / Getty Images

6 Omni Parker House © courtesy of the Omni Parker House

7 *USS Constitution* © Getty Images

8 Swan Boats / Public Garden © Steve Edson

9 Newbury Street shopping © Steve Edson

10 Bonsai collection © Richard Griswold / Arnold Arboretum

11 Head of the Charles regatta © Nicholas Devore III / Network Aspen

12 Harvard Square © Steve Edson

13 Blackstone Block © Maureen Hancock

14 Black Heritage Trail / Shaw Memorial © Jeffery Nintzel

15 Gibson House Museum © courtesy of Gibson House Museum

16 Union Oyster House © courtesy of the Union Oyster House

17 Concert at Symphony Hall © courtesy of Boston Symphony Orchestra

18 Sevens Ale House © David Paler

19 Mount Auburn Cemetery © Kellypix.com

20 Christian Science Center © Nicholas Devore III / Network Aspen

21 Old North Church © Steve Edson

22 Faneuil Hall / Sam Adams statue © Steve Edson

23 John Singer Sargent painting © 1882 John Singer Sargent; gift of Mary Louisa Boit, Julia Overing Boit, Jane Hubbard Boit and Florence D. Boit in memory of their father, Edward Darley Boit

24 Lobster Pot restaurant © Steve Edson

Chapter photos

Quincy Market and skyline © Getty Images (p.45)

Paul Revere statue © Steve Edson (p.63)

Townhouse and gaslamp © Maureen Hancock (p.79)

Fenway Park seats © Steve Edson (p.111)

Harvard from above © Nicholas Devore III / Network Aspen (p.135)

Salem Witch Memorial © Bill Bachmann / Network Aspen (p.142)

Rowes Wharf buildings © Nicholas Devore III / Network Aspen (p.161)

Boston Celtics / Paul Pierce © ALLSPORT / Getty Images (p.220)

Rough Guides travel

Europe

Algarve
Amsterdam
Andalucia
Austria
Barcelona
Belgium
  & Luxembourg
Berlin
Britain
Brittany
  & Normandy
Bruges & Ghent
Brussels
Budapest
Bulgaria
Copenhagen
Corsica
Costa Brava
Crete
Croatia
Cyprus
Czech & Slovak
  Republics
Devon & Cornwall
Dodecanese
  & East Aegean
Dordogne
  & the Lot
Dublin
Edinburgh
England
Europe
First-Time Europe
Florence
France
French Hotels
  & Restaurants
Germany
Greece
Greek Islands
Holland
Hungary
Ibiza
  & Formentera
Iceland
Ionian Islands
Ireland
Italy
Lake District

Languedoc
  & Roussillon
Lisbon
London
London Mini Guide
London
  Restaurants
Madeira
Madrid
Mallorca
Malta & Gozo
Menorca
Moscow
Norway
Paris
Paris Mini Guide
Poland
Portugal
Prague
Provence & the
  Côte d'Azur
Pyrenees
Romania
Rome
Sardinia
Scandinavia
Scotland
Scottish Highlands
  & Islands
Sicily
Spain
St Petersburg
Sweden
Switzerland
Tenerife & La
  Gomera
Turkey
Tuscany & Umbria
Venice
  & The Veneto
Vienna
Wales

Asia

Bali & Lombok
Bangkok
Beijing
Cambodia
China
First-Time Asia
Goa
Hong Kong
  & Macau
India
Indonesia
Japan
Laos
Malaysia,
  Singapore
  & Brunei
Nepal
Singapore
South India
Southeast Asia
Thailand
Thailand Beaches
  & Islands
Tokyo
Vietnam

Australasia

Australia
Gay & Lesbian
  Australia
Melbourne
New Zealand
Sydney

North America

Alaska
Big Island of
  Hawaii
Boston
California
Canada
Florida
Hawaii
Honolulu
Las Vegas
Los Angeles
Maui
Miami & the
  Florida Keys
Montréal
New England
New Orleans
New York City

New York City
  Mini Guide
New York
  Restaurants
Pacific Northwest
Rocky Mountains
San Francisco
San Francisco
  Restaurants
Seattle
Southwest USA
Toronto
USA
Vancouver
Washington DC
Yosemite

Caribbean & Latin America

Antigua & Barbuda
Argentina
Bahamas
Barbados
Belize
Bolivia
Brazil
Caribbean
Central America
Chile
Costa Rica
Cuba
Dominican
  Republic
Ecuador
Guatemala
Jamaica
Maya World
Mexico
Peru
St Lucia
Trinidad & Tobago

Africa & Middle East

Cape Town
Egypt
Israel & Palestinian
  Territories

Jerusalem
Jordan
Kenya
Morocco
South Africa,
  Lesotho
  & Swaziland
Syria
Tanzania
Tunisia
West Africa
Zanzibar
Zimbabwe

Dictionary Phrasebooks

Czech
Dutch
European
  Languages
French
German
Greek
Hungarian
Italian
Polish
Portuguese
Russian
Spanish
Turkish
Hindi & Urdu
Indonesian
Japanese
Mandarin Chinese
Thai
Vietnamese
Mexican Spanish
Egyptian Arabic
Swahili

Maps

Amsterdam
Dublin
London
Paris
San Francisco
Venice

Rough Guides publishes new books every month

TRAVEL · MUSIC · REFERENCE · PHRASEBOOKS

Rough Guides music, reference & CDs

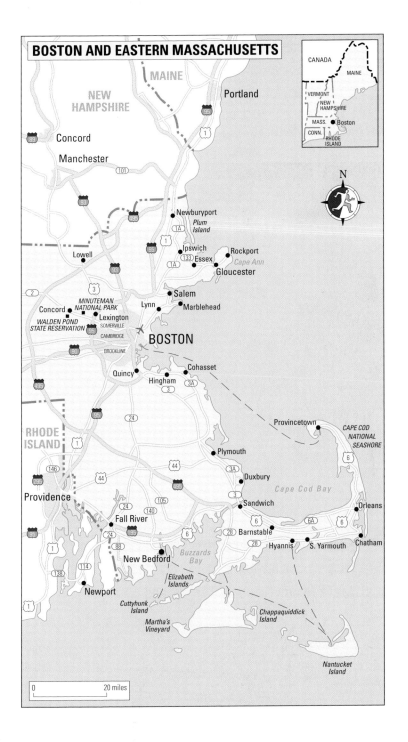
BOSTON AND EASTERN MASSACHUSETTS

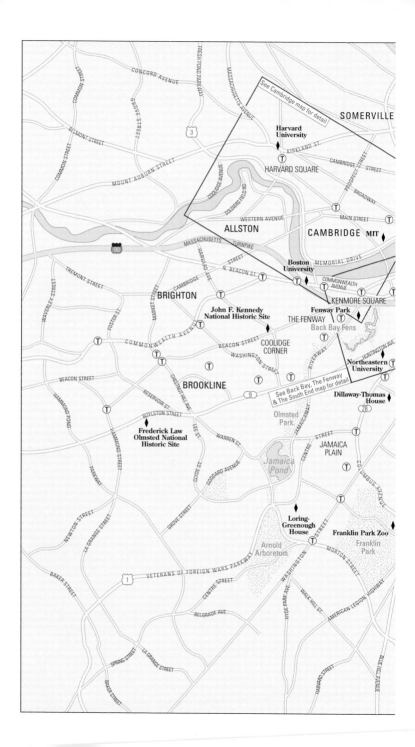

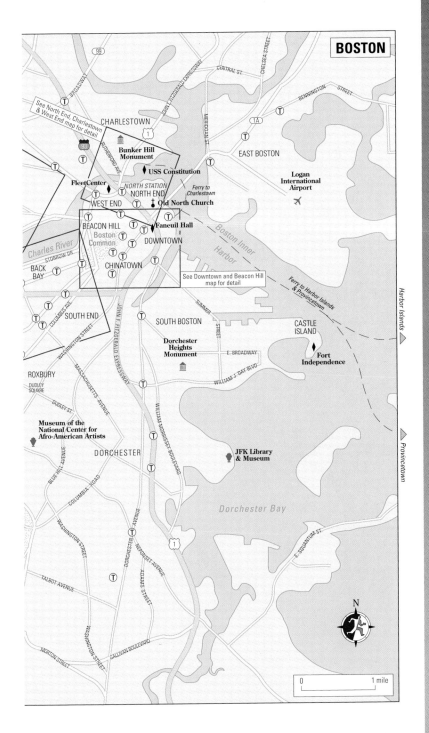

BOSTON

CHARLESTOWN

See North End, Charlestown
& West End map for detail

Bunker Hill
Monument

USS Constitution

FleetCenter

NORTH STATION
NORTH END
WEST END

Old North Church

Ferry to
Charlestown

EAST BOSTON

Logan
International
Airport

BEACON HILL

Faneuil Hall

Boston
Common

DOWNTOWN

Charles River

STORROW DR.

BACK
BAY

CHINATOWN

Boston Inner
Harbor

See Downtown and Beacon Hill
map for detail

SOUTH END

COLUMBUS AVE.

WASHINGTON STREET

JOHN F. FITZGERALD EXPRESSWAY

SOUTH BOSTON

SUMMER STREET

CASTLE
ISLAND

Fort
Independence

Ferry to Harbor Islands
& Provincetown

ROXBURY

DUDLEY
SQUARE

DUDLEY ST.

Dorchester
Heights
Monument

E. BROADWAY

WILLIAM J. DAY BLVD.

MASSACHUSETTS AVENUE

BLUE HILL AVENUE

Museum of the
National Center for
Afro-American Artists

DORCHESTER

WILLIAM T. MORRISSEY BOULEVARD

JFK Library
& Museum

COLUMBIA ROAD

WASHINGTON STREET

DORCHESTER AVENUE

NEPONSET AVENUE

ADAMS STREET

1

Dorchester Bay

E. SQUANTUM ST.

TALBOT AVENUE

MORTON STREET

WASHINGTON STREET

GALLIVAN BOULEVARD

N

0   1 mile

CENTRAL ST.

CHELSEA STREET

BENNINGTON STREET

MERIDIAN ST.

JOHN F. FITZGERALD EXPRESSWAY

BROADWAY

99

1

RUTHERFORD AVE.

99

Harbor Islands

Provincetown

WEST END

CARDINAL
O'CONNELL
WAY

Massachusetts General Hospital

NEW CHARDON ST.
BOWKER ST.
HAWKINS ST.

STANIFORD STREET

ⓣ BOWDOIN

FRUIT STREET

PARKMAN ST.

BRIDGE CT.

ADAMS PL.

BLOSSOM STREET

LYNDE ST.

R. RUSSELL ST.

JOY STREET

HANCOCK ST.

TEMPLE STREET

RIDGEWAY LA.

BOWDOIN STREET

SUDBURY ST.

SOMERSET STREET

Harrison Gray Otis House

CHARLESBANK ROAD

CHARLES STREET

CAMBRIDGE ST. AVE.

ⓣ CHARLES

GROVE ST.

LINDALL PL.

LINDALL CT.

CAMBRIDGE STREET

GARDEN ST.

IRVING

ANDERSON

SMITH CT.

African Meeting House

Abiel Smith School

PHILLIPS STREET

Lewis Hayden House

George Middleton House

W. HILL PL.

Community Boat House

REVERE STREET

MYRTLE STREET

BEACON HILL

ASHBURTON PLACE

Ashburton Park

Boston Athenæum

The Phillips School

W. CEDAR STREET

PINCKNEY ST.

Nichols House

Massachusetts State House

MT. VERNON PL.

Old Granary Burying Ground

LOUISBURG SQUARE

MYRTLE STREET

ESPLANADE

EMBANKMENT ROAD

Church of the Advent

CEDAR LANE

MOUNT VERNON STREET

WALNUT STREET

JOY PL.

Park Street Church

Charles Street Meeting House

CHESTNUT STREET

SPRUCE ST.

Somerset Club

BEACON STREET

Robert Gould Shaw Memorial

PARK STREET

ⓣ

WINTER

Hatch Shell

BRIMMER ST.

LIME ST.

BRANCH ST.

Frog Pond

CHESTNUT STREET

RIVER ST.

Bull & Finch Pub

Founder's Monument

Great Elm Site ●

ⓘ

Visitor Center

TEMPLE PL.

BEAVER PL.

Flagstaff Hill

WEST STREET

BEACON STREET

CHARLES STREET

Soldiers and Sailors Monument

HARLEM PL.

MASON STREET

TREMONT STREET

Public Garden

Gibson House Museum

㉘

George Washington Statue

Swan Boats

Boston Common

Boston Massacre Monument

AVERY ST.

WASHINGTON STREET

MARLBOROUGH ST.

ARLINGTON STREET

Baylies Mansion

COMMONWEALTH AVE.

㉘

②

Central Burying Ground

Millennium Place

BOYLSTON

ⓣ

HEAD PL.

BACK BAY

Emmanuel Church of Boston

②

②

BOYLSTON STREET

PIANO ROW

Colonial Theater

CHINATOWN

BOYLSTON SQ.

② ARLINGTON

POE WAY

BOYLSTON STREET

Majestic Theatre

LAGRANGE ST.

LADDER DISTRICT

Church of the Covenant

NEWBURY

Arlington Street Church

COMMONWEALTH AVE.

ARLINGTON STREET

PROVIDENCE STREET

CHARLES STREET

Massachusetts Transportation Building

THEATER DISTRICT

Wilbur Theatre

ELLIOT PL.

KNEELAND

BERKELEY STREET

BOYLSTON STREET

ST. JAMES AVE.

Boston Park Plaza

PIEDMONT STREET

CHURCH STREET

Shubert Theater

TREMONT ST.

PROVIDENCE

CLARENDON STREET

STUART STREET

WINCHESTER STREET

Wang Center for the Performing Arts

John Hancock Tower

TRINITY PL.

COLUMBUS AVE.

BAY VILLAGE

MELROSE STREET

FAYETTE STREET

ISABELLA STREET

ⓣ

NEW ENGLAND MEDICAL CENTER

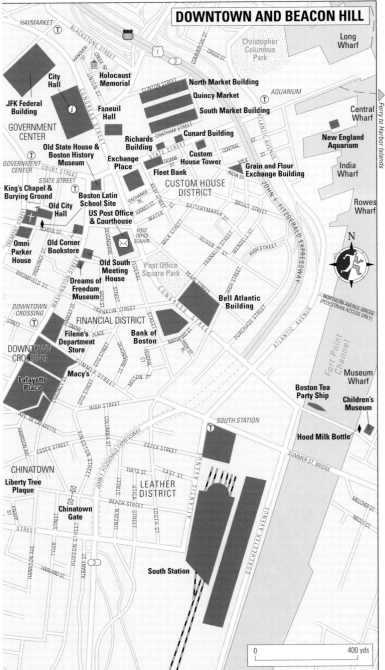

DOWNTOWN AND BEACON HILL

HAYMARKET

BLACKSTONE STREET

Long Wharf

Christopher Columbus Park

City Hall

Holocaust Memorial

North Market Building

Quincy Market

AQUARIUM

JFK Federal Building

Faneuil Hall

South Market Building

Central Wharf

Ferry to Harbor Islands

GOVERNMENT CENTER

Richards Building

Cunard Building

New England Aquarium

GOVERNMENT CENTER

Old State House & Boston History Museum

Exchange Place

Custom House Tower

Grain and Flour Exchange Building

India Wharf

COURT STREET

Fleet Bank

CUSTOM HOUSE DISTRICT

STATE STREET

King's Chapel & Burying Ground

Boston Latin School Site

Rowes Wharf

Old City Hall

US Post Office & Courthouse

BATTERYMARCH ST.

BROAD STREET

N

SCHOOL ST.

Omni Parker House

Old Corner Bookstore

POST OFFICE SQUARE

BROMFIELD ST.

Old South Meeting House

Post Office Square Park

Dreams of Freedom Museum

Bell Atlantic Building

NORTHERN AVENUE BRIDGE (PEDESTRIAN ACCESS ONLY)

DOWNTOWN CROSSING

FINANCIAL DISTRICT

Fort Point Channel

DOWNTOWN CROSSING

Filene's Department Store

Bank of Boston

Macy's

Museum Wharf

Lafayette Place

Boston Tea Party Ship

Children's Museum

HIGH STREET

SOUTH STATION

Hood Milk Bottle

SUMMER ST. BRIDGE

CHINATOWN

Liberty Tree Plaque

ESSEX STREET

TUFTS ST.

EAST ST.

LEATHER DISTRICT

MELCHER ST.

NECCO CT.

Chinatown Gate

BEACH STREET

South Station

DORCHESTER AVENUE

0   400 yds

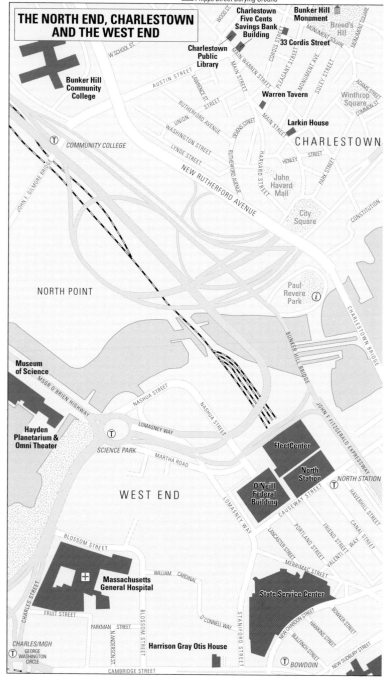

△ Phipps Street Burying Ground

THE NORTH END, CHARLESTOWN AND THE WEST END

Charlestown Five Cents Savings Bank Building

Bunker Hill Monument 🏛

33 Cordis Street

Charlestown Public Library

Bunker Hill Community College

W SCHOOL ST.

WOOD ST

Breed's Hill

MONUMENT SQUARE

AUSTIN STREET

LAWRENCE ST.

RUTHERFORD STREET

UNION STREET

WASHINGTON STREET

LYNDE STREET

MAIN STREET

MAIN WARREN STREET

PLEASANT STREET

MONUMENT AVE.

SOLEY STREET

ADAMS STREET

Winthrop Square

COMMON ST.

Warren Tavern

Larkin House

CHARLESTOWN

HENLEY STREET

PARK STREET

DICKENS STREET

MAIN STREET

HARVARD STREET

John Havard Mall

City Square

CONSTITUTION

Ⓣ COMMUNITY COLLEGE

NEW RUTHERFORD AVENUE

RUTHERFORD AVENUE

JOHN F. GILMORE BRIDGE

NORTH POINT

Paul Revere Park ⓘ

CHARLESTOWN BRIDGE

BUNKER HILL BRIDGE

Museum of Science

MSGR O'BRIEN HIGHWAY

NASHUA STREET

NASHUA STREET

JOHN FITZGERALD EXPRESSWAY

Hayden Planetarium & Omni Theater

Ⓣ SCIENCE PARK

LOMASNEY WAY

MARTHA ROAD

FleetCenter

North Station

Ⓣ NORTH STATION

WEST END

LOMASNEY WAY

O'Neill Federal Building

CAUSEWAY STREET

HAVERHILL STREET

CANAL STREET

PORTLAND STREET

FRIEND STREET

VALENTI WAY

BLOSSOM STREET

LANCASTER STREET

MERRIMAC STREET

State Service Center

WILLIAM CARDINAL

✚ Massachusetts General Hospital

O'CONNELL WAY

NEW CHARDON STREET

HAWKINS STREET

BOWKER STREET

CHARLES STREET

FRUIT STREET

PARKMAN STREET

N. ANDERSON ST.

BLOSSOM STREET

STANIFORD STREET

BULLFINCH STREET

NEW SUDBURY STREET

CHARLES/MGH Ⓣ GEORGE WASHINGTON CIRCLE

Harrison Gray Otis House

CAMBRIDGE STREET

Ⓣ BOWDOIN

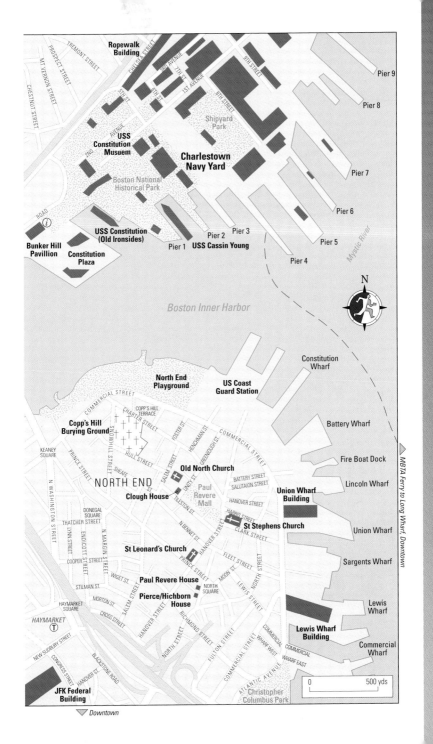

Pier 9

Pier 8

Shipyard
Park

**Charlestown
Navy Yard**

Pier 7

**Ropewalk
Building**

**USS
Constitution
Musuem**

Pier 6

Boston National
Historical Park

Pier 5

**USS Constitution
(Old Ironsides)**

Pier 2 Pier 3

Pier 1 **USS Cassin Young**

Pier 4

Mystic River

**Bunker Hill
Pavillion**

**Constitution
Plaza**

N

Boston Inner Harbor

Constitution
Wharf

**North End
Playground**

**US Coast
Guard Station**

Battery Wharf

COMMERCIAL STREET

COPP'S HILL
TERRACE

**Copp's Hill
Burying Ground**

Fire Boat Dock

Lincoln Wharf

KEANEY
SQUARE

Old North Church

NORTH END

Paul
Revere
Mall

Clough House

**Union Wharf
Building**

St Stephens Church

Union Wharf

DONEGAL
SQUARE

St Leonard's Church

Sargents Wharf

HAYMARKET
SQUARE

Paul Revere House

NORTH
SQUARE

**Pierce/Hichborn
House**

HAYMARKET Ⓣ

Lewis
Wharf

**Lewis Wharf
Building**

Commercial
Wharf

**JFK Federal
Building**

Christopher
Columbus Park

0   500 yds

MBTA Ferry to Long Wharf, Downtown ▷

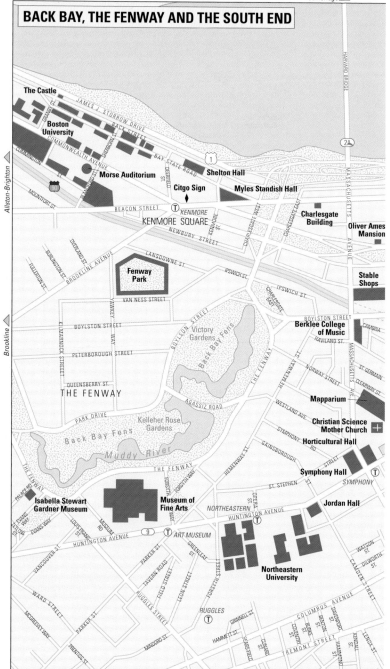

BACK BAY, THE FENWAY AND THE SOUTH END

Cambridge

The Castle

Boston University

JAMES J. STORROW DRIVE

BACK STREET

COMMONWEALTH AVENUE

BAY STATE ROAD

Morse Auditorium

Shelton Hall

Citgo Sign

Myles Standish Hall

MOUNTFORT ST.

BEACON STREET

KENMORE

KENMORE SQUARE

Charlesgate Building

NEWBURY STREET

Oliver Ames Mansion

LANSDOWNE ST.

BROOKLINE AVENUE

Fenway Park

IPSWICH ST.

Stable Shops

VAN NESS STREET

IPSWICH ST.

BOYLSTON STREET

Victory Gardens

BOYLSTON STREET

Berklee College of Music

CAMBRIA

HAVILAND ST.

PETERBOROUGH STREET

Back Bay Fens

THE FENWAY

NORWAY STREET

ST. GERMAIN

CLEARWAY ST.

QUEENSBERRY ST.

THE FENWAY

AGASSIZ ROAD

WESTLAND AVE.

Mapparium

PARK DRIVE

Kelleher Rose Gardens

Christian Science Mother Church

SYMPHONY RD.

Horticultural Hall

Back Bay Fens

GAINSBOROUGH ST.

Muddy River

THE FENWAY

Symphony Hall

SYMPHONY

ST. STEPHEN

THE FENWAY

Isabella Stewart Gardner Museum

Museum of Fine Arts

NORTHEASTERN

Jordan Hall

HUNTINGTON AVENUE

EVANS WAY

HUNTINGTON AVENUE

9

ART MUSEUM

PARKER ST.

GREENLEAF ST.

VANCOUVER ST.

TAVERN ROAD

FIELD STREET

LEON STREET

FORSYTH STREET

Northeastern University

WATSON ST.

CAMDEN ST.

WARD STREET

PARKER ST.

RUGGLES STREET

RUGGLES

COLUMBUS AVENUE

MCGREEVEY WAY

MINDORO ST.

GRINNELL ST.

HAMMETT ST.

SEARSFIELD

LINDALL ST.

TREMONT STREET

DAVENPORT ST.

KENDALL ST.

LENOX ST.

PRENTISS ST.

Alliston-Brighton

Brookline

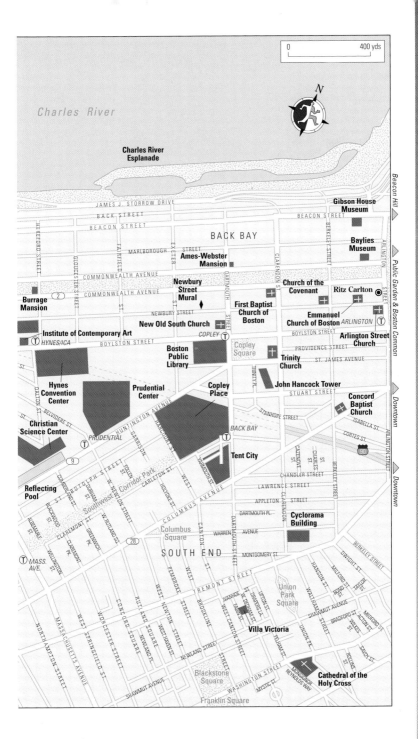

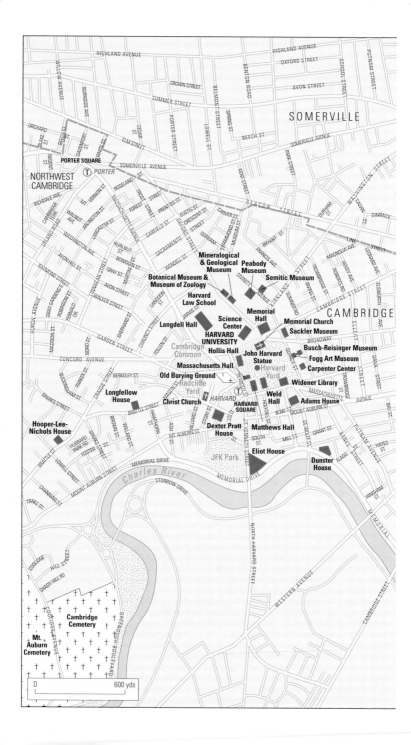

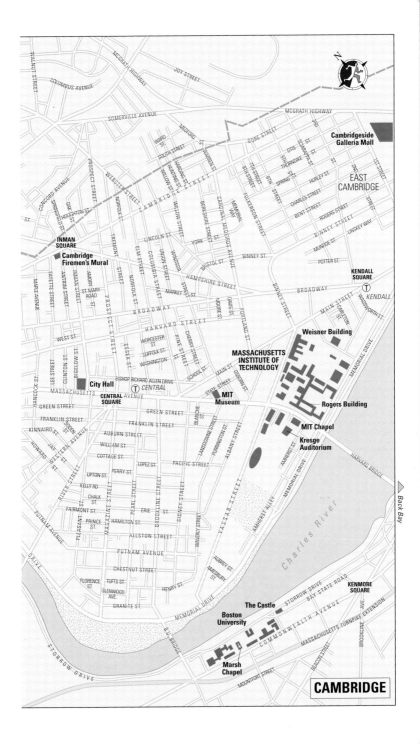

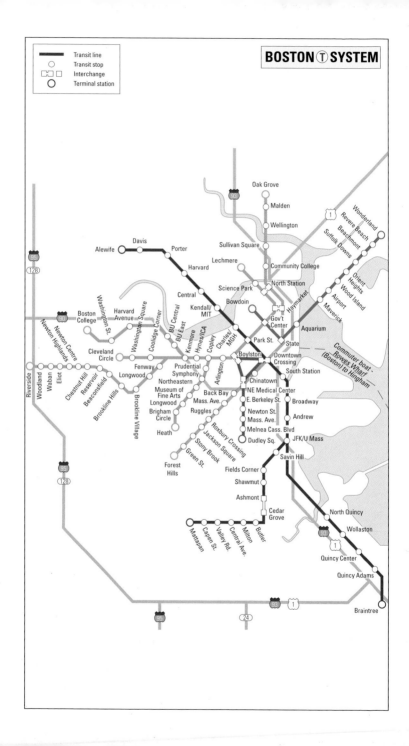